Regionalisation and Global Governance

The relationship between global governance and regionalisation is fraught with ambiguity. Understanding regionalisation in this context requires an understanding of its relationship, and reactive condition, with both the constellations of global governance and globalisation.

Regionalisation and Global Governance presents an overview and explores the distinctive but intersecting trajectories of regionalisation and global governance. It surveys:

- the theoretical debates
- the economic dimensions: multinationals, trade and investment, and labour
- the security considerations: armed conflict, conflict prevention and peacekeeping and non-traditional security in Asia
- the governing structures: managing contemporary multilevel architecture and cultural policy, leadership and the L20.

The expert and multi-disciplinary editors and contributors survey the context as well as the general character of these projects, together with their links as both parallel mediating mechanisms and distinctive choices for interjecting governance into globalisation. Examining these projects in tandem amplifies their importance and enables the authors to tease out coincidental as well as alternative possibilities in policy direction.

This book will be of interest to students and scholars of international relations, area studies, international economics, international political economy, political science, public administration and development studies.

Andrew F. Cooper is a Professor of Political Science at the University of Waterloo and Associate Director and Distinguished Fellow of the Centre for International Governance Innovation (CIGI), Waterloo, Canada.

Christopher W. Hughes is a Senior Research Fellow and Deputy Director of the ESRC Centre for the Study of Globalisation and Regionalisation at the University of Warwick, UK.

Philippe De Lombaerde is a Research Fellow at the United Nations University-Comparative Regional Integration Studies (UNU-CRIS) in Bruges, Belgium.

Routledge/Warwick Studies in Globalisation
Edited by Richard Higgott and published in association with the Centre for the Study of Globalisation and Regionalisation, University of Warwick.

What is globalisation and does it matter? How can we measure it? What are its policy implications? The Centre for the Study of Globalisation and Regionalisation at the University of Warwick is an international site for the study of key questions such as these in the theory and practice of globalisation and regionalisation. Its agenda is avowedly interdisciplinary. The work of the Centre will be showcased in this series.

This series comprises two strands:

Warwick Studies in Globalisation addresses the needs of students and teachers, and the titles will be published in hardback and paperback. Titles include:

Globalisation and the Asia-Pacific
Contested territories
Edited by Kris Olds, Peter Dicken,
Philip F. Kelly, Lily Kong and
Henry Wai-chung Yeung

Regulating the Global Information Society
Edited by Christopher Marsden

Banking on Knowledge
The genesis of the global development network
Edited by Diane Stone

Historical Materialism and Globalisation
Edited by Hazel Smith and Mark Rupert

Civil Society and Global Finance
Edited by Jan Aart Scholte with
Albrecht Schnabel

Towards a Global Polity
Edited by Morten Ougaard and
Richard Higgott

New Regionalisms in the Global Political Economy
Theories and cases
Edited by Shaun Breslin,
Christopher W. Hughes, Nicola Phillips
and Ben Rosamond

Development Issues in Global Governance
Public-private partnerships and market multilateralism
Benedicte Bull and Desmond McNeill

Globalizing Democracy
Political parties in emerging democracies
Edited by Peter Burnell

The Globalization of Political Violence
Globalization's shadow
Edited by Richard Devetak and
Christopher W. Hughes

Regionalisation and Global Governance
The taming of globalisation?
Edited by Andrew F. Cooper, Christopher
W. Hughes and Phillipe De Lombaerde

Routledge/Warwick Studies in Globalisation is a forum for innovative new research intended for a high-level specialist readership, and the titles will be available in hardback only. Titles include:

1. **Non-State Actors and Authority in the Global System**
   Edited by Richard Higgott, Geoffrey Underhill and Andreas Bieler

2. **Globalisation and Enlargement of the European Union**
   Austrian and Swedish social forces in the struggle over membership
   Andreas Bieler

3. **Rethinking Empowerment**
   Gender and development in a global/local world
   Edited by Jane L. Parpart, Shirin M. Rai and Kathleen Staudt

4. **Globalising Intellectual Property Rights**
   The TRIPs agreement
   Duncan Matthews

5. **Globalisation, Domestic Politics and Regionalism**
   The ASEAN Free Trade Area
   Helen E. S. Nesadurai

6. **Microregionalism and Governance in East Asia**
   Katsuhiro Sasuga

7. **Global Knowledge Networks and International Development**
   Edited by Diane Stone and Simon Maxwell

8. **Globalisation and Economic Security in East Asia**
   Governance and institutions
   Edited by Helen E. S. Nesadurai

9. **Regional Integration in East Asia and Europe**
   Convergence or divergence?
   Edited by Bertrand Fort and Douglas Webber

10. **The Group of Seven**
    Finance ministries, central banks and global financial governance
    Andrew Baker

11. **Globalisation and Poverty**
    Channels and policy responses
    Edited by Maurizio Bussolo and Jeffery I. Round

12. **Democratisation, Governance and Regionalism in East and Southeast Asia**
    A comparative study
    Edited by Ian Marsh

13. **Assessment and Measurement of Regional Integration**
    Edited by Philippe De Lombaerde

14. **The World Bank and Governance**
    A decade of reform and reaction
    Edited by Diane Stone and Christopher Wright

15. **Nationalism and Global Solidarities**
    Alternative projections to neoliberal globalization
    Edited by James Goodman and Paul James

16. **The Evolution of Regionalism in Asia**
    Economic and security issues
    Edited by Heribert Dieter

Regionalisation and Global Governance
The taming of globalisation?

Edited by Andrew F. Cooper, Christopher W. Hughes and Philippe De Lombaerde

Routledge
Taylor & Francis Group

LONDON AND NEW YORK

Centre for the
Study of
Globalisation and
Regionalisation

E·S·R·C
ECONOMIC
& SOCIAL
RESEARCH
COUNCIL

First published 2008
by Routledge
2 Park Square, Milton Park, Abingdon, Oxon OX14 4RN

Simultaneously published in the USA and Canada
by Routledge
270 Madison Ave, New York, NY 10016

*Routledge is an imprint of the Taylor & Francis Group, an
informa business*

Typeset in Times New Roman by
RefineCatch Limited, Bungay, Suffolk
Printed and bound in Great Britain by
MPG Books Ltd, Bodmin, Cornwall

British Library Cataloguing in Publication Data
A catalogue record for this book is available from the British Library

Library of Congress Cataloging in Publication Data
Regionalisation and global governance : the taming of globalisation? /
edited by Andrew F. Cooper, Christopher W. Hughes and Philippe De
Lombaerde.
     p. cm. – (Routledge/Warwick studies in globalisation)
  Includes bibliographical references and index.
  1. Regionalism. 2. Globalization–Political aspects.
3. International organization. I. Cooper, Andrew Fenton, 1950–
II. Hughes, Christopher W. III. Lombaerde, Philippe de.
  JZ5330.R443 2008
  341.2–dc22
  2007027003

ISBN10: 0–415–45376–3 (hbk)
ISBN10: 0–415–45377–1 (pbk)
ISBN10: 0–203–93339–7 (ebk)

ISBN13: 978–0–415–45376–9 (hbk)
ISBN13: 978–0–415–45377–6 (pbk)
ISBN13: 978–0–203–93339–8 (ebk)

Contents

List of illustrations   ix
List of contributors   x
Foreword   xii
Acknowledgements   xiii
List of abbreviations   xiv

**Introduction: regionalisation and the taming of
globalisation?**   1
ANDREW F. COOPER, CHRISTOPHER W. HUGHES AND
PHILIPPE DE LOMBAERDE

PART I
Theoretical debates: locating regionalisation theory   15

1 Enhancing global governance through regional integration   17
RAMESH THAKUR AND LUK VAN LANGENHOVE

**2 Studying regionalisation comparatively: a conceptual
framework**   43
ALEX WARLEIGH-LACK

3 The future of regionalism: old divides, new frontiers   61
BJÖRN HETTNE AND FREDRIK SÖDERBAUM

4 Rethinking classical integration theory   80
BEN ROSAMOND

PART II
**Economic dimensions: regionalisation and the need for
rule-making**   97

5   **Regional multinationals and the myth of globalisation**   99
    ALAN M. RUGMAN

6   **The role of regional agreements in trade and investment
    regimes**   118
    STEPHEN WOOLCOCK

7   **No safe havens: labour, regional integration and
    globalisation**   142
    ROBERT O'BRIEN

PART III
**Security considerations: the changing nature of strategic
regionalism**   157

8   **Regionalisation and responses to armed conflict, with
    special focus on conflict prevention and peacekeeping**   159
    KENNEDY GRAHAM

9   **Non-traditional security in Asia: the many faces of
    securitisation**   187
    MELY CABALLERO-ANTHONY

PART IV
**Governing structures: managing contemporary multilevel
architecture**   211

10 **Making cultural policy in a globalising world**   213
    PATRICIA M. GOFF

11 **Regionalism in global governance: realigning goals and
    leadership with cultures**   230
    MARTIN ALBROW AND COLIN I. BRADFORD

12 **Executive but expansive: the L20 as a project of 'new'
    multilateralism and 'new' regionalism**   249
    ANDREW F. COOPER

    Index   265

Illustrations

Figures

5.1	Upstream and downstream firm-specific advantages	107
5.2	The distinction between (F/T), (E/T) and home sales	110
5.3	ROTA and (E/T) at the mean values of the control variables	113

Tables

2.1	A typology of regionalisation	52
2.2	Independent variables of regionalisation	55
2.3	Hypotheses	56
5.1	Classification of the top 500 firms	100
5.2	Geographic sales of the world's largest home-region oriented firms	102
5.3	Intra-regional sales of the world's largest home-region firms	103
5.4	Regional sales and performance of UK multinationals	112
6.1	Elements of rule-making in trade and investment agreements	124
8.1	Metamorphosis in global threat perception (1945–2006)	164
8.2	Incidence of regional threat perceptions (2006)	165
8.3	Chapter VIII executive functions	174
8.4	Executive roles of regional, sub-regional and other agencies to date	175

Contributors

Martin Albrow is Research Professor, Social Sciences, Roehampton Institute, UK.

Colin I. Bradford is Senior Fellow, Global Economy and Development, Brookings Institution, USA.

Mely Caballero-Anthony is Assistant Professor, Institute of Defence and Strategic Studies, Nanyang Technological University, Singapore.

Andrew F. Cooper is Professor, Political Science, University of Waterloo, Canada, and Associate Director and Distinguished Fellow, the Centre for International Governance Innovation, Waterloo, Canada.

Philippe De Lombaerde is Research Fellow, United Nations University–Comparative Regional Integration Studies (UNU-CRIS), Bruges, Belgium.

Patricia M. Goff is Associate Professor, Political Science, Wilfrid Laurier University, Canada.

Kennedy Graham is Research Fellow at the School of Law, University of Canterbury, Christchurch, New Zealand, and Associate Research Fellow, United Nations University–Comparative Regional Integration Studies (UNU-CRIS), Bruges, Belgium.

Björn Hettne is Professor, Department of Peace and Development Research, Göteburg University, Sweden.

Christopher W. Hughes is Senior Research Fellow and Deputy Director, Centre for the Study of Globalisation and Regionalisation, University of Warwick, UK.

Robert O'Brien is Professor, Political Science Department, McMaster University, Canada.

Ben Rosamond is Reader, Politics and International Studies, University of Warwick, UK.

Alan M. Rugman is L.L. Waters Chair in International Business, Indiana University, USA.

Fredrik Söderbaum is Associate Professor, Department of Peace and Development Research, Göteburg University, Sweden, and Associate Research Fellow, United Nations University-Comparative Regional Integration Studies (UNU-CRIS), Bruges, Belgium.

Ramesh Thakur is Professor, Political Science, University of Waterloo, Canada, and Distinguished Fellow, the Centre for International Governance Innovation, Waterloo, Canada.

Luk Van Langenhove is Director, United Nations University–Comparative Regional Integration Studies (UNU-CRIS), Bruges, Belgium.

Alex Warleigh-Lack is Professor, International Politics and Public Policy, University of Limerick, Ireland.

Stephen Woolcock is Lecturer, International Relations, London School of Economics, UK, and Associate Research Fellow, UNU-CRIS, Bruges, Belgium.

Foreword

As globalisation proceeds apace, so it generates new demands for new forms of governance to curb its potential excesses. For many in the developing world, and even in parts of the developed world, regionalisation provides this hoped for global governance format. Regionalisation is seen to provide a meditating level of governance between the nation state and the global system, enabling states and non-state actors to collectively deal with a variety of global governance issues on a regional scale whilst not isolating themselves from the benefits of globalisation.

This latest book in the Warwick Studies in Globalisation series represents a culmination of much of the pioneering work by the Centre for the Study of Globalisation and Regionalisation (CSGR) over the past decade in the study of the interconnection of globalisation and regionalisation. The book project is the result of a joint conference held in October 2005 at the University of Warwick by the CSGR and the Centre for International Governance Innovation (CIGI), Canada. The book brings together many of the world's leading scholars on issues of regionalisation and globalisation, who themselves are drawn from a diverse range of regions, including East Asia, Europe, and North America. The volume is highly innovative, as is the hallmark of the CSGR, in drawing on multidisciplinary perspectives from Political Science, International Politics, Security Studies, Sociology, Business Studies, Social Anthropology, and Economics. It provides theory to contextualise our understanding of regionalisation and globalisation, and then moves on to examine new forms of regional and global governance in the functional domains of trade, finance, migration, traditional and non-traditional security, cultural policy, and international coordination fora.

Andrew F. Cooper, Christopher W. Hughes and Philippe De Lombaerde have done a fine job in melding these approaches together and in providing us with one of the first truly comprehensive studies of how regionalisation may help to equip the world to face the future challenges of global governance.

Richard Higgott
Foundation Director, CSGR
October 2007

Acknowledgements

This volume arose (mostly) from papers which were first presented at the 7th Annual CSGR Conference on *Regionalisation and the Taming of Globalisation? Economic, Political, Security, Social and Governance Issues*, held at Scarman House, University of Warwick, on 26–28 October 2005. The Conference was co-organised by and received financial support from the ESRC, Centre for the Study of Globalisation and Regionalisation (CSGR), University of Warwick, UK (www2.warwick.ac.uk/fac/soc/csgr), the Centre for International Governance Innovation CIGI, Canada (www.cigionline.org) and the United Nations University-Comparative Regional Integration Studies (UNU-CRIS), Belgium (www.cris.unu.edu).

We would like to thank the following people at CSGR for their Contribution to the organisation of the conference: Richard Higgott (Founding Director), Jan-Aart Scholte (Co-Director), Michela Redoana (conference co-organiser), Denise Hewlett, Dan Harris and Sian Alsop (administrative support), and Sook-Ok (Jamie) Shin (administrative support).

At CIGI we would like to acknowledge John English (Executive Director), Daniel Schwanen (Director of Research), Caroline Khoubesserian, Bessma Momani, Andrew Schrumm, Andrew Thompson, and Jennifer Jones. At UNU-CRIS we would like to thank Luk Van Langenhove (Director) and Eveline Snauwaert (administrative support).

A word of thanks also goes to Series Editor Professor Richard Higgott, and the people at Routledge, including Heidi Bagtazo, Amelia McLaurin, Steve Thompson, Cat Kennedy, and Susan Dunsmore.

Finally, this comprehensive publication would obviously not have been possible without the excellent contributions (and the patience) of the different authors.

Andrew F. Cooper, Waterloo
Christopher W. Hughes, Warwick
Philippe De Lombaerde, Bruges

Abbreviations

ACP	African, Caribbean and Pacific Group of States
AFTA	ASEAN Free Trade Area
ANZUS	Australia-New Zealand United States Defence Arrangement
APEC	Asia-Pacific Economic Cooperation
APRO	Asian and Pacific Regional Organisation
ASEAN	Association of Southeast Asian Nations
ASEAN+3	ASEAN, together with China, Japan and Korea
ASEM	Asia-Europe Meeting
AU	African Union
BSY	Bina Swadaya Yogyakarta (Malaysia)
CAN	Andean Community
CENTO	Central Treaty Organization
CIS	Commonwealth of Independent States
CIT	classical integration theory
COE	Council of Europe
CRIS	United Nations Comparative Research in Integration Studies
CRTA	Committee on Regional Trade Agreements (WTO)
CRTC	Canadian Radio-television and Telecommunications Commission
CSA	country-specific advantage
CSCE	Commission on Security and Cooperation in Europe
CSR	corporate social responsibility
CSTO	Collective Security Organization
CUSFTA	Canada-United States Free Trade Agreement
DDA	Doha Development Agenda
EC	European Community
ECCAS	Economic Community of Central African States
ECOSOC	Economic and Social Council (UN)
ECOWAS	Economic Community of West African States
ECSC	European Coal and Steel Community
EEC	European Economic Community
EMEs	emerging market economies
ERT	European Roundtable of Industrialists

EU	European Union
EWC	European Works Council
FDI	foreign direct investment
FGLS	feasible generalised least squares
FSA	firm-specific advantage
FTA	free trade agreement
G4	Group of Four (Germany, Japan, India, Brazil)
G8	Group of Eight (Industrialised Nations)
G20	Group of Twenty (Finance)
GATS	General Agreement on Trade in Services
GATT	General Agreement on Tariffs and Trade
GPA	Government Procurement Agreement
HLM	high-level meeting
ICC	International Criminal Court
ICFTU	International Confederation of Free Trade Unions
IDSS	Institute of Defence and Strategic Studies, Singapore
IGAD	International Governmental Development Authority
ILO	International Labour Organization
IMF	International Monetary Fund
INCP	International Network on Cultural Policy
IPE	International Political Economy
IPR	intellectual property rights
IR	International Relations
IT	information technology
L20	Leaders' Twenty
LAS	League of Arab States
MAI	Multilateral Agreement on Investment
MDGs	Millennium Development Goals
MDG8	Millennium Development Goal 8: Develop a global partnership for development
MEDIA	Measures to Encourage the Development of the Audiovisual Industry (European Commission)
Mercosur	Common Market of the South
MFN	most-favoured-nation
MNE	multinational enterprise
MRA	mutual recognition agreement
NAACL	North American Agreement on Labour Cooperation
NAFTA	North American Free Trade Agreement
NATO	North Atlantic Treaty Organization
NEP	National Economic Policy (Malaysia)
NGO	non-governmental organisation
NR	new regionalism
NRA	new regionalism approach
NTS	non-traditional security
OAS	Organization of American States

OAU	Organization of African Unity
OECD	Organisation for Economic Co-operation and Development
OECS	Organization of East Caribbean States
OIC	Organization of the Islamic Conference
OLS	ordinary least squares
ORCs	other restrictions on commerce
OSCE	Organization for Security and Cooperation in Europe
PIF	Pacific Islands Forum
R&D	research and development
ROE	rest of Europe
ROFA	return on foreign assets
ROTA	return on total assets
ROW	rest of the world
RTA	regional trade agreement
SAARC	South Asian Association for Regional Cooperation
SADC	Southern African Development Community
SAFTA	South Asian Free Trade Area
SAGIT	Culture Industries Sectoral Advisory Group on International Trade
SAPs	structural adjustment policies
SARS	Severe Acute Respiratory Syndrome
SC	Security Council (UN)
SCO	Shanghai Cooperation Council
SEATO	Southeast Asian Treaty Organization
SHIRBRIG	Standby High Readiness Brigade for United Nations Operations
SIGTUR	Southern Initiative on Globalization and Trade Union Rights
SPS	sanitary and phytosanitary
TBT	technical barrier to trade
TCE	transaction cost economics
TNC	transnational corporation
TRIPs	trade-related aspects of intellectual property rights
UN	United Nations
UNDP	United Nations Development Programme
UNEP	United Nations Environment Programme
UNESCO	United Nations Educational, Scientific and Cultural Organisation
UNICE	Union of Industrial and Employers' Confederations of Europe
UNSAS	United Nations Stand-By Arrangement System
UPC	Urban Poor Consortium (Malaysia)
WHO	World Health Organization
WIPO	World Intellectual Property Organization
WMD	weapons of mass destruction
WTO	World Trade Organization

Introduction

Regionalisation and the taming of globalisation?

Andrew F. Cooper, Christopher W. Hughes and Philippe De Lombaerde

The relationship between global governance and regionalisation is fraught with ambiguity.[1] If the core of global governance is about rule-setting and maintenance, the architecture of this project should be constructed at the universal level. The development of multilateral institutions, and modes of authority, trumps all other options. Global governance should also allow for an expansion of actorness beyond the traditional state-centric model. The interactive participation – including possibly some delegative responsibilities – for non-governmental organisations (NGOs) and what some proponents of global governance term civil society must be a priority here (Lipschutz 1996: 249), building on the notion of transnational advocacy networks on a global scale (Keck and Sikkink 1998). The formalistic attributes of inter-governmentalism are simply not enough. In agenda terms any embrace of global governance needs to take into account the extent to which an extensive set of issues have become trans-sovereign in nature (Cusimano 2000), with problems 'without passports' and their solutions extending across borders as well.

Yet, the first best choice, universal forms of structure and agency, comes up short on both conceptual and operational grounds. On one side, global governance has faced a backlash from critics who argue that its intellectual foundations have not lived up to expectations. A flavour of this negative reaction emerged with the appearance of the Commission on Global Governance (Commission for Global Governance 1995; Knight 2005). But this critique has been extended in a number of recent publications. The central theme of these works is that, far from offering a coherent and all-encompassing vision of the future, the notion of global governance has become increasingly imprecise and woolly. As one commentator judged the deficiencies of this project: 'It can take virtually any meaning, a vast conceptual space to be filled by content by those involved in the theory and practice of world affairs' (Friedrichs 2005: 50).

Nor has the global governance project achieved primacy in the policy struggles. As Andrew Hurrell has noted: 'strong notions of global governance are not looking very plausible' (2005: 53). By placing such considerable emphasis on norms and values – most notably justice and equity – it has lost its appreciation of the power dimension in world affairs. A huge gap exists between the professed goal of global governance and modes of credible operational commitments.

In the struggle for ascendancy the global governance project lost ground with the 'triumph' of the neo-liberal strategy of globalisation. The ingredients of this alternative model are well known: accelerated economic interaction, liberalisation, deregulation, and privatisation. Instead of the holistic menu presented by the global governance project – with checks on the hypercompetitive ethos and the sharp distinction between winners and losers – the globalisation model is self-consciously economist, rationalistic, and homogenous.

Regionalism as part of a wider constellation of projects

Regionalisation in this context cannot be viewed as a completely autonomous project. Its relevance depends on its relationship, and reactive condition, with both the constellations of global governance and globalisation. As Richard Higgott probes this constellation, any claim of regionalisation possessing a privileged condition as a project depended on its ability not just to advance but 'to manage, retard, control, regulate or mitigate market globalization' (Higgott 2003: 128).

Through this relational and reactive lens, the wider process of regionalisation is cast as constitutive of both an offensive and defensive mechanism. As the dominance of globalisation was revealed, so did the emergence of demands for more innovative types of governance to condition its effect! Regionalisation opens up one possible channel for exploring these creative enterprises. But regionalisation also provides a fall-back or compensatory option by which a retreat takes place from an over-extended approach towards the deepening of integration. Behind both responses is a measure of counterconsensus, if not a full-scale double movement, in which a social market or cultural balance is established at odds with the market-oriented variant of the globalisation process.

This dynamic – which provides the title of this book: *Regionalisation and Global Governance: The Taming of Globalisation?* – provides a number of normative and practical benefits. In some ways it complicates the construct by bringing back elements of territory or geography as the site for governance: whether in terms of institutional architecture, actorness or agenda setting. In other ways though, this shift in the framing of governance – via the elevation of physical space as a prime container – allows locality and/ spatiality to be a privileged locus of control that has many attractive features both for efficiency and legitimacy. Although done in an even fashion (Mittelman 2004), the possibility of closeness to citizens – with greater measures of accountability – can be combined with a better job of problemsolving that responds to new demands and filling gaps in policy needs.

These debates play out across a wide spectrum of contestation. From a state-centric perspective, regionalisation allows a second best or fall-back scenario. The focus on a narrower construct of 'neighbourhood' allows national governments back into policy at odds with the image of sweeping globalisation. Some degree of bargaining becomes necessary at the inter-governmental and/or at the societal level. And the emphasis on grappling back prerogatives of authority and aspects of the policy agenda provides some choice over regulatory capacity, mechanisms for social coherence, or even developmental strategies.

At the inter-state level, regionalisation allows the possibility of providing some check on the capacity of the big powers to dominate. The traditional advantages of multilateralism – whether applied through the United Nations or other institutions such as the General Agreement on Tariffs and Trade (GATT) or the World Trade Organization (WTO) – have morphed into one of the perceived advantages of regionalism. Regional hegemons are kept in the process – and in some projects continue to hold their long dominant positions, albeit by shifting means (Gamble and Payne 1996) – but the zeal-ousness of any one power is tempered in the case of other projects by the combined weight of other actors (Fawcett 2005). Smaller players have some space to provide ideas, to take on forms of entrepreneurial and technical leadership, as well as to combine in blocking coalitions of the weak.[2]

In societal terms, regionalisation has morphed from being viewed almost exclusively as either a project which promotes clubs of rich countries and/or as a precursor to globalisation, designed to accommodate liberalisation and de-regulation via regional free trade deals. Today regionalisation is cast in far more hybrid or ambivalent terms. Some projects are still fought against as a race to the bottom with an attendant loss of labour and environmental condi-tions. But this debate reveals how regionalism has become mixed in com-position as a mobilising construct with a blend of developed/developing countries. Regionalisation has been recognised by elements of civil society as unanticipated sites or layers of scepticism and resistance to – with the buffering of – neo-liberalism (Bøås *et al.* 2005: 3). Alliances have sprung up between some leaders/governments and these societal groups have taken up this cause both at a national and transnational level. As part of a wider struggle between state/societal and market forces, outcomes differ sharply among regional projects. But the fact that results are not pre-determined is salient in itself. Regionalisation changes the language and the meaning of governance. It also brings different political variables into play, as the trad-itional fixed domestic and international landscapes become blurred.

The detractors of regionalisation see a very different and more problematic outcome. Both hyper-globalists and some defenders of the multilateral order see regional projects generally and regional trade deals in particular not as a fall-back solution but as a defection strategy. Localism comes at the expense of a push towards universalism. At the very least it reveals a shrinking of ambition. At worst, it retraces its steps towards the competitive regionalism of former eras.

Advocates of stronger global regimes in human rights point out other dangers. The rich clubs of the past have become security zones in which walls are erected between insiders and outsiders. Far from being a progressive project, regionalism becomes regressive (Falk 2002), with the narratives of regionalism becoming distorted in terms of identity. Some projects – e.g. the European Union (EU) – are commonly seen as having adopted a narrower gauge of who belongs and who doesn't. Some projects – the North American Free Trade Agreement (NAFTA) comes to mind – can be divided up into concentric rings with differentiated treatment and access even among 'partners' in the same regional project.

These images of differentiation have become accentuated after 9/11. Security concerns have meant a return to harder borders at the expense of inclusiveness, never mind any sense of a 'we feeling'. Images of Fortress Europe have become associated not only with economic conditions but with respect to the movement of people. The introduction of Smart Borders in North America connotes a sharp divide between allowing the free flow of certain categories of people and heightening restrictions against others. Terrorists, of course, top the list of fears. But to this concern is added other 'bads': drugs, trafficking of people, and money laundering.

Stripping off the issues with respect to the other constellation of architecture, actorness and agenda in this fashion brings the analysis back to the disconnects and connects between global governance and regionalisation. If in some ways continuing to have rough edges at their inter-section, in other ways they mirror and reinforce each other. Indeed, as the social and cultural dimensions are added to the economic, the complexity of this relationship between global governance and regionalisation is stretched still further.

This duality leads into some of the central questions discussed in this book. What are the 'bad' and 'good' implications when the forces of regionalisation and global governance rub up against each other? Is the result a parting of the ways with exacerbated tensions? Through a different lens, what are the opportunities of extending co-existence to complementary activity in a functional vein? Are there tasks that can be shared in the pursuit of both global governance and regionalisation? And what is the distribution of the requisite resources? And it must at least be asked, what difference does it make whether there are tensions or complementariness between the two sets of projects?

Finally, the book clearly connects also to the various (more or less recent) theoretical discussions on optimal policy and governance levels and, more specifically, on the optimality of the regional level in different policy areas. These discussions include those inspired by, for example, fiscal federalism, optimal currency areas and functional integration, and will be placed in a new light.[3]

The aims and contributions of the book

The aim of this book is to provide a big picture of the distinctive but intersecting trajectories of regionalisation and global governance. By design, it is intended to provide an expansive canvass and survey of the context as well as the general character of these projects, together with their links as both parallel mediating mechanisms and distinctive choices for interjecting governance into globalisation. By looking at these projects in tandem, the importance of both is amplified, and coincidental as well as alternative possibilities in policy direction are teased out. As increasingly understood in the literature: 'governance agreements rarely operate in a vacuum; more often they interact with other agreements in complex ways' (Koenig-Archibugi 2006: 16).

What the book does not provide are up-to-the-moment detailed renditions of the different regional projects themselves. In part, this is simply a choice of comparative advantage. The authors of the individual chapters bring with them an impressive degree of expertise in being able to locate the connects and disconnects between regionalisation and global governance. Some do so as analysts who have opened up that area of study from a narrow technical endeavour to one that embraces a comprehensive methodology. Others are sophisticated commentators of global trends who have come to increasingly appreciate the need to scrutinise regional dynamics. Even those contributors considered specialists in the workings of a particular regional project have stepped out of this framework to assess the wider set of intellectual debates and practical contours.

There has also been a valuable catch-up in the literature on the various regional projects. The EU has been comprehensively studied, as has NAFTA and at a quickened pace other projects in Asia-Pacific, the Americas, and Africa.[4] While still North-oriented in focus, the gap between the scrutiny of North-centric and Southern-based projects – and those inter-regional approaches crossing geographic barriers – has been substantially closed.

Under these conditions, with an extensive and expanding specialist literature, there is little need to go over the well-rehearsed debates through a similar volume. Rather, an opportunity can now be seized to move out and beyond this valuable albeit more defined work to build on this base through a more eclectic and expansive volume.

Eclecticism and expansiveness, however, should not be confused with superficiality. By cutting into and through the debates on global governance and regionalisation via this pairing, the exploration of both projects is carried forward. This book may be free of the 'devil is in the details' account of some studies on regional projects. But the contributors are all aware of making sure their conceptual big pictures are grounded in sensitive and well-grounded empirical accounts. All of the chapters provide a mix of normative and policy-rich material.

Part I: Theoretical debates

Chapter 1 by Ramesh Thakur and Luk Van Langenhove serves as an introduction to this volume's theoretical examination of regionalisation, and an
ideal starting point for a discussion of regionalisation as a satisfactory solution to the missing elements in global governance. Recognising that the
meaning of governance has gradually changed over the decades, the authors
identify a number of governance problems, from the explosion in the number
of nation-states, to legitimacy challenges as a result of increased civil society
activity and market dominance. Their emphasis is on the paradox found
between global problems that are so often linked and the solutions that are
disconnected. As well, they highlight the dangers to the multilateral system –
especially the United Nations – associated with the rise of regionalisation.
But they also appreciate the value of regional governance as part of the
multilateral framework of governance, positing that regions may have a
comparative advantage over states in terms of effective actions on security,
development and human rights. In order for the advantages to outweigh the
disadvantages, the authors conclude that regionalisation must move beyond
economic integration, that region-building should be encouraged in vulnerable areas without strong regional mechanisms, and that non-state actors and
the tenets of subsidiarity must be added to regional projects as well.

Rather than concentrating on the relationship between regional organisations and global institutions such as the UN, in Chapter 2, Alex Warleigh-
Lack explores the many attempts to theorise regionalism. Examining the
main conceptual schisms, he argues that the well-known divide between 'new'
and 'old' regionalisms in international politics has been exaggerated. The
attempt to build a new body of theory to explain and describe recent forms
of region-building – the 'New Regionalist Approach' – is problematic. He
suggests that the separation between integration theorists/European studies
scholars and the 'new regionalism' theorists is unhelpful for the regionalism
field as a whole, arguing that both sub-fields can learn and benefit from the
mistakes and insights of the other. The two areas of study should instead be
understood not as separate paradigms, but rather as sub-divisions of the same
one. The chapter sets out a definition and typology of regionalisation and
argues for a critical theory approach to the elaboration of a conceptual
framework for its study.

In Chapter 3, Björn Hettne and Fredrik Söderbaum recognise that regionalism is now a focus in a number of social science specialisations, and that the
field of study has become fragmented and plagued by divisions, as noted by
Warleigh-Lack. This chapter concentrates on three significant schisms. The
authors first tackle the 'old' versus 'new' regionalism divide, and suggest that
while the distinction between the two is no longer useful, the new regionalism
approach is still valid as a way of analysing regionalisation. The second divide
is between the European integration theorists and the international relations/
international political economy (IR/IPE) comparative regionalism scholars.

Rather than using Europe as the standard from which to explain all other cases of regionalisation, or excluding Europe altogether in theorising attempts, it is important to 'bridge the gap', and enhance communication in comparative regional analysis. Finally, Hettne and Söderbaum discuss the 'stumbling block' versus 'stepping stone' dichotomy in the relationship between globalisation and regionalisation. They posit that moving beyond this dualism would allow a more nuanced understanding of the relationship, with a focus on process and change. Rather than encouraging the development of a single rigid theory for understanding regionalism, the authors propose that it is more helpful to approach an empirical case from multiple angles, as different theories will uncover different aspects of complex issues.

In this examination of conceptualising regionalism, in Chapter 4, Ben Rosamond continues from Hettne and Söderbaum, suggesting that 'new' regionalism has lost much of its novelty. He too advocates for a rediscovery of past theories in his chapter to augment current debates, yet he proposes a visitation of the theory that begat them all – the long marginalised classical integration theory, which once directed studies in European integration. Since that time, the regional movement in Europe has evolved into a complex institutional framework, and accordingly, multiple intricate theories have been constructed to explain and predict economic, political, legal and cultural outcomes. But in their complexity, Rosamond suggests that these theories have lost clarity and flexibility. He asserts that classical integration theory hearkens back to an approach where multiple perspectives were adapted, for a fair and frank theoretical dialogue. It was an analytical project, providing theoretical constraints to observations on theory building and hypothesis testing – a model that Rosamond argues could return order to studies of regional integration. Although the theory was developed during the period of 'old' regionalism and based upon analytical primitivism, classical integration theory provides a sound theoretical footing as we move beyond 'new' regionalism to explain emerging regional political, economic, security and cultural realities.

Part II: Economic dimensions

Regionalisation is often driven exclusively by economic motivations. Here, multiple actors with a variety of interests compete for access and influence, inevitably leading to a clash between market integration and transnational rule-making. Foreign market penetration and regional economic activity are led mostly by self-interested firms, while states and multilateral organisations are often forced to follow. This reality has fostered difficulty in policy-making and rules enforcement. In this arena, Alan Rugman, in Chapter 5, strips away what he presents as the mythology of globalisation in terms of the activities of the world's 500 largest multinational enterprises. With detailed empirical firm-level data, he advances the argument that multinational corporations are actually regional firms with global interests. In doing so, he reinforces the hold of regions as the central site of the governance of commercial activity. Rugman points to a decline of economic globalisation and to a steady increase of regional economic activity, and suggests that corporations must fully develop regional strategies for commodity sourcing, R&D, manufacturing, and logistics. The forces of regionalisation are thus, in his view, critical for firms to understand as globalisation affects only the small percentage of them that are truly global in their activities. However, beyond this recasting in terms of domain, Rugman highlights the need to showcase the activities of multinational enterprises alongside other categories of institutions and actors.

For Stephen Woolcock, an analysis of economic regionalisation must look at normative principles and institutions within and beyond the regional context. In Chapter 6, he addresses the question of how rule-making in trade and investment at the multilateral and regional level interact. Policy-making cannot exist in a vacuum, as in the global era few initiatives are unaffected by externalities. Often the process of negotiation and its ability to coordinate perspectives from a variety of interests are as important as the policy outcomes themselves. Woolcock explores how developments in regional and even bilateral trade agreements can affect the international trade and investment regimes. The key point he underscores is that recent developments suggest that some more malign features of regional initiatives have emerged. To neglect international rule-making risks the possibility of emerging competing regional systems of rules as the dominant players use bilateral or regional level negotiations to establish their own, possibly divergent systems. This trend risks further undermining the multilateral system. Woolcock thus advocates the need to conceive of rule-making as a multi-level process, and that current global trade institutions should adopt procedural reforms. In the face of the transformative effects of regionalisation and globalisation, strong and effective governance, trade and investment are necessary at all levels.

Bridging the economic and security sections of this volume, in Chapter 7, Robert O'Brien introduces the topic of labour, detailing the contradiction between labour's central and peripheral role in regionalisation. In accordance with Hettne and Söderbaum's proposition that topics should be examined from multiple angles in order to better understand the complexity of situations, O'Brien notes the variety of ways in which labour manifests itself in regionalisation, both formally and informally. On the one hand, labour is central to regional integration in the sense that labour issues and migration patterns are often explicitly considered by regional organisations. On the other hand, however, regional integration projects often undermine labour rights, placing labour at the periphery of regionalisation. O'Brien posits that in some projects, regional labour rights and mobility have moved up the policy agenda. But in the majority of cases, formal regionalisation tends to be a negative occurrence from the point of view of labour: rather than improving the position of labour, many regional agreements are eroding labour rights and entrenching the corporate position. While Thakur and Van Langenhove suggest that regionalism needs to move beyond economic integration to be most successful, O'Brien goes further, advocating the development of an alternative type of regional project not as guided by neoclassical economics, but one that is still linked to the national and global levels.

Part III: Security considerations

Kennedy Graham, in Chapter 8, shifts the attention of the volume towards the security dimension of regionalisation – especially the performance of regional organisations – in times of crisis. Whereas Thakur and Van Langenhove posit that it is problematic to argue that the creation of regional organisations is directly related to the absence of regional conflict, and instead suggest that integration on a regional level can help to control and manage conflict, Graham argues on both a conceptual and operational basis that the full potential of regions to deal with security issues has yet to be fulfilled. His chapter provides an extensive review of this regionalisation experience. Just as Thakur and Van Langenhove introduced multilevel governance into this volume, Graham also places regional security measures within this multilevel framework, detailing how regional organisations have been working in collaboration with international institutions such as the United Nations. The chapter also goes on to offer a broad framework as to how improvements could be brought about and how regionalism could function more fully to mitigate global security issues.

Adding to the discussion of security in the context of regionalism, in Chapter 9, Mely Caballero-Anthony explores the theme of non-traditional security in Asia. Moving away from the traditional linking of security with military threats to states, she considers the impact of 'securitising' issues, such as poverty and infectious disease, on both the academic field of security studies and the policy responses of state and non-state actors. She begins with an analysis of the manner by which 'security-framing' is used as a device to treat a wide number of national and transnational issues. To 'orthodox' specialists, this new language distorts the meaning of security. Notwithstanding these objections, though, the profile of these emerging issues has continued to be raised. In terms of policy responses, a key component of the decision to 'securitise' an issue is the role of the securitising actor. While the state is still a critical actor in most of the securitising process, non-state actors can also play a strong role in certain instances. In addition, regional organisations are crucial actors when non-traditional security issues are not adequately dealt with at national levels; this view corresponds to the position taken by Thakur and Van Langenhove, who posit that regional organisations may have a comparative advantage over states in terms of efficacy. Nevertheless, the decision of which issues to 'securitise' is still based on conceptions of state security, rather than human security. Caballero-Anthony suggests that institutional capacity-building at all levels of governance may provide a better alternative in addressing non-traditional security issues.

Part IV: Governing structures

Providing order and coherence in policy terms for these complex issues of regionalisation is no small task. Regardless of how one conceives the influences of regional dimensions, there are numerous policy areas that must be placed in this context. Managing political, economic, security, and cultural aspects of regional integration requires a keen understanding of the issues surrounding them and of how regionalisation affects policy-making at other levels of authority. On this basis, Patricia Goff, in Chapter 10, explores cultural components of the globalisation debate, and locates a split between those who argue that globalisation has accentuated diversity and those who see it as intertwined with standardisation. Her analysis covers all levels of cultural policy development – local, national, regional and international – with specific case studies of each and their contribution to the regionalisation of culture. Goff argues that making cultural policy in a globalising world requires a complex set of initiatives at all levels of government. In particular, she contrasts how economic integration has spurred cultural protectionism in North America while bringing about cultural standardisation in Europe. Respectively, culture is seen as an issue of sovereignty and as a regional policy sector in these two regions. Here, Goff showcases the hybrid status of culture in public policy, where governments implement liberalised initiatives at local levels to exploit the potential of economic integration while at the same time attempting to protect themselves against the negative effects of globalisation. She submits that culture, and how it is addressed in global governance, comprises an issue area that is most susceptible to the forces of globalisation and that different regions have adopted alternative approaches to cultural policies as they have differing desired ends of regional integration.

Extending this analysis over the entire constellation of projects showcased in this book – global governance, globalisation and regionalisation – Martin Albrow and Colin Bradford, in Chapter 11, seek evidence of collective political culture within regions and its external projection. They examine the potential global role of regions, in particular their ability to advance international agreements or targets as entities themselves and as competitors with other regions. What they signal – using a wide variety of lenses – is the emerging capacity of regions to play a global role, if not as part of a coherent global governance process, then at least because of a commitment to a set of global goals such as the Millennium Development Goals (MDGs). Rather than viewing cultural differentiation as a stumbling block, it is taken as a building block to more effective and wide-reaching political consensus. Here then, governance is the key to agreement. The authors submit that regions with institutionalised frameworks can play an important role in advancing international agendas like the MDGs, for they can set appropriate guidelines for their adherence regionally. Additionally, regional organisations are better equipped at assisting in the development of multinational agreements, for they credibly represent numerous states with a variety of perspectives. A collection of states with mutual interests can thus have a great impact on advancing international standards and agreements through cooperation.

In the final chapter of this volume, Andrew Cooper distinguishes between 'new' multilateralism and 'new' regionalism as sites of value for global governance. As with the construct of global governance and regionalisation more generally, he sees the parallels (not the juxtaposition) between these projects as meriting attention. The case of the proposed Leaders' Twenty (L20) is used as an extended snapshot of how new multilateralism and regionalisation can work in tandem. Where multilateralism has drifted towards issue-specific initiatives and regionalism has developed new rule-making institutions, such a forum could bring together emerging global powers and regional leaders to promptly and effectively address global issues. Cooper argues that there is space for the L20 to transform summitry from a club to a networked form of new multilateralism. The inclusion of regional anchors in this framework furthers its ability to solidify international cooperation, for the essence of the L20 is as a cross-regional project. The L20 would thus move away from the 1970s model of the G8, and recognise contemporary economic leaders and the political realities of the twenty-first century. Cooper concludes that if it can be argued that the forces of globalisation can be conditioned by any form of global governance, the major global and regional powers must be brought into the apex of power and responsibility.

Facilitating the dialogue

With both regionalisation and global governance highly complicated and contested projects, it is not surprising that the conclusions of this book take the analysis in diverse and often surprising directions. Neither the regionalisation nor the global governance project follow one easily pinned down or conventional script so a blending together pushes us beyond our comfortable boundaries. What can be safely understood is that we have already moved into a stage of complex multi-governance with a wide variety of contours and speeds for looking at and doing things. This increases the frustrations of this activity with a myriad of open possibilities and interpretations. But it also raises the stakes of expectations. Fresh ways of looking at these dynamics are necessary, then, both in terms of intellectual inquiry and in helping guide policy direction.

Notes

1 For the purpose of this Introduction we will use 'regionalisation' and 'regionalism' as synonyms. However, for the further analysis of the phenomena, a distinction where the former refers to a 'process' and the latter to a 'policy or project', is obviously most useful (see Fawcett (2005: 23–7), for a discussion of definitional issues). Regionalisation refers, then, to the regional concentration of human activity, the emergence of regional interdependencies, the emergence of regional actors and institutions, whereas regionalism as a policy or political project ranges from the

building of regional communities and the promotion of regional identities (*soft* regionalism) to the promotion and formation of formal regional organizations based on inter-state arrangements and agreements (*hard* regionalism).

2 See also Tussie (2003) on the political economy (and ambiguity) of the regionalisation–globalisation interplay in a trade context.

3 For a recent review of these approaches, see, for example, Gavin and De Lombaerde (2005) and De Lombaerde and Costea (2006).

4 For a representative sample, see Payne (2004), Phillips (2004), Söderbaum and Taylor (2003), Ravenhill (2001), and Farrell *et al.* (2005).

References

Bøås, M., Marchand, M.H. and Shaw, T.M. (2005) *The Political Economy of Regions*, New York: Palgrave Macmillan.

Commission for Global Governance (1995) *Our Global Neighbourhood*, Oxford: Oxford University Press.

Cusimano, M.K. (2000) 'Beyond Sovereignty: The Rise of Transsovereign Problems', in M.K. Cusimano (ed.) *Beyond Sovereignty: Issues for a Global Agenda*, Boston, MA: Bedford/St Martin's Press.

De Lombaerde, P. and Costea, A.C. (2006) 'Comparative Fiscal Integration Indicators', in P. De Lombaerde (ed.) *Assessment and Measurement of Regional Integration*, London: Routledge, pp. 130–45.

Falk, R. (2002) 'The Post-Westphalia Enigma', in B. Hettne and B. Odén (eds) *Global Governance in the 21st Century: Alternative Perspectives on World Order*, Stockholm: EGDI.

Farrell, M., Hettne, B. and Van Langenhove, L. (2005) *Global Politics of Regionalism: Theory and Practice*, London: Pluto Press.

Fawcett, L. (2005) 'Regionalism from an Historical Perspective', in M. Farrell, B. Hettne and L. Van Langenhove (eds) *Global Politics of Regionalism*, London: Pluto Press, pp. 21–37.

Friedrichs, J. (2005) 'Global Governance as the Hegemonic Project of Transatlantic Civil Society', in M. Lederer and P.S. Muller (eds) *Criticizing Global Governance*, New York: Palgrave Macmillan.

Gamble A. and Payne, A. (1996) *Regionalism and World Order*, London: Routledge.

Gavin, B. and De Lombaerde, P. (2005) 'Economic Theories of Regional Integration', in M. Farrell, B. Hettne and L. Van Langenhove (eds) *Global Politics of Regionalism*, London: Pluto Press, pp. 69–83.

Higgott, R. (2003) 'Economic Globalization and Global Governance: Towards a Post-Washington Consensus?', in V. Rittberger (ed.) *Global Governance and the United Nations System*, Tokyo: United Nations University Press.

Hurrell, A. (2005) 'The Regional Dimension in International Relations Theory', in M. Farrell, B. Hettne and L. Van Langenhove (eds) *Global Politics of Regionalism*, London: Pluto Press, pp. 38–53.

Keck, M.E. and Sikkink, K. (1998) *Activism Beyond Borders: Advocacy Networks in International Politics*, Ithaca, NY: Cornell University Press.

Knight, W.A. (2005) 'Equivocating on the Future of World Order: The Commission on Global Governance', in R. Thakur, A.F. Cooper and J. English (eds) *International Commissions and the Power of Ideas*, Tokyo: United Nations University Press, pp. 99–122.

Koenig-Archibugi, M. (2006) 'Introduction: Institutional Diversity in Global Governance', in M. Koenig-Arhibugi and M. Zurn (eds) *New Modes of Governance in the Global System: Exploring Publicness, Delegation and Inclusiveness*, New York: Palgrave Macmillan.

Lipschutz, R.D. (1996) *Global Civil Society and Global Environmental Governance: The Politics of Nature from Place to Planet*, New York: SUNY.

Mittelman, J.H. (2004) *Whither Globalisation?: The Vortex of Knowledge and Ideology*, London: Routledge.

Payne A. (ed.) (2004) *The New Regional Politics of Development*, New York: Palgrave Macmillan.

Phillips, N. (2004) *The Regional Cone Model: The Political Economy of Regional Capitalist Development in Latin America*, London: Routledge.

Ravenhill, J. (2001) *APEC and the Construction of Pacific Rim Regionalism*, Cambridge: Cambridge University Press.

Söderbaum, F. and Taylor, I. (2003) *Regionalism and Uneven Development in Southern Africa: The Case of the Maputo Development Corridor*, Aldershot: Ashgate.

Tussie, D. (2003) 'Regionalism: Providing a Substance to Multilateralism?', in F. Söderbaum and T.M. Shaw (eds) *Theories of New Regionalism*, Basingstoke: Palgrave, pp. 99–116.

Part I
Theoretical debates
Locating regionalisation theory

1 Enhancing global governance through regional integration

Ramesh Thakur and Luk Van Langenhove

> The United Nations and regional organizations should play complementary roles in facing the challenges to international peace and security.
>
> (Annan 2005: para. 213)

Introduction

The *problématique* of global governance may be simply stated: the evolution of institutions of international governance has lagged behind the rapid emergence of collective problems with on-border and cross-border dimensions, especially those that are global in scope or potentially so. Depending on the issue area, geographic location, and timing, there are vast disparities in power and influence among states, international organisations, corporations, and non-governmental organisations (NGOs). Consequently, today's world is governed by a 'crazy quilt' or patchwork of authority that is as diffuse as it is contingent (Rosenau 1999: 293). In particular, the international intergovernmental institutions that collectively underpin global governance are insufficient in number, inadequately resourced and sometimes incoherent in their separate policies and philosophies.

In framing global governance in this way, the nature and shortcomings in governing international peace and security become clear: the absence of any semblance of a central authority in a world of sovereign states. The Security Council and Chapter VII of the United Nations (UN) Charter exist on paper, but the overwhelming reality is what Hedley Bull immortalised as 'the anarchical society' (Bull 1997). With a few exceptions (arguably Korea, Kuwait, and responses to a few humanitarian crises in the 1990s), the dearth of any powerful institutional response ensures poor international security governance. Collective security is an idea, not a reality. The existence of vibrant market forces and proliferating NGOs does little to counteract this dominant fact.

The basic unit of international relations is and for the foreseeable future will remain the sovereign state. As such, sovereign states have to cope with the governance of global problems. This gives rise to a paradox: on the one hand, the policy authority for tackling global problems and mobilising the necessary resources is vested in states, while on the other hand, the source/ scale of the problems and potential solutions are situated at a transnational, regional or global level. The result is that member states have the capacity to disable decision-making and policy implementation by the United Nations, but lack the vision and the will to empower and enable global problem-solving. This paradox holds for many problems such as armed conflicts, environmental degradation, human trafficking, terrorism and nuclear weapons. The United Nations cannot displace the responsibility of local, state and national governments, but it can and should be the locus of multilateral diplomacy and collective action to solve problems shared in common by many countries.

So can regional organisations be the locus of multilateral diplomacy and collective action to solve problems shared in common within a region but not necessarily beyond it? As societies evolve, expand and multiply, their governing framework of rules and institutions becomes correspondingly more complex and functionally specific. A necessary consequence of increasingly differentiated structures of governance is the increased space between citizens as self-contained individuals, and the state as a collective abstraction. In contemporary societies, national governments can satisfy only a small and diminishing proportion of the needs of human beings as social animals. Consequently, citizens look more and more to additional actors and layers of governance. Civic associations channel a growing range and variety of social interactions, which in turn need a framework of governance outside the jurisdiction of the state. 'Civil society' refers, broadly speaking, to the social and political space where voluntary associations (as distinct from the automatic, binding and compulsory membership of a state) attempt to shape norms and policies to regulate public life in social, political, economic and environmental dimensions. And the layers of governance now extend from the local to the global.

The central question addressed in this chapter is whether regionalism and regionalisation can provide a satisfactory solution for the above paradox. Solving it calls for a new thinking that emphasises the networked aspects of governance in order to deal with the interdependencies across policy *levels* (from local to global) and policy *domains*. Especially in Europe, with, on the one hand, the processes of Europeanisation of policy and, on the other, the progressive upgrading of the microregional level in both national and European policy processes, there is now a wide consensus that governance is not limited to the level of the state. A novel concept has been advanced – multi-level governance – in order to emphasise power-sharing between different levels of government with

> no centre of accumulated authority. Instead, variable combinations of governments on multiple layers of authority – European, national, and subnational – form policy networks for collaboration. The relations are

characterised by mutual interdependence on each other's resources, not by competition for scarce resources.

(Hooghe 1996: 18)

Such multilevel governance can be defined as 'the dispersion of authoritative decision-making across multiple territorial levels' (Hooghe and Marks 2001: xi). From this perspective, European integration is a polity-creating process in which authority and policy-making influence are shared across the multiple levels of government.

The United Nations University has developed in the past decade an Interlinkages Initiative (Velasquez and Piest 2003), which is based on the recognition that nowadays the problems are linked but the solutions are often disjointed. Interlinkages is a strategic approach to managing sustainable development which stems from the premise that different issues arise across different levels and planning phases (negotiation and ratification, implementation, monitoring). Responses need to take these levels into account and have to be tailored to specific requirements. To take better advantage of the interlinkages between our problems and ensure the effective implementation of our solutions, we need to understand the challenges and opportunities that exist at the various levels of governance.

Considerable potential exists to develop and apply interlinkages at and across all levels of governance. In recent years, attention has been focusing on improving inter-agency coordination at the global institutional level. However, while efforts to enhance synergies at the global level must continue, challenges and opportunities for enhanced coordination at the regional and national levels also need to be addressed. Secretary-General Kofi Annan spoke evocatively of problems without passports that require solutions without passports. The one continent where passport-less borders have become at least a partial reality (in the Schengen area) is Europe (although a UN passport by itself is not sufficient to gain entry into this area).

We shall argue that there is indeed a place for regional governance in the multilateral framework of global governance. But only if regional integration processes go beyond economic integration and only if they have sufficient support from civil society, will regional integration have the power to combat the dark sides and unlock the development potential of globalisation. The argument is developed in relation to the UN's two great normative mandates, namely, underwriting international peace and security and promoting sustainable development. The difference between the two mandates is important, for two reasons. First, at the global level, in the trade and economic sector there probably still is a degree of genuine multipolarity that has disappeared in the peace and security sector. And, second, reflecting this, regionalism in the economic arena can more easily be self-sufficient than in the security sector. Thus the European Union (EU) is comprised of Europeans, but the North Atlantic Treaty Organization (NATO) is trans-atlantic, anchoring the United States (US) to Europe. Similarly in Asia-Pacific, the experience and memory of the financial crisis of 1997–98 have generated deepening intra-Asian institutionalisation in the finance and trade sectors while the US remains the pivot of regional security arrangements because of persisting and confrontational nationalist sentiments in the political relations among the major East Asian nations.

Global governance [1]

Traditionally, governance has been associated with 'governing', or with political authority and institutions and, ultimately, control. Governance in this particular sense denotes formal political institutions that aim to coordinate and control interdependent social relations. In recent years, however, analysts of global affairs have used 'governance' to denote the regulation of interdependent relations in the *absence* of an overarching political authority, such as in the international system.

Three definitions related to governance would be helpful. *Governance* refers to the complex of power, control, and authority; how they are exercised; and how the relationships between their holders, wielders, and objects are mediated and transformed over time. *Good governance* incorporates participation and empowerment with respect to public policies, choices, and offices; rule of law and an independent judiciary to which the executive and legislative branches of government are subject, along with citizens and other actors and entities; and standards of probity and incorruptibility, transparency, accountability, and responsibility. It includes, essentially, institutions and national integrity systems in which these principles and values find ongoing expression. *Global governance*, which can be good or bad, refers to concrete cooperative problem-solving arrangements on the global plane. These may be rules (laws, norms, codes of behaviour) as well as constituted institutions and practices (formal and informal) to manage collective affairs by a variety of actors (state authorities, intergovernmental organisations, NGOs, private sector entities, and other civil society actors). It thus refers to the complex of formal and informal institutions, mechanisms, relationships, and processes between and among states, markets, citizens and organisations, both intergovernmental and non-governmental, through which collective interests are articulated, rights and obligations are established, and differences are mediated.

At the national level, governance implies 'government plus' – a range of technical, private, economic, and civil society quasi-public authorities that supplement and work with (and sometimes against) governments. At the global level, governance entails 'government minus' – a range of state, intergovernmental, and only in very exceptional cases supranational public authorities. However, they are supplemented by technical, multinational economic, and transnational civil society actors interacting with one another and promoting public and contestable rules and norms even in the absence of world government.[2]

The business of the world has changed almost beyond recognition in the past century. The locus of power and influence is shifting. When the UN was founded, its membership consisted of 51 states. Today it stands at 192. Alongside the growth in the number of states there has occurred the rise of civil society actors who have mediated state–citizen relations and given flesh and blood to the concept of 'We the peoples of the world'. The international policy-making stage is increasingly congested as private and public non-state actors jostle alongside national governments in setting and implementing the agenda of the new century.

The dominance of the market, the rise of civil society and the emergence of international 'uncivil' society have all created problems of governance. This is self-evident with respect to uncivil society but worth explaining with regard to the other two, briefly. While economic goals, resources and instruments have always been significant elements in international affairs, the interdependence of national economies has increased with accelerated and expanded flows of trade, investment and technology across political frontiers. Conversely, because states provide the indispensable political, legal and military context for market operations, international economic relations cannot be explained fully without acknowledgement of the enduring and assertive role of the states: 'Markets cannot play a dominant role in the way in which a political economy functions unless allowed to do so by whoever wields power and possesses authority' (Strange 1988: 23). Rules governing international commerce, like those governing international politics, reflect the interests of the dominant players.

The dislocation of market power from political authority has led to a crisis of legitimacy. It is now accepted that globalisation entails risks as well as opportunities, and the sceptical dissenters in the streets offer an antidote to the unbridled enthusiasts in boardrooms and finance departments. Financial crises of the 1990s in Asia, Latin America, and Russia showed how much, and how quickly, regional crises take on a systemic character through rapid contagion. The experience demonstrated the potential vulnerability of the G7 economies to crises originating in the emerging market economies. And, of course, the reverse direction of causality is even stronger. Hence the claim by the former managing director of the International Monetary Fund (IMF) that to the duty of domestic excellence and rectitude we must add the ethic of global responsibility in the management of national economies. He goes on to describe the widening inequality within and among nations as 'morally outrageous, economically wasteful, and socially explosive' (Camdessus 2001).

NGOs face many challenges to their legitimacy as they are often seen as unelected, unaccountable, unrepresentative, self-serving and irresponsible. Can they claim to speak on behalf of anyone but themselves? What mechanisms exist to hold them accountable to their constituents? Hugo Slim writes of 'voice accountability': the reliability and credibility of *what* they say (an empirical question: can you prove it?), and the *locus of their authority* for saying it (a political question: from where do you get your authority to speak?) (2002: 6). They can behave like 'five star activists' indulging their pet causes without taking responsibility for trying to effect changes. According to Chidi Odinkalu, in Africa, 'Far from being a badge of honour, human rights activism is . . . increasingly a certificate of privilege' (ibid.: 2). UN engagement with unelected civil society actors can sometimes cut across and undermine the role of democratically-elected representatives (see Johns 2004). Recipient countries, for example Afghanistan, can resent the NGO community as competitors for siphoning off aid from governments (D'Cruz 2004). In their unrestrained eagerness to capitalise on worldwide public sympathy after the earthquake and tsunami of 26 December 2004, NGOs paid little heed to how much they could actually do by way of relief work that could not be done better by governments and the UN system.

> For all the talk of coordination and accountability, the need to maintain market share continues to trump sound humanitarian practice – at least in crises like the tsunami, where the Western public and Western donor governments are attentive and engaged.
>
> (Rieff 2005: 50)

The organising principle of global governance is multilateralism, and the UN lies at the very core of the multilateral system of global governance – governance without global government. According to Anne-Marie Slaughter, the glue binding the contemporary system of global governance is governing networks, both horizontal and vertical. Horizontal networks link counterpart national officials across borders, such as police investigators or financial regulators. Vertical networks are relationships between national officials and supranational organisations to which they have ceded authority, such as the European Court of Justice. The world needs global governance to combat problems without passports. Most people fear the idea of a centralised, all-powerful world government. The solution lies in strengthening existing networks and developing new ones that could create a genuine global rule of law without centralised global institutions (Slaughter 2004).

Unlike many in earlier generations of analysts of international organisation, the goal of most contemporary proponents of global governance is *not* the creation of world government, but of an additional layer of consultations and decision-making between and alongside governments and intergovernmental organisations. Although improved global problem-solving may or may not involve the creation of more powerful global institutions, there exists a need for specific agents to take action rather than relying upon any 'invisible hand'. Agency is important; there is no guarantee that the supply of global public goods will follow the clear demand.

The goal of *global economic governance* is to manage the world's economic activity without undermining state sovereignty, maintain international financial stability, promote cooperative solutions to global problems, and encourage and facilitate market efficiencies around the world. The goal of *global security governance* is to minimise conflict and violence across the planet, once again while respecting state sovereignty, and to try to resolve the security dilemma through global intergovernmental modalities, institutional arrangements and diplomatic practices.

Global financial governance refers to the rules and procedures by which international financial institutions are regulated. The *architecture* of international financial governance refers to the intergovernmental mechanisms by and through which the rules of global financial governance themselves are authoritatively allocated (Germain 2001: 411). And the *infrastructure* of global financial governance (Sinclair 2001) includes the major debt rating agencies like Moody's Investor Service (Moody's) and Standard and Poor's (S&P), whose decisions move markets (and capital) independently of governmental policies and actions.

Global governance is thus a chameleon-like concept that can be adapted to suit the meaning of the analyst. There is no single model or form of global governance, nor is there a single structure or set of structures. It refers to a broad, dynamic, complex process of interactive decision-making that is constantly evolving and responding to changing circumstances. The report of the Commission on Global Governance emphasised that the challenge of global governance is to set up a global system of rules in such a way that 'the management of global affairs is responsive to the interests of all peoples in a sustainable future', that it is 'guided by basic human values' and that it makes global organisations 'conform to the reality of global diversity' (Commission on Global Governance 1995: xvii).

Global governance and the United Nations

The principal objective of the United Nations at its inception in 1945 was to establish a mechanism to prevent the repeat of devastating world wars and also to promote human rights and international economic and social cooperation. The maintenance of international peace and security was the stated primary purpose of the UN, and the Security Council was conceived as the core of the international law-enforcement system. The ordering in the Preamble begins with the words to 'save succeeding generations from war' and later mentions the need 'to promote social progress and better standards of life'. A reading of other declarations, actions and documents demonstrates that governments were creating a set of institutions that reflected what they perceived as their immediate postwar interests. First and foremost, they sought to create an intergovernmental organisation powerful enough to deter aggression, while preserving state sovereignty.

During the course of the second half of the twentieth century, many new issues appeared on the global agenda, and they were seen as requiring cooperative approaches. For example, such issues as the environment and population increasingly were seen by experts and many governments as requiring collective responses. These issues were explored through global ad hoc conferences organised by the United Nations. These debates, as well as the oil shocks of the 1970s and the debt crisis of the 1980s, led to the notion that the international system was increasingly characterised by a complex global interdependence.

This recognition led to discussions about the potential role of multilateral institutions in mitigating the adverse effects of interdependence. Hence, we moved from a discourse of dependency in the 1960s to one of interdependence in the 1970s and 1980s. The vocabulary maintained a 'Keynesian flavour' in that international regulation and more muscular intergovernmental organisations remained high on most lists of policy recommendations. In the 1990s, however, the discourse switched to global governance, a fuzzier but more accurate depiction of the nebulous nature of the global drivers of order and justice. The concept is premised on devising new ways of fostering greater synergy among state and non-state actors who must be engaged to solve global problems. The logic is that more attention can and should be paid to possible synergies among various levels of efforts because world government, and perhaps even more muscular intergovernmental organisations, are out of the question in the foreseeable future.

The UN's traditional role of improving government policy and formulating intergovernmental institutional policies – a logical role for an institution whose members are states – is giving way to new emphases. In view of the increasingly transnational character of many problems and of the importance of non-state actors, the UN's conceptualisation of global governance has expanded to encompass both transnational market forces and civil society as a regular bill-of-fare instead of an occasional snack. The insertion of the idea of 'human security' in development discourse at the UN in the 1990s, the Security Council's session on HIV/AIDS in January 2000, and the High-Level Panel embrace of a significantly broader conception of security threats (United Nations 2004: 7–19) are recent illustrations of an expanded international agenda. As a result, the operative concept is governance for the globe, rather than world government.

Few will claim that these changes and challenges call for less multilateralism and global governance. On the contrary. But, as Secretary-General Kofi Annan noted, 'we can no longer take it for granted that our multilateral institutions are strong enough to cope with all of the challenges facing them' (United Nations Press Release 2003).

Regionalism

So far we have tried to argue that both the nature of global governance is changing as are the players who constitute the system of global governance. In the remainder of this chapter we will now focus on the actual and potential roles of the regional level in solving the authority/manifestation paradox and in realising an effective global governance. In doing so, it will be argued that: (1) regional governance is not incompatible with and does not negate global governance – on the contrary, it has the potential to strengthen global governance; and (2) we are today witnessing a new current in multilateral governance that gives a prominent role to regions but still has a series of problematic issues that need to be settled. To return to some of the definitional distinctions above, 'good' global governance may well imply, not exclusive policy jurisdiction, but rather an optimal partnership between the state, regional and global *levels* of actors, and between state, intergovernmental and nongovernmental *categories* of actors.

The principle of regionalism has become a major trend in recent times (Farrell *et al.* 2005). Indeed, it is argued by some that the nation-state has become an unnatural, perhaps even dysfunctional, unit for organising human activity and economic interactions in a borderless world. It does not represent any genuine community of economic interests. Instead, the natural economic zones are 'region states' whose boundaries are drawn not by politicians but by the invisible hand of the global market for goods and services. And their primary links are not with host countries but with the global economy (Ohmae 1993).

It is not generally remembered today that originally, a principal impulse to West European integration was the political motive of avoiding another major war in Europe. Economic unification was seen as a means of securing European peace. When French Foreign Minister Robert Schuman announced his famous plan to unify Europe's coal and steel markets in 1950, he said that the European Coal and Steel Community (ECSC) would make war between France and Germany not just unthinkable but materially impossible (Nye 1971: 117). With their economies integrated, the major European powers would lack the means to wage war against one another.

There has been no major war or expectation of war among the West European powers since the Second World War. But it is problematical to try to attribute a causal relationship between the creation of the ECSC and its transformation into the EU, and the absence of war. Another leading contender for having helped to keep the peace in Europe from 1945 to 1990 is nuclear deterrence. A third possible explanation would be the progressive democratisation of Europe. More general studies have concluded that regional organisations do help to create webs of functional links which then improve relations between the member-states, and they do help to control some types of conflicts between their member-states and prevent them from spreading (ibid.). They produce these results because functional interdependence promotes a sense of common identity or community among members; raises the threshold of tolerance of irritating behaviour from other members because perceived benefits exceed perceived challenges; increases the cost of violent conflict to all members; and provides mechanisms, experience and expectations of 'integrative solutions'.

But the more general relationship between the dependent variable of conflict and the independent variable of integration is curvilinear rather than linear. In other words, there is some relationship between the incidence of conflict and integration between states. But it is not a straightforward relationship in either direction (positive or negative). Instead, initially conflicts seem to increase as countries come into greater contact, but then conflicts peak and begin to decline beyond an unspecified threshold of integration.

While these conclusions might appear to be counter-intuitive, on closer reflection, they are not so surprising. Total independence from one another signifies a complete lack of contact and therefore the absence of any opportunity for a clash of interests. Increasing interdependence multiplies the number of issues over which states interact and therefore expands the potential universe of a competitive clash of interests. But once states are heavily integrated, their economies become so thickly intertwined that the costs of extricating from the mutually beneficial relationship are far greater than any possible gains that might accrue from going to war. It is cheaper, quicker, more efficient and less deadly today to buy what you need in the marketplace than to fight for it on the battlefield.

The number of armed conflicts rose steadily until the end of the Cold War, peaked in the early 1990s, but has declined since then (see Mack 2005). The nature of armed conflict has changed. Until the Second World War, war was an institution of the states system, with distinctive rules, etiquette, norms and stable patterns of practices (Holsti 1996). In recent times the line between war as a political act and organised criminality has become increasingly blurred. The weakness of state structures and institutions in many countries has heightened the challenges and risks of nation-building and sometimes tempted armed groups to try to seize the levers of political power in order to exploit the resources of economic wealth, including 'conflict diamonds'. Internal conflicts are made more complex and lethal by modern technology and communications, and in particular by the proliferation of cheap, highly destructive small arms. Violence becomes a way of life with catastrophic consequences for civilians caught in the crossfire.

Yet few modern conflicts are purely internal. The networks that sustain them can involve a range of ancillary problems like trafficking in arms, drugs and children; terrorism; and refugee flows. Whole regions can quickly be destabilised. Sometimes the rich world is deeply implicated. Civil conflicts are fuelled by arms and monetary transfers that originate in the developed world, and in turn their destabilising effects are felt in the developed world in everything from globally interconnected terrorism to refugee flows, the export of drugs and the spread of infectious disease and organised crime. All the signs are that the markets for illicit trafficking in drugs and humans (e.g. for the sex trade) are regional and interregional rather than purely national.

As conflict resolution actors, regional organisations would have the advantages of closeness to the conflicts, deeper familiarity with the issues underlying the conflict and the social and political contexts encasing them, and awareness of the urgency to deal with the crisis to hand. The handicaps under which regional arrangements operate include local rivalries, partisanship, the tendency to replicate local power imbalances within the regional organisations, and the fear of establishing precedents for intervention in the internal affairs of member countries.

In order to take on a security role, regional organisations would need to overcome an obstacle and resolve a paradox. They would need to possess the requisite financial, institutional and military capacity to play a regional conflict management role. This is not a trivial obstacle, for example, to the African Union (AU) assuming a credible and effective managerial role. Regional arrangements would also need to be synchronous with the regional security complexes which emphasise the 'interdependence of rivalry as well as that of shared interests' (Buzan 1991: 190). That is, all the parties that are central to a regional security complex must be included within the regional arrangements for the latter to have real meaning. Thus sub-regional organisations like the Association of Southeast Asian Nations (ASEAN) cannot play a regional conflict management role because they do not coincide with the regional security complex. But if all relevant regional actors are included, then the regional arrangements can be rendered impotent because of the refusal of the parties to permit security discussions for fear of derailing regional cooperation on non-security issues, as is the case with the South Asian Association for Regional Cooperation (SAARC). The question of China–Taiwan relations could play a similar spoiling role in Northeast Asia.

Integration-cum-fragmentation

Regional governance has to be seen as something that emerges out of the interplay between two organising forces that shape all policy issues: integration and disintegration.

The common usage of the term 'integration' is often confusing and the notion of integration has traditionally been the subject of much debate, due to the lack of consensus on its meaning and properties. Indeed, not only has the concept been used imprecisely, there also does not seem to be a single definition of 'integration' that has gained widespread acceptance. Inherent in the term is the concept of interactions, since any situation other than complete isolation will inevitably give rise to some kind of interactive relationship. The concept of integration refers to a process in which units move from a condition of total or partial isolation towards a complete or partial unification. Applied to the interaction between independent sovereign states, the concept refers to a process of complex social transformations, which may or may not imply some kind of permanent institutional structure or mutual cooperation. Integration between sovereign states is a process of large-scale territorial differentiation characterised by the progressive lowering of internal boundaries and the slow raising of new external boundaries. As a result, the volume of flows – of people, goods, services, capital, etc. – between the integrating actors becomes proportionately greater compared to their total global transactions. Such processes liberate conflicting energies and tensions at all levels. This has consequences for states, their welfare system, economic trade, national identities, and so on.

Regional integration thus applies conceptions of interactions to the study of the modern world system. More specifically, it refers to a process of complex social transformation that is characterised by the intensification of relations between independent sovereign states and that gives rise to some kind of structure for mutual cooperation based on recurring and stable patterns of behaviour, that is, to institutionalisation.

The salience of state boundaries diminishes even with respect to sub-national flows and transactions. And this is reflected just as powerfully in the changing sense of identity. In terms of affective identity, it is possible to think of oneself simultaneously as a member of a micro-regional (e.g. Catalan), national (e.g. Spanish) and macro-regional or continental (e.g. European) person. The international community, in this sense, remains more of an imagined and constructed community of strangers than a point of affective identity. It is worth making the point that in this sense of transnational regionalism, we can have identities such as Arab as well as continental. In the latter sense, while there would appear to be some sense of being European, African or Latin American, however inchoate, there is very little sense of being Asian (as opposed to Central, South, Southeast or East Asian).

In other words, identity has both flowed upwards from the state to trans-national or continental levels and devolved downwards to sub-national levels. Or, to put it another way, there has occurred simultaneously both integration and fragmentation. Conceptualisation of this paradox has to take into account the multidirectional and hybrid nature of the process of integration, which also implies greater attention to the concept of disintegration and a normative revision of its objective value: no given level of political or economic organisation is *a priori* sacrosanct, good or bad.

Processes of integration and disintegration have played an important role in constituting the Westphalian world order. Many modern 'nation-states' are products of the consolidation of loose federations of states into more centralised federations. Such integration has been driven by the desire to create larger free trade areas or by needs to increase the capacity for defence. Since the end of the Second World War, the number of independent countries has increased dramatically.

As a consequence of this increase in the number of sovereign units of governance, the world now comprises a large number of relatively small countries. In 1995, 87 countries in the world had a population of less than 5 million (Alesina *et al.* 2000: 1276; Alesina and Spolaore 2003). In addition, there is evidence that many of the richest countries are small. So there seems to be a tendency to favour decentralisation. However, the stability of the Westphalian system together with globalisation seems also to favour integration between states. Federation and cooperation between relatively small units of governance are growing. Meanwhile the tendencies towards decentralisation within countries continue as well. But both integration and decentralisation now occur in most cases without challenging the existing states. As a result, the 'theatre' of governance also comprises regions that complement the global/national governance in two ways: as units of governance within states (micro-regions) and as units of governance that unite states (macro-regions). From a global governance perspective, three aspects of this situation deserve to be highlighted:

1 the growth of macro-regional governance;
2 the increasing inter-macro-regional relations (outside the existing multi-lateral system);
3 the emerging roles of macro-regions within the multilateral system.

Macro-regional governance

Regional organisations have proliferated over the past few decades to a world-wide phenomenon. The jury is still out on whether bilateral and regional alternatives undermine or complement progressive liberalisation on a truly global, universal and non-discriminatory basis. That debate is beyond the scope of this chapter. The growth in number and geographical coverage is also matched by an increased diversity in the 'substance' or 'content' of integration. There is a wide spectrum of regional processes nowadays, with organisations belonging to different 'waves' of regional integration cohabiting next to each other. First of all, there are regional integration agreements primarily focusing on the achievement of a linear process of economic integration involving the combination of separate (national) economies into larger economic regions. According to the World Trade Organization (WTO) Committee on Regional Trade Agreements, by July 2003, only three WTO members (Macau China, Mongolia and Chinese Taipei) were not yet parties to such agreements. By May 2003, over 265 had been notified to the WTO (and its predecessor, the General Agreement on Tariffs and Trade). Of these, 138 were notified after the WTO was created in January 1995. Over 190 are currently in force; another 60 are believed to be operational although not yet notified. Judging by the number of agreements reportedly planned or already under negotiation, the total number of regional trade agreements in force might well approach 300 by 2005 (WTO Committee on Regional Trade Agreements 2005). Regions not covered by such agreements before are now on the way towards creating regional economic integration fora. To give but a few examples, in East Asia, the 1992 ASEAN Singapore Summit launched the creation of an ASEAN Free Trade Area (AFTA), while in South Asia, a newly created South Asian Free Trade Area (SAFTA) came into force on 1st January 2006 (Twelfth SAARC Summit 2004).

Next to these agreements there are regional organisations, created especially in the 1980s and 1990s, which have undergone a deepening of the integration between member states beyond purely economic concerns:

a multidimensional form of integration which includes economic, political, social and cultural aspects and thus goes far beyond the goal of creating region-based free trade regimes or security alliances. Rather, the political ambition of establishing regional coherence and identity seems to be of primary importance.

(Hettne 1999: xvi)

This phenomenon coined under the term of 'new regionalism' is based on the idea that one cannot isolate trade and economy from the rest of society: integration can also imply non-economic matters such as justice, security, culture and policy harmonisation on such subjects as migration.

The emergence of the 'new regionalism' needs to be historically related to a series of transformations of the world. Schultz *et al.* summarise the trends observed by previous studies:

(1) the move from bipolarity towards a multipolar or perhaps tripolar structure, centred around the EU, [the North American Free Trade Agreement] NAFTA, and the Asia-Pacific, with a new division of power and new division of labour; (2) the relative decline of American hegemony in combination with a more permissive attitude on the part of the United States toward regionalism; (3) the restructuring of the nation-state and the growth of interdependence, transnationalisation and globalisation; (4) recurrent fears over the stability of the multilateral trading order, hand in hand with the growing importance of non-tariff barriers (NTBs) to trade; (5) the changed attitudes towards (neo-liberal) economic development and political systems in developing countries as well as in the post-communist countries.

(2001: 3)

'New regionalism' organisations have therefore several important characteristics:

1   deep economic integration plus political elements;
2   multilevel governance;
3   devolution within states;
4   strong international legal framework;
5   cooperation along many dimensions.

At the same time, the 'new regionalism' aims to promote certain 'world values' such as security, development, ecological sustainability, rather than globalism *per se* (Hettne 1999: xvi).

The European Union has been the first and the most advanced case of 'new regionalism', as it has managed to develop a model of integration that incorporates political elements in a deep economic integration. But nowadays this type of regional integration is no longer an exclusively European phenomenon. It has spread to the other continents through the creation of new organisations or the upgrading of previously existing regional economic organisations. Examples of 'new regionalism' comprise the Economic Community of West African States (ECOWAS), the Common Market for Eastern and Southern Africa (COMESA) and the Southern African Development Community (SADC) on the African continent; ASEAN and SAARC on the Asian continent; and the Common Market of the South (Mercosur), the Andean Community (CAN) and the Caribbean Community and Common Market (CARICOM) in Latin America and the Caribbean.

Each region of the world has at present several regional organisations which can be classified under the categories presented above, and most countries belong to multiple regional organisations. But, when looking at the world map, one can easily notice that regionalism is still an *uneven* phenomenon: regional organisations are particularly prominent in Europe, Africa and the Americas. It is also in these regions that the average number of regional organisations' membership per country, or what we might call *regional intensity*, is the highest (Kati 2005: 10).

Inter-regional interaction

In parallel with the evolution and growth of regional integration, a new phenomenon has gradually started to take shape – inter-regionalism – which signifies in the most general sense 'the condition or process whereby two regions interact as regions' (Söderbaum *et al.* 2005: 257). There are several examples of region-to-region relations between first-generation regional arrangements. However, inter-regionalism is beginning to have deeper ramifications for world order and it is a new level of interaction and a distinct phenomenon which needs consideration in its own right (Gilson 2002).

Following a period dominated by the EU in this field, regional organisations from all continents (e.g. ASEAN, Mercosur, SADC) have started in the past decade to be more proactive, engaging in inter-regional arrangements and agreements that can have effects on relations at the global level. In Asia, the EU has institutionalised inter-regional relations with ASEAN through the creation of the Asia-Europe Meeting (ASEM). In Latin America, it is leading political and trade negotiations of the Inter-regional Association Agreement with Mercosur, and has prepared the ground, at the third Europe–Latin America and the Caribbean (EU-LAC) Summit in Guadalajara, towards the opening of negotiations on Association Agreements with Central America and the Andean Community. In the framework of the EU-African, Caribbean and Pacific Group of States (ACP) process, in 2004 the EU launched economic partnership agreements, involving negotiations on the establishment of a free trade area with the six ACP sub-regions: Central and Western Africa, East and Southern African states, the Caribbean, the Southern African Development Community, and the Pacific islands.

The European Union is undoubtedly the biggest initiator of inter-regional agreements, but has been increasingly followed on this path by regional organisations on other continents as well. In April 2004, Mercosur and CAN strengthened their ties through the conclusion of the negotiations on a free trade agreement between the two regions, conceived as a first step towards the establishment of a South American Community of Nations. Also in 2004, the Andean Community and the Asia-Pacific Economic Cooperation (APEC) launched the implementation of the 'CAN-APEC 2008' programme aiming to strengthen the relationship between the two organisations and to increase the presence of Andean countries in the Asia-Pacific Basin (Andean Community 2004).

Although inter-regional interactions are primarily focused upon economic and trade issues, it is interesting to note that there is also a civil society interaction between the two regions, for instance, in the case of ASEM. The Asia-Europe Foundation, launched in 1997, aims to promote cultural and intellectual exchange and inter-regional mobility (de Prado Yepes 2004). However, labour organisations have complained about their exclusion from the ASEM process (Yeates 2005: 22).

As pointed out in a special issue of the *Journal of European Integration*, co-edited by UNU-CRIS and the University of Göteburg, focusing on the EU's interregional relations (Söderbaum *et al.* 2005), assessing regionalism raises important questions regarding world order and global governance. What are the implications of inter-regionalism for the patterns of foreign policy and world order? Does the EU try to construct regions and inter-regional partnerships in order to deal with regions through inter-regionalism, rather than the old-style (bilateral) state-to-state foreign policy relations? Does inter-regionalism imply a shift from a world order based on nation-states towards one based on regions and inter-regional relations? How does inter-regionalism relate to bilateralism? Does the EU have suitable partners to engage in inter-regional relations?

UN interaction with regional organisations

The United Nations since its creation has been based exclusively on state membership. Yet geographical groupings are pervasive to the organisation and functioning of the UN system, from the composition of the Security Council, Economic and Social Council and the Human Rights Commission/ Council to the appointment of personnel at all levels. Many regional group-ings function as a caucus within the UN. There are also the regional commis-sions and economic regional sub-structures set up by the UN. Then there are the non-UN regional organisations that have obtained observer status within the UN. A special case here is the European Commission: in the WTO and in the Food and Agriculture Organization (FAO), the European Commission is present as a truly regional representation with voting rights. The European Commission also has a special status of 'regional economic international organisation' that allows it to fully participate in the UN Framework

Convention on Climate Change and cast votes of all its member states. The existence of all these structures corroborates the claim that a regional philosophy, far from being incompatible with UN goals, is integral to the organisation. Exploring all aspects of UN-regional organisation interactions is beyond the scope of this chapter. Hence, the rest of this section will only deal with interactions in the field of peace and security.

Already in 1992 the Secretary-General's report *An Agenda for Peace* had called for a greater involvement of regional organisations in the UN activities regarding peace and security. Both the *Agenda for Peace* and the *Supplement to an Agenda for Peace* highlighted the advantages and potential for the division of labour in using the regional arrangements for the different mechanisms such as preventive diplomacy, peace-keeping, peace-making and post-conflict peace-building. Since then, a formal cooperation between regional organisations and the UN has also started developing at the initiative of the UN Secretary-General, who convened in the period 1993–2005 six 'high-level meetings' with regional organisations involved in security matters from all continents (EU, NATO, ECOWAS, the Organization for Security and Cooperation in Europe [OSCE], the Commonwealth of Independent States [CIS], the Organization of the Islamic Conference [OIC], ASEAN, the AU, and the League of Arab States [LAS]). The discussions focused on challenges to international peace and security, the role of regional organisations in peace-building activities and practical measures to promote greater coordination and cooperation in peace-keeping and peace-building.

The meetings so far have allowed the drafting of a 'framework for cooperation' between the UN and regional agencies comprising 'modalities for conflict prevention' and 'principles for peace-building'. As underlined by Graham and Felício (2005; 2006), this normative framework for cooperation is based on nine principles:

1   A 'flexible and pragmatic approach' to regional crises, with no 'universal model'.
2   UN primacy in all crises.
3   A clear division of labour between the UN and regional agencies.
4   Regular consultations between the UN and regional agencies.
5   Mutual support in diplomatic and operational activities.
6   Joint operational deployment where appropriate.
7   Regional impartiality in handling conflicts.
8   Common conflict prevention modalities.
9   Common peace-building principles.

Next to these high-level meetings, the Security Council has also given more attention to regional organisations. In 2003, it held a meeting on the topic 'The Security Council and regional organisations: facing the new challenges to international peace and security'. An important step in this debate was taken by Romania which, during its July 2004 presidency of the Security

Council, encouraged the debate on the role of regions within its functioning. Additionally, on 20 July 2004, a second 'open meeting' between the Security Council and regional organisations aimed to identify new methods of cooperation in conflict resolution and stabilisation processes. In the presidential statement issued at the conclusion of this occasion, the Council invited regional organisations

> to take the necessary steps to increase collaboration with the United Nations in order to maximise efficiency in stabilisation processes, and encouraged enhanced cooperation and coordination among regional and sub-regional organisations themselves, in particular through exchange of information and sharing experience and best practices.
>
> (UN Security Council 2004)

The 2005 reform effort

Not surprisingly, the topic of the optimum relationship between the United Nations and regional organisations was discussed by the Secretary-General's High-Level Panel on Threats, Challenges and Change. Its report dealt with the subject in four paragraphs, and made the following remarks (United Nations 2004: paras 270-3). If the UN Security Council is to be more active and effective in preventing and responding to threats, it needs to utilise Chapter VIII provisions of the UN Charter dealing with regional organisations and arrangements more and more productively. In the past sixty years, many regional and sub-regional groupings have been established. They have made important contributions to regional stability and prosperity and some of them have assumed direct peace and security roles. The United Nations was advised to promote the establishment of such groupings.

Most crucially for present purposes, the High-Level Panel's report explicitly recognised that regional organisations can be a vital part of the multilateral system. Their efforts neither contradict those of the UN, nor absolve the United Nations of its primary responsibility for the maintenance of international peace and security. Rather, the critical requirements are: (1) regional action should be organised within the framework of the UN Charter and consistent with its purposes and principles; and (2) the United Nations and regional organisations work together in a more integrated fashion than has been the case so far.

In practice, this means that:

1   Regional organisations should undertake peace operations only with the authorisation of the UN Security Council, although sometimes the exigencies of the situation may make it necessary to obtain such authorisation after the operations have commenced.
2   Consultation and cooperation between the United Nations and regional organisations, covering issues such as meetings of the heads of the

organisations, more frequent exchange of information and early warning, co-training of civilian and military personnel, and exchange of personnel within peace operations, should be expanded and could be formalised in memoranda of agreements.

3   Donor countries should commit to a ten-year programme of capacity development for African regional and sub-regional organisations.

4   Conversely, regional organisations with a capacity for conflict prevention or peace-keeping should place such capacities in the framework of the UN Standby Arrangements System.

5   Member States should agree to allow the United Nations to provide equipment support from UN-owned sources to regional operations as needed, and to finance regional operations authorised by the Security Council with assessed contributions.

In his three-paragraph response, the Secretary-General accepted the broad thrust of the analysis in the High-Level Panel's report with regard to the complementary roles of the UN and regional organisations and endorsed points 2–5 (Annan 2005: para. 213–15).

At the sixth high-level meeting between the United Nations and regional organisations on 25–26 July 2005, Annan said that strengthening the UN relationship with regional and other intergovernmental organisations was a critical part of the effort to reform the UN. At the meeting it was concluded that indeed a more structured relationship between the UN and regional and other intergovernmental organisations needs to be developed 'creating a truly interlocking system that guarantees greater coordination in both policy and action. This partnership should build on the comparative strengths of each organisation' (Sixth High-Level Meeting 2005). The geographical proximity and close historical, economic and cultural ties between members of regional organisations give them the advantage of perhaps understanding the root causes of regional conflicts and thus of developing peaceful solutions to these problems.

The sixth high-level meeting also endorsed the High-Level Panel's call for the establishment of regional and sub-regional groupings in highly vulnerable parts of the world where no effective security organisations currently exist (see ibid: Conclusions of the Chairmanship). However, it was also viewed as important that initiatives and mandates for any such new groupings should come from within the region and that such mandates could cover economic and social development as well as international peace and security. Consequently the meeting decided upon a number of concrete measures such as creating a standing committee and setting future meetings – now on an annual basis – to coincide with the meetings that the Security Council holds with regional organisations. In order to increase coordination, it was decided to identify one high-level official in each organisation for the purpose of liaising with the United Nations and with one another. Participants supported the establishment of a Human Rights Council and a Peacebuilding Commission, while stressing the latter's role also in conflict prevention. Also, the Secretary-General was mandated to conclude agreements of appropriate kinds with individual organisations.

The document finally negotiated at the September 2005 UN summit acknowledges the special contribution of regional organisations to peace and security, the importance of partnerships between the UN and regional organisations, and the special needs of Africa. In this context, it supports efforts by the EU and others to develop rapid deployment, stand-by and bridging capacities, and the development and implementation of a ten-year plan for African Union capacity building. More generally, the declaration endorses a stronger relationship between the UN and regional and sub-regional organisations within the framework of Chapter VIII of the UN Charter; encourages more consultation and cooperation between them through formalised agreements and the involvement of regional organisations in the work of the UN Security Council; encourages regional organisations with peace-keeping capacity to place these at the disposal of the United Nations through the stand-by arrangements; and encourages economic, social and cultural cooperation as well (United Nations 2005: paras 93, 170).

Conclusion

Globalisation is eroding the legitimacy and effectiveness of national governments and intergovernmental organisations. There has been a corresponding decline in levels of resources and support for international organisations, including the UN. In the meantime, new actors, including regional organisations, have become progressively more assertive. In some respects, the metropolitan governments of megacities have more in common with each other in confronting challenges of urban governance than with the small municipal authorities of their own countries. As such, macro-regional governance will continue to grow and change the global governance landscape.

This holds some promises and threats. The major threat is that it will further weaken the multilateral system and the UN if the processes of regionalism and inter-regionalism develop into a world order based upon shifting alliances between regional blocs. The promises are that a worldwide network of regional integration schemes injects fresh oxygen to both states and the UN and permits all levels of governance to exploit the principle of subsidiarity.

If, as the sub-title of this book suggests, regional integration is to 'tame' globalisation, a number of conditions have to be met. First, macro-regions need a proper global institutional framework in which their inter-regional interactions can be organised. Only the UN can provide such a global framework. Inter-regional interactions outside such a framework are analogous to bilateral relations between states. But unlike states and international organisations, the system of regional organisations has yet to be fully conceptualised as a system. One of the main issues is the heterogeneity of regional organisations. For instance, at the sixth high-level meeting between the Secretary

General of the United Nations and Heads of Regional and other Inter-governmental Organisations, 22 organisations showed up. But as the very title of the meeting suggests, next to major regional organisations such as the African Union, the EU, or the League of Arab States, there were also other organisations present such as the Community of Portuguese-speaking Coun-tries or the Organisation for the Prohibition of Chemical Weapons. Such a diverse membership makes focused discussions – and thus effective govern-ance – difficult.

Second, there is the uneven spread of regional organisations across the world. Leonard (2005) has recently introduced the notion of 'regional domino effect': more and more regional clubs will emerge as regions want to do busi-ness with other regions. According to Leonard, one will need to be part of a (regional) club to have a seat at the table of global governance. While it is true that all geographical areas of the world have several regional organisations and most countries belong to one or more regional organisations, it cannot be denied that regionalism is still most prominent in Europe, Africa and the Americas. And rich countries are more prominent in regionalism than poor countries. It thus becomes very important to step up region-building in the highly vulnerable parts of the world where no effective regional security or regional trade mechanisms exist. Of course, initiatives and mandates for any new groupings should come from within the region. At present we see that especially the EU is taking up the role of region builder. The question is to what extent the UN should also be involved in promoting regionalism.

Third, regional integration projects need to increase the active participation of civil society and local governments. At the end of the day, global govern-ance needs to be democratically accountable and inclusive of civil society actors.

The central theme of this chapter has been whether regionalism/region-alisation can provide a satisfactory solution to the authority/manifestation paradox of global governance. It has been argued that there is indeed a place for regional governance in the multilateral framework for global governance. But only if regional integration processes go beyond economic integration and only if they have sufficient support from civil society, will regional inte-gration have the power to combat the dark sides of globalisation and unlock the development potential of globalisation.

States will continue to offer the legitimacy to multilateralism and global governance, but regions have the comparative advantage to become a primary locus for effective actions that realise the ideals of multilateralism. While this chapter has canvassed the argument with respect to the two dominant UN mandates of security and development, in principle the argument could be developed just as well with respect to the emerging third leg of UN policy discourse, namely human rights. For with human rights as well, regional-level governance can provide a mediating solution to the persisting challenge of particularism versus universalism. Norms and values may be global and uni-versal, for example, murder is bad. Their translation into rules of behaviour and laws nevertheless is done within particular spatial and temporal contexts, for example, viewing capital punishment, abortion, euthanasia or killing in war as murder or not. Often the wider transnational community that shares both the abstract value and its rule manifestation may exist at the regional but break down at the global level. That is, potentially the European Court of Human Rights may provide valuable pointers to other regions as a happy medium between embedding human rights in national laws and institutions, international accountability and complementary mechanisms at the regional level. The broader import of this example is how Europe has witnessed an *institutionalisation of the process of policy-making* at the regional level across a range of policy domains.

Let us take two further examples from current and prospective debates about the United Nations. The so-far abortive debate on Security Council enlargement, including with respect to new permanent members, is couched in terms of regional representation. But which one of the existing permanent five members has a record of speaking and voting as a representative of its region as opposed to on the basis of how it conceives and calculates its own national interests being affected? Where is the assurance that new members would be any different? Can Spanish-speaking Latin America be represented by Portuguese-speaking Brazil? And if regionalism is to be the determining factor in permanent membership, then would it not be better to re-conceive the unit of Security Council membership, for example, agreeing to the EU as one permanent member? One can even imagine the Security Council becoming a hybrid forum composed of both nations to be considered as global actors and regional organisations that group the other nations into global actors.

The second example pertains to the Secretary-General appointment process. Once again, the firmly established convention is for the office to rotate between the different regional groupings in the UN scheme. But the whole point of the office is that the person chosen represents the international community, not any particular region. Thus the paradox of regionalism-universalism is inherent in the UN concept.

There are two possible explanations for the underwhelming outcome, one cynical, the other charitable. For a UN official, it is a toss-up as to which is the more dispiriting. The cynical explanation is that all sides pushed their own interests, blocked items not of interest to them, and criticised others for not elevating the common interest. While pushing items of importance to themselves, they rejected others as not being all that urgent and distracting attention from their own pet reforms.

South African President Thabo Mbeki criticised 'rich and powerful nations' for allegedly blocking attempts to widen the Security Council to include more developing nations (BBC News 2005). He chose to ignore Africa's role in bringing to a halt the head of momentum that had been built up by the G4 campaign because the African Union insisted on full veto powers for all new permanent members. Had the AU combined with the G4, they might well have had the votes. The Western countries blamed the developing countries for blocking efforts at management reform that would have given greater discretionary authority to the Secretary-General in hiring and firing UN personnel, for fear that Americans and Europeans would stand to gain if the General Assembly surrendered its prerogatives in this regard. This ignores the existing severe distortions in the senior ranks of the UN system that are disproportionately dominated by Westerners.

Washington wanted to focus on non-proliferation and management reform, but betrayed an instinct for mismanaging international diplomacy in presenting a list of demands for 750 amendments at the eleventh hour to a text that had been under negotiation for months, and in the refusal to link non-proliferation to disarmament. For their part, Americans have yet to receive a convincing answer as to why the world's only superpower should acquiesce in its own 'Gulliverisation', bound and tethered by the many fine strands of international treaties and conventions. Or why they should not seek to refashion institutions to reflect their pre-eminence. Or why indeed the growing circle of democratic countries should accept moral equivalence with regimes which are anything but when it comes to collective decision-making.

The charitable interpretation is that the sense of shared values and solidarity that makes up an international community may have frayed a thread too far. The UN membership has not just quadrupled since 1945, but has grown far more diverse. There are many more states today, with markedly diverging interests and perspectives. The range of issues they have to confront are more numerous, complex and challenging, for example, hot-button items like global warming, HIV/AIDS and nuclear terrorism that were not on the international agenda in 1945. There are also many more non-state actors. A 'community' exists if members share core values and agree on legitimate behaviour. The values underpinning the European Community find expression as norms and laws and are embedded in institutions and structures, including regulatory frameworks and dispute-resolution mechanisms. The serious disagreements between the states of the world on many key issues may be evidence of a growing loss, not betrayal, of the sense of international solidarity on which the UN is predicated.

The UN sceptics might well feel vindicated by the outcome of the grandiloquently entitled World Summit in New York in September 2005. The agreed outcome document is so underwhelming as to lend credence to critics who insist that the world body is reform proof. The lack of progress on major reform items will only heighten moves away from a single international organisation to ad hoc, shifting and issue-specific networks of coalitions of convenience and the willing. If this reflects a turning away from affective identity or even its global symbolism, then the search for such identity beyond the state may focus more sharply on regional entities. If that is the case, then 'community' as such may well be a more realistic aspiration at the regional (EU, AU, Latin American) and sub-regional (ASEAN, ECOWAS, Mercosur) level alongside continuing cooperation and collaboration within the UN framework at the global level.

Notes

1 This section is adapted from a forthcoming book in the UN Intellectual History Project series. See Thakur and Weiss (forthcoming).
2 These different types of public and private authorities are discussed in Porter (2001).

References

Alesina, A. and Spolaore, E. (2003) *The Size of Nations*, Cambridge, MA: MIT Press.
Alesina A., Spolaore, E. and Wcziarg, R. (2000) 'Economic Integration and Political Disintegration', *American Economic Review*, 90(5): 1276–96.
Andean Community (2004) 'Following a Meeting with APEC Executive Director Wagner Announces Program CAN-APEC 2008', *Andean Community Press, Release*, Lima, 20 October.
Annan, Kofi A. (2005) *In Larger Freedom: Towards Development, Security and Human Rights for All*, Report of the Secretary-General A/59/2005, 21 March, New York: United Nations.
BBC News (2005) 'UN Summit Agrees Reform Document', *BBC News International Version*, 17 September. Available at: http://news.bbc.co.uk/2/hi/americas/4253358.stm.
Bull, Hedley (1977) *The Anarchical Society*, New York: Macmillan.
Buzan, Barry (1991) *People, States and Fear: An Agenda for International Security Studies in the Post-Cold War Era*, 2nd edn, Boulder, CO: Lynne Rienner.
Camdessus, Michel (2001) 'The IMF at the Beginning of the Twenty-first Century: Can We Establish a Humanized Globalization?' *Global Governance*, 7(4): 363–5.
Commission on Global Governance (1995) *Our Global Neighbourhood*, Oxford: Oxford University Press.
D'Cruz, Don (2004) 'Tracking Aid Dollars', *Canberra Times*, 31 December.
De Prado Yepes, Cesar (2004) 'ASEM's Extra-Regionalism: A Proposal for Europe's and East Asia's Joint Backing of World Regionalism', in Wim Stockhof, Paul Van der Velde and Yeo Lay-Hwee (eds) *Eurasian Space: More than Two Continents*, Leiden: International Institute of Asian Studies and Singapore: Institute of Southeast Asian Studies.
Farrell, Mary, Hettne, Björn and Van Langenhove, Luk (eds) (2005) *Global Politics of Regionalism: Theory and Practice*, London: Pluto Press.
Germain, Randall D. (2001) 'Global Financial Governance and the Problem of Inclusion', *Global Governance*, 7(4): 411–26.
Gilson, J. (2002) *Asia Meets Europe: Inter-Regionalism and the Asia-Europe Meeting*, Cheltenham: Edward Elgar.
Graham, K. and Felício, T. (2005) 'Regional Security and Global Governance: A Proposal for a "Regional-Global Security Mechanism" in the Light of the UN High-Level Panel's Report', *Egmont Paper No. 4*, Brussels: Royal Institute for International Relations.
—— (2006) *Regional Security and Global Governance: A Study of the Interaction between Regional Agencies and the UN Security Council*, Brussels: VUB Press.
Hettne, B. (1999) 'The New Regionalism: A Prologue', in B. Hettne, A. Inotai and O. Sunkel (eds) *Globalism and the New Regionalism*, London: Macmillan.
Holsti, Kal J. (1996) *War, the State, and the State of War*, Cambridge: Cambridge University Press.

Hooghe, L. (ed.) (1996) *Cohesion Policy and European Integration: Building Multi-Level Governance*, Oxford: Oxford University Press.

—— and Marks, G. (2001) *Multi-level Governance and European Integration*, Lanham, MD: Rowman and Littlefield.

Johns, Gary (2004) 'Relations with Nongovernmental Organizations: Lessons for the UN', *Seton Hall Journal of Diplomacy and International Relations*, 5(2): 51–65.

Kati, Suominen (2005) 'Globalizing Regionalism: Harnessing Regional Organizations to Meet Global Threats', *UNU-CRIS Occasional Paper O-2005/11*. Available at: http://www.cris.unu.edu/admin/documents/20050905115653.o-2005–11.pdf.

Leonard, M. (2005) *Why Europe Will Run the 21st Century*, London: Fourth Estate.

Mack, Andrew (ed.) (2005) *Human Security Report*, New York: Oxford University Press.

Nye, J.S. (1971) *Peace in Parts: Integration and Conflict in Regional Organizations*, Boston: Little, Brown & Co.

Ohmae, Kenichi (2003) 'The Rise of the Region State', *Foreign Affairs*, 72(Spring): 78–87.

Porter, Tony (2001) 'The Democratic Deficit in the Institutional Arrangements for Regulating Global Finance', *Global Governance*, 7(4): 427–39.

Rieff, David (2005) 'Tsunamis, Accountability and the Humanitarian Circus', *Humanitarian Exchange*, no. 29, March. Available at: http://www.odihpn.org/report.asp?id=2711.

Rosenau, James N. (1999) 'Toward an Ontology for Global Governance', in Martin Hewson and Timothy J. Sinclair (eds) *Approaches to Global Governance Theory*, Albany, NY: State University of New York.

Schulz, M., F. Söderbaum and J. Öjendal (2001) 'Introduction: A Framework for Understanding Regionalization', in M. Schulz, F. Söderbaum, and J. Öjendal (eds) *Regionalization in a Globalizing World*, London: Zed Books.

Sinclair, Timothy J. (2001) 'The Infrastructure of Global Governance: Quasi-regulatory Mechanisms and the New Global Finance', *Global Governance*, 7(4): 441–51.

Sixth High-Level Meeting (2005) 'Joint Statement by Participants in the Sixth High-Level Meeting between the United Nations and Regional and Other Intergovernmental Organizations', meeting held at United Nations Headquarters, New York, 25–26 July.

Slaughter, Anne-Marie (2004) *A New World Order*, Princeton, NJ: Princeton University Press.

Slim, Hugo (2002) *By What Authority? The Legitimacy and Accountability of Non-governmental Organisations*, Geneva: International Council on Human Rights Policy. Available at: http://www.ichrp.org/paper_files/119_w_02.doc.

Söderbaum, F., Stalgren, P. and Van Langenhove, L. (2005) 'Introduction: The EU as a Global Actor and the Dynamics of Interregionalism: A Comparative Analysis', *Journal of European Integration*, 27(3): 249–62.

Strange, Susan (1988) *States and Markets: An Introduction to International Political Economy*, London: Pinter Publishers.

Thakur, Ramesh and Weiss, Thomas G. (forthcoming) *The UN and Global Governance: An Idea and Its Prospects*. Bloomington, IN: Indiana University Press.

Twelfth SAARC Summit (2004) *Agreement on South Asian Free Trade Area*, 4–6 January, Islamabad.

United Nations (2004) *A More Secure World: Our Shared Responsibility. Report of the*

High-Level Panel on Threats, Challenges and Change, A/59/565, 2 December, New York: United Nations.

—— (2005) 'Draft Outcome Document', UN General Assembly 2005 World Summit, A/59/HLPM/CRP.1/Rev.2, 13 September.

United Nations Development Programme (2005) *Human Development Report 2005. International Cooperation at a Crossroads: Aid, Trade and Security in an Unequal World*, New York: United Nations Development Programme.

United Nations Press Release (2003) *Secretary-General's Address to the General Assembly*, SG/SM/8891,GA/10157, 23 September.

United Nations Security Council (2004) *Statement by the President of the Security Council*, S/PRST/2004/27, 20 July.

Velasquez, J. and Piest, U. (2003) 'Introducing the UNU Inter-Linkages Initiative: Focusing on the Implementation of Sustainable Development', *Work in Progress: A Review of Research Activities of the United Nations University*, 17(1): 1–3.

WTO Committee on Regional Trade Agreements (2005) 'Regionalism: Friends or Rivals', *Understanding the WTO: Cross-cutting and New Issues*, Available at: http://www.wto.org/english/thewto_e/whatis_e/tif_e/bey1_e.htm.

Yeates, Nicola (2005) *'Globalisation' and Social Policy in a Development Context: Regional Responses*, Social Policy and Development Programme Paper No. 18, Geneva: United Nations Research Institute for Social Development.

2 Studying regionalisation comparatively

A conceptual framework

Alex Warleigh-Lack

Introduction: regionalisms 'old' and 'new' and the problem of theory

Theorising regionalism has never been straightforward. The well-worn dialectic between neofunctionalism and intergovernmentalism in European Union (EU) studies ultimately has failed to generate workable theories, and scholars in this field – historically the prime example of regional integration[1] studies – now find themselves working with a 'mosaic' (Diez and Wiener 2004) of various concepts, approaches and projects in a period of revision and experimentation. On the other hand, scholars of the so-called 'new regionalism' – in terms of quantity, primarily an extra-European phenomenon, but one which includes and was even initiated by the *reliance* of the EU (Fawcett 1995: 9; Schulz *et al.* 2001: 3) – have generally eschewed orthodox integration theory as represented by the *acquis* in EU studies. Instead such scholars have sought to generate their own corpus of theory on the ground that their dependent variable – 'new regionalism' – was too different from the 'old regionalism' of the pre-Single European Act EU to be meaningfully studied using the traditional conceptual lenses of EU studies scholars.[2] Thus, these scholars have sought to elaborate a self-consciously separate 'new regionalism approach' (NRA), an excellent critical overview of which is represented by the essays in Söderbaum and Shaw (2003).

Scholars have begun to question this intellectual separatism, and there is a growing body of work which disputes the idea of a neat or even workable distinction between the two fields (Warleigh 2004: 304–8). Current thinking is that scholars in both sub-fields have much to gain from a pooling of resources and the undertaking of explicitly comparative studies: witness the plea made by the chief proponent of the NRA, Björn Hettne (Hettne 2003). Such cooperation would also help reorient work in EU studies away from what has become a rather worthy-but-dull focus on the middle range, in which the ultimate goal of the middle-range theory – the generation of a holistic understanding – appears to have been forgotten. Furthermore, it would liberate EU studies from its untenable *sui generis* assumptions and enable a new range of work to be undertaken through the use of a different range of comparators from those most often employed – other regional integration projects, rather than federal polities of the nation-state kind.

However, the theoretical implications of such a step have not yet been fully addressed by scholars in either sub-field. In this chapter it is argued that the price to be paid for such an advance is that both NRA and EU studies scholars must admit that they are all essentially interested in the same phenomenon, focus on agreeing to a workable definition of the phenomenon they study, and cooperate in joint research endeavours which explore a common list of independent variables in order to test hypotheses and move towards a new theoretical framework.

The structure of the chapter is as follows. The second section explores in more depth the weaknesses of existing theory in the field(s). The third section discusses the metatheoretical issues inherent in trying to form a new corpus of theory from two fields of scholarship which auto-define as discrete entities. The fourth section sets out a putative understanding of the dependent variable of integration studies across the NRA-EU studies divide, which here is called 'regionalisation'. Finally, the fifth section discusses the independent variables to be investigated in order to advance the project and sets out tentative hypotheses to be put to the test in future comparative empirical work.

Theorising new regionalism/regional integration: overcoming the conceptual divide

The problems of orthodox integration theory are well documented and need not be rehearsed here.[3] What counts in this context is the importance of the differences that scholars of the 'new regionalism' perceived between their subject of study and the classic regional integration literature, and in particular its most advanced theorisation, neofunctionalism. In this section, therefore, we explore the principal differences between 'new regionalism' and 'regional integration' as set out by scholars of the former and proceed to argue that the theoretical salience of these differences is far less than has generally been assumed. This is for four main reasons. First, because the claimed differences between new regionalism and its antecedents are, to some extent, exaggerated. Second, because EU scholars themselves no longer tend to use neofunctionalism and its attendant ontologies/epistemologies – thus, the theoretical basis for the NRA claim that regionalism in Europe and elsewhere cannot be studied in the same way is metatheoretically and methodologically unsound. Third, because the fact that the EU has itself been just as much a form of 'new regionalism' as the North American Free Trade Agreement (NAFTA), or Asia-Pacific Economic Cooperation (APEC), etc., tends to be acknowledged, but glossed over, by scholars in both fields. And finally, because the 'new regionalism approach' is itself being revised, and several of the grounds on which it set itself apart from previous bodies of theory are being questioned.

Questioning the 'new regionalism'

For many scholars in the field, new regionalism (NR) can be differentiated from its predecessor in several ways.[4] Andrew Hurrell (1995a: 332) lists five major distinguishing factors. First, NR is very diverse in its nature, comprising a range of models/structures/processes of region-building rather than the single norm expected of, and advocated for, first wave regionalism by neofunctionalists. Second, it can involve partnerships between states in the 'North' and 'South' (i.e. developed and developing countries respectively), whereas previous regionalisms presupposed only North–North or South–South cooperation. Third, NR varies enormously in the level of institutionalisation of the various regions, whereas neofunctionalism/'old' regionalism had a very formal understanding of region-building that saw a lack of new joint institutions as a sign of weakness. Fourth, NR is multi-dimensional, and fundamentally blurs the distinction between the economic and the political, in contrast with its predecessor. Fifth, NR reflects, shapes and requires the development of a regional sense of identity, whereas neofunctionalism (and indeed first wave regionalism as represented by its European variant), for all its interest in the development of a new political community, notoriously underplayed and misunderstood issues of legitimacy, identity and popular support.

To this list should be added other factors. Hettne (2000: xxi) argues that new regionalism is not dependent on spillover for its survival or success, as instead the policy objectives of the region are set out explicitly at the outset. Further core features claimed for new regionalism are that unlike its predecessor(s) it is both global in scope (rather than effectively limited to Europe), based on economic openness/neoliberalism rather than protectionism, independent of superpower politics, and shaped voluntarily by actors from the bottom-up rather than imposed by foreign powers or cultivated by actors at the new centre (on these various points, see Hettne 2002; Söderbaum 2003).

How accurate is this picture of difference? Of Hurrell's five distinguishing features, only the second and the fifth (respectively the North–South element of new regionalism and the lack of emphasis on issues of identity and legitimacy in the 'old' version) seem to stand up to reflection. It is true that neofunctionalists saw the lack of institutionalisation as a sign of a regional organisation's likely failure to prosper (points one and three), but that is entirely different from assuming that the first wave of regionalism resulted from a single design; neofunctionalism may in this regard be narrowly prescriptive, but, if so, that is a point about theory rather than about the nature of 'old regionalism' (which was undertaken in diverse ways in Latin America, Europe, Africa and Asia). The fourth point – the allegation that old regionalism was not multi-dimensional and separated economics and politics – is similarly misconceived. Just by taking the EU case, it can be seen that a broad range of tasks was anticipated in the very idea of the 'Community Method'

(Coombes 1970) of integration, whereby cooperation in coal and steel production was intended to 'spill over' into other fields of policy – and to a
significant extent did so even before the Single European Act, as is evidenced
by the extent of legal integration during the 1960s and 1970s as well as extent
of the European Economic Community (EEC) competence from the outset
of European integration in areas such as agricultural policy. By the same
token, the mixture of economics and politics in 'old regionalism' has always
been a matter of controversy; the EU began as a matter of high politics
(peace preservation and economic recovery), and many of its controversies
and legitimacy problems have resulted from its leaders' attempts to pass
highly political measures off as matters of economics and trade (Warleigh
2003, Ch. 2).

   Similar caution should be displayed in addressing the issues raised respectively by Hettne and Söderbaum. It is true that 'old regionalism' depended on
the cultivation of spillover by actors at the new central level (as well as interest groups) for its success, and underestimated the ability and will of national
governments to resist this pressure. The stress on spillover cultivation is clear
from both the memoirs of key political actors (Monnet 1978) and neofunctionalist theory (Haas 1958, 1964). On that point, new regionalism is clearly
different. It is also valid to state that, economically speaking, 'new regionalism' is neoliberal in nature reflecting the changing fashions and ideologies
of the times. However, it is at least questionable whether old regionalism
(as represented by both neofunctionalism and EU politics in the pre-Single
Act era) really failed to focus on social actors' role in the process of region-
building. As pointed out above, interest groups were considered by neofunctionalists to be likely to play a key part in the process; and empirical evidence
shows that, although the Single Act certainly caused a flurry of interest
in group activity at EU level, this was by no means absent beforehand
(Greenwood 1997).

   Whether new issues can or cannot be added to the remit of a 'new' regional
organisation once it has been set up must remain an open question, given
the youth of the various 'new' regional integration projects. Equally it is
simply incorrect that old regionalism was (usually) involuntary, whereas new
regionalism is freely chosen. 'Regional integration' was classically defined by
neofunctionalists as a voluntary process, in order to distinguish it from previous methods of unifying territories such as nation-building or empire (Haas
1970). It might be argued that neofunctionalists under-played the role of
American dominance in supporting/dictating regional integration in Europe;
but then, involvement of the United States (US) in NAFTA (Hurrell 1995b)
and APEC (Foot 1995) has been crucial in determining the policies towards
regionalism of the two organisations' respective member states. Perhaps it
might be argued that the 'Community Method' of European integration
sought a system-shaping, and even system-building, role for the European
Commission. However, it is conventional wisdom that the Commission's ability to play this role has been severely truncated, and certainly has never

amounted to the power to dictate the pace of EU politics without a broad coalition of member state and interest group support (for an overview, see Cini 2002).

Thus, a certain degree of caution is necessary when attempting to make distinctions between regionalisms old and new. Hettne (2003: 24–5) argues that the theoretically salient differences between 'new regionalism' and its antecedent are in fact very few, and relate principally to the need to focus analytically on a broad range of actors, to study both non-institutional and institutional factors in the region-building process, to refer specifically to globalisation and the global political economy as exogenous factors having an impact on the regional organisation/process, and to adopt a multi-disciplinary, multi-dimensional focus. These requirements for theory-building are helpful, and are addressed in the final section of this chapter.

'Old regionalism' studies beyond neofunctionalism

A further ground on which the distinction between the NRA and theories of integration/'old regionalism' can be questioned is the caricature of theory-building in the latter that is often to be found in NRA theory. With the exception of a few diehards (e.g. Schmitter 2004) or recasters of traditional approaches (Moravcsik 1999), and an unsuccessful attempt to synthesise neo-functionalism and intergovernmentalism in the early 1990s, integration theory is no longer within the narrow confines of the debates of the 1950s–1970s. Indeed, it has witnessed an explosion of new concepts and approaches in recent years.[5] Neither neofunctionalism nor intergovernmentalism continue to enjoy conceptual hegemony in the field; the very processes which sparked the creation of the NRA sparked conceptual renewal in integration theory too. The current focus is on middle-range theory, with the general rationalists versus constructivists debate in international relations becoming something of a new orthodoxy (see Wiener and Diez 2004 for an overview). Here is not the place to comment on the strengths and weaknesses of the various new approaches; what counts in the present analysis is the fact that integration theory is as different today from neofunctionalist-intergovernmentalist orthodoxy of yore as the NRA itself – and arguably more diverse.

Taking the EU as 'new regionalism' seriously

Moreover, it is necessary to take seriously the fact that the EU (the prime case study of 'old regionalism') itself is part of the 'new regionalism'. As mentioned above, it was in the EU that the shoots of the new regionalism first broke the soil; and in its continuing experimentation with a range of policy styles and regimes the EU gives as good an example of network governance dependent on links to the global political economy as well as the constituent units (the member states) as any. This fact has, however, not been given theoretical centrality. Instead, NR scholars have tended to emphasise the differences between regionalisms old and new, and been extremely wary of the idea that the European experience might be treated as a template to follow slavishly elsewhere (Acharya 2002; Hettne 2002). In their turn, 'old regionalism' scholars (at least, those concerned with EU studies) have tended to ignore the new regionalism in their own theoretical endeavours.[6] Of course, certain scholars in EU studies have engaged with new regionalism – to give but three examples, Ben Rosamond, Walter Mattli and Mario Telò have all produced interesting work in this field (Mattli 1999; Telò 2001; Breslin *et al.* 2002) – but these scholars remain few in number. Explicit 'new regionalist' readings of the EU are few (for an exception, see Wunderlich 2004). It therefore remains to give proper weight to the EU's 'new regionalism' characteristics, a shortcoming from which scholars in both 'new' and 'old' regionalisms suffer (Warleigh 2004: 304–9).

Revising 'new regionalism'

A fourth and final reason to overcome the false divide between 'new' and 'old' regionalism studies is the fact that the NRA has entered an explicit revision phase. Björn Hettne, the NRA's chief proponent, has in recent work undertaken reflexive analysis of the NRA and called for change (Hettne 2003). In particular, Hettne argues in this piece that the NRA exaggerated the differences between first and second wave regionalisms, over-stated the dependence of regional projects on globalisation, and misjudged the growth potential of new regionalism. Other scholars in the field have made similar pleas for more and better work in regional theory (Söderbaum 2003: 2; Laursen 2003a, 2003b). Comparative analyses of different regional integration projects are singled out as a useful way forward (Katzenstein 1996; Higgott 1998; Hettne 2001: 1). This reflexive phase of development in the NRA sits extremely well with the 'normative turn' and metatheoretical phase in EU studies (Bellamy and Castiglione 2003; Warleigh 2003: 16–23), providing an opportunity for collaboration in theory-building which ought not to be missed.

Theory-building across paradigms? Towards a conceptual framework

However, is such collaboration possible? Certainly, the auto-definition of the 'new regionalism' as a separate field of study gives pause for thought; the intellectual parochialism of much theory work in EU studies does the same. One of the key concepts in social science theory is that of the paradigm (Kuhn 1970) – a body of thought adopted as a matter of faith (ibid.: 156) which allows us to make sense of the world/our chosen phenomena for study, and which must be accepted or rejected wholesale (Doyal and Harris 1989: 14). Only internal critique of a paradigm is possible, for 'outside' criticism is easily written off on the ground that it starts from a false basis or fails to understand the subtleties of the paradigm under examination. If we interpret 'integration theory' and the NRA as different paradigms, then there must be significant doubt about the feasibility of the collaboration between scholars in the two sub-fields called for immediately above.[7]

However, and following from section two, I maintain that the NRA and integration theory are not separate paradigms, but rather sub-fields of the same one. Although they often use different terminology, both sets of scholars study the same dependent variable: the formation of regional blocs, processes and clusters in the global political economy. They both start from political science perspectives to embrace interdisciplinarity and to focus on the functions, scope, development and impact of regional organisations.[8] They are not reflections of different meta-understandings of international relations (idealism and realism);[9] instead, within each field, scholars who might be called idealists or realists contribute to the debate. Such paradigm sub-sections as the NRA and integration theory are thus not accurately conceived as incommensurable rivals. This is partly because debate between paradigms is always circular and inconclusive, meaning that they cannot compete in any meaningful sense of the word and thus to speak of rival paradigms is always problematic (Kuhn 1970); however, it is chiefly because the alleged differences between the two sub-fields of study are revealed upon hard analysis to be meagre, and therefore capable of deliberation, adaptation and expression in a new shared understanding.

Nonetheless, sub-paradigms can and do proceed as if the other did not exist, either considering themselves as true paradigms or in real or affected ignorance of each other. It is this problem which must be addressed if the various useful insights generated by both sets of scholars are to be harnessed with optimal benefit. This requires explicit attention to the strengths and weaknesses of each approach and dialogue between their respective proponents.[10] Each sub-field will gain from this.[11] 'New regionalism' scholars would thereby embrace a more complex understanding of interdisciplinarity (law, sociology, anthropology as well as politics and economics), broaden their focus and range by no longer seeing the EU as 'the Other', and learn from the various mistakes that integration theorists/EU studies scholars have made as well as the insights they have generated. 'Old regionalism' scholars would rediscover the importance of critical theory and political economy, both of which are under-represented in EU studies, and engage more explicitly with global/international issues that affect their dependent variable. Both sets of scholars would gain from explicit investigation of what may not after all be quirks of the EU system as it advances (e.g. flexibility, heavy reliance upon informal politics, legitimacy issues, complex inter-linkages between the new centre and the component states) but rather inherent features of regionalism wherever practised.

How is this process of engagement to be undertaken, however? What kind of approach to theory-building does it require? Two initial points are obvious, but also important: first, if we undertake this task, we are not starting in a vacuum; we therefore need to take stock of what we already 'know' or claim, and use the resultant audit as a starting point. Second, progress will come gradually through dialogue, comparative research around a shared research agenda, and critique.

This indicates that at the metatheoretical level a critical approach to theory is likely to be beneficial. Critical theories aim to liberate scholars (and non-academics too) from hegemonic/dominant but unhelpful perceptions – in this case, the false divide between the NRA and 'old regionalism' studies. Acknowledging the impossibility of complete objectivity, critical theorists nonetheless eschew extreme forms of relativism as unhelpful, on the ground that the world can be known even if each of us perceives it differently, and knowledge can meaningfully be communicated (Mjøset 1999). Critical theorists also engage in explicitly reflective practice, seeking 'truth' not by correspondence with 'facts' as in Popperian positivism but by consensus (i.e. through reflection and deliberation about the most plausible explanation of a phenomenon or the best course of action). Of course, there is a strong ethical flavour to critical theory – it seeks to uncover ways of making the world better, and not just better understood. The ultimate goal of uncovering ways in which regional organisations might work more effectively, or more democratically, is surely one worth supporting.

A further advantage of critical theory is that it can be undertaken more or less 'scientifically'.[12] In other words, it can define dependent variables, list and justify independent variables, specify hypotheses and collect evidence which is then deliberated upon in order to draw conclusions and, if appropriate, prescribe a course of action. In this way, it seeks ultimately to elaborate generalisable theory, not as Grand Theory but as a conceptual framework – a 'frame of reference in which reality can be examined . . . [by] providing interpretations of relationships between variables' (Stoker 1995: 18). In the next section we take the initial steps in this process by defining the dependent variable for such studies.

Defining the dependent variable: 'regionalisation' as an offer

Trying to define what a 'region' is has been fraught with difficulty in the NRA. Do regions have to be (heavily) institutionalised? Do they have to be geographically distinct and coherent? Do they have to be at a certain stage of economic development before they qualify for the label? Calleya (1997: 34) argues that there is no agreement in the literature on this head, arguing that regions are *de facto* defined by the interactions (social/cultural flows) that they contain.[13] Typologies of regions abound; they can be 'transnational' (network-based, led by cross-border interest groups and informal interaction), 'intergovernmental' (led by governments) or 'comprehensive' (led by both governments and interest groups) (ibid.: 38). They can be 'core' or 'periphery' regions (Hettne 2000: xvii–xix). They can be 'hegemonic' (dominated by one state), 'international' (where all component states are roughly equal), or 'transnational' (of which there are two sub-categories:

corporate transnational regions, which seek to promote economic growth, and *societal transnational regions*, which seek to tackle wealth inequalities) (Hveem 2003: 86–91). Moreover, regions can fluctuate along a continuum comprising five stages of 'region-ness' according *inter alia* to internal flows of senses of regional identity and global level variables (Hettne 2002; Hettne and Söderbaum 2002).[14] There is thus an emergent view that attempting a narrow definition of the term 'region' is not likely to be productive, and that instead theorists should concentrate on understanding the various processes of regionalisation that are unfurling across the globe (Schulz *et al.* 2001; Laursen 2003b).

That said, good theory-building requires clarity about the nature of the dependent variable. To that end, I propose the term 'regionalisation' as one which could be usefully adopted, and offer a typology to help understand and conceptually manage the diversity of this phenomenon. I intend 'regionalisation' to mean: an explicit, but not necessarily formally institutionalised, process of adapting participant state norms, policy-making processes, policy styles, policy content, political opportunity structures, economies and identity (potentially at both elite and popular levels) to both align with and shape a new collective set of priorities, norms and interests at regional level, which may itself then evolve, dissolve or reach stasis.

Regionalisation focuses by definition on process rather than outcome; this helps avoid unnecessary battles over defining the likely or desired end-point, since there may in fact be no such thing. By the same token, no particular end-point for, or institutional configuration of, regionalisation is prioritised. In this way, teleological assumptions such as those of early neofunctionalists can be avoided. Moreover, the term can be applied to processes of region-construction which have diverse natures and core rationales. Table 2.1 presents a typology of regionalisation.

'Regionalisation' is a dynamic term, implying fluidity and movement. However, it is not intended to imply that processes of regionalisation can, or should, only progress/deepen. Moreover, the term connotes a non-monolithic and multi-level focus, because it brings the scholar's attention to transformations of structures, process and agency at the regional level, the level of the component states, and within those states (groups, institutions, individuals): one cannot make or recast a region without altering its component parts and the individual people swept up in, or partly causing, the process. Additionally, 'regionalisation' should be understood as a two-way, or multi-way, process in which complex constellations of variables at regional, global, national, local, and even personal/individual levels can combine to produce outcomes at any given time.

Thus, the term is generalisable, by which I mean that it could be applied to any instance of cross-border international region-formation in world politics. It expects a link between politics and economics, but does not privilege one over the other. It allows for security issues to be a causal factor, but does not expect this always to be the case, at least if by 'security' we mean military

Table 2.1 A typology of regionalisation

Type of regionalisation	Features	Examples
Structured regionalisation	A complex multi-issue entity, using informal politics despite deep institutionalisation. No hegemon exists; substantial power is delegated to the new centre in many policy areas, and is costly to 'repatriate'.	European Union (EU); African Union (in aspiration)
Dominance regionalisation	An alternative to a global regime, established by regional/global hegemon to counter threats to its power from other regionalisation processes or states. Focuses on narrow range of issues, with emphasis on trade.	North American Free Trade Area (NAFTA)
Security regionalisation	Focus on security issues, either military or socio-economic. May be geographically contiguous or transregional in membership.	Euro-Mediterranean Partnership; North Atlantic Treaty Organisation (NATO)
Network regionalisation	Regional identity-driven response to globalisation. May acquire significant or more limited range of powers, but relies primarily on non-institutionalised or intergovernmental working methods.	Association of Southeast Asian Nations (ASEAN); African Union (in actuality); South American Common Market (Mercosur)
Conjoined regionalisation	Strategic partnership of one regionalisation process with either another such process or with key states outside the region for the sake of economic or foreign policy advantage	Asia-Pacific Economic Cooperation (APEC); putative Free Trade Area of the Americas

issues. It allows for both normative and more instrumental factors to play a causal role, again without stating which is the more important. Such matters should be explored empirically rather than simply stated at the outset. As a final benefit, it avoids loaded terminology such as 'old regionalism', 'new regionalism', and 'integration' (which NRA scholars, with some justification, see as an irretrievably neofunctionalist term, and thus too closely bound to teleological accounts of regional polity-formation for general use – viz. Söderbaum 2003).

Understanding 'regionalisation' as the dependent variable in such a way thus has much to offer. It might also be seen to have shortcomings: it does not specify the policy areas in which regionalisation must/should occur, or set out precise mechanisms by which the process might be deepened. Nor does it say why states might undertake regionalisation in the first place, or even whether the choice is actually theirs to make. Nor does it specify precisely the range of actors involved and their roles in the process; instead it lists actors who are *potentially* involved. All these problems are, however, capable of solution by comparative empirical research. In the next section, I set out and justify a list of independent variables to study in such a manner, and to such an end.

Independent variables of regionalisation and issues for research

Ernst Haas (1970: 614–16) argued that regional integration projects (his terminology) depended on certain key factors for their success: transaction levels between participant states had to increase relative to those with third countries, in order to increase actor perceptions of interdependence; all involved actors/states had to perceive benefits from the process, even if those benefits were distributed unequally; the readiness of wealthier participant states to provide side-payments when necessary was more important for success than relative homogeneity of either wealth or size between participant states; formal institution-building helped cement senses of interdependence; and although certain issue areas may always be resistant to regionalisation, and others may reach a plateau at an early stage of the process, the key catalyst was the creation of a common market for and between the component states. This set of variables, generated on the back of impressive empirical work, is nonetheless clearly neofunctionalist: witness, for example, the emphasis on institutions, the perceived importance of progress/deepening, the idea of protectionist market-formation. Thus, it should be treated with as much caution as respect in regionalisation studies, even if we recall (again) that the so-called 'new regionalism' began with the very act of protectionist market-creation in what is now the EU that Haas identified as key.

More recent literature suggests a range of independent variables to study. Hveem (2003) argues that perceptions of output legitimacy are crucial for regionalisation to continue or progress; Bøås, Marchand and Shaw (2003) urge scholars to focus explicitly on the interplay between formal and informal aspects of regionalisation.

Walter Mattli (1999: 42) suggests that if we wish to understand the likely success of a regionalisation process (although, like Haas, he uses the term 'regional integration'), we should focus on four key variables: (1) the likelihood of significant economic gain; (2) likely gain for key national actors, e.g. increased legitimacy/popularity; (3) the existence of credible and accepted leadership; and (4) joint formal institutions (although Mattli argues that these are helpful rather than vital). In later work (Mattli 2003), he also argues that 'horizontal' factors – essentially the willingness of the component states or regional organisation to delegate power to the private sector – are vital for successful economic regionalisation, and therefore need to be studied as key variables.

Finn Laursen (Laursen 2003b) argues that comparative study of regionalisation (my term) projects should focus on four key variables: (1) the functional scope of the various entities; (2) their respective institutional systems; (3) the size of their membership; and (4) their respective impacts. The level of regionalisation (how much economic regionalisation? Political as well as economic regionalisation?) can be understood by exploring three issues: (1) the interests of the component states; (2) the roles and capacities of regional institutions; and (3) the impact of exogenous factors, e.g. globalisation. Breslin *et al.* (2002: 19) agree with Laursen's first and third issues, but add a different complementary variable – the existence of a sense of regional identity. All these lists of variables provide useful points of departure, but they require harnessing in a consolidated format and attention both to contradictions and to hidden (rather than explicitly articulated) assumptions of a neofunctionalist/NRA kind. The following is an attempt to do just that, while also adding variables (or issues to explore in order to assign the proper weight to those variables).

There are, I submit, four principal independent variables which require exploration. All of them have sub-variables, or, perhaps better expressed, issues to address empirically in order to generate an understanding of the variable in question. The principal independent variables are: the rationale for the beginning of the regionalisation process (*genesis*); the way the regionalisation process works (*functionality*); the ideational/affective factors at work in the process (*socialisation*); and the effects of regionalisation on its component states/other states (*impact*). Table 2.2 lists each principal independent variable in turn, and then sets out issues for empirical research in order to explore them.

The list of suggested research issues for each of the independent variables appears to me to be comprehensive at the present time. However, nothing precludes the addition of further questions should this prove necessary. Table 2.3 contains a tentative hypothesis for each of the independent variables. Each hypothesis is intended to involve as many of the relevant research issues as possible. Each hypothesis is capable of being tested using research questions formulated on the basis of the research issues listed above, and is capable of partial or complete falsification.

In lieu of a conclusion – summary and aspiration

In this chapter it has been argued that the divide between 'new' and 'old' regionalisms is conceptually untenable as well as unhelpful. The stated differences between 'new' and 'old' regionalisms as politico-economic projects are exaggerated, and only two (the North–South element of some new regionalist projects such as NAFTA, and the relative lack of emphasis on issues of identity and legitimacy in the 'old' regionalist projects and scholarship) stand up to scrutiny. These two issues do not constitute justification for the creation of another sub-field of social science. Furthermore, in conceptual terms, the 'new regional approach' often caricatures classical integration theory, and is far less different from current theoretical work in the epitome of 'old

Table 2.2 Independent variables of regionalisation

Genesis	Functionality	Socialisation	Impact
Why do states participate?	Who leads, how and why?	Impact on senses of identity (at elite and mass levels)	On global economy
Why do states continue as participants?	Who makes day-to-day decisions? With which decision rules?	Policy learning (exchange of models/ideas, or convergence to new norm)	On democracy in the component states
What are the stated purpose and objectives of the regionalisation process?	What role, if any, is played by non-state actors?	Transaction flows (social, cultural, economic)	On distribution of wealth (state-state, and intra-state)
How is the regionalisation process defined (inclusion/ exclusion)?	Which policy issues are addressed, and why?	Popular awareness and understanding	On influence of the component states (both on each other and *vis-à-vis* third countries)
	Is the regionalisation process stop–go, linear, reversible, or static?	Popular support (legitimacy)	Are certain policy styles/ types imposed or made impossible?
	Do the actors involved also collaborate outside the regionalisation process? If so, how and why?	Increase in trust (elite or mass)	Are the structures/ constitutions of the component states changed?
	What mixture of informal and formal mechanisms?		Does the regionalisation process deepen? Why?
	Implementation and enforcement mechanisms		Does the regionalisation process take on more states over time?
	Performance (output)		

Table 2.3 Hypotheses

Independent variable	Hypothesis
Genesis	States participate in regionalisation because they perceive a specific common interest in managing the economic and/or security consequences of globalisation that is not shared with states outside the region
Functionality	Regionalisation is a stop–go process dominated by the governments of component states and dictated by their perceived interests, with a tendency towards informal methods of decision-making
Socialisation	Policy learning and joint problem-solving are more apparent than regionalised identities at either elite or mass level
Impact	Regionalisation empowers the component states as a collective *vis-à-vis* third countries and has significant structural (constitutional) impact on its component states

regionalism', EU studies, than might be thought from this misrepresentation. Equally, the fact that the NRA has highlighted issues which could very usefully be addressed in EU studies has gone largely unnoticed because scholars in both sub-fields of study have tended to gloss over, or at least fail to give adequate conceptual weight to, the fact that the EU itself is a form, and even the crucible, of 'new regionalism'. It was argued that the divide between new and old regionalism was therefore erroneous, and capable of being understood as an unfortunate schism within a single paradigm rather than as evidence of separate paradigms incapable of meaningful communication between themselves.

In order to repair this schism, the chapter elaborated a new understanding of the dependent variable, the process by which states work together in regional clusters, which was called 'regionalisation' and which was deliberately defined in terms that are *a priori* acceptable to scholars of both new and old forms of regionalism (or at least to contemporary adherents of the NRA and EU studies). This definition focuses on process rather than outcome, and sets the basis for the stipulation of independent variables, issues to be explored in research, and tentative hypotheses for such work. Empirical work may of course indicate that the typologies require revision, or that a given state can take part in different regionalisation processes simultaneously but for different reasons. It may also show that regionalisation processes change their nature over time. Comparative study may be as useful within each 'type' as between each type, at least in this early stage of reaching for a pre-theory. Thus, the conceptual framework set out here is intended as a guide for future research, to be revisited and revised as necessary.

In sum, the chapter argues for a critical theory approach to the development of a conceptual framework for the study and theorisation of regionalisation, both in terms of the kind of theory that is being sought and in the approach taken to its elaboration. In that respect it is both a homage to, and (hopefully) a refinement of, the scholarship of theorists such as Joseph Nye (1968), who saw the back-to-basics, cards-on-the-table approach as the only way to solve the problems of first generation neofunctionalism. My intention here has not been to reinvigorate that body of scholarship, but rather to emulate the approach Nye adopted to the solution of a difficult, paradigm-shaping research problem. It is my hope that as regionalisation scholars we can therefore avoid continuing intra-paradigm schism and seize the available opportunities for both cross-fertilisation and conceptual clarity.

Notes

1 In the fourth section of this chapter, I advocate the use of a new term, 'regionalisa-tion'. Terms such as 'regionalism' and 'regional integration' are used in the earlier sections in two ways. First, in a general sense and for the sake of variety, as synonyms. Second, and more precisely, as appropriate to reflect the ontologies of the scholars who worked with the two concepts.
2 The value of EU studies and integration theory for new regionalism scholars, and the differences between 'old' and 'new' forms of regionalism have been matters of controversy; see the second section.
3 For an excellent account of the relevant issues, see Rosamond (2000). For a set of essays exploring the main trends in current (European) integration theory, see Wiener and Diez (2004).
4 As will be clear from what follows, it is not always apparent whether such distinc-tions are considered to be essentially empirical (i.e. differences between 'new' and 'old' regional projects) or theoretical (i.e. differences between the NRA and integration theory *à la* neofunctionalism).
5 For a discussion of this attempted synthesis, see Warleigh (1998).
6 For instance, the otherwise impressive volume on integration theory edited by Antje Wiener and Thomas Diez (2004) has no chapter on the new regionalism approach.
7 Kuhn (1970: 151) argued that communication between paradigms is possible, and in very rare cases scholars can even 'convert' from one paradigm to another – note the religious terminology. However, the complementarity of paradigms is not high, since although no single paradigm can explain everything, decisions about which questions are the most important to answer, how answers should be sought, and even which evidence is accepted, drive the individual back into the creation of an established corpus of thought and rules – a vicious circle. Paradigms, therefore, change or collapse only when they become incapable of explaining a critical mass of matters considered by the paradigm-subscribers to be significant, and when there is another putative paradigm to adopt instead (ibid.: 77).
8 I use the term 'organisation' as shorthand, for the sake of convenience rather than to imply that all regionalisation processes must be heavily institutionalised.
9 On these two traditions, see Hollis and Smith (1991).
10 The fourth and fifth sections make a tentative attempt at this.
11 The remainder of this paragraph draws on Warleigh (2004: 303–7).
12 This capacity is far less clear in the constructivism – see the lucid thoughts of Alexander Wendt on 'science' and constructivism (Wendt 1999: 372–3).
13 Calleya (1997: 36) does, however, put forward his own definition of a region, arguing that regions require: regularly inter-acting states whose foreign policy has

an impact on each other's domestic policy; member states which have geographical proximity to each other; a ruling group of at least two states; and positive external influence from third states.

14 These stages are described by Hettne (2002: 327–8) as: 'regional space' (a geographical unit bound together by trade and settlement links); 'regional complex' (embryonic interdependence); 'regional society' (formal membership organisation covering issues of culture, economics, defence/security and politics); 'regional community' (based on shared values and transnational civil society); and 'regional institutionalised polity' (fixed regional political structures with a degree of autonomous power).

References

Acharya, A. (2002) 'Regionalism and the Emerging World Order: Sovereignty, Autonomy, Identity', in S. Breslin, C. Hughes, N. Phillips and B. Rosamond (eds) *New Regionalisms in the Global Political Economy*, London: Routledge, pp. 20–32.

Bellamy, R. and Castiglione, D. (2003) 'Legitimizing the "Euro-Polity" and its "Regime": The Normative Turn in EU Studies', *European Journal of Political Theory*, 2(1): 7–34.

Bøås, M., Marchand, M. and Shaw, T. (2003) 'The Weave-World: The Regional Interweaving of Economies, Ideas and Identities', in F. Söderbaum and T. Shaw (eds) *Theories of New Regionalism* Basingstoke: Palgrave, pp. 197–210.

Breslin, S., Higgott, R. and Rosamond, R. (2002) 'Regions in Comparative Perspective', in S. Breslin, C. Hughes, N. Phillips and B. Rosamond (eds) *New Regionalisms in the Global Political Economy*, London: Routledge, pp. 1–19.

Breslin, S., Hughes, C., Phillips, N. and Rosamond, B. (eds) (2002) *New Regionalisms in the Global Political Economy*, London: Routledge.

Calleya, S. (1997) *Navigating Regional Dynamics in the Post-Cold War World*, Aldershot: Dartmouth.

Cini, M. (2002) 'The European Commission', in A. Warleigh (ed.) *Understanding European Union Institutions*, London: Routledge, pp. 41–60.

Coombes, D. (1970) *Politics and Bureaucracy in the European Community*, London: George Allen and Unwin.

Diez, T. and Wiener, A. (2004) 'Introducing the Mosaic of Integration Theory', in A. Wiener and T. Diez (eds) *European Integration Theory*, Oxford: Oxford University Press, pp. 1–21.

Doyal, L. and Harris, R. (1989) *Empiricism, Explanation and Rationality: An Introduction to the Philosophy of the Social Sciences*, London: Routledge.

Fawcett, L. (1995) 'Regionalism in Historical Perspective', in L. Fawcett and A. Hurrell (eds) *Regionalism in World Politics: Regional Organization and International Order*, Oxford: Oxford University Press, pp. 9–36.

Foot, R. (1995) 'Pacific Asia: The Development of Regional Dialogue', in L. Fawcett and A. Hurrell (eds) *Regionalism in World Politics: Regional Organization and International Order*, Oxford: Oxford University Press, pp. 228–49.

Greenwood, J. (1997) *Representing Interests in the European Union*, Basingstoke: Macmillan.

Haas, E. (1958) *The Uniting of Europe: Political, Social and Economic Forces, 1950–57*, Stanford, CA: Stanford University Press.

—— (1964) *Beyond the Nation State: Functionalism and International Organization*, Stanford, CA: Stanford University Press.

—— (1970) 'The Study of Regional Integration: Reflections on the Joy and Anguish of Pretheorizing', *International Organization*, 24: 607–46.

Hettne, B. (2000) 'The New Regionalism: A Prologue', in B. Hettne, A. Inotai and O. Sunkel (eds) *National Perspectives on the New Regionalism in the North*, Basingstoke: Macmillan, pp. xv–xix.

—— (2001) 'Regionalism, Security and Development: A Comparative Perspective', in B. Hettne, A. Inotai and O. Sunkel (eds) *Comparing Regionalisms: Implications for Global Development*, Basingstoke: Palgrave, pp. 1–53.

—— (2002) 'The Europeanisation of Europe: Endogenous and Exogenous Dimensions', *Journal of European Integration*, 24(4): 325–40.

—— (2003) 'The New Regionalism Revisited', in F. Söderbaum and T. Shaw (eds) *Theories of New Regionalism*, Basingstoke: Palgrave, pp. 22–42.

—— and Söderbaum, F. (2002) 'Theorising the Rise of Regionness', in S. Breslin, C. Hughes, N. Phillips and B. Rosamond (eds) *New Regionalisms in the Global Political Economy*, London: Routledge, pp. 33–47.

Higgott, R. (1998) 'Globalisation and Regionalisation: New Trends in World Politics', the 1998 Emirates Lecture no.13, Abu Dhabi.

Hollis, M. and Smith, S. (1991) *Explaining and Understanding International Relations*, Oxford: Clarendon Press.

Hurrell, A. (1995a) 'Explaining the Resurgence of Regionalism in World Politics', *Review of International Studies*, 21: 331–58.

—— (1995b) 'Regionalism in the Americas', in L. Fawcett and A. Hurrell (eds) *Regionalism in World Politics: Regional Organization and International Order*, Oxford: Oxford University Press, pp. 250–82.

Hveem, H. (2003) 'The Regional Project in Global Governance', in F. Söderbaum and T. Shaw (eds) *Theories of New Regionalism*, Basingstoke: Palgrave, pp. 81–98.

Katzenstein, P. (1996) 'Regionalism in Comparative Perspective', *Cooperation and Conflict* 31(2): 123–59.

Kuhn, T. (1970) *The Structure of Scientific Revolutions*, 2nd edn, Chicago: University of Chicago Press.

Laursen, F. (2003a) 'International Regimes or Would-be Polities? Some Concluding Questions and Remarks', in F. Laursen (ed.) *Comparative Regional Integration: Theoretical Perspectives*, Aldershot: Ashgate, pp. 283–93.

—— (2003b) 'Theoretical Perspectives on Comparative Regional Integration', in F. Laursen (ed.) *Comparative Regional Integration: Theoretical Perspectives*, Aldershot: Ashgate, pp. 3–28.

Mattli, W. (1999) *The Logic of Regional Integration: Europe and Beyond*, Cambridge: Cambridge University Press.

—— (2003) 'The Vertical and Horizontal Dimensions of Regional Integration: A Concluding Note', in F. Laursen (ed.) *Comparative Regional Integration: Theoretical Perspectives*, Aldershot: Ashgate.

Mjøset, L. (1999) *Understanding of Theory in Social Sciences*, ARENA Working Paper 99/33, Oslo: ARENA.

Monnet, J. (1978) *Memoirs*, London: Collins.

Moravcsik, A. (1999) *The Choice for Europe: Social Purpose and State Power from Messina to Maastricht*, London: UCL Press.

Nye, J. (1968) 'Comparative Regional Integration: Concept and Measurement', *International Organization*, 22(4): 855–80.

Rosamond, B. (2000) *Theories of European Integration*, Basingstoke: Macmillan.

Schmitter, P. (2004) 'Neo-neofunctionalism', in A. Wiener and T. Diez (eds) *European Integration Theory*, Oxford: Oxford University Press, pp. 45–74.

Schulz, M., Söderbaum, F. and Öjendal, J. (2001) 'Introduction: A Framework for Understanding Regionalization', in M. Schulz, F. Söderbaum and J. Öjendal (eds) *Regionalization in a Globalizing World*, London: Zed, pp. 1–21.

Söderbaum, F. (2003) 'Introduction: Theories of New Regionalism', in F. Söderbaum and T. Shaw (eds) *Theories of New Regionalism*, Basingstoke: Palgrave, pp. 1–21.

—— and Shaw, T. (eds) (2003) *Theories of New Regionalism*, Basingstoke: Palgrave.

Stoker, G. (1995) 'Introduction', in D. Marsh and G. Stoker (eds) *Theory and Methods in Political Science*, London: Macmillan.

Telò, M. (ed.) (2001) *European Union and New Regionalism: Regional Actors and Global Governance in a Post-hegemonic Era*, Aldershot: Ashgate.

Warleigh, A. (1998) 'Better the Devil You Know? Synthetic and Confederal Understandings of European Integration', *West European Politics*, 21(3): 1–18.

—— (2003) *Democracy in the European Union: Theory, Practice and Reform*, London: Sage.

—— (2004) 'In Defence of Intra-disciplinarity: "European Studies", the "New Regionalism" and the Issue of Democratisation', *Cambridge Review of International Affairs*, 17(2): 301–18.

Wendt, A. (1999) *Social Theory of International Politics*, Cambridge: Cambridge University Press.

Wiener, A. and Diez, T. (eds) (2004) *European Integration Theory*, Oxford: Oxford University Press.

Wunderlich, U. (2004) 'Conceptualising the European Union: A New Regionalism Approach', paper presented at the 34th UACES Annual Conference and 9th Research Conference, University of Birmingham, 6–8 September.

3   The future of regionalism

Old divides, new frontiers

Björn Hettne and Fredrik Söderbaum

Introduction

Over the past decade regionalism has become somewhat of an academic growth industry in a number of social science specialisations: European studies, comparative politics, international economics, international geography, international relations (IR) and international political economy (IPE). The approach of these different academic specialisations varies considerably, which means that regionalism means different things to different people. The field of regionalism is fragmented and plagued by divisions which, in our view, need to be transcended in order to reach new research frontiers. In response, this chapter seeks to contribute to a more productive debate between different theoretical standpoints in the research field.

The study of regionalism contains a significant number of different theoretical approaches to regionalism, from a revival of neofunctionalism to a variety of constructivist, critical and 'new regionalism' approaches, and with neorealism, neoliberal institutionalism and liberal intergovernmentalism in between. There are quite a few interesting theoretical explanations of specified aspects of regionalism. The problem with rigid theorising is that it must delimit the object for study, even while the object refuses too much reductionism. An empirical case can (or rather should) be approached from different theoretical angles. Different theories illuminate different dimensions of a multidimensional phenomenon. Therefore we will not propose any preferred theory in this chapter. Our purpose is instead to point at the divides that tend to fragment the research field and which need to be overcome and left behind.

Our study centres around what is here considered to be the three main divides in the research field. The first is between what has been termed 'old' and 'new' regionalism. After two decades of so-called 'new regionalism', we propose its dissolution. The second unfortunate divide is between European integration scholars and IR/IPE scholars, who are continuously speaking past one another. In our view, the study of regionalism would be greatly enhanced if scholars from these two camps would learn to communicate and build on each other's research results (see Warleigh-Lack, Chapter 2 in this volume). The third divide is that globalisation and regionalism are often treated in a grossly simplified way, especially in the sense that regionalism is often seen as either an integral part of economic globalisation (a stepping stone) or as a political instrument to resist economic globalisation (a stumbling block). It is not until we transcend such simplified conceptualisations that we will be able to better understand the complex and multifold relationships between globalisation and regionalism. As will become evident below, even if our analysis is structured according to the three divides, there are important overlaps between the themes.

Transcending old and new regionalism [1]

It has become commonplace in the field to distinguish between an older or earlier wave of regionalism (then often referred to as 'regional integration') in the 1950s and 1960s and a more recent new 'wave' or 'generation' of regionalism starting in the latter half of the 1980s and today being a prevalent phenomenon throughout the world. There are, however, both continuities and similarities between so-called 'old' and 'new' regionalism, so that when studying contemporary regionalism one can easily get a feeling of *déjà vu*. For instance, many regional projects and regional organisations were actually initiated in the 1960s, 1970s or early 1980s, and then simply renewed or re-inaugurated (sometimes with a new name and sometimes with a few different members) in the mid-1980s and 1990s. Under such circumstances it is often difficult to separate the historical from the contemporary. In response to these continuities we have argued elsewhere for identifying 'new' patterns of regionalisation co-existing with 'older' forms (Hettne 1999: 8; Söderbaum 2004a). But after two decades of so-called 'new regionalism', the distinction has lost much of its original meaning (or been too much misused), and we are herewith proposing that it is time to bury the distinction.

Having said this, it is still relevant to identify continuities and discontinuities, both in terms of empirical practices and theoretical perspectives, and for this purpose we find it more useful to distinguish between the early and the more recent debate. In what follows, we describe the first 'generation' of regionalism studies, focused on regional integration in Europe, and the subsequent 'big leap' from the 'early debate' to the more 'recent debate', which really was the study of regionalisms in the context of globalisation.

In this context it needs saying that even if the distinction between old and new regionalism has been misused and has also lost much of its meaning, it is still consistent to argue for the continued relevance of so-called 'new regionalism' *theory*, including the new regionalism approach (NRA) which we have both been trying to develop elsewhere (Hettne 2003, 2005; Hettne *et al.* 1999–2001; Hettne and Söderbaum 2000; Söderbaum 2004a; Söderbaum and Shaw 2003). The new regionalism approach/theory is a particular way (or rather ways) of analyzing the phenomenon of regionalism and is not dependent on a tight distinction between old and new regionalism.

The early debate

The early theories or approaches to regionalism were all concerned with peace, and tended to see the nation-state as the problem rather than the solution. The most relevant theories were federalism, functionalism and neo-functionalism. Federalism, which inspired the pioneers of European integration, was not really a theory but rather a political programme; it was sceptical of the nation-state, although what was to be created was in fact a new kind of state. There was no obvious theorist associated with federalism. In contrast, functionalism has been much identified with one particular name, that of David Mitrany (1965). This was also an approach to peace-building rather than a theory. The question for functionalists was on which political level various human needs (often defined in a rather technical way) could best be met. Usually, the best way was found to be going beyond the nation-state, but not necessarily going regional. Thus, both federalism and functionalism wanted the nation-state to go, but through different routes and by different means. For the functionalists, international organisations should be established in the promotion of cooperation and transnational activities around basic functional needs, such as transportation, trade, production and welfare. Economics was seen as more important than politics. Functionalism was rather technocratic and therefore unrealistic. Form, in the functionalist view, was supposed to follow function, whereas for federalists it was really form that mattered. Mitrany criticised both federalism and regional integration in general because both were primarily based on territory rather than function. For functional solutions there should be no territorial boundaries. Territoriality was seen as part of the Westphalian logic and Westphalia implied conflict and war. However, in contrast to the European Community (EC), which was a political community, the European Coal and Steel Community was, according to Mitrany, a functional and therefore acceptable organisation (for here the technical question was: how can coal and steel production best be organised?).

One early approach that to a larger extent had theoretical ambitions was neofunctionalism: the theory (but also strategy) of European integration. The central figure here was Ernst Haas. He challenged the functionalist assumption of the 'separability' of politics, claiming that the technical realm was in fact made technical by a prior political decision. Neofunctionalists argued that raising levels of interdependence would set in motion a process eventually leading to political integration. The emphasis was on process and purposeful actors, far away from functional 'automaticity'. Haas in fact theorised the 'community method' of Jean Monnet. Even if the outcome of this method could be a federation, the way of building it was not by constitutional design. The basic mechanism was 'spill-over', this key concept being defined as 'the way in which the creation and deepening of integration in one economic sector would create pressures for further economic integration within and beyond that sector, and greater authoritative capacity at the

European level' (Rosamond 2000: 60; also cf. Rosamond, Chapter 4 in this volume).

Europe was the centre of the debate about old regionalism. In the 1960s, the fit between the neofunctional description (and prescription) and the empirical world, now dominated by de Gaulle's nationalism, disappeared. Stanley Hoffmann (1966) asserted that integration could not spread from low politics (economics) to the sphere of high politics (security). Integration happened only as long as it coincided with the national interest. The image of the EC began to diverge. According to Alan Milward (1992), the EC should be seen as a 'rescue of the nation-state'. The EC could furthermore be understood as a confederation rather than a federation, according to the intergovernmentalist turn in the study of European integration. The ontological shift thus implied an epistemological shift towards a more state-centric, realist analysis.

Haas responded to his critics by calling the study of integration 'pre-theory' (since there was no clear idea about dependent and independent variables), then spoke about the field in terms of obsolescence, and ended up suggesting that the study of regional integration should cease to be a subject in its own right. Rather, it should be seen as an aspect of the study of interdependence (a concept then popularised by Robert Keohane and Joseph Nye). This was again a new turn. The global context was not really considered by old regionalism theory, concerned as it was with regional integration as a planned merger of national economies through cooperation among a group of nation-states. Comparative studies were for obvious reasons rare. Haas listed a number of background factors for successful integration and Philippe Schmitter focused particularly on Latin America and Joseph Nye on Africa (Haas 1961; Haas and Schmitter 1964). In retrospect, it is particularly interesting to see that the early theorists looked for post-Westphalian trends, but the global dynamics were then stifled by the bipolar structure. In the post-Westphalian context emerging after end of Cold War the earlier theorising is becoming more relevant (see Rosamond, Chapter 4 in this volume).

The recent debate

In the real world, the 1970s was a period of 'Eurosclerosis' within the European Communities. Elsewhere, attempts to create regional organisations were failing and most of these organisations fell dormant. However, the 1985 White Paper on the internal market started a new dynamic process of European integration. This was also the start of the 'new regionalism' elsewhere; after some time, everywhere. Naturally, this attracted a lot of interest in the late 1980s and early 1990s. What was striking, though, was the lack of correspondence in this respect between economics and political science.

The studies of the so-called 'new regionalism' considered new aspects, particularly those focused on conditions related to what increasingly came to be called globalisation (Hettne *et al.* 1999; Farrell *et al.* 2005; Fawcett and

Hurrell 1995; Gamble and Payne 1996; Schulz *et al.* 2001; Söderbaum and Shaw, 2003). Regionalism is strongly related to globalisation, but there are, as we shall see below, different views on the nature of this relationship. Much of the more recent debate on regionalism is strongly related to the relationship between globalisation and regionalism.

It is obvious that an understanding of contemporary regionalism requires both an *endogenous perspective*, according to which regionalisation is shaped from within the region by a large number of different actors, and an *exogenous perspective*, according to which regionalisation and globalisation are intertwined articulations, contradictory as well as complementary, of global transformation (see Hettne 2002; 2003). The endogenous perspective strongly underlines the connection between old and new regionalism, for instance, the relevant continuities back to functionalist and neofunctionalist theorising about the integration of Europe, the role of agency, as well as the long-term transformation of territorial identities.

Whereas the early debate was heavily focused on the concept of regional integration and to some extent regional cooperation, the more recent debate (with the exception of European integration studies) is more centred around the concepts of regionalism and regionalisation. At least from the view of its users, this is assumed to be more appropriate for covering the multidimensional features of current regionalism and transcending the limitations and state-centrism inherent in the concept of regional integration.[2] Regionalism refers to a tendency and a political commitment to organise the world in terms of regions; more narrowly, the concept refers to a specific regional project. In some definitions the actors behind this political commitment are states; in other definitions the actors are not confined to states. According to Anthony Payne and Andrew Gamble, 'regionalism is a state-led or states-led project designed to reorganise a particular regional space along defined economic and political lines' (Payne and Gamble 1996: 17). Due to the fact that their main concern lies with state-centred conceptions and projects of regional cooperation and integration they also share some important features with several earlier theories. But there are also discontinuities. Payne and Gamble say that 'regionalism is seen as something that is being constructed, and constantly reconstructed, by collective human action' (ibid.: 17), which sounds like a more comprehensive view as far as agency is concerned.

Other authors find it difficult to confine the regionalism project to states. The project on the 'new regionalism', financed by the United Nations University-World Institute for Development Economics Research (UNU-WIDER), suggested that, in the context of globalisation, the state was being 'unbundled', with the result that actors other than the state were gaining strength (Hettne *et al.* 1999–2001). By implication, the focus of analysis should not only be on state actors and formal inter-state frameworks, but also on non-state actors and what is sometimes referred to broadly as non-state regionalisation.[3]

Business interests are often supposed to be globalist in their orientation. However, this seems to be a myth. Globalisation strategies and multinationals actually tend to end up creating more regionalised patterns of economic activity (see Rugman, Chapter 5 in this volume). Civil societies are still generally neglected in the description and explanation of new regionalism (for exceptions, see Söderbaum 2004a, and O'Brien in this volume). Similarly, even if the external environment and globalisation are often readily called into account, extra-regional actors themselves are also generally weakly described and conceptualised within the study of regionalism. This is somewhat surprising, given the considerable attention which 'external' actors – such as foreign powers, donors, international financial institutions, non-governmental organisations, transnational corporations, and so on – receive in the study of national and local transformation processes, especially in the South. In the final analysis, it is not really a question of state-led regionalism versus non-state-led regionalism. On the contrary, state, market, civil society and external actors often come together in a variety of mixed-actor coalitions, networks and modes of governance (Söderbaum 2004a).

We are not throwing out the baby with the bathwater and claiming the irrelevance of the state. On the contrary, states continue to be crucial actors in the process of regionalisation, but in at least partly different ways compared to in the past and in mainstream theorising. Therefore, we need to complement conventional conceptualisations and notions about the role of states in regionalism. In a recent book on the political economy of regionalism in Southern Africa, one of us has 'unpacked' the state and addressed the question for whom and for what purpose regionalism and regionalisation is being pursued (ibid.). The study shows that ruling political leaders engage in a rather intense diplomatic game, whereby they praise regionalism and sign treaties, such as free trade agreements and water protocols. In so doing, they can be perceived as promoters of the goals and values of regionalism, which enables them to raise the profile and status of their authoritarian regimes. What is particularly important is that often the 'state' is not much more than a (neopatrimonial) interest group. Furthermore, although the rhetoric and ritual of regional diplomacy serve the goal of the reproduction and legitimisation of the state, it can also be a means to create a façade that enables certain regime actors to engage together with other non-state market actors in more informal modes of regionalism, such as trans-state regionalism or networks of plunder. This has also been referred to as 'shadow regionalism' (Söderbaum 2004b).

Summing up, in contrast to the time when Haas was writing, there are today many regionalisms and thus a very different base for comparative studies (see Bøås *et al.* 1999). 'Old' regional organisations continued but with at least partly new functions, while new regional organisations were formed to meet new challenges. At the same time various actors (especially non-state actors) have began to operate in these regional arenas, dealing with regional and global problems and providing regional and global public goods. In view of all of this, it is rather obvious that neither the object for study (ontology) nor the way of studying it (epistemology) have remained the same.

Bridging European integration and IR regionalism

After the Second World War, the study of regionalism, especially the 'old regionalism', was dominated by an empirical focus on Europe. Although the neofunctionalists were somewhat conscious of their own Eurocentrism, in their comparative analyses they searched for those 'background conditions' and 'spill-over' effects that could be found in Europe (Haas 1961; Hettne 2003). During the era of such old regionalism, European integration theories were developed for and from the European experience and then more or less re-applied or exported around the world. All too often (but not always) the EC/EU was then seen and advocated as the model, and other looser and informal modes of regionalism were, wherever they appeared, characterised as 'different' or 'weaker'. This bias still prevails in parts of the scholarly literature. For instance, Christiansen (2001: 517) illustrates the dangers of this privileging of Europe-centric understandings of regionalism in his assertion that 'on the whole, these forms of regionalism [in the rest of the world] differ from European integration in only focusing on economic matters and relying on a very limited degree of institutionalisation'. Hence, regionalism in (Western) Europe is, according to this view, considered multidimensional and highly institutionalised – both a descriptive and prescriptive contention – whereas regionalism in the rest of the world is seen as only weakly institutionalised and reduced to an economic phenomenon. In our view, these types of generalisations are problematic and often misleading.

This weakness in the field is confirmed by two renowned scholars of European integration, Alex Warleigh and Ben Rosamond (2006), who argue that large parts of recent EU studies scholars have considered the EU as a nascent, if unconventional, polity in its own right ('the famous *n = 1* problem'). This parochialism has contributed little, Warleigh and Rosamond assert, to deepening our understanding of the EU as a political system, and it has ironically also reinforced the notion that the EU is *sui generis*, thereby down-playing the respects in which the EU remains more like other regionalist projects around the world. We agree with Warleigh and Rosamond's solution, namely that EU studies need to return to the broader ambitions of the comparative (and classical) regional integration theory, at least as far as the development of generalisable and comparative conceptual and theoretical frameworks are concerned. Here it needs saying that, according to Rosamond, the early neofunctionalists were not Eurocentric and actually had genuinely comparative ambitions (cf. Rosamond, Chapter 4 in this volume).

If focus is changed from EU integration studies to IR/IPE theories of comparative regionalism, we can detect that variants of realist and liberal frameworks are also plagued by Europe-centred generalisations, which limit their ability to contribute to a more 'globally' applicable comparative regionalism.

Attention to North America and Asia-Pacific has indeed been significant, but has been marked by a dominant concern simply to explain variation from the 'standard' – European – case. As one authoritative scholar asserts, 'The study of comparative regionalism has been hindered by so-called theories of regionalism which turn out to be little more than the translation of a particular set of European experiences into a more abstract theoretical language' (Hurrell 2005: 39).

Related to this is the fact that much of the mainstream IR literature has a rather narrow empirical selection. It is, for instance, revealing that one of the key mainstream contributions to IR regionalism, that of Mansfield and Milner (1997), entirely ignores Africa and all regional organisations on that continent. This and several similar volumes seem to believe that meaningful and efficient regionalism is happening only, or primarily, in the 'core' regions of Europe and North America (Coleman and Underhill 1998). Apart from the inherent problems of such a narrow empirical selection for theorising about comparative regionalism, the problem lies in the ways the underlying assumptions and understandings about the nature of regionalism, which stem from a particular reading of European integration, influence the description of what regionalism in the rest of the world does – and, moreover, should – look like. It bears reiterating, as well, that the overwhelming majority of mainstream IR scholars maintain a limiting focus on states as aggregated and unitary units, and/or on formal regional intergovernmental organisations. This is highly problematic. As Bach (1999: 1) points out with regard to African regionalism, 'Outside Europe, the rebirth of regionalism during the late-1980s often had little to do with the numerous international organisations that were supposed to promote its development.' In sum, mainstream approaches in the field of IR and comparative regionalism can be characterised as introverted, ignorant of critical and reflective approaches and, at worst, largely irrelevant to an analysis and understanding of regionalisms outside Western Europe and North America. Breslin and Higgott (2000: 343) are correct in saying that: 'Ironically, the EU as an exercise in regional integration is one of the major obstacles to the development of analytical and theoretical comparative studies of regional integration.'

Whereas the mainstream IR literature has been biased towards a rather conventional interpretation of the EU, the problem has been the reverse in much of the so-called 'new regionalism' literature in IR, in our view especially the radical and postmodern variants. According to Warleigh and Rosamond (2006), many of these IR scholars have made a caricature of the EU and/or of orthodox integration theory (especially neofunctionalism), which has resulted in a failure to learn from both its successes and its failures. Presumably because of the exaggeration of differences between old and new forms of regionalism, Warleigh and Rosamond argue, the new regionalism scholars in IR have not engaged with EU studies scholars or older forms of integration theory. Some new regionalism scholars (such as Bøås *et al.* 1999) have deliberately rejected the case of Europe and instead developed a regional approach specifically for the South. Their theorising efforts are both innovative and thought-provoking, but they are upholding the rather misleading $n = 1$ problem that some EU integration scholars have constructed on their side. There is clearly a somewhat sceptical attitude towards Europe in critical new regionalism studies. As an example, one of us once called Europe 'the paradigm' for new regionalism (Hettne 2001), which, although it was not meant as a model to apply, was fiercely criticised by our more radical colleagues. Similarly, our efforts to theorise the rise of 'regionness' as a heuristic tool for comparative analysis (Hettne 1993; 2003; 2005; Hettne and Söderbaum 2000), have also been heavily criticised by the same scholars for being overly Eurocentric and too similar to classical integration theory.

In many ways we agree with Warleigh's and Rosamond's assertion that many of the so-called new regionalism scholars in the critical and radical camp (in some ways including ourselves) have missed the opportunity to take advantage of the richness of the EU as a project and the impressive research on the project. Few can dispute that the EU as a region is diverse and, as a result, there has been an explosion of interesting theorising. Hence, there is no single EU mode of governance but a series of different interpretations of the EU (see Wiener and Diez 2003), and, that this richness as well as ambitious theorising ought to have at least a potential positive influence on IR regionalism. Warleigh's and Rosamond's (2006) prescription is that IR and comparative regionalism 'cannot afford to lock itself away from the most advanced instance of regionalism in world politics' (i.e. the EU). But, as emphasised by Warleigh and Rosamond, there is a need for a conceptual and theoretical framework that can address the complexity of the field, and at the same time transcend the case of Europe itself. This is why there is such a great potential for bridging the gap between EU integration studies and IR regionalism.

The comparative method is certainly needed for the development of the field of regionalism, and for 'bridging the gap'. Since theory necessarily relies on some generalisations (beyond a single case), comparative analysis is also crucial for theory-building. Comparative analysis helps to guard against ethnocentric bias and culture-bound interpretations that can arise in too specialised or isolated an area of study, as well as 'ethnocentric universalism' that can arise when the case of Europe misleadingly becomes the standard framework for analysing regionalism in the rest of the world.

Hence, it is crucial to move beyond the false universalism inherent in a selective reading of regionalism in the core, and in the EU in particular, and instead to conduct analysis through 'genuinely' comparative regionalism. As Hurrell (2005: 39) insists, rather than try and understand other regions through the distorting mirror of Europe, it is better to think in general theoretical terms and in ways that draw both on traditional IR theory and on other areas of social thought. But, as already indicated, it is important not to reinforce the dividing lines between European integration studies and IR regionalism, and instead enhance communication and make the two fields of specialisation mutually reinforcing. This is only possible if the case of Europe is integrated within a larger and more general discourse of comparative IR regionalism, built around general concepts and theories (but still showing cultural sensitivity); hence a comparative IR regionalism which is not 'afraid' of European integration.

Our argument is that there is certainly a need for detailed analyses and case studies of various regions around the world, including European integration (as well as other regional specialisations). The main limitation of such specialisations is that it is difficult to generalise and build theories on the basis of these regions alone. There is a real need for comparison:

> when conducted properly, the comparative approach is an excellent tool ... In particular, it is a key mechanism for bringing area studies and disciplinary studies together, and enhancing both. It provides new ways of thinking about the case studies whilst at the same time allowing for the theories to be tested, adapted and advanced.
>
> (Breslin and Higgott 2000: 341)

In this sense we agree with Warleigh and Rosamond (2006) and their quest for a new research agenda on comparative regional integration. But comparative regionalism is not enough in itself, and we would like to add a third component that is required for a more complete understanding of regions and regionalism, namely to go beyond regionalism *per se* and understand the regional dimension in global transformation. The meaning of this component is elaborated in detail in the next section.

Bridging globalisation and regionalism

Much of the more recent debate on regionalism is strongly focused on conditions related to globalisation or world order. In particular, as indicated in the subtitle of this volume, the relationship between globalisation and regionalism constitutes one of the main concerns in the research field. This contrasts with many (but not all) earlier regionalism theories, which were heavily concerned with the endogenous forces of regional integration or intra-regional theorising (Hurrell 2005). Contemporary regionalism is thus strongly related to globalisation, but there are, as we shall see below, different views about the nature of this relationship. Our analysis rejects any simplified notions about how globalisation and regionalism hang together, instead drawing attention to the diversity of relationships. In fact, in a globalised world, regionalism as such is not the appropriate object for theorising; the focus should rather be on the regional factor or dimension of global transformation.

From dichotomy to diversity

Trade blocs have been a crucial aspect in the discussion of regionalism ever since the 1950s. According to neoclassical economics, regional trading arrangements are often seen as a 'second-best' and therefore judged accord-ing to whether they contribute to a more closed or more open multilateral trading system, embodied in the so-called 'stumbling block vs stepping stone' dichotomy. Many of the regional trading arrangements that existed during the era of regionalism in the 1950s and 1960s were inward-looking and protectionist, and were often regarded by contemporary economists as fail-ures. At the time, however, they were widely considered to be instruments for enhancing industrial production, as in the strand of development think-ing associated with the United Nations Economic Commission for Latin America (ECLA) and the even more ambitious strategy of the United Nations Conference on Trade and Development (UNCTAD), both led by Raúl Prebisch. The culmination of this process was the demand for a new international economic order. Regionalism developed into a form of global mobilisation against an unequal world order, but lost some of its strength in the process.

When regionalism returned in the mid-1980s the stumbling block vs step-ping stone dichotomy reappeared, sometimes under the banner of 'the new protectionism' vs 'open regionalism'. The new protectionism was basically an early interpretation of the new wave of regionalism by neoliberal economists who feared that the sudden interest in regionalism heralded a new protection-ism. Thus, for the neoliberals, regionalism was 'new' mainly in the sense that it represented a revival of protectionism or neomercantilism, whereas other economists and liberal observers drew attention to the fact that closure of regions was not on the agenda; rather, the current regionalism was 'open regionalism', which emphasised that the integration project should be market-driven and outward-looking, should avoid high levels of protection and should form part of the ongoing globalisation and internationalisation process of the world political economy (Anderson and Blackhurst 1993; de Melo and Panagariya 1993). Cable and Henderson (1994: 8) defined 'open regionalism' as a 'negotiating framework consistent with and complementary to GATT [the General Agreement on Tariffs and Trade]'. To say the least there are a significant number of economists and IPE scholars of a liberal orientation who favour the current drive towards such open regionalism.

Many critical scholars (in IR/IPE) also agree that current regionalism is above all to be understood as open regionalism, but consider it to be a prob-lem rather than a virtue. For instance, a pair of the most eminent scholars in the field, Andrew Gamble and Anthony Payne (1996: 251), claim that 'one of the most striking characteristics common to all the regionalist projects is their commitment to open regionalism', which tends to reinforce the detrimental effects of economic globalisation and global capitalism. Gamble and Payne believe that there is a long way to go before contemporary regionalism con-tributes to social regulation and social control, which in their view could be achieved by regulatory regionalism rather than neoliberal 'open regionalism' (also see Payne and Gamble 2003).

It is misleading to argue that globalisation is a singular and linear project;

alternative reactions and directions are also possible. Still, the conventional discussion – about whether regionalism constitutes a stumbling block vs building block – continues to influence much of the discussion on the topic. To a large extent globalisation and regionalism have become competing ways of understanding the world, and much analytical work has been devoted (or wasted?) in trying to clarify how the two processes are related.

Our message is that we need to transcend simple dichotomies, which are reinforced by the stumbling block vs stepping stone controversy, and instead take into account the diversity of relationships between globalisation and regionalism. A recent edited volume grouping some of the most prominent theorists in the field, *Theories of New Regionalism* (Söderbaum and Shaw 2003), clearly emphasises that any simple relationship between globalisation/ multilateralism and regionalism needs to be challenged. In fact, more or less all theorists in this edited collection (albeit some more than others) state that globalisation and regionalisation produce their own 'counterforces' with mixed outcomes in different regions. In addition, the infamous dichotomy is reductionist in its content since both 'economic globalists' as well as pro- ponents of regions as 'stepping stones' neglect the turbulence and contradic- tions inherent in the globalisation/regionalisation dyad. One group of authors in the volume, Morten Bøås, Marianne H. Marchand, and Timothy M. Shaw, claim that we are dealing with different layers and overlapping processes and nexuses of globalisation and regionalisation simultaneously, what these authors refer to as the 'weave-world'. Another contributor, Bob Jessop, high- lights a large number of micro-regional and rescaling activities that lead to new cross-border micro-regions – all of which are closely related and occur- ring within contexts of both globalisation and macro/meso-regionalisation (Jessop 2003).

Yet another of the respected authors in the volume, Helge Hveem, draws particular attention to regional projects and the alternative ways whereby these can ride on, reinforce, reject, hinder or hedge globalisation (Hveem 2003). In a somewhat similar fashion, but referring specifically to multi- lateralism, Diana Tussie also argues for a more subtle understanding:

> regionalism thrives in the policy spaces left by multilateralism but that at the same time when these lacunae are too many or too wide these ten- sions are then re-played in the multilateral sphere. In this sense the focus on these neglected games allows us to move away from one-dimensional views that posit regionalism and multilateralism as dilemmas of building blocks versus stumbling blocks.
>
> (2003: 100)

It also needs saying that the stumbling block vs building block dichotomy is formulated and defined from a particular standpoint whereby the end-goal of globalisation/multilateralism automatically becomes the 'best of all worlds'. Thus, the dichotomy has, clearly, been formulated 'for someone and for some purpose' to use Coxian language. One result of this critical attitude of the project of economic globalisation is that *politics* of assorted kinds has again been recognised to be important for both empirical and normative reasons. Building on the thinking of Karl Polanyi, Hettne (2003) develops a comprehensive argument in favour of 'the return of the political' in the overall context of globalisation. The argument is that, according to a non-liberal and more sceptical view, the liberal project of globalism is not realistic; the unregulated market system is analogous to political anarchy, and consequently there is a need to 'politicise the global', which in our view is the same thing as 'taming globalisation'. This serves as an example of how we may understand the regional dimension in the context of global transformation. Such analysis depends on a global perspective and therefore has to go 'beyond regionalism' in itself, including comparative regionalism (cf. Hettne 2005), and which also has been referred to as *The Global Politics of Regionalism* (Farrell *et al.* 2005).

Taming globalisation: 'politicising the global'[4]

In a comprehensive research programme on regionalism carried out during the second half of the 1990s, one of the basic assumptions was that regionalism constituted an integral, albeit contradictory part of globalisation (Hettne *et al.* 1999–2001). This raised the issue of how to conceive globalisation in theoretical terms. Since globalisation by definition is a worldwide, multi-dimensional process about which there can be no meaningful explanatory theory, we have to choose a more specific and delimited entry point for the study of globalisation and the role of regionalism. In the theory of economic history associated with Karl Polanyi, an expansion and deepening of the market is supposedly followed by a political intervention 'in defence of society'; the expansion of market exchange constituting the *first*, and the societal response the *second* movement, together making 'the double movement' (Hettne 1999; 2003).

This represents a dialectic and, in our view, a more nuanced understanding of globalisation compared to the simplified dichotomy discussed above, hence emphasising contradiction and change. Regionalism is thus part of both the first and second movement, with a neoliberal face in the first, and a more interventionist orientation in the second. There is thus a transnational struggle over the political content of regionalism/regionalisation, as well as over that of globalisation. It is important to note that both movements, albeit through different dynamics, are engineered by political forces and actors. The first sequence of the double movement implies a deliberate institutionalisation of market exchange and the destruction of institutions built for social protection, a destruction euphemistically called 'deregulation' or even 'liberalisation' in line with the ideology of globalism. According to Polanyi, the resulting turbulence and social unrest lead to attempts at re-regulation, new institutions of social welfare adapted to the new political economy created through this transformation. In the historical transformation analysed by Polanyi, these institutions were an integral part of the modern nation-state.

The re-embedding of the economy is never final. The dysfunctions typically associated with the second movement and its various forms of political intervention and regulation lead to a renewed defence and increased popularity of market solutions. Regulation becomes the problem. Friedrich von Hayek, disgusted with the interventionist ideological menu of the 1930s, expressed early warnings against political regulation, described as *The Road to Serfdom*, the title of his famous book, published in the same year as Karl Polanyi's equally classic *The Great Transformation* (1944). However, he had to wait a long while, until the 1970s, for market solutions to become the predominant approach.

Let us now apply the Polanyian dialectical approach to the current situation of growing dissent about the benefits of neoliberalism and the view of the market as a bad master rather than as a good servant. In accordance with the double movement thesis – that market exchange and political regulation (mediated by social movements) constitute the basic dialectics of a changing political economy – contemporary economic globalisation, or the globalist project, can be seen as an effort to institutionalise the market system on a global scale. This means that the trend towards the creation of regional formations throughout the world can be seen as one political attempt (among others) to manage the social turbulence implied in such a radical deregulation, unprecedented in terms of its global scope. This does not mean that globalisation is uniformly 'economic' and regionalisation 'political'. In both processes political decisions shaped by contesting social and political forces are crucial, and the consequences in terms of distribution of resources are deeply political. As stressed above, the distinction between economic and political must not be exaggerated. Here 'political' will normally refer to efforts at creating political communities on various levels of the world system; but depoliticisation or deregulation is nevertheless also political in its redistributive consequences.

Karl Polanyi's account of the rise and fall of market society was very simple, perhaps even simplistic, but he nevertheless pointed at one very strong and useful generalisation. An institutionalised balance between society, state and market – as a dialectic outcome of the two processes forming part of the Great Transformation – can be called a 'Great Compromise'. The Bretton Woods system that emerged after the Second World War was in fact such a compromise. Using a Polanyian term, Ruggie (1998: 62) labelled this system 'embedded liberalism', more precisely defined as transnational economic multilateralism combined with domestic interventionism. If the past two decades have been characterised by the predominance of economics, the time seems to have come for a 'return of the political' in order for another balance, or Great Compromise, to be established. From a Polanyian perspective the point is not only a return of 'the political' but equally much a 'return of the social', and even a 'return of the moral'. Thus the second movement is something much wider than state intervention, or for that matter regionalism. Regionalism is only one possible political response, important for its effort to retain the territorial imperative.

If the globalist project to institutionalise the market system on a global scale can be seen as the first phase of a (second) 'great transformation' in Polanyi's sense of the word, we should thus expect various political forces to shape the future course of globalisation; in other words to 'politicise' it (in the sense of democratic, civil society control). This will be done in competition between forces that are neither mutually compatible nor necessarily benevolent. Stated in this open way, there is little in Polanyi's theorising that provides a firm base for forecasting the design of future political structures. Furthermore, 'the second great transformation' takes place in a global context, with different manifestations in different parts of the world. Some of these manifestations are local protests, many of which are not very dissimilar from the countermovements in the original transformation. To be counted as part of a 'second' transformation the countermovements should, however, address global issues, even in their local manifestations. This means that they search for a global agenda, realising that local power-holders do not exercise full control and that challenges as well as counterforces express relations between different societal levels. 'Resistance is localised, regionalised, and globalised at the same time that economic globalisation slices across geopolitical borders' (Mittelman 2000: 177). We should not expect a uniform response to this 'great transformation', but rather, as history shows, many forms of resistance, constructive as well as destructive (Gills 2000). And regionalism is only one of them.

Conclusion

Regionalism is a multidimensional phenomenon that explains the richness of concepts, theories and perspectives on the topic. Although this pluralism is desirable in many ways, the research field is plagued by a lack of communication between different theoretical perspectives and standpoints. This chapter pinpoints that three divides in particular can be overcome: (1) the divide between 'old' and 'new' regionalism; (2) the divide between European integration scholars and IR regionalism; and (3) the simplified notions about how globalisation and regionalism are related.

The first part of the chapter discussed the transition from old to new regionalism, and the continuities and discontinuities involved. Since the new regionalism now has two decades behind it, this may be the time to bury the distinction and recognise the study of regionalism as a search for a moving target, even if this leaves us with a complicated ontological problem. We are not quite sure about the object of study.

One discontinuity that emerges in retrospect is thus the stronger normative and prescriptive nature of the early debate, whether the point of departure was federalism, functionalism or neofunctionalism. The idea was to achieve peace by moving beyond the Westphalian logic to find institutionalised forms of permanent international cooperation. The more recent debate is generated much more by the erosion of national borders and the urgent question of how to find an alternative order beyond Westphalia. Neofunctionalism, the only one of the three early approaches with theoretical ambitions, was dismissed before regionalism (or regional integration which was the preferred concept) had shown its real face. There was a lively debate without much happening on the ground, or perhaps it is more correct to say that whatever happened in the field of regional integration was distorted by the bipolar world order. Based on this poor showing in the real, empirical world, the critics, mostly realists, had a fairly easy task in questioning the viability of and the case for regional integration. The new wave of interest in regionalism should thus be seen in the context of an ending of the Cold War and a beginning of globalisation. The challenge now, in other words, is to theorise a fast emerging empirical phenomenon without much theory to work from. In order to meet this challenge there is a need to consolidate the research field and bridge the gap between earlier and more recent theorising.

Regarding the second divide, EU integration studies has largely been separated from IR regionalism studies, even if mainstream IR literature have focused heavily on the European experience and tried to generalise from this example. Important sections of radical and critical IR regionalism have, for their part, deliberately avoided the case of Europe, thereby reinforcing the misinterpretation that Europe is 'different' from the rest of the world, a belief which prevails in large parts of European integration studies. But the lack of communication between EU integration studies and IR regionalism can be overcome. Our argument is that we need a three-fold approach to the study of regionalism, which can be combined in different ways: (1) there is a need for detailed analyses and case studies of various regions around the world, including European integration and any other regional specification (mono-, inter- or multidisciplinary); (2) there is a need for genuine comparative regionalism studies, which include but also go beyond the case of Europe, but this is not enough; and (3) there is a need to go beyond comparative regionalism in itself, and analyse the regional dimension in global transformation, especially the taming of globalisation through politicising the global, which is related to the third divide.

Much of the more recent debate on regionalism is above all concerned about the relationship between globalisation and regionalism. Hence, regionalism is strongly related to globalisation, but there are many oversimplified ways to describe how they hang together. Important sections of the literature are dichotomising globalisation and regionalism, whereby regionalism is simply seen as either a stumbling block or a stepping-stone towards the latter. This dichotomy has at least two major weaknesses. First, it is built on a particular ideological and theoretical perspective which is biased in favour of multilateralism at the expense of other notions about world order and the regulation of the global political economy. Second, it is built on a simplified dichotomy which neglects the diversity of relationships between globalisation and regionalism. In our view, there is a need for more nuanced perspective that is capable of analysing and explaining the variety of ways whereby globalisation and regionalism are related and impact on each other. There are of course several possible perspectives, but our preferred model is the dialectical approach associated with Karl Polanyi, whereby globalisation can be tamed through 'politicising the global'. Regionalism can make up such political and countermovement strategy, which will take on different manifestations in different parts of the world.

Notes

1 This section draws mainly on Hettne (2005), which in turn is inspired by Rosamond (2000).
2 For broader definitions of regional integration, see both Rosamond and Warleigh-Lack in this volume, as well as the approach adopted by the United Nations University-Comparative Regional Integration Studies (UNU-CRIS), available online at http://www.cris.unu.edu.
3 A large number of labels have been used in the debate to capture these two similar (but not always identical) phenomena, such as 'top-down' and 'bottom-up' region-alisation; *de jure* and *de facto* regionalisation; states-led regionalism and market and society-induced regionalisation; and formal/informal regionalism.
4 This section draws on Hettne (2003).

References

Anderson, Kym and Blackhurst, Richard (eds) (1993) *Regional Integration and the Global Trading System*, Harvester: Wheatsheaf.

Bach, Daniel C. (1999) 'Revisiting a Paradigm', in Daniel C. Bach (ed.) *Regionalisation in Africa: Integration and Disintegration*, London: James Currey.

Bøås, Morten, Marchand, Marianne H. and Shaw, Timothy M. (eds) (1999) *New Regionalisms in the New Millennium*, special issue of *Third World Quarterly*, 20(5).

—— (2003) 'The Weave-World: The Regional Interweaving of Economies, Ideas and Identitities', in Fredrik Söderbaum and Timothy M. Shaw (eds) *Theories of New Regionalism*, Basingstoke: Palgrave.

Breslin, Shaun and Higgott, Richard (2000) 'Studying Regions: Learning from the Old, Constructing the New', *New Political Economy*, 5(3): 333–52.

Cable, Vincent and Henderson, David (eds) (1994) *Trade Blocs? The Future of Regional Integration*, London: Royal Institute of International Affairs.

Christiansen, Thomas (2001) 'European and Regional Integration', in John Baylis and Steve Smith (eds) *The Globalization of World Politics: An Introduction to International Relations*, Oxford: Oxford University Press.

Coleman, William D. and Underhill, Geoffry R. D. (eds) (1998) *Regionalism and Global Economic Integration: Europe, Asia and the Americas*, London: Routledge.

Farrell, Mary, Hettne, Björn and Van Langenhove, Luk (eds) (2005) *The Global Politics of Regionalism: Theory and Practice*, London: Pluto Press.

Fawcett, Louise and Hurrell, Andrew (eds) (1995) *Regionalism in World Politics: Regional Organization and International Order*, Oxford: Oxford University Press.

—— (2003) 'World Order Approach', in Fredrik Söderbaum and Timothy M. Shaw (eds) *Theories of New Regionalism*, Basingstoke: Palgrave.

Gamble, Andrew and Payne, Anthony (eds) (1996) *Regionalism and Global Order*, Basingstoke: Macmillan.

Gills, Barry (ed.) (2000) *Globalization and the Politics of Resistance*, Basingstoke: Macmillan.

Haas, Ernst B. (1961) 'International Integration: The European and the Universal Process', *International Organization*, 15(4): 366–92.

—— and Schmitter, Philippe (1964) 'Economics and Differential Patterns of Integration: Projections about Unity in Latin America', *International Organization*, 18(4): 259–99.

Hayek, Friedrich A. von (1944) *The Road to Serfdom*, London: G. Routledge & Sons.

Hettne, Björn (1993) 'Neo-Mercantilism: The Pursuit of Regionness', *Cooperation and Conflict*, 28(3): 211–32.

—— (1999) 'Globalization and the New Regionalism: The Second Great Transformation', in Björn Hettne *et al.* (eds) *Globalism and the New Regionalism*, Basingstoke: Macmillan.

—— (2001) 'Europe: Paradigm and Paradox', in Michael Schulz, Fredrik Söderbaum and Joakim Öjendal (eds) *Regionalization in a Globalizing World: A Comparative Perspective on Forms, Actors and Processes*, London: Zed Books.

—— (2002) 'The New Regionalism and the Return of the Political', Paper presented at XIII Nordic Political Association, 15–17 August, Aarlborg, Denmark.

—— (2003) 'The New Regionalism Revisited', in Fredrik Söderbaum and Timothy M. Shaw (eds) *Theories of New Regionalism*, Basingstoke: Palgrave.

—— (2005) 'Beyond the "New" Regionalism, *New Political Economy*, 10(4): 543–72.

—— and Fredrik Söderbaum (2000) 'Theorising the Rise of Regionness', *New Political Economy*, 5(3): 457–74.

——, Inotai, Andras and Sunkel, Osvaldo (eds) (1999) *Globalism and the New Regionalism*, Basingstoke: Macmillan.

—— (eds) (1999–2001) *The New Regionalism Series*, Vols I–V, Basingstoke: Macmillan.

Hoffmann, Stanley (1966) 'Obstinate or Obsolete? The Fate of the Nation State and the Case of Western Europe', *Daedalus*, 95: 865–85.

Hurrell, Andrew (2005) 'The Regional Dimension in International Relations Theory', in Mary Farrell, Björn Hettne and Luk Van Langenhove (eds) *The Global Politics of Regionalism: Theory and Practice*, London: Pluto Press.

Hveem, Helge (2003) 'The Regional Project in Global Governance', in Fredrik Söderbaum and Timothy M. Shaw (eds) *Theories of New Regionalism*, Basingstoke: Palgrave.

Jessop, Robert (2003) 'The Political Economy of Scale and the Construction of Cross-Border Regions', in Fredrik Söderbaum and Timothy M. Shaw (eds) *Theories of New Regionalism*, Basingstoke: Palgrave.

Mansfield, Edward D. and Milner, Helen V. (eds) (1997) *The Political Economy of Regionalism*, New York: Columbia University Press.

Mattli, Walter (1999) *The Logic of Regional Integration: Europe and Beyond*, Cambridge: Cambridge University Press.

Melo, Jaime de and Panagariya, Arvind (eds) (1993) *New Dimensions in Regional Integration*, Cambridge: Cambridge University Press.

Milward, Alan S. (1992) *The European Rescue of the Nation State*, London: Routledge.

Mitrany, David (1943) *A Working Peace System*, Chicago: Quadrangle Books.

—— (1965) 'The Prospect of Integration: Federal or Functional?', *Journal of Common Market Studies*, 4(1): 119–49.

Mittelman, James H. (2000) *The Globalization Syndrome: Transformation and Resistance*, Princeton, NJ: Princeton University Press.

Payne, Anthony and Gamble, Andrew (1996) 'Introduction: The Political Economy of Regionalism and World Order', in Andrew Gamble and Anthony Payne (eds) *Regionalism and World Order*, Basingstoke: Macmillan.

—— (2003) 'The World Order Approach'. in F. Söderbaum and T. Shaw (eds) *Theories of New Regionalism*, Basingstoke: Palgrave, pp. 43–62.

Polanyi, Karl (1944) *The Great Transformation*, Boston: Beacon Press.

Rosamond, Ben (2000) *Theories of European Integration*, Basingstoke: Macmillan.

Ruggie, John G. (1998) *Constructing the World Polity*, London: Routledge.

Schulz, Michael, Söderbaum, Fredrik and Öjendal, Joakim (eds) (2001) *Regionalization in a Globalizing World: A Comparative Perspective on Actors, Forms and Processes*, London: Zed Books.

Söderbaum, Fredrik (2004a) *The Political Economy of Regionalism: The Case of Southern Africa*, Basingstoke: Palgrave.

—— (2004b) 'Modes of Regional Governance in Africa: Neoliberalism, Sovereignty-boosting and Shadow Networks', *Global Governance: A Review of Multilateralism and International Organizations*, 10(4): 419–36.

—— and Shaw, Timothy M. (eds) (2003) *Theories of New Regionalism*, Basingstoke: Palgrave.

Tussie, Diana (2003) 'Regionalism: Providing a Substance to Multilateralism?', in Fredrik Söderbaum and Timothy M. Shaw (eds) *Theories of New Regionalism*, Basingstoke: Palgrave.

Warleigh, Alex and Rosamond, Ben (2006) 'Comparative Regional Integration: Towards a Research Agenda', description of Workshop for the ECPR Joint Sessions, Nicosia, Cyprus, 25–30 April.

Wiener, A. and Diez. T. (eds) (2003) *European Integration Theory*, Oxford: Oxford University Press.

4 Rethinking classical integration theory

Ben Rosamond

Introduction

The study of regional integration has undergone a well-documented revival in recent years. As with all intellectual endeavours, much effort has been placed upon the business of conceptual reflection and the selection of appropriate theoretical apparatuses to study the 'new regionalism'. Indeed, the use of the epithet 'new' to announce this field suggests dissatisfaction with longer-established (that is 'old') theories and concepts. Thus the growth of the 'new regionalism' over the past decade and a half describes not only an alternative manifestation of an apparently familiar phenomenon, but also a new type of analysis. There is, in short, a claimed reciprocal relationship between the recent emergence of regional projects within the global political economy, on the one hand, and the need for new analytical tools, on the other. Of course, the primary casualties of this double move have been the European Union (EU) as a benchmark case of regionalism and the theoretical tools that have been developed over half a century to study European integration. There is much to be said for abandoning the idea of the EU as a 'typical' or 'advanced' case of regional integration and this chapter will make no attempt to present an alternative case. However, what this chapter will argue is that the abandonment of the EU as a static comparator in regional integration studies does not justify neglect of the theoretical legacy of EU studies. Alex Warleigh-Lack's Chapter 2 in this volume makes a compelling case for how studies of regionalism can be reconnected with ongoing dynamic currents in EU studies. The focus here is on what might be thought of as a rather harder body of work to rehabilitate: 'classical' integration theory.

Making the case for revisiting and rethinking classical integration theory is made all the more difficult because such work is increasingly overlooked or discounted within EU studies itself. The argument here is that the lack of continuing attention to theories such as neofunctionalism in both EU studies and comparative regionalism studies leaves contemporary scholars bereft of a rich and enduring theoretical legacy. Moreover, this chapter suggests that the summary discounting of classical theory is premised normally on extremely partial, static and stereotypical readings of the theories in question. It follows that the 'rethinking' referred to in the title of this piece is directed less at the theories themselves and more at the standard ways in which these bodies of work are described and re-described. Therefore, the chapter commences with a brief discussion of what is meant by 'classical' integration theory before moving to an analysis of how and why this body of work has been marginalised with both EU studies and the recent resurgence of work on regionalism. There then follows a case for intellectual recovery based upon rediscovering themes within the original texts that have been forgotten. This requires a re-reading of classical integration theory to show that it has been subjected to stylised readings. The chapter, therefore, mobilises an argument that draws upon themes from the sociology of knowledge and critical disciplinary history. The chapter finally develops a clear statement of the key themes that remain largely latent within classical theory that might usefully inform the present study of comparative regional integration.

Classical integration theory and its critics

For the purposes of this chapter, 'classical integration theory' (hereafter CIT) is taken to refer to the work of a group of (mostly US-based) scholars spanning two decades from the mid-1950s to the mid-1970s. The primary empirical context within which this work arose was the developing project of European institution-building exemplified by first the European Coal and Steel Community (ECSC) after 1951 and the European Economic Community (EEC) after 1957. It is important to recognise from the outset that, while the European Communities provided a vital empirical laboratory, integration theorists aspired to develop general testable propositions that could be applied to all cases of regional integration. The most obvious variant of this integration theory movement came to be called neofunctionalism and was most associated with the work of prominent scholars such as Ernst B. Haas, Leon N. Lindberg, Philippe Schmitter and Joseph Nye. The designation 'neofunctionalism' – a classification endorsed by some of its leading exponents (Haas 2004; Schmitter 2004) – as a separate and discrete school prompts two initial observations.

The first is that for much of CIT's active life, its practitioners saw themselves less as adherents to a particular school and rather more as colleagues in a collective endeavour called 'integration theory' (see Lindberg and Scheingold 1971). Moravscik puts this another way: '[f]rom 1958 to the late 1980s, neofunctionalism was the only game in town' (2005: 357). This is not to be pedantic. It is important because the story of CIT is often re-told, especially within EU studies, as a titanic clash between two 'grand' schools of thought: neofunctionalism and intergovernmentalism. There is some merit in this imagery, not least because the most obvious recent attempt to articulate a cogent and all-embracing intergovernmental theory of European integration (Moravcsik 1998) deliberately presents a version of neofunctionalism as its coherent 'other'. However, the danger – elaborated below – is that the acceptance of a simple opposition between intergovernmental and neofunctionalist theories of integration acts as an inducement to present somewhat stylised, static and simplistic versions of each position. And indeed, while two undeniably powerful state-centred critiques of the integration theorists were presented in the 1960s (Hoffmann 1966; Hansen 1969), it is difficult to regard these as confirming evidence of a coherent intergovernmentalist school to rival the obvious collective endeavours of the self-designated collective of integration theorists.

The second preliminary observation is that the exponents of CIT saw their work as far from isolated. In particular, the legacy of Karl Deutsch's earlier work on security communities (the communications or transactionalist view of integration) was evident (Deutsch *et al.* 1957). Meanwhile, older functionalist theory (most associated with the work of David Mitrany) provided an obvious point of departure for CIT. The rather obvious difference was CIT's interest in the creation of institutions and projects on a *regional* scale, which stood in marked contrast to Mitrany's variegated 'form follows function' principle for the construction of post-national functional agencies (Mitrany's eloquent critique of CIT can be found in Mitrany 1965). An equally important distinguishing feature was CIT's allegiance to standard social scientific norms of theory building, a commitment it shared with the research of Deutsch and his colleagues (De Vree 1972; Kaiser 1965; Rosamond 2005b; Ruggie *et al.* 2005). While Mitrany's functionalism was driven primarily by a *normative* concern to apply de-ideologised, rational and technocratic design to the governance of human welfare needs, CIT was an *analytical* project seeking to explain the dynamics of regional integration through standard processes of theory-building and hypothesis-testing.

CIT sought to develop deductive theory, but it also chose the European experiment of the 1950s and 1960s as an empirical venue to derive grounded propositions. This inductive quality of CIT became the principal complaint against it, particularly from scholars of the 'new regionalism'. The 'new regionalist' case against CIT is easily stated. Perhaps most obviously, CIT is tainted by its association with the 'old regionalism' as an empirical phenomenon, of which European integration (at least as manifested in the 1950s and 1960s) is deemed to be an instance. Moreover the use of the EU (and its post-1951 antecedents) as a paradigm case of regionalism invites the problematic assumption that all cases of regionalism will come to resemble the form taken by the (West) European variant. Using the EU as a benchmark biases the analysis and prevents proper grounded analysis of post-Cold War regional forms. This implies that the 'new' regionalisms that have taken hold since the late 1980s have (1) been occasioned by quite different stimuli to those confronting West European decision-makers three decades earlier and (2) are propelled by quite different dynamics to those which have fashioned the modern EU. To this way of thinking, the EU is better seen as a peculiar path-dependent consequence of a remarkably specific set of imperatives (the Franco-German security dilemma, the emergent Cold War order, particular technocratic and federalist mind sets) that were local to the time and space of the Communities' foundations. The EU is most obviously distinct from 'new' regionalisms in terms of its level of institutionalisation. Its member-states have over time delegated agency to powerful supranational bodies and are now subject to an emphatic corpus of law that is adjudicated above the nation-state via the European Court of Justice. CIT offers – at best – a set of hypotheses that help us to understand how this unparalleled state of affairs came about. And even if CIT did generate meaningful comparative applications, its insights (in so far as there are any) do not travel from the 1960s to the analysis of recent regional forms.

CIT has also been subject to considerable criticism within contemporary EU studies. While most scholarly and pedagogic expositions of the theoretical coordinates of the field place neofunctionalism (and its supposed great debate with intergovernmentalism) at centre-stage, the general impression given is that CIT is a facet of EU studies *past* rather than an ongoing dynamic feature of EU studies *present* (and by implication of EU studies *future*). EU studies' auto-critique of its theoretical past tends to rely upon four propositions. The first identifies a disjuncture between the hypotheses and the predictive inclinations of CIT, on the one hand, and the actuality of the progress of European integration, on the other. For example, one of the earliest (and perennially stickiest) criticisms of neofunctionalism concerned its neglect of both nationalist sentiments and the pervasive influence of self-regarding national actors within the emerging Community system of the 1960s (Hoffmann 1966).

If this initial line of critique took CIT to task for the inaccuracy of its predictions, the second strand of criticism cast doubt on whether integration theory was ever properly a rigorous 'scientific' theory. This argument tends to emerge from discussions of more recent movements and interventions in the field that are designated as attempts to apply the highest standards of social scientific rigour to the study of the European Union (see for example, Caporaso 1999; Moravcsik 1998; Schneider *et al.* 2000). The heavy implication is that the earliest theoretical work on European integration took place at a less advanced moment in the social scientific evolutionary scale.

The third argument from EU studies against CIT suggests that such work was premised on the idea that European integration was a phenomenon to be studied from the disciplinary vantage point of international relations (IR). In contrast, critics of CIT suggest that there is – at best – only limited insight to be obtained by studying the EU in this way. Rather the EU is better understood as a political system or a polity, which should be theorised via the tools of political science and policy analysis (Hix 2005). So the displacement of IR as EU studies' 'parent discipline' brings with it, somewhat axiomatically, the marginalisation of CIT. Interestingly, the disconnect between EU studies and IR means that the newer academic discourses of regionalism that have emerged out of debates within IR in general and international political economy (IPE) in particular have not shown (as least as prominently as they should) on the radar screens of contemporary scholars of the EU.

Finally, criticisms of CIT from within EU studies touch base with those from scholars of new regionalism in terms of the failure to account for patterns of regional integration beyond (Western) Europe. This is both an empirical argument (that the experience of European integration has not been replicated elsewhere) and an analytical one. The analytical side of the argument is particularly important and powerful because it suggests that CIT became unsustainable due to its loss of analytical leverage as the dynamics discovered in the grounded study of Europe failed to reproduce themselves in other regions. Of particular concern here was the concept of 'spillover', which, in neofunctionalist theory, appeared to carry a good deal of the burden of explaining how integration proceeded, expanded to new sectors and became institutionalised or politicised. If, as seemed to be the case, 'spillover' was not a general driving dynamic that would take hold in all regional integration projects, but rather a very peculiar set of processes that operated under the specific local conditions of the early European Communities, then the theoretical credentials of CIT were in serious peril. If CIT's major discovery was a *sui generis* phenomenon, then the best that could be said for CIT was that it was an exercise in thick descriptive social science. In other words, it was a failure in it own terms. The problem – from the point of view of theoretically inclined EU studies – was that CIT left European integration/ EU in a hopeless $n = 1$ situation, where there were no obvious comparators. Analytical leverage would need to be achieved through other means. Armed with this premise, the virtues of standard political science and policy analysis become obvious. By recasting the EU less as a case of 'integration' and more as a polity/policy system, they allow for analytical leverage through the provision of obvious multiple comparators (other polities/policy systems).

Contemporary EU studies

The combined weight of critiques from scholars of both the new regionalism and EU studies have left CIT largely discredited, as an 'other' against which current, more 'advanced' theoretical efforts might be measured and as little more than a 'relic' of past theoretical efforts (though within the EU studies context, see Haas 2001, 2004; Rosamond 2005b, 2005c; Schmitter 2004). Contemporary EU studies now tends to characterise its CIT phase as a failed experiment in 'grand theorising', with a consequent emphasis on the utility of mid-range conceptualisation and theory-building. The only concerted attempt to revisit CIT emerged in the late 1980s and early 1990s following the apparent revitalisation of market integration following the ratification of the Single European Act (1987). Yet the same period was characterised by an increasingly vocal academic realisation that the Communities were characterised by complexity and as such were not amenable to capture by a single theoretical school (Anderson 1995).

How we carve up the field of EU studies for the purpose of classification is, inevitably, the subject of some debate (Rosamond 2007), but Pollack's (2005a, 2005b) threefold classification of (1) a metatheoretic opposition between rationalists and constructivists; (2) a tight community of scholars working from the precepts of mainstream US political science; and (3) a looser grouping of scholars working in both orthodox and heterodox ways with the concept of 'governance' is fair and inclusive. It is important to recognise that these oppositions operate at different levels of theorising. The differentiation between rationalists and constructivists within the field is, at heart, an ontological disagreement that is found more broadly within political science (Hay 2002) and particularly within IR following the challenge to realist and liberal orthodoxies posed by the likes of Wendt (1999). But the migration of this debate into EU studies has not been a matter of straightforward transplantation. There is, for one thing, considerable disagreement among EU studies constructivists (Christiansen, *et al.* 2001), reflecting *inter alia* quite distinct epistemological commitments as well as perhaps a greater propensity to draw upon more obviously 'European' social theory. Pollack's second and third groupings capture much diverse work, but at its heart are disagreements about two things: (1) the analytical status of the object of analysis (that is the EU); and (2) what the appropriate social scientific tools are to undertake its study.

Those scholars who prefer to embed their work within the analytical frame of mainstream US political science ultimately treat the EU as a polity whose rules of action conform to those of any political system. So we are able to explore classical political science questions of the 'who gets what, when, how?' variety, which translate into standard topics such as cleavage formation, interest intermediation, the implication of formal voting rules within institutionalised settings, how 'principals' delegate common tasks to institutional 'agents', and so on. Moreover, it invites the application of models – notably of a rational choice institutionalist variety (Dowding 2000) – that profess (usually aggressively and somewhat triumphantly) a commitment to rigorous theory building and the achievement of 'normal scientific' practices. This work is clearly susceptible to the kind of critique that draws attention to its reliance on standard benchmarks that more often than not rely upon the assumption of an analogy between the EU polity and national (Weberian) states in general and the US political system in particular (Manners 2003).

In many ways the broad and variegated collection of work that falls under the 'governance' banner rejects the axiom that the EU is familiar (for a detailed summary of such work, see Jachtenfuchs 2007). Of course, this does not necessarily imply that the EU is not comparable to national polities, not least because the foundational assumption here is that public authority in one way or another is being re-scaled and recalibrated via processes such as the transfer of authoritative capacity to non-state agencies, the emphasis on regulation at the expense of other traditional state functions and the breakdown of hierarchical 'command and control' modes of government. So while the

EU can be read as part of a broader set of transformative political processes, it is – in all probability – transcendent of established forms of political order. Such a move carries with it (although not necessarily of course) analytical implications. If the EU is something new and unfamiliar to social scientists, then it must follow that social scientists should redouble their efforts to develop new analytical tools to understand this new moment. Such arguments perhaps explain the explosion of self-consciously 'critical' work on the EU that had emerged in recent years, drawing as it does on the likes of Foucauldian social theory, post-structuralism and feminism (Manners 2007).

There is much to discuss in the foregoing. But the point that should concern us here is a relatively simple one. What is lacking (pretty much consistently) from all of this work, in its infinite variety, is the conceptualisation of the EU as a 'region'. There is, in other words, a systematic disengagement from work that seeks to develop the comparative analysis of regional forms. Even if we regard CIT as error-strewn and ultimately a failed project (which this chapter manifestly does not), then it is important to recognise that among its many merits was the understanding of the EU as an institutional manifestation of processes operating at the regional level. The concentration on 'integration' (as well as, it should be noted, the operation of the Communities as a political system) as its object forced its adherents into discussing the construction of a region-level politico-legal form and its relationship to a variety of social and economic processes, emanating from both within and beyond the component units of the region.

New regionalism and comparative analysis

It is worth dwelling a little on some of the characteristic ways in which 'new' regional projects (i.e. those initiated over the past two decades) have been analysed. As Söderbaum (2005) rightly observes, much – perhaps most – of the work has been located within the problem-solving rationalist mainstream of political science, international economics and IPE. He advances three more 'critical' approaches, which perhaps add up to a 'new' turn in studies of regionalism characterised by the common impulse to move away from established theoretical toolkits. As such, it is not only EU studies as a field, but standard rationalist analyses more generally that fall prey to the appetite to capture analytically the 'new' regionalism. It should be said here that one line of argument – labelled the 'new regionalisms/new realist' approach by Söderbaum (ibid.: 236–7) are inherently suspicious of moves toward comparative analysis. The reasoning here follows from attentiveness to the local specificities of distinctive regional projects – an idiographic defence against the generalising ambitions of deductive nomothetic social science. In common with much of the cultural, anthropological and sociological literature on globalisation (for example, Appadurai 1996), such work wishes to emphasise the profound particularities and differences that attend the reorganisation of social space on a trans-territorial scale. By extension, this might induce a paradoxical rehabilitation of CIT 'through the back door' since CIT, as noted above, has been criticised precisely because of its supposedly pathological tendency to produce a thick, non-generalisable *description* of the European case.

Söderbaum's other two categories are consistent with forms of general comparative analysis. The first – the 'world order approach' – is centred on the idea that regions represent, in one way or another, collective state-led responses to the onset of globalisation. Attention is directed to ongoing struggles between manifestations of state and market power. This is consistent with the identification of deep asymmetries within a regionalised world order, but is able to place the analysis of the recent growth of state formations within a common frame of reference. There is also an in-built assumption that recent efforts at region-building are qualitatively different from projects of earlier periods, because they take place within the context of important recent transformations in global capitalism (i.e. globalisation). The assumption that new regionalism is analytically distinct is shared with Söderbaum's third identifiable current, the 'new regionalism approach'. The most obvious defining characteristic of this school is the treatment of regions as constructions rather than as self-evident geographic spaces. This allows: (1) a particular emphasis upon ideational variables as key components of the research agenda; and (2) an understanding of the particularities of different regions. The 'new regionalism approach' claims for itself a more subtle understanding of the state and its capacities. This means that regionalism represents a reaction to global pressures, but it is a reaction that has transformative impacts upon the shape, scope and capacity of publicly-oriented governance.

This summary offers further evidence of a disconnect between the two fields of EU and new regionalism studies. The latter draws attention, in the way EU studies perhaps does not, to the significance of ideational variables in the construction of 'regionness' and to the interaction between regional and global processes. But the field's eagerness to escape Eurocentrism and to carve out a distinctive niche for itself does potentially excuse scholars from a proper engagement with currents in EU studies present and past.

That said, we should not dismiss either new regionalism's critique of EU studies or its own subtle evolution into an insightful field. Therefore, the challenge for any attempt to rehabilitate CIT might be summarised as follows. Three obvious things are required:

1   The provision of demonstrable added value to extant efforts directed at developing a critically-informed comparative analysis of regional formations.
2   The supply of an argument to show why theories designed in the context of 'old' regionalism can travel safely into analyses of the 'new'.
3   Reassurance that CIT need not rely overly upon a nomothetic approach to knowledge production where the preference for general deductive theory: (1) prohibits the historicised analysis of regional particularities; and

(2) allows the norms of social science orthodoxy to muscle in upon the critical spirit of more recent approaches.

The remainder of the chapter attempts to deliver an argument for CIT's intellectual recovery along these lines. It does so in two steps. The first mounts a general challenge to the critiques of CIT found in the new regionalism and EU studies literatures, while the second turns to CIT itself in search of a plausible defence.

The case for intellectual recovery

It is important to be clear again about what this chapter is not advocating. It is not saying that only a rehabilitation of CIT can solve the conundrum of how the study of regionalism can be reunited with the study of the EU. However, it is arguing that CIT has been dismissed too easily by its critics both within EU studies and within the analysis of the new regionalism. Moreover, it is suggesting that a reliance on secondary narratives of CIT tends to yield caricatures that prevent effective conversations taking place between EU studies and discussants of the political economy of regionalism. It is part of the broader process that has cordoned off EU studies from contemporary IR analysis (Warleigh 2006).

It follows that a first crucial step in the act of intellectual recovery involves an interrogation of the way in which CIT is conventionally read. The intention here is quite deliberately to unsettle the mainstream representation of CIT and to cast doubts upon the conventional wisdom about the theoretical legacy of EU studies. Standard accounts of CIT are not only produced through textbooks or formal exegetical statements. Indeed, they appear, reappear and are reinforced through the routine acts of framing that characterise everyday scholarship and contribute to a widely shared understanding of what CIT was about, how it contributed to the past of EU studies and why it failed. At this point it becomes important to recognise the importance of insights from the sociology of knowledge. From here we learn that constructions of a field's past are absolutely critical to the constructions of (1) that field's identity in the present, and (2) its appropriate future trajectory. More often than not, these constructions of the past are ultimately contentious, but are rarely contended. If a particular narrative of a field becomes accepted or embedded, then certain logics are unleashed and it is these logics that drive and shape work in the present (for relevant discussions in the political sciences, see Collini *et al.* 1983; Schmidt 1998; Wæver 2003).

As suggested already, the common assumption driving the trajectories of both EU studies and scholarship on the new regionalism is that of a failed past intellectual project bound up with the experience of CIT. Moreover, this premise drives the new regionalism towards forms of analysis that are inherently suspicious of EU studies as a source of insight and of the EU as a feasible comparator. Meanwhile, EU studies' displacement of its own intellectual past means that it is no longer predisposed to think of its object as an instance of regional integration, preferring instead to study, in both orthodox and heterodox ways, the operation of the supranational polity.

Of course, one rather obvious problem is the very term 'integration' that sits at the heart of EU studies past. The concept of 'integration' is not only suggestive of a process that follows predictable steps towards a defined outcome. It also carries within itself, the connotation of the weakening of the state and its replacement with a new locus of political authority at a regional level. Scholars of region-building elsewhere are struck by the refusal of states to compromise core aspects of their autonomy or sovereignty and the almost systematic tendency to *not* delegate authority to new supranational institutions. The preferred buzzwords are 'cooperation', which implies non-autonomy-threatening forms of collective action, and 'construction', which places the ongoing agency of principal actors (states) at centre-stage. While EU studies has its own variants of such reasoning that connect to mainstream debates in IR and political science in the respective forms of liberal intergovernmentalism (Moravcsik 1998) and principal-agent analysis (Pollack 2003), it is CIT that is most obviously criticised for its adherence to a non-transportable idea of 'integration'.

Within neofunctionlism, the concept of 'spillover' appeared to carry much of the weight in explaining how integration deepens, transfers from one sector to another and becomes politicised – roughly how economic integration yields political integration (for a full discussion, see Rosamond 2000: 59–65). Indeed, the presentation of neofunctionalism (as the paradigm case of CIT) tends to reduce this theory to its claims about 'spillover'. If 'spillover' was Euro-specific – a process discernible in the first decade or so of the Communities' existence but nowhere else – then the undoubted generalising ambitions of neofunctionalism could be said to have failed. The dynamics that allowed integration in one sector to force integration in other sectors would not be a general phenomenon. The accompanying rational processes of loyalty transference from the national polity to the supranational polity among non-state actors would equally not be seen elsewhere.

Yet, contrary to this prevailing and static picture of CIT's understanding of spillover, neofunctionalists were acutely aware of the danger of falling into the inductive trap of assuming that a phenomenon discovered in the European setting should be treated as a generalisable dynamic. For one thing, the neofunctionalists were perfectly well aware of this problem. It was they (rather than their critics) who sought to work it through (Nye 1971). Within three years of the publication of the first edition of *The Uniting of Europe* (Haas 1958), its author was arguing that 'spillover' was most likely to occur in situations where states actively delegated control of an economic sector to institutions whose mission was 'inherently expansive' (Haas 1961). In other words, the burden of explanation was taken away from 'spillover' and given to the circumstances within which acts of institutional creation occurred. The idea that 'spillover' was somehow automatic was also rejected, not least via the strenuous work of Schmitter (1971), who built a complex model of various processes (of which 'spillover' was but one) and which ultimately sought to understand the complicated dynamics that might occur within certain institutional conditions. Moreover, neofunctionalism was recast as much as a theory of *dis*integration as it was theory of integration (Schmitter 2004).

To argue that CIT/neofunctionalism, failed to predict the failure of integration initiatives elsewhere is simply wrong. Haas and Schmitter (1964) showed how some regional organisations are prone to 'spillover', while others are not. Here again, the emphasis was on what neofunctionalists called 'background conditions': the array of potential independent variables (levels of democracy, rates of inter-societal transactions, elite predispositions, the operation of organised interests, and so on) that might aid the assessment of both the initiation of regional projects and the capacity for the building of a regional order once initiated. Moreover, what that regional order should be was open to question. Haas (1971) came to prefer the designation of the dependent variable (what it was that CIT sought to explain) as 'putative', non-teleological and thus not necessarily needing to resemble the peculiar institutional form developed in Western Europe.

This more open-ended, less Euro-centric version of neofunctionalism is rarely seen in standard accounts of CIT. The recovery – via a re-reading of the original texts – reveals an unfinished quest for rigorous comparative enquiry that refused to posit general laws solely out of the European case. When this came to be a danger, the collection of scholars working within CIT adjusted their sites to develop better independent variables and a looser, less Euro-specific dependent variable (Rosamond 2005b). These observations also cast serious doubt on the contemporary impression that CIT lacked social scientific rigour or was somehow rooted in a ghetto of IR conceptual primitivism. Indeed, contemporaneous reviewers of CIT were more than happy to celebrate CIT as a case of 'advanced' social science (Kaiser 1965: De Vree 1972).

At this point it might be worth asking why, given its apparent advantages, did CIT fall out of favour, not least with its most conspicuous proponents? (Haas 1975; 1976). The answer lies, to some degree with the exhaustion of an intellectual project, but as ever it is impossible to detach the fate of a field from the broader social scientific context within which it is located. The quest to develop a broad theory of regional integration fell foul of a growing distaste for 'grand theorising' and the emerging preference for 'mid-range' explanations. Meanwhile, emerging debates in IR and the newly (re)constituted IPE were yielding persuasive ideas about 'transnationalism' and 'interdependence' (Keohane and Nye 1971; 1977), within which a good deal of thinking about regional processes was subsumed.

Bringing classical integration theory back in

The previous section briefly attempted to disrupt some of the prevailing conventional wisdom about CIT. It questioned the assumption of CIT as a failed intellectual enterprise by recommending a re-reading of neofunctionalism as a strong, dynamic theoretical apparatus that kept open the possibility of the rigorous comparative analysis of regional forms without privileging the particular European variant. This is what can be termed a 'negative' rationale for intellectual recovery – the claim that CIT has been unfairly treated and thus misconstrued, which in turn justifies the re-opening of books and journals that have lain unread for too long.

But what of the 'positive' rationale? What can a re-read CIT contribute to the ongoing quest for the development of a critically informed comparative analysis of regional forms? Again it needs to be said that CIT does not possess all the answers and that bringing CIT back in is not intended to displace the huge volume of productive work both within EU studies and the new regionalism literature.

As Söderbaum (2005) reminds us, one of the key characteristic of the new regionalism is an emphasis on 'regionness'; on regions as constructed and imagined spaces. This is suggestive of the usefulness of constructivism as a fruitful approach to the study of regional forms and of work that emphasises the social processes that sit at the heart of regional construction. At first sight, there appears to be a disconnect between the 'soft rationalism' of CIT's neofunctionalist variant (Haas 2004) and the constructivist's emphasis upon the endogeneity of interests and identities. Yet, the role of knowledge, values, actor expectations (and their evolution) and cognitions was elemental to neofunctionalism from its formative stages, as were the sociological dimensions of institutional interaction. Nye (1971) developed the neofunctionalists' concern with background conditions to the point where he included perceptual factors as a candidate independent variable. This implies that regionalism requires a set of subjective conditions to take hold before such projects emerge. The adage that contemporary regionalism represents a collective states-led response to globalisation is fair enough, but it leaves open many questions. Not least among these is how and why the external environment comes to be imagined in ways that create logics of appropriateness that suggest regional building as a correct technical response and logics of appropriateness that place value upon the region as a valid and desirable collective project.

Beyond the initiation phase, the practitioners of CIT were interested in the ways in which regional orders created complex policy environments riven with uncertainty. In a particularly rich essay, Haas (1976) showed that an act of integration did not automatically beget more integration, but rather a policy environment in which further integrative solutions might arise among actors operating without a clearly objective appreciation of their interests. Unlike much of the hard rationalism currently at work within EU studies, neofunctionalism preceded so that actors' interests did not self-evidently follow from their material circumstances: 'values shape interests, and values include many nonmaterial elements' (Haas 2004: xv). As such there is considerable scope for scholars with an interest in comparative regionalism to follow up and develop the reflections contained in the final essay on integration theory by Haas (2004).

It is not simply that CIT can touch base with constructivism in productive ways. The positive case for bringing CIT back in is also bound up with how its story exemplifies a productive approach to theory building from which much can be learned in the contemporary period. The practitioners of CIT were, at one level, engaged in a tight collective endeavour that – in its neofunctionalist manifestation – extended from the late 1950s to the mid-1970s. But they did not operate as a monkish sect cut off from the ebb and flow of social and political science, seeking to normalise their pursuit. This produced a profoundly productive spirit of intellectual honesty and a powerful culture of auto-critique, which not only generated self-criticism, but sought to find creative, yet rigorous, ways to overcome problems that inhered within their theoretical apparatus. An open-minded, critical approach to comparative regionalism will seek to dissolve the divisions between past and present and between EU studies and the new regionalism. One step is to re-engage the (accurate) legacy of CIT.

Conclusion

This chapter identified three conditions which would need to be fulfilled in order to justify the re-inspection of CIT as a potential contributor to the comparative study of contemporary regional forms. The concluding section of this chapter is organised around a discussion of each in turn.

The first condition is that CIT should be able to offer some sort of added value to the construction of a critically informed analysis of regional forms. The substantive contribution is that CIT in general, and neofunctionalism in particular, are to offer a ready-made (though, of course, not necessarily perfect) theory of the variables that influence both the initiation and evolution of regional orders allied to an understanding of how the construction of a regional organisation/regional collaboration can induce polity-like effects. Less substantive, but equally important, is the positive demonstration effect of an open, self-critical project – connected to (and certainly not isolated from) emerging currents in social science.

The second condition asked for an argument to show why theories designed in the context of 'old' regionalism can travel safely into analyses of the 'new'. The issue here is the constitutive effect of the differentiation between 'new' and 'old', which helps to construct CIT as rooted in an empirical irrelevance and based upon analytical primitivism. The way we carve up the world into empirical sequences needs constant scrutiny, not least because it invites the marginalisation of all that is analytically resident in the old.

The final condition is in part about a reassurance that CIT was not simply a thick localised description dressed up as general theory. A clear reading of the evolution of CIT shows, at the very least, that CIT scholars strove hard to avoid this problem by careful refinement of their dependent and independent variables. It also asks that theories need to avoid the presumption that a specific localised object (in this case the EU and its antecedents) does not act as a benchmark against which comparators are measured. It may be the case that the neofunctionalists' inductive discovery of spillover led them to think about the specific conditions within which expansive sector-to-sector integration might emerge, but this ultimately pushed them away from a quest for localised independent variables and towards a more sensitive understanding of the dependent variable.

Together these add up to a persuasive argument for bringing CIT back onto the agenda. It may be that we end up inspecting CIT and concluding that we can do without its insights. But at least this would amount to disposing of a body of work for the right reasons. At present, both EU studies and studies of comparative regionalism are too hasty in the dismissal of their common intellectual ancestor.

References

Anderson, Jeffrey J. (1995) 'The State of the (European) Union: From the Singular Event to General Theories', *World Politics*, 47(3): 441–65.

Appadurai, Arjun (1996) *Modernity at Large: Cultural Dimensions of Globalization*, Minneapolis: University of Minnesota Press.

Caporaso, James A. (1999) 'Toward a Normal Science of Regional Integration', *Journal of European Public Policy*, 6(1): 160–4.

Christiansen, Thomas, Jørgensen, Knud Erik and Wiener, Antje (2001) 'Introduction', in T. Christiansen, K.E. Jørgensen, and A. Wiener (eds) *The Social Construction of Europe*, London: Sage, pp. 1–19.

Collini, Stefan, Winch, Donald and Burrow, J.W. (1983) *That Noble Science of Politics: A Study in Nineteenth Century Intellectual History*, Cambridge: Cambridge University Press.

Deutsch, Karl W. *et al.* (1957) *Political Community in the North Atlantic Area: International Organization in the Light of Historical Experience*, Princeton, NJ: Princeton University Press.

De Vree, Johan K. (1972) *Political Integration: The Formation of Theory and its Problems*, The Hague: Mouton.

Dowding, Keith (2000) 'Institutional Research on the European Union: A Critical Review', *European Union Politics*, 1(1): 125–44.

Haas, Ernst B. (1958) *The Uniting of Europe: Political, Social and Economic Forces, 1950–1957*, Stanford, CA: Stanford University Press.

—— (1961) 'International Integration: The European and the Universal Process', *International Organization*, 15: 366–92.

—— (1971) 'The Study of Regional Integration: Reflections on the Joy and Anguish of Pretheorizing', in L.N. Lindberg and S.A. Scheingold (eds) *Regional Integration: Theory and Research*, Cambridge, MA: Harvard University Press, pp. 3–42.

—— (1975) *The Obsolescence of Regional Integration Theory*, working paper, Berkeley, CA: Institute of International Studies.

—— (1976) 'Turbulent Fields and the Study of Regional Integration, *International Organization*, 30(2): 173–212.

—— (2001) 'Does Constructivism Subsume Neofunctionalism?', in T. Christiansen, K.E. Jørgensen, and A. Wiener (eds) *The Social Construction of Europe*, London: Sage, pp. 22–31.

—— (2004) 'Introduction: Institutionalism or Constructivism?', in E.B. Haas, *The Uniting of Europe: Political, Social and Economic Forces, 1950–1957*, 3rd edn, Notre Dame, IN: University of Notre Dame Press.

—— and Schmitter, Philippe C. (1964) 'Economics and Differential Patterns of Integration: Projections about Unity in Latin America', *International Organization*, 18(4): 705–37.

Hansen, Roger D. (1969) 'European Integration: Reflections on a Decade of Theoretical Efforts', *World Politics*, 21(2): 242–71.

Hay, Colin (2002) *Political Analysis: A Critical Introduction*, Basingstoke: Palgrave.

Hix, Simon (2005) *The Political System of the European Union*, 2nd edn, Basingstoke and New York: Palgrave Macmillan.

Hoffmann, Stanley (1966) 'Obstinate or Obsolete? The Fate of the Nation-State and the Case of Western Europe', *Daedalus*, 95(3): 862–915.

Jachtenfuchs, Markus (2007) 'The EU as a Polity (2)', in Knud Erik Jørgensen, Mark A. Pollack, and Ben Rosamond (eds) *Handbook of European Union Politics*, London: Sage.

Kaiser, Karl (1965) 'L'Europe des Savants: European Integration and the Social Sciences', *Journal of Common Market Studies*, 4(1): 36–47.

Keohane, Robert O. and Nye, Joseph S. (1971) 'Transnational Relations and World Politics', *International Organization*, 25(3): 161–3.

—— (1977) *Power and Interdependence: World Politics in Transition*, Boston, MA: Little, Brown and Co.

Lindberg, Leon N. and Scheingold, Stuart A. (eds) (1971) *Regional Integration: Theory and Research*, Cambridge, MA: Harvard University Press.

Manners, Ian (2003) 'European Studies', *Journal of Contemporary European Studies*, 11(1): 67–83.

—— (2007) 'Another Europe is Possible: Critical Approaches to European Union Politics', in Knud Erik Jørgensen, Mark A. Pollack, and Ben Rosamond (eds) *Handbook of European Union Politics*, London: Sage.

Mitrany, David (1965) 'The Prospect of Integration: Federal or Functional?', *Journal of Common Market Studies*, 4(1): 119–49.

Moravcsik, Andrew (1998) *The Choice for Europe: Social Purpose and State Power from Messina to Maastricht*, Ithaca, NY: Cornell University Press.

—— (2005) 'The European Constitutional Compromise and the Neofunctionalist Legacy', *Journal of European Public Policy*, 12(2): 349–86.

Nye, Joseph S. (1971) 'Comparing Common Markets: A Revised Neofunctionalist Model', in Leon N. Lindberg and Stuart A. Scheingold (eds) *Regional Integration: Theory and Research*, Cambridge, MA: Harvard University Press.

Pollack, Mark A. (2003) *The Engines of European Integration: Delegation, Agency and Agenda-Setting in the EU*, Oxford: Oxford University Press.

—— (2005a) 'Theorizing EU Policy-Making', in Helen Wallace, William Wallace, and

Mark A. Pollack (eds) *Policy-Making in the European Union*, 5th edn, Oxford: Oxford University Press, pp. 13–48.

—— (2005b) 'Theorizing the European Union: International Organization, Domestic Polity or Experiment in New Governance?', *Annual Review of Political Science*, 8: 357–98.

Rosamond, Ben (2000) *Theories of European Integration*, Basingstoke and New York: Macmillan and St. Martin's Press.

—— (2005a) 'Globalization, the Ambivalence of European Integration and the Possibilities for Post-disciplinary EU Studies', *Innovation*, 18(1): 23–43.

—— (2005b) 'The Uniting of Europe and the Foundation of EU Studies: Revisiting the Neofunctionalism of Ernst B. Haas', *Journal of European Public Policy*, 12(2): 237–54.

—— (2005c) 'Conceptualizing the EU Model of Governance in World Politics', *European Foreign Affairs Review*, 10(4): 463–78.

—— (2007) 'The Political Sciences of European Integration: Disciplinary History and EU Studies', in Knud Erik Jørgensen, Mark A. Pollack, and Ben Rosamond (eds) *Handbook of European Union Politics*, London: Sage.

Ruggie, John J., Katzenstein, Peter J., Keohane, Robert O. and Schmitter Philippe C. (2005) 'Transformations in World Politics: The Intellectual Contributions of Ernst B. Haas', *Annual Review of Political Science*, 8: 271–96.

Schmidt, Brian C. (1998) *The Political Discourse of Anarchy: A Disciplinary History of International Relations*, Albany, NY: SUNY Press.

Schmitter, Philippe C. (1971) 'A Revised Theory of European Regional Integration', in Leon N. Lindberg and Stuart A. Scheingold (eds) *Regional Integration: Theory and Research*, Cambridge, MA: Harvard University Press.

—— (2004) 'Neo-neo-functionalism?', in Antje Wiener and Thomas Diez (eds) *European Integration Theory*, Oxford: Oxford University Press, pp. 45–74.

Schneider, Gerald, Gabel, Matthew and Hix, Simon (2000) '*European Union Politics* Editorial Statement', *European Union Politics*, 1(1): 5–8.

Söderbaum, Fredrik (2005) 'The International Political Economy of Regionalism', in Nicola Phillips (ed.) *Globalizing International Political Economy*, Basingstoke: Palgrave.

Wæver, Ole (2003) 'The Structure of the IR Discipline: A Proto-Comparative Analysis', presentation to the Annual Convention of the International Studies Association, Portland, OR, 25 February–1 March.

Warleigh, Alex (2006) 'Learning from Europe? EU Studies and the Rethinking of International Relations', *European Journal of International Relations*, 12(1): 31–51.

Wendt, Alexander (1999) *Social Theory of International Politics*, Cambridge: Cambridge University Press.

Part II

Economic dimensions

Regionalisation and the need for rule-making

5   Regional multinationals and the myth of globalisation

Alan M. Rugman

Introduction

A dialogue on globalisation needs to be framed by informed commentary based on empirical evidence. In a wide variety of previous publications, I have presented data showing that the vast majority of world economic activity is organised within the triad regions and not globally. Yet many authors still fail to address this empirical evidence on the lack of globalisation. I suggest that my fellow scholars need to confront the lack of evidence on globalisation. More recently I have shown that the vast majority of the world's 500 largest multinational enterprises operate intra-regionally. They average 75 per cent of their sales in their home region and 85 per cent of their foreign assets are also in their home region of the triad. In this chapter I explore some unresolved aspects of the economic, social and business implications of the regional nature of the world's multinationals. From a business school viewpoint, my main concern is to debunk the notion of global strategy and present a case for corporate level regional strategy. This implies that public policy should also reflect the observed empirical reality of regional business activity.

Definitions and data on regional multinationals

One of the puzzles of international business research is that the key actor, the multinational enterprise (MNE), appears to have a very unevenly distributed geographic dispersion of sales. The MNE is usually a regionalised rather than a globalised business. Three definitions matter:

1   *multinational enterprise*: a firm with operations across national borders;
2   *global business*: a firm with major operations (at least 20 per cent of its total sales) in each of the three regions of the 'broad triad' of the European Union (EU), North America, and Asia-Pacific;
3   *regional business*: a firm with the majority of its sales inside one of the triad regions, usually its home region.

Given these definitions, the following empirical observations can be made based on Rugman (2005):

1   The world's 500 largest MNEs account for over 90 per cent of the world's stock of foreign direct investment (FDI) and over half of world trade, the latter usually in the form of intra-firm sales.
2   Of these 500 MNEs, only nine are 'global' in the sense of having a substantial presence (at least 20 per cent of sales) in each region of the triad.
3   The vast majority of the 500 MNEs (320 of the 380 for which data are available) have an average of 80 per cent of their sales in their home region of the broad triad. The overall intra-regional sales figure for all 380 firms is 71.9 per cent. See Table 5.1.

These stylised facts suggest a new research agenda for the international business field, as requested by Buckley (2002). In Rugman (2005), I explored some aspects of this in terms of the regional solution. A somewhat similar point about the possible myth of globalisation has been raised by Hirst and Thompson (1999). However, they do not develop the business-level focus of this chapter. The observed empirical regionalisation can be given a simple transaction cost economics (TCE) explanation. Host regions require substantial 'linking' or 'melding' investments (a form of asset specificity), in order to integrate the MNE's existing firm-specific advantages (FSAs) and exogenous country-specific advantages (CSAs), whereas such investments, driven by cultural, administrative, geographic and economic distance, are much lower in the home region. This perspective on international business leads to a new 'big question' for the field: why are we still teaching global business when much of it is actually regional?

Table 5.1 Classification of the top 500 firms

Type of MNE	No. of MNEs	Per cent of 500	Per cent of 380	Per cent intra-regional sales
Global	9	1.8	2.4	38.3
Bi-regional	25	5.0	6.6	42.0
Host-Region Oriented	11	2.2	2.9	30.9
Home-Region Oriented (1)	320	64.0	84.2	80.3
Insufficient Data	15	3.0	3.9	40.9
No Data	120	24.0		NA
Total	**500**	**100.0**	**100.0**	71.9

Note: Data is for 2001, from the 'Fortune Global 500', *Fortune*, 2002.

Source: Rugman (2005).

Data on the regional multinationals

As a challenge to our thinking provided by the lack of evidence on globalisation, let us revisit the key data presented (Rugman 2005). This book was the first to report data on intra-regional sales of the 500 largest firms in the world. The data bank was constructed over the 2002–3 period based on basic listings in the *Fortune* of August 2002, which reports the published data from the annual reports of the top 500 firms for the year 2001. When the 2001 data were updated for 60 firms for 2002, the latest year available at the time of writing, the addition of 2002 data only caused reclassification of two firms: Nokia ceased being global; and GlaxoSmithKline became a host-region bi-regional.

As another final check on the reliability of the 2001 data, let us consider the main group of 320 home-regional firms identified in Rugman (2005). In Table 5.2, we report the 2002 sales data for a set of 32 home-region-based firms. (This is every tenth firm in the list of the world's top 500 for which data are available on geographic sales, from Rugman [2005]). All the firms remain in the home-region classification based on 2001 data. The average intra-regional sales for the 32 firms actually increased slightly from 82.4 per cent to 84.6 per cent.

Table 5.3 shows that the average intra-regional sales of this sample of 32 firms with 2001 data are 82.4 per cent. The intra-regional sales increased, to 84.6 per cent, for 2002 data. Far from a trend towards globalisation, these home-region firms are becoming even more regional. Of the 32 firms in the sample, 6 have 100 per cent of their sales in the home region. Twelve of the 32 experienced an increase in intra-regional sales between 2001 and 2002, whereas 11 experienced a decrease. However, the large increases in intra-regional sales of ConocoPhillips at 26.4 per cent; Saint-Gobain at 10.4 per cent; Dynergy at 8.8 per cent; and Volvo at 8 per cent offset the much smaller decreases in intra-regional sales, with only Bank of Nova Scotia at 5.8 per cent; Pemex at 5.7 per cent; Eli Lilly at 4.8 per cent; and Honeywell at 4 per cent; showing significant increases in intra-regional sales.

It can be concluded that the 2001 sales data provide reliable classifications of firms and that using data for a later year in Table 5.2 provides no changes. Indeed, Table 5.3 shows that firms became more intra-regional over the 2002 period than in 2001. Similarly, sales data for earlier periods are highly unlikely to provide much new information or cause us to reclassify more than a handful of the 380 firms of the top 500 for which a classification was possible.

Yet some colleagues still seem to question these data. They say there must be a trend towards globalisation over time. In actuality, the aggregate data strongly suggest the opposite. Over the past 25 years there has been a trend towards increased intra-regional trade and investment (Rugman 2000). Naturally, these aggregate data trends are likely to be mirrored in the firm-level data. At the very least the latest data on sales present an up-to-date snapshot

Table 5.2 Geographic sales of the world's largest home-region oriented firms

2002 Fortune Rank	Company	Revenues in billion $US	F/T Sales	N. America per cent of total	Europe per cent of total	Asia per cent of total
1	Wal-Mart Stores[a]	246.5	16.7	94.5	4.6	0.5
21	Siemens	77.2	77.0	25.0[b]	57.0	12.0
26	Hitachi	67.2	32.0	11.0	7.0	80.0
46	Fiat	52.6	64.0	13.0	74.0	na
50	Merck	51.8	16.0	84.0	na	na
na	Dynegy	5.6	13.5	99.5[c]	0.5	na
95	Pemex[a]	38.0	34.3	86.0	2.1	na
121	Kmart	30.8	–	100.0[d]	–	–
36	ConocoPhillips	56.7	17.8	84.0[c]	na	na
120	United Parcel Service	31.3	16.0	84.0[d]	na	na
133	Saint-Gobain	28.6	68.8	22.4	74.3	na
138	Enel	28.3	5.1	1.7	98.3	na
153	Lockheed Martin	26.8	14.0	86.0[d]	na	na
197	Honeywell Intl.	22.3	30.3	69.7[d]	18.8	na
176	America Express	23.8	21.3	78.7[d]	7.9	6.9
233	Royal & Sun Alliance	19.7	58.3	26.5[b]	63.1[e]	10.4
188	Best Buy	22.7	7.2	100.0	na	na
243	Volvo	19.2	na	24.1	59.6	9.0
246	Washington Mutual	19.0	–	100.0[d]	–	–
320	U.S. Bancorp	15.4	–	100.0	–	–
67	AmericansourceBergen	45.2	–	100.0	–	–
150	Valero Energy	27.0	–	100.0[b]	–	–
376	May Dept. Stores	13.5	–	100.0	–	–
432	Bank of Nova Scotia[a]	11.6	43.7	65.4	na	na
436	Accenture[a]	11.6	na	50.4[b]	42.9[e]	6.7
369	Anheuser-Busch	13.6	6.9	93.1[d]	na	na
272	WellPoint Health Netwks.	17.3	–	100.0	–	–
429	British Airways	11.9	52.7	19.3[b]	63.8	7.4
456	Eli Lilly	11.1	41.0	59.0	19.5	na
366	Old Mutual[a]	13.7	na	na	na	na
323	Sun Life Financial	15.3	72.0	80.0[c]	8.0	3.0
479	Manulife Financial[a]	10.5	67.2	73.9	na	21.4

Notes: (a) *Wal-Mart*: Estimated using number of stores. *Pemex*: Estimated using 1999 date (latest available) North America refers to Mexico and the US; *Bank of Nova Scotia*: Revenues are estimated using income figures as reported in the Annual Report; *Accenture*: Includes information on India in its EMEA geographic segment; *Old Mutual*: *Fortune* Magazine reports Old Mutual as a British company because it is headquartered there. However, the company is South African. Data for 2002 is not available; *Manulife Financial*: The data are estimated using sales by division (US, Canada and Asia) as reported in the Annual Report.

(b) includes Latin America;
(c) Canada and the United States;
(d) United States only;
(e) Europe, Middle East and Africa.

Source: Rugman (2005).

Table 5.3 Intra-regional sales of the world's largest home-region firms

Company	Region	Intra-regional Sales (%)		Change
		2001	*2002*	
Wal-Mart Stores	North America	94.1	94.5	0.4
Siemens	Europe	52.0	57.0	5.0
Hitachi	Asia-Pacific	80.0	80.0	–
Fiat	Europe	73.3	74.0	0.7
Merck	North America	83.6	84.0	0.3
Dynegy	North America	90.7	99.5	8.8
Pemex	North America	91.7	86.0	(5.7)
Kmart	North America	100.0	100.0	–
ConocoPhillips	North America	57.6	84.0	26.4
United Parcel Service	North America	86.3	84.0	(2.3)
Saint-Gobain	Europe	63.9	74.3	10.4
Enel	Europe	98.6	98.3	(0.3)
Lockheed Martin	North America	83.0	86.0	3.0
Honeywell Intl.	North America	73.7	69.7	(4.0)
America Express	North America	75.3	78.7	3.4
Royal & Sun Alliance	Europe	64.8	63.1	(1.7)
Best Buy	North America	100.0	100.0	–
Volvo	Europe	51.6	59.6	8.0
Washington Mutual	North America	100.0	100.0	–
U.S. Bancorp	North America	100.0	100.0	–
AmericansourceBergen	North America	100.0	100.0	–
Valero Energy	North America	100.0	100.0	–
May Dept. Stores	North America	100.0	100.0	–
Bank of Nova Scotia	North America	71.2	65.4	(5.8)
Accenture	North America	54.8	50.4	(4.4)
Anheuser-Busch	North America	94.7	93.1	(1.6)
WellPoint Health Netwks.	North America	100.0	100.0	–
British Airways	Europe	64.8	63.8	(1.0)
Eli Lilly	North America	63.8	59.0	(4.8)
Old Mutual	Europe	93.4	na	na
Sun Life Financial	North America	83.5	80.0	(3.5)
Manulife Financial	North America	71.1	73.9	2.8
	Average	**82.4**	**84.6**	**2.2**

Source: Author's calculations.

of the lack of globalisation and the dominance of regional firm-level economic activity. It is now up to other scholars to advance on this research and to extend the debate on global versus regional strategy.

Some comments on the globalisation literature

There will be little progress in the debate on globalisation unless we can agree on some basic definitions, as above, and then apply them. Here are five examples of unresolved issues:

1   My definition of globalisation appears in Rugman (2000: 5–6), as 'the worldwide production and marketing of goods and services by multi-national enterprises'. In turn, I explain that the 'economic' data actually reveal that MNEs operate regionally, so a global MNE is defined as having a significant market presence in each of the three regions of the world. In Rugman and Verbeke (2004), we define significant as 20 per cent or more. For purposes of strategic management, anything less than 20 per cent is highly unlikely to be strategic.

2   In Rugman (2000), Chapter 7, it is shown that regional economic activity is increasing over time and that economic globalisation is decreasing over time. A high percentage of foreign-to-total operations is not robust evidence of globalisation; only significant foreign operations in all three regions can be considered as generating a global firm. Wal-Mart is a home-region firm with 94 per cent of its sales in North America; its strategy is better explained by regional agreements, such as NAFTA, than by any globalisation logic. The vast majority of the world's 500 largest MNEs are like Wal-Mart, i.e. home-region firms. Absolute values are not as relevant as percentages in the formulation and operation of strategy; as most MNEs operate regionally, they do not need a global strategy.

3   Rugman (2000) also has data in Chapter 8 demonstrating that the 500 largest multinational enterprises dominate world trade (over 50 per cent) and FDI (over 90 per cent). Yet these 500 firms cannot be defined as global; most are regional. This point has been elaborated with theoretical and empirical rigor by Rugman and Verbeke (2004) and offers the same finding as Ghemawat (2003) does in his work on semi-globalisation. Authors who support globalisation are swimming against the tide of recent empirical research and they are guilty of thinking that confuses internationalisation with globalisation. It should now be clear that we need to be much more careful in the definition and analysis of global and regional strategy.

4   These large MNEs are the key instruments for economic integration, usually at the hubs of clusters acting as, what we call 'flagship firms' (Rugman and D'Cruz 2000). Recent trends in mergers and acquisitions lead to the further growth of the large 500 firms, e.g. in pharmaceuticals, banking, retail, etc. There is an ever increasing concentration of world economic power in the world's very largest firms. They serve as systems integrators and many other firms are linked to them in networks of alliances and partnerships. This type of flagship firm network development is reinforcing the regional nature of international business and is not best described as globalisation.

5   As indicated in Rugman (2005), the data that I have assembled came from the annual reports of the 500 firms. In an appendix to Rugman (2005), I list the regional sales of the 380 firms for which data are available. I analyse the strategies of some 50–60 of these in some detail.

However, I do believe that any serious scholar needs to take ownership of his/her data, so scholars are advised to go and read some annual reports and construct their own data bank. If they find any global firms that I have not identified (only 9 out of the largest 500), then please let me know. But until scholars undertake actual research, there cannot be an informed debate.

The social implications of regionalisation

The implications of MNE activity for social welfare and public policy have been the subject of a particularly large and varied literature in economics and political science (Rugman and Verbeke 1998). The topic of the integration impacts resulting from regional trade and investment agreements has been studied extensively, especially in the context of North American and European integration processes (for an extensive review, see Pomfret 2001). Much of the relevant literature has focused on two issues. First, the problem of trade creation versus trade diversion, whereby insiders and outsiders may be affected differently by a regional integration program. Second, the relative merits of regionalisation *vis-à-vis* efforts toward multilateralism, such as through the General Agreement on Tariffs and Trade (GATT) and the World Trade Organization (WTO).

Here, four contradictory perspectives have been formulated (Poon 1997). The first is an emphasis on the economic inferiority of regional *vis-à-vis* multilateral integration outcomes (Bhagwati 2002). The second is the view that regionalism is an efficient substitute for ill-functioning multilateral institutions in terms of economic outcomes (Rugman 2005). The third is a focus on the comparative ease of conducting a regional integration process (with only a limited number of participants that are geographically close) *vis-à-vis* a multilateral integration process that could involve all the 144 countries in the WTO. And the fourth is a focus on the organic nature of economic integration in regional clusters (Krugman 1993). Here, regional integration is not driven primarily by the strategic intent of government agencies and powerful economic actors to increase or consolidate economic exchange within a region through new institutions in a top-down fashion. Rather, it reflects efforts by multiple sets of economic actors who wish to expand their geographical business horizon, guided by immediate opportunities that are geographically close and associated with low transaction costs, as well as a high potential for agglomeration economies. In the long run, such agglomeration, in the sense of improved 'regional diamond conditions', may improve the MNEs' capabilities to penetrate other triad markets (Rugman and Verbeke 2003).

None of these four perspectives has paid much attention to the MNE as the appropriate unit of analysis, with some exceptions that include Rugman and Verbeke (1990), and Rugman (2005). This is a fruitful avenue for future research, for five reasons.

First, the role of individual MNEs in the institutional processes of regional integration could be investigated in more depth, without starting from the ideological assumption that all MNEs pursue a narrow and homogenous business agenda. Each firm's regional integration preferences and role will depend upon its FSA configuration, much in line with its preferences regarding trade and investment protection at the national level (Milner 1988). These preferences may even vary from business to business in a single firm. The main question for the MNE is to assess how regional integration may reduce the need for location-specific adaptation investments in the various national markets, when expanding the geographic scope of activities.

Second, rather than merely analysing macro-economic or sectoral data, it is useful to analyse the FSAs and the firm-level adaptation processes to regional integration. This needs a focus on the region-specific adaptation investments needed to link the MNEs' existing FSAs (non-location-bound and location-bound ones) with the regional-location advantages, and on the nature of these investments (internal development versus external acquisition) (Rugman and Verbeke 1990). An analysis of such new knowledge development in MNEs may be critical to fully understand the societal effects of increased regionalisation.

Third, the impacts of regional trading agreements have often been interpreted in terms of changes in entry barriers facing insiders and outsiders at the macro, industry, and strategic-group levels. From a resource-based perspective, however, there is a real need to understand how regional integration processes affect the creation or elimination of isolating mechanisms, and thereby economic performance, at the level of individual MNEs and subunits within MNEs.

Fourth, regional integration also has implications for knowledge exchange, as it is likely to increase the geographic reach of MNEs' networks in terms of backward and forward linkages, and even the MNEs broader flagship networks (Rugman and D'Cruz 2000). To the extent that such linkages and networks are associated with knowledge diffusion spillovers, these should also be taken into account in any analysis of the regional integration welfare effects.

Finally, regional integration can have an impact on the MNEs' internal distribution of resources and FSAs; more specifically, firm-level investments in regional adaptation often imply the relocation of specific production facilities to the most efficient subunits, in order to capture regional scale economies and a re-assessment of subsidiary charters. This implies to some extent a zero sum game with 'winning' and 'losing' subsidiaries.

Interestingly, it has also been observed that regional integration may energise subsidiaries to start new initiatives and to develop new capabilities, which really implies a non-zero sum game (Birkinshaw 2000), again with macro-level welfare improvements as an outcome. Will the deepening of a regional trading block, even if it has positive net welfare effects inside the region and at the world level, strengthen the affected insider MNEs in other legs of the triad? Or will it, on the contrary, act as an incentive to focus these MNEs' resource allocation processes and market expansion plans even more on intra-regional growth opportunities? The empirical data in Rugman (2005) indicate that regional integration during the past decade has had little effect on the abilities of MNEs to increase their globalisation capabilities.

Regional strategies of multinational enterprises

An asymmetry may exist between the MNEs' downstream and upstream firm-specific advantages. We have presented data above on sales, representing the downstream end of the firms. We need also to consider the possibility that the upstream end of production could be globalised, i.e. is there a global supply chain? We shall consider the organisational structure of an MNE, whereby many tasks within R&D, sourcing, manufacturing, and logistics operations are structurally divorced from customer-related subunits. This explains why many MNEs have been able to develop internally efficient global operations, with a possible wide geographic dispersion across units of the upstream activities (and FSAs) involved, but have simultaneously been incapable of capitalising on such strengths at the downstream end, in terms of sales achieved.

Figure 5.1 constitutes a re-conceptualisation of Bartlett and Ghoshal's (1989) framework on the organisational structures of the MNE. We amend this to take account of the empirical and analytical insights on the pervasive nature of 'regional' activities of MNEs.

Figure 5.1 makes a distinction among the various generic roles of strategic business units within the company. The horizontal axis measures the strength of the FSAs, embedded in each strategic business unit, which may consist of either a single national affiliate, or a set of affiliates, possibly located in various nations and bundled into a geographic or product division. MNEs

Geographic Scope of FSAs

	1 triad region	2 triad region	3 triad region
Downstream FSAs	1	3	5
Upstream FSAs	2	4	6

Figure 5.1 Upstream and downstream firm-specific advantages.

evaluate business operations at various levels; here, the relevant level is the one at which performance is assessed as the basis of company-wide capital budget allocation. The strategic business unit's FSAs may be deployable at the national level, in the home region, in two triad regions, or in all triad regions, as reflected by business performance. Figure 5.1 also makes a distinction, on the vertical axis, between downstream or customer-end, and upstream FSAs. Strong upstream FSAs are required to create an efficient internal production system within the nation, one region, or inter-regionally. Strong downstream FSAs are necessary to achieve market success in the market considered, again at the national, regional, or inter-regional levels. Conceptually, individual strategic business units may have both upstream and downstream FSAs, which would make them span two vertical cells in Figure 5.1.

When using Figure 5.1, we can identify the business units in MNEs that perform the role of global market leaders in the firm, as measured, not by their location inside a large national market *per se*, but by their ability to achieve a satisfactory market penetration in each of the three broad regions of the triad. This is a reflection of strong downstream FSAs. The reality for most MNEs is that they may lack even a single global market leader. In contrast, some MNEs have global production units, with upstream activities spread across continents, especially to take advantage of market imperfections in markets for raw materials, labour, components and other intermediate goods, and even to source final goods, but without an equivalent geographic distribution of sales. In addition, most of the large firms have units with the status of national or intra-regional market leaders but usually confined to the home region. Where inter-regional market success is achieved, namely by a strong position in at least a second triad market, this often occurs through a distinct strategic business unit. The strong market position in the second leg of the triad then usually reflects cooperative behaviour, such as joint venture activity, mergers and acquisitions, etc.

In a recent paper, Rugman and Collinson (2006) applied this framework to analyse the operations of the 64 Japanese MNEs in the world's 500 largest firms. Based on published information in annual reports we find that for 2003, the average intra-regional sales of these 64 firms is 81.1 per cent, whereas their average intra-regional foreign assets is 83 per cent.

In terms of Figure 5.1, 58 of the 64 Japanese MNEs are home-region firms in cell 1; three are in cell 3 (these bi-regionals are Toyota, Nissan and Bridgestone); while there are three global firms in cell 5 (Canon, Sony and Mazda). These data are for 2003, and the classifications confirm those with 2001 sales data in Rugman (2005). It again shows that the vast majority of MNEs are home-region based (58 of the 64 Japanese MNEs). Further, when data on foreign assets are compiled (for the first time), we find all of the 64 Japanese MNEs are in cell 2. There are no Japanese MNEs that operate bi-regionally or globally in terms of foreign production: all foreign production (as measured by foreign assets) is home-region based. We believe that these new findings on the regional nature of foreign assets generalise to the other large 500 MNEs.

We conclude that there is a lack of evidence for globalisation of the supply chain of MNEs; rather, the supply chain is regional. Delios and Beamish (2005) also find that the majority of Japanese MNEs follow a home-region strategy over time and that their production-based activities, such as R&D, also tend to be concentrated in their home region. Related to this is the recent concern about offshoring (i.e. the outsourcing of some manufacturing and service activities to foreign countries). Yet, again, such offshoring is mainly intra-regional, with the exception of IT work by American and European MNEs in India. However, this is a small part of their activities. For example, the US Department of Labor found that only 2 per cent of all job changes in the United States in 2002 were due to outsourcing. So the popular concern about the globalisation of the value chain is, again, factually incorrect.

Some economic and business implications of regionalisation

This thinking on the regional solution to strategy can be applied to the case of UK-based MNEs. Yip *et al.* (2005) and Rugman *et al.* (2005) have conducted empirical analyses of the effect of intra-regional sales on the performance of UK MNEs. Using the OSIRIS database of about 30,000 publicly listed companies, a set of UK firms can be identified and analysed. The central independent variable in this analysis is a measure of regionalisation (E/T), which is a ratio of sales in a home region (Europe) to the total sales of a multinational enterprise (Rugman 2005). Hence, this measure includes home country (UK) sales, subsidiaries' sales in the region (Europe) and the UK firm's exports to the rest of Europe. Inclusion of such export data is partly governed by data availability, but it is also appropriate as exporting obviously generates foreign sales. Both exports and foreign subsidiary sales are components of foreign sales. According to internalisation theory, an internationalising firm chooses the most cost-efficient way among all possible modes of foreign sales (Buckley and Casson 1976; Rugman 1981).

As a performance measure, we use return on foreign assets (ROFA). We use ROFA as it measures the performance of the subsidiaries of the MNE, which is our main concern, and we set this against the regional measure (E/T), for the first time. Usually return on total assets (ROTA) is used, or another firm-level metric. We also regress ROTA against (E/T), and compare the difference between ROFA and ROTA as dependent variables.

To further understand these relationships, consider Figure 5.2. This reports the mean value of the (F/T) and (E/T) variables for the set of UK MNEs in the *Fortune* 500 for 2001. The average (F/T) is 48 per cent, which gives an average home-market sales of 52 per cent. We also find that the average (E/T) is 64 per cent. This means that the 'foreign' sales of UK firms in the rest of Europe, 1-(E/T) is 16 per cent. It also means that the 'foreign' sales outside of Europe, i.e. the rest of the world (ROW), amount to an average of 36 per cent.

Given the evidence and insights confirming the regional nature of MNE activity in Rugman (2005) and Rugman and Verbeke (2004), we are able to use these regional sales (E/T) to address the issue of generating more accurate proxies for geographical configuration. Figure 5.2 confirms the existing theory and evidence of the regional multinationals, in that the majority of the largest UK MNEs are home-region orientated, namely, that they have over 50 per cent of sales in the home region.

To further test the relationship between multinationality and the performance of UK firms, we conduct a wider test across a large set of UK firms. From the OSIRIS database we select the UK companies present in the top 100 across 89 sectors as classified by Dow Jones. This gives a total of 587 UK companies from the European total of 8,900, according to the OSIRIS database. However, not all of these UK companies report the necessary regional segment data, so we found only 210 companies for which we are able to calculate both: (1) the regionalisation measure (E/T); and (2) the ROFA. These companies constitute our sample (those companies that reported the data for only one of the years under consideration were excluded from the sample). The data were collected for four years: 2003, 2001, 1998 and 1993, thus creating an unbalanced panel of 495 observations.

A number of control variables allow us to moderate the effects of other factors which have been shown to have a significant impact on a firm's performance according to earlier research. First, we control for a firm's size effect by including a logarithm of company's total revenues into the

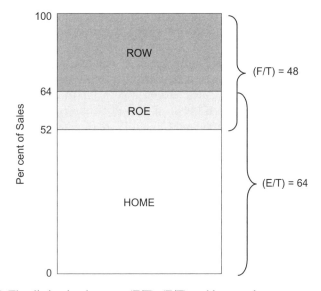

Figure 5.2 The distinction between (F/T), (E/T) and home sales.

Notes: For UK firms, their mean home sales = 52 per cent; their mean (F/T) = 48 per cent; and their mean (E/T) = 64 per cent.
Rest of Europe (ROE) Rest of World; (ROW).

regressors (Tallman and Li 1996; Hitt *et al.* 1997; Gomes and Ramaswamy 1999). Second, recognising the importance of industry effects in explaining firm performance in a multi-industry study (Schmalensee 1985; Grant *et al.* 1988; Montgomery and Porter 1991; Tallman and Li 1996), we use the corresponding Dow Jones industry's average return on assets measured for all public companies: (1) in the world in a particular industry; and (2) in the UK in a particular industry as additional controls (based on the OSIRIS database again). Third, we also control for the global competitiveness of British companies in an industry by including the global market share of all British companies in each Dow Jones industry sector. Finally, we include a time trend to mediate a year or temporal effect in profitability data, as the former was shown to have a significant effect in previous research (Cowley 1988; Mascarenhas and Aaker 1989; Haskel and Martin 1992; Li 2005).

We estimate the following two major specifications:

$$S1: ROFA_{it} = \beta_0 + \beta_1 (E/T_{it}) + \beta_2 (E/T_{it})^2 + \Sigma_j \beta_j \, Control \, Variable_{ijt} + \varepsilon_{it,}$$

$$S3: ROTA_{it} = \beta_0 + \beta_1 (E/T_{it}) + \beta_2 (E/T_{it})^{2+} \beta_3 (E/T_{it})^3 +$$
$$\Sigma_j \beta_j \, Control \, Variable_{ijt} + \varepsilon_{it,}$$

Where $ROFA_{it}$ is return on foreign assets of company i in year t, $ROTA_{it}$ is return on total assets of company i in year t, E/T_{it} is a ratio of European sales to total sales of company i in year t, *Control Variable*$_{ijt}$ is a control variable j for a company i (or industry k) in year t ($log(TR_{it})$ is a natural logarithm of total revenues of company i in year t, $ROTAW_{kt}$ is an average return on assets of all public companies in the world of industry k in year t, $ROTAUK_{kt}$ is an average return on assets of all public UK companies in industry k in year t, and $MSHUK_{kt}$ is a market share of UK companies in industry k in year t, $YEAR_t$ is a time trend), and $\varepsilon_{it,}$ is a corresponding error term.

Since the time series is short in our dataset, we are not able to estimate reliably either fixed or random effects models. Therefore, here we use a feasible generalised least squares (FGLS) estimator, which is more efficient than a pooled ordinary least squares (OLS) estimator when the series exhibit heteroskedasticity (that is a concern in the analysed data set). By downweighting estimated coefficients by an estimate of the cross-section residual standard deviation, FGLS allows assigning a smaller weight to observations coming from populations with greater variance and a larger weight to the ones coming from populations with smaller variance. In this way, cross-sectional heteroskedasticity is addressed.

Additionally, we use White heteroskedasticity consisted covariances to obtain estimates which are robust to general heteroskedasticity; that is, we allow for inter-temporal differences in variances along with cross-sectional heteroskedasticity, which is traditionally addressed by FGLS. A similar estimation technique was used in studies by Gomes and Ramaswamy (1999), Contractor *et al.* (2003), and Li (2005).

We found a significant quadratic relationship (inverted U-shape) between our measures of multinationality (E/T) and performance (ROFA) in the two specifications we have tested. The difference between specifications is in control variables used that address a concern about the importance of moderator variables articulated in Grant (1987). We have also tested for a possible cubic relationship between (E/T) and ROFA, yet no significant association was found. However, there is a significant cubic fit for ROTA, see S3 and S4 in Table 5.4. We also find significant size and industry effects, an overall competitiveness effect (measured by market share), and a time effect.

In general, this analysis demonstrates that regional sales have a significant association with the financial performance of a multinational's subsidiaries. However, the relationship is not linear. At smaller regionalisation levels (that is, with a high dispersion of the UK MNE's international operations), there is a negative effect on the performance of foreign operations (due to, for instance, a strong liability of foreignness [Zaheer and Mosakowski 1997], and overexpansion problems [Contractor *et al.* 2003]). In contrast, a larger

Table 5.4 Regional sales and performance of UK multinationals

Dependent variable	Return on Foreign Assets (ROFA)		Return on Total Assets (ROTA)	
Independent variables	S1	S2	S3	S4
European/Total sales	0.095*** (0.000)	0.014 (0.411)	−0.147*** (0.000)	−0.153*** (0.000)
European/Total sales^2	−0.001*** (0.000)	−0.001*** (0.000)	0.003*** (0.000)	0.003*** (0.000)
European/Total sales^3	–	–	−0.00002*** (0.000)	−0.00002*** (0.000)
Total revenues (log)	0.560*** (0.000)	0.697*** (0.000)	0.633*** (0.000)	0.738*** (0.000)
Industry return on total assets (world)	0.326*** (0.000)	0.345*** (0.000)	0.302*** (0.000)	0.412*** (0.000)
Market share	–	−0.085*** (0.000)	–	−0.029*** (0.000)
Time Trend	−1.149*** (0.000)	−1.994*** (0.000)	−0.929*** (0.000)	−1.000*** (0.000)
Constant term	17.002*** (0.000)	22.648*** (0.000)	5.607*** (0.000)	4.484*** (0.000)
Adjusted R-Squared	0.689	0.912	0.751	0.990
F-statistics	5333***	1623***	249***	7202***
Number of observations	495	495	495	495

Note: p-values in parentheses. *** $p = < 000.1$.

Source: Author's calculations, see also Rugman (2005).

amount of regional sales has a positive effect on the subsidiaries' performance (perhaps because the liability of foreignness is reduced once the company operates in a more familiar environment). Overall, this analysis shows that regional sales have a significant positive performance impact on the international operations of UK multinational enterprises.

Table 5.4 reports the results from estimation of four models: the first two models (S1 and S2) have ROFA as a dependent variable, whereas the other two use ROTA for the same purpose. In this way we can easily compare the four specifications as we use the same sets of control variables for estimation. Whereas specifications 1 and 2 show an inverted U-shaped quadratic relationship between the ROFA and (E/T), the ROTA models (specifications 3 and 4) are considerably different as they reveal a significant cubic relationship between ROTA and (E/T).

This difference in fit with an inverted U-shape for ROFA and a cubic fit for ROTA can perhaps be better understood if we consider the nature of two of the key variables: ROTA and (E/T). ROTA is the overall profitability of a multinational enterprise (it includes domestic profitability) while (E/T) also includes a significant proportion of home sales. Hence, low levels of (E/T) indicate a highly (non-European) internationalised company, whereas a high (E/T) ratio is a sign of a more regionalised company, where there are also larger home sales. Consequently, a reported S-shaped relationship between (E/T) and ROTA confirms the earlier studies by Contractor *et al.* (2003). However, if we draw a chart depicting the relationship between ROTA and (E/T) at mean values of other variables for eligible values of (E/T) (that is between 0 and 100), we observe again only the U-shaped part of the S-curve (Figure 5.3). Hence, we can apply the same logic as we did for ROFA to rationalise this finding.

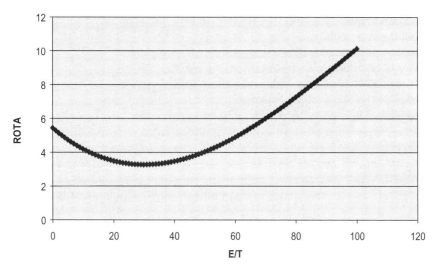

Figure 5.3 ROTA and (E/T) at the mean values of the control variables.

In general, this analysis demonstrates that regional sales (E/T) have a significant positive association with the financial performance of a multinational's subsidiaries (ROFA) and its overall performance (ROTA). However, the relationship is not linear, but quadratic for ROFA and cubic for ROTA. At smaller regionalisation levels (that is, with a high dispersion of the UK MNE's international operations) there is a negative effect on the performance of foreign operations (due to, for instance, a strong liability of foreignness [Zaheer and Mosakowski 1997], and overexpansion problems [Contractor *et al.* 2003]). In contrast, a larger amount of regional sales has a positive effect on the subsidiaries' performance, and also on the firm (perhaps because the liability of foreignness is reduced once the company operates in a more familiar environment). Overall, this analysis shows that regional sales (E/T) have a significant positive performance impact on the international operations of UK multinational enterprises.

Conclusion

The evidence is that most of the world's largest firms are regional multinationals. The great majority of MNEs (320 out of 380 with available data) have, on average, 80 per cent of all their sales in their home region of the triad. The world of international business is a regional one, not a global one. Only a handful of MNEs (a total of nine) actually operate successfully as key players in each region of the triad. For 320 of 365 cases of MNEs for which data are available and classifiable, the data indicate they operate on a home-triad basis. This is very strong evidence of regional/triad activity. There are 25 bi-regional MNEs and another 11 host-country based ones. Data on foreign assets suggest that production is even more intra-regional than sales. There are so few 'global' MNEs as to render the concept of 'globalisation' meaningless. This research suggests that scholars of international business need to pay less attention to models of 'global' strategy – as this is a special case. The 'big question' for research in international business is: why do MNEs succeed as regional organisations without becoming global?

Transaction cost economics reasoning largely explains this regional phenomenon: market-seeking expansion by firms in host regions is often associated with high, location-specific adaptation investments to link the MNE's existing knowledge base with host-region location advantages. Firm (FSAs) and country factors (CSAs) do not simply meld together without managerial intervention. As the required investments to meld FSAs and CSAs become larger, driven by the cultural, administrative, geographic, and economic distance between home country/region and host regions, the attractiveness of foreign markets declines, and regional, rather than global, strategies are needed to reflect the differential need for 'linking' investments in each region. Only in a few sectors, such as consumer electronics, can a balanced, global distribution of sales be achieved.

Based on preliminary tests of the logic of Figure 5.1, it is likely that the upstream end of the value chain can be globalised more easily than the customer end, because upstream location-specific investments are not one-sided (in the sense of lacking reciprocal commitments from the other economic actors involved, which is a critical problem at the customer end). Upstream globalisation obviously need not be expressed in a balanced geographic distribution of R&D, manufacturing, etc., but rather in the MNE's ability to choose and access locations around the globe where the firm's upstream FSAs can easily be melded with foreign-location advantages, without the need for major, location-specific adaptation investments. Yet the available data on production also suggest the dominance of home-region-based production clusters and networks, as in the automobile sector. This suggests that the hazards of cultural, administrative, geographic, and economic distance between the home country/region and host regions are often also present at the upstream side.

In terms of the definitions outlined in the introduction to this chapter we can make the following conclusions:

1   The largest 500 firms are all MNEs as they operate across national borders, but about 120 of them are not reporting data on the geographic distribution of sales (these include the Chinese firms in the top 500).
2   There is evidence that only nine of 380 MNEs reporting sales data for 2001 are 'global' firms defined as firms with a significant presence of 20 per cent plus of sales in each broad region of the triad. There are up to 36 bi-regional firms.
3   The typical large MNE is an extremely home-regional-based business, as 320 of the 380 firms reporting data have an average of 80 per cent of their sales in their home region.

Recent data on foreign assets also show a strong home-region bias with 83 per cent of the foreign assets of Japanese firms being in Asia. This is evidence of a regional supply chain, rather than a global one. It has also been reported here that a regional sales variable (E/T) helps to explain the performance of UK MNEs. We expect that this is a generalised result, but further research is required. Overall, these firm-level data on regional MNEs strongly support the more aggregate, country-level data reported in Rugman (2000), where it was first shown that globalisation is a myth and that regionalisation explains world business activity.

References

Bartlett, C. A. and Ghoshal, S. (1989) *Managing across Borders: The Transnational Solution*, Cambridge, MA: Harvard Business School Press.
Bhagwati, J. (2002) *Free Trade Today*, Princeton, NJ: Princeton University Press.
Birkinshaw, J. (2000) *Entrepreneurship in the Global Firm*, London: Sage.
Buckley, P. J. (2002) 'Is the International Business Research Agenda Running Out of Steam?', *Journal of International Business Studies*, 33(2): 365–73.

—— and Casson, M. (1976) *The Future of the Multinational Enterprise*, London: Macmillan.

Contractor, F. J., Kundu, S.K. and Hsu, C.C. (2003) 'Three-stage Theory of International Expansion: The Link Between Multinationality and Performance in the Service Sector', *Journal of International Business Studies*, 34(1): 5–18.

Cowley, P. R (1988) 'Market Structure and Business Performance: An Evaluation of Buyer/Seller Power in PIMS Database', *Strategic Management Journal*, 9(3): 271–9.

Delios, A. and Beamish, P.W. (2005) 'Regional and Global Strategies of Japanese Firms', *Management International Review*, 45(1): 19–36.

Ghemawat, P. (2003) 'Semiglobalization and International Business Strategy', *Journal of International Business Studies*, 34(2): 138–52.

Gomes, L. and Ramaswamy, K. (1999) 'An Empirical Examination of the Form of the Relationship Between Multinationality and Performance', *Journal of International Business Studies*, 30(1): 173–88.

Grant, R. M. (1987) 'Multinationality and Performance among British Manufacturing Companies', *Journal of International Business Studies*, 18(3): 79–89.

——, Jammine, A.P. and Thomas, H. (1988) 'Diversity, Diversification, and Profitability among British Manufacturing Companies, 1972–1984', *Academy of Management Journal*, 31: 771–801.

Haskel, J. and Martin, C. (1992) 'Margins, Concentration, Unions and Business Cycle', *International Journal of Industrial Organisation*, 10(4): 611–31.

Hirst, P. and Thompson, G. (1999) *Globalization in Question*, Malden, MA: Blackwell.

Hitt, M.A, Hoskisson, R.E. and Kim, H. (1997) 'International Diversification: Effects on Innovation and Firm Performance in Product-Diversified Firms', *Academy of Management Journal*, 40(4): 767–98.

Krugman, P. (1993) 'Regionalism Versus Multilateralism: Analytical Note', in J. de Melo and A. Panagarily (eds) *New Dimensions in Regional Integration*, New York: Cambridge University Press, pp. 58–79.

Li, L. (2005) 'Is Regional Strategy More Effective than Global Strategy in the US Service Industries?' *Management International Review*, 45(1): 19–37.

Mascarenhas, B. and Aaker, D. (1989) 'Strategy over the Business Cycle', *Strategic Management Journal*, 10(3): 199–211.

Milner, H.V. (1988) *Resisting Protectionism: Global Industries and the Policies of International Trade*, Princeton, NJ: Princeton University Press.

Montgomery, C.A. and Porter, M.E. (1991) *Strategy: Seeking and Securing Competitive Advantage*, Boston, MA: Harvard Business School Publishing.

Pomfret, R. (2001) *The Economics of Regional Trading Arrangements*, Oxford: Oxford University Press.

Poon, J. (1997) 'The Cosmopolitanization of Trade Regions: Global Trends and Implications', *Economic Geography*, 73: 390–404.

Rugman, A.M. (1981) *Inside the Multinationals: The Economics of Internal Markets*, London: Croom Helm.

—— (2000) *The End of Globalization*, London and New York: Random House and Amacom-McGraw Hill.

—— (2005) *The Regional Multinationals*. Cambridge: Cambridge University Press.

—— and Collinson, S. (2006) 'Asian Business is Regional, not Global', in M. Fratianni *et al.* (eds) *Regional Economic Integration*, London: Elsevier.

—— and D'Cruz, J. (2000) *Multinationals as Flagship Firms: Regional Business Networks*, Oxford: Oxford University Press.

—— and Verbeke, A. (1990) *Global Corporate Strategy and Trade Policy*, London and New York: Routledge.

—— (1998) 'Multinational Enterprises and Public Policy', *Journal of International Business Studies*, 29(1): 115–36.

—— (2003) 'Extending the Theory of the Multinational Enterprise: Internationalization and Strategic Management Perspectives', *Journal of International Business Studies*, 34(2): 125–37.

—— (2004) 'A Perspective on Regional and Global Strategies of Multinational Enterprises', *Journal of International Business Studies*, 35(1): 1–15.

——, Kudina, Alina and Yip, George S. (2005) *The Regional Dimension of UK Multinationals*, mimeo.

Schmalensee, T. (1985) 'Do Markets Differ Much?' *American Economic Review*, 75: 341–51.

Tallman, S. and Li, J.T. (1996) 'Effects of International Diversity and Product Diversity on the Performance of Multinational Firms', *Academy of Management Journal*, 39: 179–96.

Yip, George S., Rugman, Alan M. and Kudina, Alina (2005) 'International Competitiveness of British Companies', mimeo, London Business School, Dept. of Strategic and International Management.

Zaheer, S. and Mosakowski, E. (1997) 'The Dynamics of the Liability of Foreignness: A Global Study of Survival in Financial Services', *Strategic Management Journal*, 18(6): 439–63.

6   The role of regional agreements in trade and investment regimes

Stephen Woolcock

Introduction

Two themes have been central to recent work on international trade and investment agreements; the scope and legitimacy of the World Trade Organization (WTO), in particular with regard to the so-called 'behind the border' issues, and the growth of regional agreements. While much has been written on the trade-creating and trade-diverting effects of regional agreements, there has been much less work on the role of regional agreements in rule-making in trade and investment. This chapter addresses the question of how rule-making at the multilateral and regional level interact. After outlining the two central themes in the current trade and investment debate, it then offers a framework for analysing the relatively neglected question of how developments at the regional (or bilateral) level shape the evolution of the international trade and investment regime. The chapter draws on a number of recent case studies that deal with the evolution of rules for behind the border issues, the findings of which are summarised. The chapter argues that it is necessary to view rule-making (or regime formation) in trade and investment as a multi-level process. It suggests that in this process the regional level played a broadly benign role in the period between the mid-1980s and mid-1990s, but that recent developments suggest that some more malign features of regional initiatives are now creeping in.[1] To overcome this, there is a need for meaningful negotiations on new rule-making within the WTO even if this may require a plurilateral approach.

Two broad themes in research on the international trade and investment system

The first theme concerns the scope of WTO rules. In other words, should there be common rules established at the multilateral level for policy areas such as public procurement, intellectual property, competition, investment etc., and, if so, how far should these rules go in constraining national policy autonomy? On the one hand, it is argued that as tariffs and other measures at the border have been reduced, there is a need to address such 'behind the border' issues that can limit or distort competition in trade and investment. On the other hand, it is argued that multilateral rules for behind the border issues take the WTO 'too far' by limiting national policy autonomy, undermining accountability, reducing beneficial 'policy competition' between national jurisdictions and imposing unsuitable rules on developing countries.

In practice, the trade and investment regimes of today do constitute a balance between the adoption of common rules and policy autonomy; the issue is, what sort of balance is struck and at which level of policy-making, bilateral, regional, plurilateral or multilateral? Compared to earlier decades, when the rules of the General Agreement on Tariffs and Trade (GATT) were drawn up on a range of behind the border issues from technical regulations to services and intellectual property, the WTO rules have become more inclusive. In the 1960s and 1970s, a core group of developed countries led by the US shaped rule-making. In the 1980s, the plurilateral level of the Organisation for Economic Co-operation and Development (OECD), with the active involvement of other developed countries, played a key role. In addition to this 'club' model of rule-making, there was also close transatlantic co-operation between the two major proponents of trade and investment rules. Now there are more countries with an effective voice (and veto) in negotiations on rule-making. This change in the nature of decision-making in the WTO makes the task of finding the right balance between rules and policy autonomy more difficult. As a result the WTO member governments have effectively decided that significant new rule-making is too difficult to handle in the current Doha Development Agenda (DDA).

The second theme concerns the role of regional (or bilateral) trade agreements (RTAs). Although the debate over customs unions and free trade agreements (FTAs) goes back at least a century, the recent significant increase in the number of RTAs concluded or being negotiated has brought the issue to the top of the trade agenda (Irwin 1993). In the 'first phase' of regionalism in the 1960s Europe provided a model for countries in Africa and Latin America to emulate but without much success. Economic integration in Europe stagnated in the 1970s also. Things changed in the 1980s with the 'second phase of regionalisation' in which the European Union moved forward again with the single European market and monetary union projects, and the US began to conclude (bilateral) free trade agreements. Since the early-to-mid-1990s there has been a veritable explosion of regional and bilateral trade agreements that has stimulated a great volume of research (World Bank 2005; WTO 2005).

The trade economic literature on RTAs drew heavily on customs union theory and on tariff-based models. Much of the work took the form of quantitative assessments of the trade-creating and trade-diverting effects of tariff preferences, an important field but one of diminishing importance as tariffs, at least among the major economies of the world, have continued to come down (Winters 1996). Imperfect competition models assessed also the dynamic and growth effects of deeper or positive integration in regions, with studies being especially focused on the EU (Baldwin and Venables 1996). There has also been a good deal of economic literature on the question of whether RTAs constitute building blocks or stumbling blocks for the multi-lateral system (Bhagwati *et al.* 1999). But this work, like the rest of the trade literature, has neglected rule-making that is not immediately trade-related. In other words the focus has been on areas such as anti-dumping and safeguard rules. What literature there is on rule-making has either argued that the deep integration associated with rule-making does not normally lead to prefer-ences or that it creates a spaghetti bowl of conflicting rules. The case for the former is that rules are at least *de jure* applied in a non-discriminatory manner. For example, establishing environmental or safety standards or regu-lating risk does not explicitly discriminate between national and foreign-produced goods or services. The difficulty here of course is that experience has shown that there is significant scope for *de facto* discrimination, either because the rules reflect domestic supplier interests or in the way they are applied. The case for the latter is that regional and bilateral rules create conflicting norms or standards. Bhagwati has made this case most persist-ently, but has done so on the basis of an assessment of rules of origin. While there is no question that different rules of origin hinder trade and add to the frictional costs of trade, one cannot conclude that all rule-making creates a spaghetti bowl of rules.

Legal studies have looked at the question of the legal compatibility of RTAs with the provisions of GATT Article XXIV and Article V of the General Agreement on Trade in Services (GATS), but these have been encumbered by the loose wording of these provisions and the lack of any operational criteria for assessing the impact of rule-making in RTAs and FTAs. The GATT 1994 Article XXIV stipulates that preferential agreements must not result in an increased incidence of protection as a result of 'other restrictions on com-merce' (ORCs) in addition to tariffs. There has been work on how to apply Art. XXIV to tariff preferences and ORCs clearly applies to border measures such as quotas or other quantitative restrictions (Trachtmann 2002). But there is no consensus on how to apply Article XXIV or GATS Article V to common rules on behind the border issues within a region. Without oper-ational criteria for the impact of rule-making at the bilateral or regional level, the current discussions on how to improve WTO disciplines on RTAs in Geneva are going nowhere, because there is no way of assessing whether common regional rules restrict or facilitate trade and investment.

Political economists have also studied RTAs and have in particular addressed the question of the motivation behind such preferential agree-ments. Broadly speaking, this work suggests that there are a number of different motives ranging from strategic and foreign policy considerations to commercial interests in gaining new markets or locking in reforms in signa-tory states (Schott 2004). But the political economy research has tended not to look at the detailed substance of the agreements themselves and has, in particular, not looked at the rule-making aspects (Krueger 1999).

In general terms, therefore, the increased debate on RTAs and the outpouring of new studies have not resulted in any consensus on whether they are building blocks or stumbling blocks and the rule-making dimension has not been covered much. The case has been made that RTAs are creating a 'spaghetti bowl' of different rules, but this argument relies essentially on the indisputably 'spaghetti bowl-like' rules of origin (Bhagwati and Kreuger 1995). With little work done on other areas of rule-making, it is unsound to draw wider conclusions from just one case. Equally, the case that deep integration is likely to be benign because rules in this area are less likely to be applied in a discriminatory fashion (Lawrence 1995; Winters 1996), appears to require some more empirical testing that involves looking at the substance of the various RTAs.

What is needed therefore is more work on how the two themes of the scope of the WTO and the growth of regional agreements interact. The recent research that gets closest to addressing this question is that which deals with the question of whether RTAs or bilateral agreements go 'beyond the WTO'. This work has to some extent been undertaken by the WTO itself, which keeps an inventory of RTAs including the rule-making elements of these agreements. The OECD has also produced a number of studies comparing RTA provisions in a range of behind the border issues (OECD 2002). This chapter draws on this work as well as a number of horizontal case studies (i.e. studies in specific policy areas such as investment, that assess rule-making on all levels) conducted in a research project funded by the United Nations University-Comparative Research in Integration Studies in Bruges and additional case studies carried out by the author (Ullrich 2004; Reiter 2006; Pugatch 2004; Garay and De Lombaerde 2006).

Towards a multi-level analysis of trade and investment regimes

The proposition here is that existing research has been constrained by a number of assumptions. First, it has been assumed that there is a clear distinction between trade and non-trade issues or between market access and rule-making. This assumption has simplified things for those looking at the impact of RTAs, who have, by and large, focused only on the tariff and market access issues. The distinction between market access and rule-making has also been used to simplify negotiations. But in reality there never has been and is unlikely to be any clear distinction between rules and access. Rules have and will continue to have important consequences for the degree of openness of economies and must therefore be considered alongside market access in assessments of trade policy. This includes an assessment of rule-making in RTAs.

Second, much of the literature on RTAs tends to assume that the issue at hand is the extent to which trade policy (and investment policy) is regional or multilateral. Regional agreements are often presented as a new development that threatens the existing multilateral order. The assumption in this chapter is that multi-level rule-making is normal and that multilateral rule-making is the exception. In other words, rule-making in terms of trade and investment regimes has always been multi-level in nature, involving unilateral, bilateral, regional, plurilateral and multilateral rule-making. The issue at hand is therefore how the role of the regional level might be changing, rather than whether regionalism is undermining multilateralism.

If rule-making cannot be distinguished from other aspects of trade and investment policy and the process of regime formation is multi-level in nature, it is important to understand the role of regional/bilateral agreements in rule-making. This necessitates analysing the substance of RTA (and bilateral) rules on trade and investment in some detail, which is something that few studies have done until recently.[2]

An analytical framework

When assessing the impact of RTAs it may help to equate the effects of rules in RTAs with the generally understood effects of tariffs. There are three analogies that might be made with conventional trade theory. First, there is the question of what degree of preference the regional rules represent. As will be shown below, this varies between elements of rule-making. Second, there is the question of trade creation and diversion. Rule-making in RTAs can be said to facilitate trade and investment (analogous to trade creation) when common regional rules replace divergent national rules and thus reduce frictional and compliance costs for third parties (as well as for the signatories). Trade and investment restricting (diversion) effects could be said to result when the stringency of the rules (norms or standards) exceeds the level of the previous national rules. In GATT terminology, would the RTA then result in a higher incidence of protection due to 'other restrictions on commerce'?

For example, the introduction of common contract award procedures for public contracts within a region to replace diverse national procedures could be said to facilitate trade and investment because third country suppliers, as regional suppliers, will henceforth only need to conform to a unified set of rules. If, on the other hand, regional technical regulations are introduced that exceed the level of regulation of the previous national regulations, these will have both trade (and investment) facilitating effects in the form of a common technical regulation, and trade (and investment) limiting effects in the shape of the higher regulatory standard.[3]

A third analogy can perhaps be made with optimal tariffs that may help us to understand how RTAs might have wider systemic effects. Optimal tariff theory envisages the use of asymmetric bargaining power to shape international prices and thus shift the terms of trade. It is easy to see how, by analogy, dominant actors such as the US and EU or other 'hubs' might use a network of RTAs (or bilateral agreements) to promote rules to shape international rules to match their narrow national interest and thus enhance their 'terms of trade'. From international political economy, one can also use the analogy of regional hegemons. But hegemony can be both benign and malign. In this sense benign regional hegemons would be those that promote regulatory best practice or rules that enhance sustainable development throughout the region. In contrast, the malign or 'selfish hegemon' would promote rules that predominantly serve their own narrow vested interests, such as rules aimed primarily at enhancing market access in regional partners.

In order to address these questions we need an analytical framework that enables us to make qualitative assessments of the impact of regional rules. A summary version of this framework is set out in Table 6.1. Table 6.1 illustrates the typical elements in rule-making in any trade or investment agreement, the likely impact of each element, the scope of WTO rules (in very general terms as these will of course differ from case to case), and the nature and degree of preference.

Coverage

Regional rules will be deeper, the greater their coverage. Coverage can be defined by sector schedules, regulatory entities covered, for example, whether rules apply to state and local government, and regulatory agencies as well as central government, and the type of instruments covered. Rules that cover only legislation are shallower than those that also cover secondary instruments or regulatory decisions. The greater the coverage, the more 'liberal' the regime if the rules constrain the scope for the use of regulatory instruments as means of protection. The degree of preference is then determined by the greater coverage of regional rules than wider multilateral rules. Analogous to tariffs, preferences in terms of the coverage of rules are subject to erosion through increased coverage of equivalent multilateral rules. For example, a regional preference resulting from greater sector coverage for services is subject to erosion by further negotiations in the GATS.

Non-discrimination

Principles, such as non-discrimination, are common to all regimes. Here the nature of the preference is clear in the sense that the extension of national treatment or most-favoured-nation (MFN) status only to regional partners constitutes a clear preference. How important this preference is will depend very much on the specific case. For example, the North American Free Trade Agreement (NAFTA) requires national treatment for technical barriers to trade, as opposed to policy approximation. But the NAFTA parties are already bound to provide *de jure* national treatment under the WTO, so there is no preference. On the other hand, NAFTA also provides for pre-investment national treatment. This is equivalent to the right of establishment and therefore a significant preference for investors from within the region because

Table 6.1 Elements of rule-making in trade and investment agreements

Rule element	Typical provisions	Likely impact	Typical scope of WTO rules	Nature and degree of preference
Coverage	Sector schedules Type of entity, e.g central, state, local, independent regulator or private entities (iv) Regulatory instruments covered	More extensive coverage Implies greater 'liberalisation'	(i) Use of positive and negative lists (ii) Generally limited to central government and 'best endeavours' for other entities (iii) Full coverage of legislation but less of secondary instruments	Third parties do not benefit from the greater WTO-plus coverage of sectors, entities or regulatory instruments Analogous to tariff preference subject to erosion
Principles	National treatment MFN status	(i) Precludes discrimination against foreign suppliers (ii) No discrimination between third parties	MFN and national treatment central to WTO rules but exceptions, specifically for customs unions and free trade agreements	Third parties do not benefit from non-discrimination provisions Limited scope for preference as most areas subject to WTO rules
Transparency	Notification of legislation (and) secondary instruments Opportunity to make submissions on proposed regulation Obligation on regulator to respond to submissions	Facilitates compliance with national rules Promotes regulatory best practice Helps guide against regulatory capture by national interests	Transparency is principle of WTO rules but often does not reach to secondary instruments Some agreements also require (ii) and (iii)	Information generally public so no preference Third parties might be denied right to make submissions, but in practice regulatory procedures unlikely to discriminate
Substantive measures	Harmonisation Partial harmonisation Approximation as a general aim Equivalence Mutual recognition	(i)–(iii) Eliminate or reduce 'frictional' costs (iv)–(v) Reduce costs while retaining regulatory autonomy	Selective harmonisation, e.g telecommunications and financial services Encourages but does not require mutual recognition or equivalence	Preference for regional norms or rules over international rules and preference in the form of mutual recognition Degree of preference potentially great

Co-operation	Joint bodies (ii) Inter-govt. committee to oversee agreement (iii) Specialist committees Technical cooperation and capacity building	(i) Promotes convergence on rules and/or best practice (ii) Helps identify regulatory barriers before these create disputes (iii) Helps less developed economies develop best practice	(i) Exist but unwieldy (ii) General provisions for cooperation and technical assistance (iii) Specialist committees in key policy areas (iv) Limited resources for technical assistance	Third parties excluded from more intensive cooperation within the RTA No third parties benefit from technical assistance under RTA Could be important for developing countries
Regulatory safeguards	Tight controls on the use of 'safeguard' measures General exceptions permitting discrimination	(i) Tight controls promote confidence and thus trade and investment (ii) Broad scope for exceptions has a chilling effect	Generally broad exceptions that offer considerable scope for regulatory discretion, but some tightening, e.g. SPS agreement	Loose discipline enables scope to discriminate against third parties Could be significant but case dependent
Enforcement implementation	States or private legal persons have standing Ind. reviews Remedies (e.g financial penalties) Regional dispute settlement	Effective implementation Promotes confidence and thus trade and investment flows	State-to-state dispute settlement only	Third parties have no recourse to tougher and more immediate remedies and reviews

there are no equivalent multilateral rules requiring pre-investment national treatment except in some service sectors under the GATS.

Transparency

Transparency provisions can also be found in virtually every agreement. These may cover statutes, or in cases of deeper integration secondary instruments. Transparency can also extend to decision-making procedures in the form of 'due process' provisions. For example, there may be regional rules, as in NAFTA, that grant parties the right to make submissions to regulators and require regulators to respond to these submissions. Taken together, such transparency rules can facilitate trade and investment and promote regulatory best practice by shedding light on any abuse of regulatory discretion to restrict trade or investment. Transparency provisions in regional agreements therefore tend not to constitute a preference.

Substantive provisions

In the area of substantive rules RTAs can have both benign and malign effects. Common rules or standards can facilitate trade and investment by replacing different national rules. But full or partial harmonisation of rules or standards may set higher standards than the national rules and thus represent a form of preference for regional suppliers that are more able to comply with these standards. Regional rules may also threaten to undermine multilateralism if, for example, they promote competing interpretations or norms. For example, in the area of sanitary and phytosanitary (SPS) rules the EU promotes the precautionary principle in the FTAs it concludes with third parties. This differs from the approach to precaution in US-centred FTAs and arguably that in the WTO SPS agreement. Another example of this is the interpretation of detailed provisions in intellectual property rights incorporated in recent US FTAs that appears to be seeking to make up some of the 'ground lost' at the multilateral level in the shape of the codification of greater flexibility in trade-related aspects of intellectual property rights (TRIPs) provisions in the Doha Declaration of 2001. In other words, FTAs can be used to promote competing sets of norms, which can be expected to have malign effects on third countries and the trading system as a whole in that they will tend to create competing sets of rules.

Mutual recognition

Mutual recognition is another typical substantive provision that can constitute a clear preference, but one that will be subject to erosion only if mutual recognition agreements (MRAs) are open to third parties that satisfy the same criteria as the original signatories.

Co-operation

Many RTAs include both general and specific cooperation commitments. General commitments to cooperate in specific policy areas can be found in many RTAs. For example, the EU association agreements call for cooperation in policy issues such as competition and environment policy, but without specific implementing provisions. There are, however, provisions in RTAs that explicitly require cooperation at the level of specific policies, such as technical barriers to trade (TBTs), or competition. These may also provide for the exchange of regulators or funding for expert technical assistance. In such cases the resources made available are likely to be greater than those under general cooperation clauses or under multilateral rules where resources are much more thinly spread. In this sense the RTA might constitute a modest form of preference, but one that will be of some importance to developing countries.

Regulatory safeguards

All trade and investment agreements contain safeguards. Rule-making therefore also generally includes a form of 'regulatory safeguard' that offers scope for exemptions from commitments in agreements. In terms of rule-making these may often take the form of 'right to regulate' provisions. The degree of stringency of regional rules with respect to these regulatory safeguards is therefore important. Do regional rules leave less scope for national regulatory discretion? If so, this could be seen as a form of preference because regulators within the region would be able to use more discretion in their treatment of third party investors or products. On the other hand, tighter rules on the use of regulatory safeguards, if applied to all comers, would be seen as a step towards wider liberalisation.

Enforcement

Finally, rules generally include provisions on enforcement. If RTAs include more effective or far-reaching enforcement provisions, these may facilitate trade and investment, for example, if they implement agreed upon international rules more effectively. Regional rules may, however, offer better access to reviews and remedies for regional suppliers or investors through, for example, investor-state dispute settlement or rights for legal persons to have regulatory decisions reviewed or set aside. Regional rules may also offer specific regional dispute settlement procedures. These could be seen as a form of preference. 'Jurisprudence' from regional dispute cases may also help shape future rule-making. The interpretation of 'regulatory taking' investment protection under NAFTA is an example of this.

Empirical evidence

This section summarises the findings of a number of horizontal case studies of rule-making.[4] These case studies are illustrative and given space constraints cannot be comprehensive. The following section provides broad conclusions based on these case studies.

Rules of origin

Rules of origin is the classic case of how a number of regional preferential agreements can create the 'spaghetti bowl' effect described by Bhagwati. Diverse and often restrictive rules of origin – including preferential rules of origin – have emerged to fill the vacuum left by the absence of adequate international rules. World Customs Council provisions specify that substantial transformation should be the test of origin, but different regional agreements have set different criteria for what constitutes 'substantial transformation'. Some rules are based on change of tariff heading, some on value added and some on specific processes that must be carried out in the customs territory to impart origin.

Divergent rules of origin can be said to be restrictive on trade rather than facilitating trade (Krueger 1993). The complexity of rules also means that they are the antithesis of transparency. Divergent rules add to costs for third country suppliers and thus represent a degree of protection.

A more detailed look at the evolution of rules in this area shows there is a trend towards the consolidation of rules of origin around two dominant approaches: the NAFTA approach and the Pan-Euro system, although there remain a large number of different rules in particular in Latin America (Estevadeordal and Suominen 2003). Although consolidation around two major approaches might be said to have some advantages, the complexity of both approaches provides considerable scope for the rules to be used to protect sensitive sectors (Garay and De Lombaerde 2006).

Technical barriers to trade

Technical barriers to trade constitute an important impediment to trade and are therefore often the first 'behind the border' issue to be addressed in trade agreements (Chen and Mattoo 2004). Rules are needed to ensure a balance between liberalisation and the right to regulate to satisfy other legitimate policy objectives, such as health and safety and consumer protection. In this policy area, rule-making has been multi-level for many years. The first work on TBTs was carried out in the OECD in the 1960s. Thus formed the basis of the qualified MFN 'Standards Code' negotiated during the Tokyo Round between 1973 and 1979. These plurilateral rules required non-discrimination and transparency, but they were ineffective and national technical barriers continued to develop. Nor were the various

international standards-making bodies able to keep up with national voluntary standards.

Rule-making in TBTs was revitalised by initiatives at the regional level,
especially in the EU after 1985. The EU 'new approach' to TBTs extended
coverage, enhanced transparency and facilitated trade both within the EU
and for third parties because access to one EU Member State market meant
access to all due to the system of mutual recognition within the EU (European
Commission 1985). In terms of substantive rules, neither the EU nor the
other RTA provisions on TBT went much – if anything – beyond the WTO
rules. Indeed, the regional initiatives tended to take WTO approaches and
implement them more effectively. In the field of voluntary standards Europe
remained dominant, but rather than develop a stronger regional identity in
standards-making, the European standards bodies concluded cooperation
agreement with international standards-making bodies to ensure the maximum coherence between European and international standards (Joerges *et al.*
1998). In other words, regional initiatives had a benign effect on trade. They
built on existing agreed approaches by introducing new methods and more
effective implementation of what were essentially the agreed multilateral
(or at least plurilateral) rules.

A mutual recognition agreement is a potentially less benign aspect of rule-
making in TBTs in the sense that it creates preferences and could result in two
sets of rules: one for the developed economies that can meet the conditions of
MRAs and one for the developing economies that cannot because they lack
the domestic institutional capacity in the shape of effective compliance testing and accreditation bodies (Baldwin 2000). But if regional and bilateral
agreements contribute to establishing such institutional capacity, they may
facilitate the entry of developing countries into the regimes maintained by the
developed economies (OECD 2000).

Sanitary and phytosanitary measures

Work on SPS rule-making suggests that two dominant regional models
for rule-making are emerging, in this case despite the existence of strong
multilateral rules in the shape of the WTO SPS agreement (Isaac 2003). It
has been argued that the existence of these dominant models threatens the
long-term viability of the multilateral rules. The fact that the EU rules are
based on a social rationality could, in particular, threaten the sustainability
of the multilateral rules in that this EU approach is behind the push
for changes in the SPS rules to include, for example, the precautionary
principle.

It is worth noting that rule-making in the SPS field started at the (European)
regional level and in particular with European regional standards for food
safety back in the 1950s and then moved to international standards in the
shape of the World Health Organization's Codex Alimentarius. A major
change in the nature of the multilateral rules occurred in the Uruguay Round

when the Codex standards were linked with trade rules in the sense that the SPS Agreement draws on Codex standards.

The SPS case points to the danger of divergent regulatory norms and standards leading to 'regulatory regionalism' or the emergence of divergent, competing approaches to rule-making in major world regions. The WTO rules are based on the scientific rationality approach used in North America so that it is pressure from the EU for more flexibility in these rules to enable scope for the social rationality model that appears to be the force for change. The issue is to what degree regional or other agreements will be used by the EU to push its agenda. All EU RTAs that include SPS provisions are based on the social rationality model of the EU and, as one would expect, all RTAs concluded by the US or Canada are based on the scientific rationality model.

The SPS case study therefore shows that trade and investment regimes are not static, even if there are multilateral rules that may be undermined if there are divergent interpretations of agreed norms. WTO SPS rules are much less ambiguous than those on rules of origin, but what scope there is may be used by the EU to push its social rationality model and by the US and Canada and others to strengthen the existing scientific rationality.

Services and public procurement

In the cases of services and public procurement, which are both of major economic significance (Evenett and Hoekman 2004), there appears to have been a positive synergy between regional and multilateral rule-making in which developments at one level have complemented developments at the other. The work in these sectors (Ullrich 2004; Woolcock 2006) argues that international rules have been built up by a kind of iterative process in which regional/bilateral, plurilateral and multilateral levels of negotiation have all played a role. For example, in the case of public procurement, work at the plurilateral level of the OEEC (the regional precursor to the OECD) in the 1960s led to the plurilateral/multilateral code of the Tokyo Round (Blank and Marceau 1997). The approach and principles established in this code were then applied at the regional level, first in the EU and then in the Canada-United States Free Trade Agreement (CUSFTA) and in NAFTA. But these regional/bilateral level agreements improved on the plurilateral rules and implemented them more effectively. Enhancements at the regional level were then subsequently incorporated in the 1994 GPA plurilateral rules. The fact that rules on procurement are substantially about transparency means that the regional rules have facilitated trade rather than restricted it.

The procurement case study shows that this synergy between the regional and plurilateral/multilateral levels was particularly marked during the Uruguay Round negotiations. The fact that there were multilateral negotiations underway served as a reference point for negotiators and rule-making at the regional level. The case is special in the sense that it was characterised by very close EU-US cooperation. After the Uruguay Round the interaction between the regional and multilateral levels appears to have changed, with both the EU and US using the FTAs they negotiated to effectively increase the number of countries adopting the rules (1994 Government Procurement Agreement [GPA]) agreed to at the plurilateral level. In some cases, signature of the GPA is a condition for the EU and US concluding an FTA with the third party. In other cases, the rules on procurement in the FTAs are equivalent to the GPA.

The case of services in general and the case of telecommunications in particular exhibit some of the same features as procurement. These cases also show that the interaction between the levels of rule-making has tended to be synergistic, with, for example, developments at the regional/bilateral level facilitating more progress at the multilateral level. At the same time, multi-laterally/plurilaterally agreed rules, such as in the case of the Telecommunications Reference Paper under the GATS sector negotiations, have subsequently been used as the basis for RTA provisions on telecommunications.

The services sector more generally illustrates how the coverage of RTAs can be wider than multilateral rules. Sector commitments in services are often wider in RTAs than in the GATS. This is especially the case for NAFTA-type FTAs that use the negative list approach. The RTAs concluded by the EU tend to be more GATS compatible than GATS plus in terms of coverage. In the case of procurement, regional agreements tend to have greater coverage, including, for example, more entities such as the sub-national purchasing entities that were excluded from the coverage of the plurilateral rules. Here there is a clear case of regional preferences, but one that is likely to be subject to preference erosion over time as the coverage of the WTO rules is extended.

Investment and intellectual property rights

Finally, the cases of investment and intellectual property illustrate how regional level agreements can and are being used by dominant players to push a particular approach to rule-making.

The case of investment illustrates how a *de facto* international regime of investment rules can be created by means of a patchwork of rules at different levels (Reiter 2006). Similar to the procurement and services case study, investment shows how the bilateral, regional, plurilateral and multilateral levels have all played a role in establishing investment rules. In the case of investment, efforts to establish multilateral rules (for investment protection) go back to the 1920s and 1930s. In the 1950s and 1960s, bilateral investment treaties provided the model for investment protection agreements and the plurilateral OECD Codes the model for investment liberalisation agreements. In the 1980s, US-centred regional/bilateral agreements (i.e. NAFTA) provided the model for comprehensive agreements covering both investment protection and liberalisation. Finally, the multilateral level agreements on GATS and trade-related investment measures (TRIMs) provided rules for investment in services and performance requires (OECD 2004; UNCTAD 2004).

The investment case appears to show how sequential negotiations at different levels can be used to promote a particular model of investment rules. Thus, the US first established a comprehensive model for investment, covering investment protection as well as liberalisation in the NAFTA, before seeking to apply this model at the plurilateral level in the Multilateral Agreement on Investment (MAI) negotiations from 1996 to 1998. When the MAI failed, the US opted to promote the NAFTA model for investment rules in regional/bilateral agreements rather than in the multilateral setting of the WTO, because opposition from developing countries stood in the way of any high standard rules for investment in the WTO.

In contrast, the EU approach to investment rules has made less use of such sequential negotiations. First, the EU favoured negotiations in the WTO over the OECD in the late 1990s, and, second, it has not used RTAs or bilateral agreements to promote a coherent model for investment rules. This appears to be due to 'domestic' factors in the EU concerning competence over investment in international negotiations as much as anything else (Reiter 2006).

Compared to the procurement and telecoms cases, therefore, investment appears to be a case in which RTAs/bilaterals have been used as an alternative for those seeking a high standard for investment rules. RTAs are thus likely to detract from any efforts to agree to multilateral level rules that will inevitably be much more modest. The fact that a range of developing countries have been willing to sign up to RTAs that include investment while blocking any substantive progress in the WTO on a wider investment agreement has contributed to this strategic use of RTAs to push investment rules.

The case of intellectual property rights (IPR) is another instance in which binding multilateral rules were adopted during the Uruguay Round of negotiations. Existing international IPR standards in the World Intellectual Property Organization (WIPO) were integrated into the trading regime through the TRIPs agreement. The reasons why this integration should occur with IPR (and SPS) rather than in industrial, labour or the environment, where there were equally agreed international standards, was clearly due to pressure from sector interests in a number of key countries.

The intellectual property rights case raises questions as to the sustainability of the multilateral rules in this field. Similar to the SPS case, the TRIPs agreement in the Uruguay Round established binding rules of considerable scope, but, inevitably left a number of ambiguities. These ambiguities have been the substance of much subsequent debate and conflict. The details of this debate need not concern us here and have been adequately described elsewhere. But one of the implications of the Doha Declaration on TRIPs has been a growth in the TRIPs – plus provisions in RTAs. A close look at the substance of recent IPR provisions in RTAs suggests that these may be being used as a means of regaining some of the ground lost at the multilateral level in the sense of introducing binding interpretations of the rules favouring the owners of intellectual property rights. In other words, the major sectoral interests, such as in the pharmaceutical sector, have become disillusioned with the WTO following the Doha Declaration on TRIPs and how it has been interpreted, and have shifted the focus of their lobbying to FTAs. Here – as in the case of investment – one can therefore find elements of a more malign strategic use of multiple levels of rule-making which major interests switch between in order to further their own narrow agenda.

Assessing the benign and malign effects of regional/bilateral rule-making

All the policy areas summarised above show that the issue is not regionalism versus multilateralism, but that rule-making has always been multi-level and is likely to continue to be multi-level. It is certainly true that the role of regional (and bilateral) rule-making has increased in importance relative to plurilateral and multilateral levels, so the aim must be to determine what role the regional level plays, and in particular whether it is benign or malign.

Benign and malign effects of preferential rules

It is necessary to be clear about what is meant by benign and malign effects of RTAs in rule-making. The analytical framework provides a basis for assessing the impact of regional level rule-making.

First of all, rule-making in RTAs will tend to be benign if the margin of preference is limited and national preferences are not replaced by regional preferences in rules. From the discussion of the elements of any rules system, it was argued that transparency measures and cooperation arrangements are least likely to represent a form of preference, so agreements that emphasise such procedural measures are likely to be benign. Rules that improve transparency and due process in rule-making, both of which tend to promote better regulatory practices and reduce the scope for discretion and thus discrimination in regulation, are also benign. This is because better, more consistent and objective regulatory practices facilitate trade and investment with third countries as well as improving economic performance within the region.

Equally, RTA rules that facilitate trade and investment by replacing divergent national rules but do not set the common regulatory norms or standards at such a level as to restrict competition from third parties will also be benign. Those that set high standards could, on the contrary, be malign.

Finally, as a general rule of thumb, RTAs in which substantive provisions are consistent with generally agreed international standards will be benign whereas RTAs thus go significantly beyond the prevailing agreed rules to pose more of a risk. Jurisprudence or precedents set in implementation might also take effect and RTAs may also go beyond generally agreed international norms (or the interpretation of equivalent rules in the WTO), for example, in how to define the scope for regulatory safeguards or the right to regulate.

Regional rules that are benign for the trading system as a whole would be those that complement multilateral rules. This may take the form of regional agreements implementing principles adopted multilaterally. Often, however, regional initiatives are likely to be developed alongside wider multilateral rules. Here they could be said to be benign if there is synergy between the two levels of rule-making in which developments on one level enhance progress on the other level. Regional or preferential rules would also have a malign influence if they serve narrow vested interests by seeking to strengthen relative gains for one party over another rather than seek to establish an agreed framework of rules from which all can benefit. In the past, rule-making has been closely linked to market access and/or the interests of specific sector interests. For example, the TRIPs agreement at a multilateral level clearly served a narrow set of interests and is generally not seen to have achieved a sustainable balance between the interests of intellectual property right holders and consumers and health policy objectives. Rule-making initiatives to curb subsidies and to promote liberalisation of public procurement markets also served narrow sector interests, such as the US steel industry and the telecommunications and energy equipment sectors in the US. The fact that vested interests captured multilateral rule-making illustrates that the threat of such malign rule-making is not just one at the regional level.

Another example of rule-making that has a malign effect on the trading system as a whole is that which tends to lead towards 'regulatory regionalism'. Regulatory regionalism occurs when regional or preferential rules go beyond the existing agreed (WTO) rules, either in terms of substantive provisions in preferential agreements or how they are interpreted. The respective regional approaches then compete by ensuring that their preferred approach is included in future bilateral or regional agreements. Competition between the two approaches to rule-making is then conducted through preferential agreements. For example, it has been argued elsewhere that the European and North American approaches to rules in the field of SPS are divergent and that both the EU and US/Canada seek to promote their respective approaches through bilateral agreements with third countries (Isaac 2006).

Once again it depends on which elements of rule-making in the preferential agreements go beyond the WTO rules. If they go beyond the WTO in terms of the sectors or activities covered, then a preference is created, but one that will be subject to erosion, provided multilateral negotiations result in an extension of the multilateral coverage. Equally, if preferential rules exceed the WTO with regard to transparency, there is unlikely to be a threat to the system. It is mainly the area of substantive rules that pose a systemic threat. Interpretations of rules that diverge from the accepted multilateral interpretation may also pose a systemic threat.

Benign effects during the second phase of regionalism

The findings from recent research suggest that regional agreements during the period between the mid-1980s and mid-1990s had, on balance, a benign effect. In terms of the impact on third parties, regional agreements did not constitute much by way of a preference. National preferences do not appear to have been replaced by regional preferences. Rules were mostly in line with existing WTO rules and when they did go beyond the WTO this was predominantly in terms of coverage, closer cooperation, enhanced transparency and 'due process' rather than substantive measures.

This finding is consistent with the view that deep integration will be less discriminatory, but at odds with the image of a 'spaghetti bowl' of conflicting rules. The close interaction between rule-making at different levels would suggest that the appropriate analogy is 'lasagne' not spaghetti. In other words trade and investment rules are often built-up layer upon layer through decisions on the bilateral, regional, plurilateral and multilateral levels. There are a number of features of the mid-1980s to mid-1990s period that may have contributed to this generally benign impact of RTAs in the field of rule-making.

First, it was a period shaped by a liberal paradigm in which progressive liberalisation at the regional and other levels went hand-in-hand. Second, the rule-making at the RTA and bilateral level during the late 1980s and early 1990s could draw on a reservoir of norms and approaches developed in the (plurilateral) OECD. In all the cases reported on, the OECD provided the source of norms and rules. Third, regional rule-making occurred against the background of active multilateral negotiations on new rule-making. This appears to have acted as a real constraint on negotiators, who went to considerable lengths to ensure that the regional initiatives were consistent with the emerging multilateral rules. This was clearly shown in the cases of services, TBTs and public procurement, although to a lesser degree for investment due to the absence of any negotiation on comprehensive investment rules at a multilateral level. Fourth, it was a period in which there was close cooperation between the EU and US. Indeed, the Uruguay Round was, like the previous Tokyo Round of the GATT, characterised by the central importance of the transatlantic negotiations. This was especially the case with regard to rule-making in which the US and EU were the main protagonists.

Less benign effects post Uruguay Round

Comparing the 'second phase' of regionalism with the period after the end of the Uruguay Round, one comes to a less benign balance on the impact of regional and preferential agreements. In the policy areas discussed above there are a number of indicators that preferential agreements are being used to promote the interests of the 'selfish' hegemon by going beyond the prevailing international rules or indeed by seeking to undermine agreed international rules.

Investment illustrates how a series of bilateral free trade agreements have extended NAFTA-type rules to a range of US trading partners. These rules combine high standards of investment protection, negative list liberalisation of investment and tough rules on performance requirements with investor-state dispute settlement. These provisions go well beyond existing agreed multilateral rules. In the case of public procurement, bilateral free trade agreements are being used by both the EU and US to increase the number of countries signing up to GPA-type rules, because the public procurement provisions in these bilateral agreements are essentially based on the GPA. At least in this case the GPA represents a set of agreed rules even if they were only agreed by a core group of countries.

In terms of the systemic effects of the post-Uruguay Round agreements, there must be some concern that regional and other preferential agreements are being used to push divergent regional approaches. In the case of TBTs, differences between the US and EU approaches have not had much impact because of the difficulties making rapid progress in this field. The EU has not made as much progress towards concluding mutual recognition agreements with its major trading partners because of the ambition of the EU approach and the reluctance of its trading partners, including the US, to cede regulatory sovereignty. But in SPS there are two distinct regulatory approaches being promoted at all levels of negotiation. In the public procurement case, the EU and US approaches are in fact very close – so close indeed that Mexico has been able to conclude agreements with both the EU and the US (within NAFTA) covering public procurement without having to adopt different rules. In the case of investment, the US is pressing ahead with its NAFTA standard of high levels of investment protection and liberal rules for foreign direct investment in its bilateral FTAs. Here, it has had some success in having this approach adopted by other countries, such as Mexico and Singapore, that are pursuing region hub strategies and wish to attract foreign investment. The EU has not included significant investment rules in its bilateral agreements because of 'domestic' issues within the EU. But if the EU were to include investment it would probably use a more modest framework based on positive listing for coverage, conventional expropriation clauses (rather than the 'regulatory taking' type clause) in the NAFTA model and eschew investor state dispute settlement.

A US-EU comparison

There has been much general debate about the respective US and EU approaches to preferential/bilateral agreements and what motivates the respective policies, but there has been much less discussion of the substance of the US and EU preferential agreements. Detailed differences exist in each of the policy areas that have been covered by recent studies.[5] Detailed differences can be very important. For example, the North American and European approaches to the regulation of biotechnology are in general terms very similar, but differences on how to interpret 'precaution' in regulating products have been enough to create major problems.

Aside from the detailed differences, it is possible to identify some general differences between the EU and US approaches to RTAs/bilateral agreements. There are some general differences between the European and US approaches to rule-making in RTAs, as well as some detailed but important differences in their respective approaches in each of the case studies covered here. In general terms, the EU appears to adopt a more comprehensive approach to rule-making with more extensive rules covering more aspects of policy, and the development and use of international standards in most policy areas. The US, on the other hand, tends to favour a policed, non-discrimination approach consisting of framework rules backed up by extensive enforcement provisions that facilitate private access to judicial reviews. The stress on private access to reviews is illustrated in the bid challenge rule for public procurement first introduced in the CUSFTA and investor–state dispute settlement in NAFTA. This, of course, is the approach used in the US for its domestic regulatory reviews and remedies.

Prescription

Finally, there is the question of what this all means in terms of policy. The first general conclusion with relevance to the policy debate is that RTAs can be good or bad when it comes to rule-making, just as they can be good or bad in terms of tariff preferences, such as in trade creation or diversion. It all depends on the substance of the specific RTA and how it interacts with other levels of rule-making.

The conclusion that multilateral or plurilateral negotiations serve to constrain negotiators of RTAs who ensure conformity as much as possible, would argue for effective multilateral negotiations on rules. At present, this is not happening and the DDA has dropped new rule-making agenda items in a search for consensus among the developed and developing country members of the WTO. If multilateral rule-making is blocked because of the difficulties finding a consensus among all the WTO members, then plurilateral approaches would offer a second-best option. The negotiation of plurilateral rules on some of the issues covered in this volume will be second best because they will exclude some countries, but agreement among a core group of major economies on the kinds of norms that should form the basis of rule-making would be better than leaving rule-making to the bilateral or regional level. To neglect international rule-making risks seeing the emergence of competing regional systems of rules as the dominant players use bilateral or regional level negotiations to establish their own, possibly divergent systems. While dropping new rule-making from the DDA may be expedient in the short term, rule-making at the plurilateral or multilateral level cannot be neglected for too long without risking competing systems developing that will be difficult, if not impossible, to reconcile in the future. Divergent systems of rules will then undermine multilateralism.

If formal binding agreements are not possible in multilateral or plurilateral negotiations, there should at least be efforts to find convergence on the core regulatory approaches and norms, as for example, the various networks in the field of competition policy are seeking to do. As the case studies discussed here have shown, such agreed norms can provide the basis for rule-making over decades.

In terms of how RTAs might be structured in order to promote benign rather than malign effects, the conclusions that might be drawn from the case studies are that regional rules that promote transparency and cooperation are unlikely to represent much of a preference if any and are unlikely to pose much of a threat to the trading system. RTAs that go beyond agreed multilateral rules in terms of coverage, such as sector coverage or coverage of more entities represent a preference, but a preference that one can expect to be eroded over time, provided work continues on international rule-making. Therefore such provisions in an RTA may have some impact on third parties, but do not pose a long-term systemic threat to the system.

Systemic threat would be expected to come from RTAs that go beyond existing substantive rules. Therefore this kind of provision in an RTA should be looked at carefully in any scrutiny process such as in the Committee on Regional Trade Agreements (CRTA) in the WTO. Substantive provisions in RTAs should therefore make use of existing agreed international standards, such as those of the ISO, Codex or agreed standards for intellectual property, etc. Unless such rules are used, there will be little incentive for governments to put resources into developing international standards and regulatory norms.

The approach proposed here is therefore to break down regional rule-making into its component elements in order to assess their impact. Such an approach could then help to develop criteria that could result in operational criteria for the work of the CRTA of the WTO and in particular help with the question of how to assess 'other restrictions to commerce' under Article XXIV of the GATT.

Finally, the major protagonists in rule-making should seek to cooperate more closely. In the past, US-EU cooperation was sufficient to ensure that the broad approaches adopted were consistent. But transatlantic regulatory cooperation is not what it was, despite repeated attempts to strengthen the bilateral dialogue. But if the transatlantic cooperation is no longer sufficient, it will be necessary to reach out to include other major economies, including developing economies, in effective negotiations or dialogue on rules. This will mean setting more modest objectives for rule-making even to achieve plurilateral agreements.

Notes

1 In this context, a benign impact is defined as one that contributes to a predictable framework of rules for trade and investment and one in which regional and bilateral approaches are broadly consistent with multilateral rules. A malign impact is then one in which regional or bilateral agreements are used to promote rules that benefit the narrow vested interests of one or more of the signatories, such as the use of bilateral rules by selfish hegemons to shape rules in their narrow self-interest.

2 Among the first studies of whether RTAs go beyond the WTO were OECD (2002); and Sampson and Woolcock (2003).
3 With suitable econometric models one might well be able to estimate the real trade-creating and trade-diverting effects of such common rules
4 The case studies are drawn from a number of recent sources. There are general compilations of case studies assessing the role of regional agreements in rule-making. See OECD (2002); Sampson and Woolcock (2003); and Woolcock (2006). In addition, there have been a number of studies looking at the role of regional agreements in specific policy areas. These are cited at the relevant points.
5 Official reports such as those produced by the OECD or WTO tend to avoid any direct comparison of US and EU approaches. For a more comprehensive comparison, see Woolcock (2006).

References

Baldwin, Richard (1993) 'A Domino Theory of Regionalism', National Bureau of Economic Research (NBER), *Working Paper*, no. 4465, September.
—— (1997) 'The Causes of Regionalism', *The World Economy*, 20(7): 865–88.
—— (2000) 'Regulatory Protectionism, Developing Nations and a Two-Tier World Trade System', Centre for Economic Policy Research (CEPR), *Discussion Papers*, no. 2574.
—— and Venables, A. (1996) 'Regional Economic Integration', in G.M. Grossman and K. Rogoff (eds) *Handbook of International Economics*, vol. III, North Holland: Elsevier.
Bhagwati, Jagdish (1991) *The World Trading System at Risk*, Princeton, NJ: Princeton University Press.
—— and Kreuger, Anne O. (1995) *The Dangerous Drift to Preferential Trade Agreements*, Washington, DC: American Enterprise Institute Press.
—— Krishna, Pravin and Panagariya, Arvind (1999) *Trading Blocs: Alternative Approaches to Analyzing Preferential Trade Agreements*, Cambridge, MA: MIT Press.
Blank, Annet and Marceau, Gabrielle (1997) 'A History of Multilateral Negotiations on Procurement: From ITO to WTO', in B. Hoekman and P. Mavroidi (eds) *Law and Policy in Public Purchasing: The WTO Agreement on Government Procurement*, Ann Arbor, MI: Michigan University Press.
Chen, Maggie Xiaoyang and Mattoo, Aaditya (2004) 'Regionalism in Standards: Good or Bad for Trade?' World Bank, *Policy Research Working Paper* no. 3458, November.
Estevadeordal, A. and Suominen, K. (2003) 'Rules of Origin in the World Trading System', paper prepared for the seminar on regional trade agreements and the WTO, 14 November.
European Commission (1985) *Communication from the Commission to the Council on Technical Harmonization and Standards: A New Approach*, COM(85) 19 final.
Evenett, Simon and Hoekman, Bernard (2004) 'Government Procurement: Market Access, Transparency and Multilateral Trade Rules', World Bank, *Policy Research Working Paper*, no. 3195, January.
Feinberg, Richard (2003) 'The Political Economy of United States' Free Trade Arrangements', *The World Economy*, 26(7): 1019–40.
Garay, Luis and De Lombaerde, Jorge Philippe (2006) 'Preferential Rules of Origin: Models and Levels of Rule-making', in S. Woolcock (ed.) *Trade and Investment*

Rule-making: The Role of Bilateral and Regional Agreements, Tokyo: UN University Press.

Grossman, G. and Helpman, E. (1995) 'The Politics of Free Trade Arrangement', *American Economic Review*, 85: 667–90.

Irwin, Douglas A. (1993) 'Multilateral and Bilateral Trade Policies in the World Trading System', in J. De Melo and A. Panagariya (eds) *New Dimensions in Regional Integration*, Cambridge: Cambridge University Press.

Isaac, Grant (2003) 'Sanitary and Phytosanitary Measures' in G. Sampson and S. Woolcock (eds) *Multilateralism and Regional Integration Agreements: The Recent Experience*, Tokyo: UN University Press.

—— (2006) 'Sanitary and Phytosanitary Measures' in S. Woolcock (ed.) *Trade and Investment Rule-making: The Role of Bilateral and Regional Agreements*, Tokyo: UN University Press.

Joerges, Christian *et al.* (1998) ' "Delegation" and European Polity: The Law's Problems with the Role of Standardisation Organisations in European Legislation', paper for the conference, 'The Political Economy of Standards Setting', European University Institute, Florence, 4–5 June.

—— (1999) 'Are Preferential Trading Arrangements Trade Liberalizing or Protectionist?' *Journal of Economic Perspectives*, 13(4): 105–24.

Krueger, Ann (1993) 'Free Trade Agreements as Protectionist Devices: Rules of Origin', National Bureau of Economic Research (NBER), *Working Paper*, no. 4352.

Lawrence, Robert (1995) *Regionalism, Multilateralism and Deep Integration*, Washington, DC: Brookings Institute.

Mattoo, Aaditya and Fink, Carsten (2002) 'Regional Agreements and Trade in Services: Policy Issues', paper for the WTO Seminar, April.

Organisation for Economic Co-operation and Development (2000) *Standardisation and Regulatory Reform: Selected Cases*, TD/TC/WP(99) 47 final, Paris: OECD.

—— (2002) *Regional Trade Agreements and the Multilateral Trading System*, Paris: OECD, November.

—— (2004) *Relationships between International Investment Agreements*, Paris: OECD, May.

Pugatch, Meir (2004) 'The International Regulation of IPRs in TRIPs and TRIPs *Plus* Worlds', paper for the UNU CRIS/LSE workshop on the interaction between levels of rule-making in trade and investment, Brussels, December. Available at: www.lse.ac.uk/collections/internationaltradepolicyunit.

Reiter, Joakim (2006) 'Investment', in S. Woolcock (ed.) *Trade and Investment Rule-making: The Role of Bilateral and Regional Agreements*, Tokyo: UN University Press.

Sampson, Gary and Woolcock, Stephen (eds) (2003) *Multilateralism and Regional Integration Agreements: The Recent Experience*, Toyko: UN University Press.

Schott, Jeffrey (ed.) (2004) *Free Trade Agreements: US Strategies and Priorities*, Washington, DC: Institute for International Economics.

Trachtmann, J. (2002) 'Toward Open Regionalism? Standardization and Regional Integration Under Article XXIV of GATT', *Journal of International Economic Law*, 6(2): 459–92.

Ullrich, Heidi (2004) 'Assessing the Interaction between Multiple Levels of Rule-Making in Trade in Telecommunications Services', paper for the UNU CRIS/ LSE Workshop on the interaction between levels of rule-making in trade and investment, Brussels, December. Available at: http://www.lse.ac.uk/collections/internationalTradePolicyUnit/Events/December2004/TelecomsServices.doc

UNCTAD (2004) *International Investment Agreements: Key Issues*, vol. I, UNCTAD/IIE/IIT/2004/10, December.

Winters, Alan (1996) 'Assessing Regional Integration Arrangements', World Bank, *Policy Research Working Paper*, no. 1687.

Woolcock, Stephen (ed.) (2006) *Trade and Investment Rule-making: The Role of Bilateral and Regional Agreements*, Tokyo: UN University Press.

World Bank (2005) *Global Economic Prospects: Trade, Regionalism and Development*, Washington, DC: World Bank.

World Trade Organization (WTO) (2005) 'The Changing Landscape of Regional Trade Agreements', *WTO Working Paper*, no. 8.

7 No safe havens

Labour, regional integration and globalisation

Robert O'Brien

Introduction

Labour is both central and peripheral to regional integration. It is central because the conditions under which labour works and the ability of business groups to access particular types of labour are integral components of regional economic agreements. Indeed, one could build a regional integration typology based upon provisions for labour rights and mobility. This would have the European Union (EU) with some common labour rights and representation on one end of the spectrum and Asia Pacific Economic Cooperation (APEC) at the opposite end, because it only deals with labour issues under the heading of human resources. Labour is also central to the regional project because migration patterns and investment strategies are working at the non-state level to bind regions together.

At another level, however, labour is peripheral to regional integration projects because labour rights are often undermined and the lives of individual workers are placed at risk by the form that regional integration takes. Labour as a commodity is of utmost concern to the designers of inter-state regional integration projects, but labour as a political actor and the interests it articulates are marginalised and undermined.

In order to come to some conclusion about the relationship between labour, regional integration and globalisation, this chapter examines regional integration both in its formal institutionalised sense and its informal incarnation. Many regional integration analysts (Gamble and Payne 1996) prefer to use the terms 'regionalism' to capture state agreements and 'regionalisation' for the activity of other actors, but these two terms are easily confused and not as accurate descriptively as 'formal' and 'informal'. The term formal refers to the official inter-state treaties that set out the rules and procedures of regional integration. This includes agreements such as the North American Free Trade Agreement (NAFTA) and elaborate political structures such as the EU. The informal aspect of regional integration refers to the activity of non-state actors which bind regions together by their behaviour. This includes the activity of transnational investors and the movement of economic migrants. Their actions may or may not be effectively governed by state regulation, but they also contribute to regional integration and have a role in influencing labour's condition.

The aim of this chapter is to reply to the questions: Do regions act as a space for labour groups to defend their interests in an era of globalisation? and Do regions make a positive difference for labour? The analysis is advanced in five stages. First, key terms are defined because they can be used in a number of contradictory ways. These terms are regions and regional integration, globalisation and labour. Second, the theoretical approach to understanding regional integration is outlined. The approach of 'Everyday IPE' (International Political Economy) is contrasted to elite-focused interpretations of regional integration such as state-centric theories in the realist or liberal international relations traditions. The third section gives an overview of some of the key elements of formal inter-state regional integration agreements and their implications for labour. The effect of these agreements is, similar to much globalisation, to shift the relative balance of power between capital and labour by dramatically entrenching corporate rights with minor changes in labour rights. The fourth section considers the implications of labour migration and political mobilisation as elements of informal regional integration. The chapter concludes by reconsidering the relationship between regionalisation and globalisation, as well as the implications of regionalisation for labour in a globalising world. It argues that regions do not act as a safe haven for labour. If anything, regions accentuate the competitive pressure channelled through the globalisation process.

It is an overly ambitious task to give an overview of all the regions of the world. This is a short chapter and the author's understanding of several regions is preliminary, at best. Rather than offering detailed regional case studies, the focus will be on the Americas, Europe and parts of the Asia-Pacific region to the degree that they are relevant for the argument. Regrettably, this reproduces a weakness of existing literature which neglects many useful experiences outside of the European and American models (Söderbaum 2005). Operating at this macro level runs the risk of overgeneralisation. Further research will be required to determine whether the propositions advanced here are justified or not.

Key concepts

The term region has been used to refer to a wide range of spaces all the way from the hinterlands of cities to the large number of countries touching the Pacific Ocean. It is an imprecise term and its use requires some clarification (Schmitt-Egner 2002). In this chapter, regional integration refers to activity that spans macro regions such as Europe, North America, Latin America, Southeast Asia and the Asia-Pacific region. It refers both to the creation of international agreements between states (formal regional integration) and the activities of non-state actors such as migrants or transnational corporations (informal regional integration). This focus does not imply that other types of regions are unimportant. It simply highlights the author's own interest in macro regions and their interaction with global processes.

Globalisation means many different things to many different people. Here, the concept is used to refer to processes that can be either transworld or supraterritorial (Scholte 2005). Transworld processes are those that span the macro regions analysed in this chapter. They need not be universal, but they should impact all of the continents. Supraterritorial processes refer to those that are relatively unencumbered by geographic space. Examples include the internet or telecommunications. In the context of this chapter, globalisation refers both to worldwide flow of goods, services, people, money and ideas, as well as the world-spanning creation of political authority that governs that activity, such as the World Trade Organization (WTO).

It is also necessary to clarify what is meant by labour in this chapter. 'Labour' refers to a wide range of people acting in their capacity as workers (O'Brien 2005). It includes workers organised in unions and engaged in bargaining with firms and states. In some states such unions may be autonomous, acting on the instructions of their members. In other states the unions may be penetrated by state or party officials and adopt a relatively passive role. Most people are familiar with the existence of organised workers in the form of unions. However, these categories of workers only make up a small percentage of the labour force. Labour also refers to the majority of people who can be classified as 'unprotected workers' (Harrod 1987). These vulnerable people labour in forms of work which receive little union, political party or state protection from power holders. Examples of such workers are people engaged in subsistence agriculture, peasants working for landholders, informal sector workers forced to scavenge employment on the streets and workers within the household (usually women and children). Most migrants also work under such conditions.

Theorising regions and globalisation

Studies of regionalisation and globalisation operate from a variety of theoretical perspectives and concerns. From realist or power politics viewpoints the primary concern is the impact that regionalism has on state power and the pursuit of 'national interest'. More liberal approaches are concerned with the development of cooperation between states in the political field or increasing efficiency in the economic realm (Söderbaum 2005).

This chapter begins from a different starting point, a concern about the relationship between regionalism, globalisation and the conditions under which non-elite people work and live. Its purpose is to develop understanding about the implications of the regionalism-globalism dynamic for labour. It is written for people concerned with such issues, rather than people wanting to understand state or corporate policy-making. Instead of focusing upon elite regulation of the global economy, attention is paid to what Hobson and Seabrooke call 'Everyday IPE' (Hobson and Seabrooke n.d.). Everyday IPE begins by examining the condition and agency of the bottom 90 per cent of the world's population, which is usually glossed over or ignored by regulatory (mainstream) IPE.

Implicit in this approach is the assumption that state 'interests' are often the articulation of particular groups' desires rather than the general interests of the societies they govern. This position does not deny that state elites can approach regional integration in a strategic manner as theorised by realist or neoliberal institutionalist studies. However, everyday IPE goes further in arguing that interstate arrangements have intended unequal distributional implications within and across states. Thus, regional agreements may not be in the broader general interests of the societies which they join together. This is contrary to many rationalist approaches which start from the premise that state actors are acting in the national interest.

Another difference in this approach to international political economy is that it locates agency in a large number of places in addition to the state or corporate elites. Non-elites influence political and economic structures through proposing alternative arrangements, resisting dominant powers or, alternatively, complying with more powerful interests. Thus, contrary to a perspective which ignores labour or sees it as a passive recipient of elite projects, this approach locates agency in labour, as well as in capital and state forces (Herod 1997; O'Brien 2000). Labour groups and labourers influence the course of regional integration by opposing particular projects, proposing alternatives or bolstering regional links through migration and transnational political mobilisation.

After investigating formal and informal regional integration below, the chapter's conclusion will consider implications of this approach for theorising the relationship between globalisation and regionalisation.

Formal regional integration

Assessing the implications of inter-state regional economic agreements requires two steps. First, the provision or non-provision of labour issues within and around the agreements needs to be judged. Second, these provisions should be compared to the institutional arrangements for other interests, such as investors.

We begin our survey in one of the least elaborate regional agreements, APEC (Asia-Pacific Economic Cooperation). A lack of consensus about the degree of institutionalisation for APEC resulted in an inability of participants to even agree if it should be called an organisation or agreement. Not surprisingly, given this low degree of institutionalisation, APEC exists primarily as a forum for discussion and coordination. While attempts have been made to liberalise trade and capital flows in the region, labour rights have been avoided. Labour issues have gradually crept on to APEC's agenda under the guise of human resource management (Haworth and Hughes 2002). Trade unions have pushed for the issue of labour rights to be considered as part of APEC's activities, but even the discussion of tripartite arrangements has been halting as the majority of states remain opposed to dealing with labour in any context other than training or increasing competitiveness (Price 2000). Labour is seen to be relevant only to the degree that it can be mobilised for state and corporate competitiveness.

The focus on labour compliance to the competitive state/business agenda also marks ASEAN's (the Association of Southeast Asian Nations) approach. ASEAN Labour Ministers or officials have met on an annual basis since 1975 (eight years after its founding). Since 2001, they have been joined by labour officials from China, Korea and Japan. The ASEAN vision for labour is of a well-educated, productive workforce. ASEAN communications and work plans focus upon human resource development and fail to mention labour rights.

Another element of ASEAN's approach is a respect for national sovereignty. Each state is encouraged to find its own 'culturally appropriate' path for developing its human resources (ASEAN 2000). Its unwillingness to press member states on basic labour rights was highlighted when ASEAN held its 13th Labour Ministers conference in Myanmar (Burma). Burma's record on forced labour is so outrageous that it holds the dubious distinction of being the only country the International Labour Organization (ILO) has asked member states to sanction by reviewing and reconsidering all their economic relations with the country. The ASEAN Burma meeting communiqué did not mention the issue of forced labour. ASEAN has similarly been unwilling to address the serious issue of mistreatment of migrant workers within and across its borders.

An alternative strategy to ignoring labour rights is to pre-empt transnational regulation by relying upon national enforcement of national standards. This is evident in North America's economic constitution, NAFTA. In an effort to blunt public criticism in the United States during the negotiation of NAFTA, labour and environmental side accords were added to the agreement. The resulting North American Agreement on Labour Cooperation (NAALC) was particularly weak in two areas. First, rather than harmonising standards upwards to create new robust continental standards, the side accord simply urged the three signatories (Canada, the United States and Mexico) to faithfully apply existing laws. Second, the scope of issues in which governments may be fined was severely limited. Relevant violations are confined to the issues of minimum wage, child labour and health and safety. The core labour rights of freedom of association, collective bargaining, and freedom from discrimination are not covered by this 'hard law' section of the agreement (Compa 2001). The core enabling rights can be the subject of discussion, but not enforcement. Even for the enforceable standards, states must be shown to have tolerated a persistent pattern of failing to enforce regulation in these areas.

While the NAALC has stimulated substantial cross-border union activity, its limited legal and practical impact pales in comparison to the corporate rights enshrined in NAFTA (Ayers 2004). The most dramatic of these is NAFTA's 'Chapter 11', which gives corporations the right to sue member governments in the event that public policy initiatives threaten corporate profits. This subordinates public policy initiatives to a legal corporate veto if the public interest legislation threatens corporate profits.

Moving beyond NAFTA to a regional agreement in the Americas, which is often put forward as a more social democratic model, we find similar imbalances in the Common Market of the South or Mercosur. Mercosur was founded in 1991 with the aim of creating a common market between Brazil, Argentina, Paraguay, and Uruguay. Originally Mercosur did not make any provision for labour rights. It was only after trade union agitation that a working group (Subgroup 11, subsequently changed to Subgroup 10) was set up on 'Labour relations, employment and social security'. The subgroup provided a forum for discussion of labour issues and the development of recommendations to member states. For example, it has recommended that governments ratify basic ILO conventions (Weeks 2000). Later initiatives have included a Socio-Labor Declaration and a Social-Labor Commission (da Motta Veiga and Lengyel 2003). Both of these vehicles have been created in lieu of a more compulsory and wide-ranging Social Charter. While these institutions do conduct some useful work on minimum standard setting, they are advisory rather than enforcement institutions. In contrast to the freedom of movement guaranteed to investors, this is not very useful protection.

European integration has always contained a more social democratic and explicitly political element than other integration projects, but progress on labour issues still faces large obstacles. The rejuvenation of the European project in the mid-1980s centred on the liberalisation of economic activity required to build a single market. The strict deflationary discipline of the Maastricht Treaty and implementation of intrusive national requirements for monetary union contrast with an EU Social Protocol which left national regulation of labour affairs largely intact (Stevis 2002). Despite this imbalance, some progress on labour issues has been made. Social directives on parental leave, and part-time and contract work have improved many workers' rights. In addition, a prominent institutional innovation has been the initiation of European Works Councils (EWCs) (Wills 2004). The EWC Directive of 1994 required that all companies of more than 1,000 employers that had at least 150 located in more than one country establish a forum for consulting employees across Europe. These forums have enjoyed different rates of success. While they have provided workers with a chance to communicate with each other and gain information, they are a long distance from facilitating transnational collective bargaining.

These developments must be offset against the general trend of elevating and legalising liberal economic practices at the regional level while subordinating employment and welfare policies (Scharpf 2002). The regional integration project has taken away a whole series of policy instruments that states might use to influence employment levels, but has provided only meagre compensatory mechanisms for states. Examples include adjusting exchange rates, capital controls, blocking imports, using the public sector and state aids (subsidies) for employment creation or regional development. This forces states to turn to supply side strategies of restructuring the labour market through deregulation (flexibility in the language of its advocates). In addition, the prioritising of liberalisation on a continental basis runs the risk of EU legal measures undermining state provision of social services. For example, is it fair from a competitive perspective that private corporations are prevented from providing social services in some EU states? The European Court of Justice has not yet ruled on the issue, but given the existing domination of the regional drive for competitive practices, such a threat is possible.

While European workers feel the pressure for labour deregulation at the national level and defences at the regional level have been meagre, voluntary global initiatives are used as an excuse not to act on a European basis. For example, when EU bureaucrats, in the wake of the Enron scandal, proposed that corporate social responsibility (CSR) should be pursued through EU regulations, the European Roundtable of Industrialists (ERT) and the Union of Industrial and Employers' Confederations of Europe (UNICE) both argued that such regulation was unnecessary given the existence of global initiatives such as the Global Compact and the Organisation for Economic Co-operation and Development (OECD) Guidelines (along with the ILO Tripartite Declaration) (Greenwood 2003).

The point here is not that labour provisions of regional agreements are useless. Hopeful analysts find some benefit in weak agreements such as the NAALC (Compa 2001; Teague 2003). However, the advances in labour rights are so minimal in contrast to the entrenching of corporate rights that one must conclude that these agreements are shifting the balance even further away from labour to capital. This is true even in the European case where some gains in worker rights are overshadowed by a general drift to increased labour flexibility and the erosion of rights and universal services (Bieler 2006).

While trade unions have generally been opposed to the neoliberal thrust of regional integration, this has varied according to the degree to which particular unions enjoyed state protections and to the ideology of the unions themselves. Unions from countries with relatively poor labour protection have tended to see possible benefits in regional integration while those enjoying more protection see more costs. For example, Mexican unions have tended to be more favourable to the NAALC than US or Canadian unions. While Mexican workers occasionally use the side accord to publicise their plight, Canadian and US unions have now concluded that the side accord is useless for their purposes. In Europe, British unions favoured the EU as an escape from poor domestic protection while Swedish unions have been much more sceptical.

Given the nature of regional integration agreements it may even be difficult to imagine what more balanced regulation would entail. Labour groups have pressed for social clauses which guarantee fundamental core rights such as freedom of association and collective bargaining. A labour-friendly arrangement could guarantee the right to organise, bargain and strike. The right to strike without intimidation from employers or security forces would go some way to match the mobility of capital and investors' rights provided by regional integration agreements. What a distance that is from today's capital and trade liberalisation deals!

Is this process substantially different from what takes place on a transworld basis? The precise arrangements are different but both reflect a form of 'selective regulation' (O'Brien 1998). Selective regulation refers to a system of interstate regulation which entails elaborate mechanisms and enforcement procedures for corporate rights and weak or non-existent mechanisms for social rights. It is economic regulation, but only in selective areas. Global institutions created since the second wave of regionalism in the 1980s marginalise labour issues. A good example is the contrast between the ILO and the WTO. The ILO is a much older institution with an elaborate organisational arrangement for promoting workers' rights, but little ability to enforce its standards. In contrast, the WTO has moved to strict enforcement of intellectual property rights on behalf of transnational corporations (TNCs) (Sell 2003). This mirrors the uneven treatment accorded to investor and worker rights at the regional level. Economic globalisation and regionalisation both require increased economic regulation to create and maintain the rules of the global marketplace. Business has been largely successful in shaping that regulation so it furthers corporate rights but does not strengthen the rights of other non-state actors (such as labour unions).

If formal regional integration has strengthened the hand of business and weakened labour rights, what has been the experience in the informal realm?

Informal regional integration

Regions are not just the creation of inter-state agreements. For example, some regions' inter-state arrangements are relatively modest but they have significant connections through direct foreign investment. Labour activity also plays a role in binding regions together. From a labour perspective there are two elements that are most significant. The first is migration and the second is transnational political mobilisation.

Many regional integration agreements pay little attention to the issue of migration. It is absent from agreements in Asia and provision for easier travel for economic purposes in NAFTA is restricted to business travellers. The case is different for common markets such as the EU, which are designed to facilitate the mobility of all factors of production including labour.

The relationship between formal regional integration and migration patterns is not clear and has been the subject of some dispute. For example, in the run-up to the negotiation of NAFTA, partisans set out two different projections. One side argued that NAFTA would strengthen the Mexican economy and thus reduce the supply of Mexican migrants while other groups suggested that the inequalities between the countries would widen and migration pressure would increase. Closer examination of the issue indicates that NAFTA, by itself, has very little impact on migration changes. NAFTA institutionalises capital mobility and encourages transnational competition which does have an impact. However, the most significant factor is the under-lying production regimes in the US and Mexico which encourage Mexican migrants to seek employment in the US (Canales 2000). The process of struc-tural adjustment and emphasis on export processing zones has increased insecurity in the Mexican labour market and brought new sectors of the Mexican population into the flow of migrants. In the US a polarisation of the labour market has led to a large increase in low wage occupations in the service and manufacturing sectors, self-employment and day labour. This has increased the supply of employment available for migrant workers.

In the case of migration in Asia, one sees different patterns at the regional and global levels. More skilled and professional labour flows out of the region (e.g. Indian IT specialists, Filipino nurses to the US) while unskilled or lower skilled labour moves within regions such as Southeast and East Asia. This labour is treated as a disposable asset which can be returned when no longer needed. Traditional sources of female migrant labour from the Philippines have come under increased pressure as new sources of female labour become available. Thus, Filipino domestic workers are being replaced by cheaper and less well-organised migrants from Vietnam, Indonesia and Sri Lanka (Piper 2004).

A central element of the migration story is the tremendously important role that remittances are now playing in the global economy. A few statistics from the Americas illustrates the point: In 2003, the value of remittances (mainly from the US) to Latin America exceeded all combined foreign direct investment and official development assistance to the region (IDB 2004). For Mexico, remittances were only exceeded by oil as a source of foreign earnings. In El Salvador the earnings of Salvadorans in the US exceeded the country's GDP!

The increase in the significance of remittances is worrying. While it is evidence of some wealth redistribution from North to South and it provides some individuals and families with a better life, it is a sign of economic failure. People leave their own countries because of poor economic pros-pects. The money they send home as remittances provides some relief in the short run but it often results in a development trap (Ellerman 2005). The communities that migrants leave come to depend upon remittances for sur-vival, but little local prosperity is generated. A generation after remittances begin to flow the communities are often as poor as they were before the migrants left. Increasing migration patterns are reinforcing a North–South divide, whereby citizens of Southern countries engage in employment activi-ties and conditions unacceptable for citizens of developed states. In an age of easier migration the difference is that the workers must now engage in long distance travel and endure lengthy separation from their families and communities.

It is possible that migration issues could offer an opening for labour groups to challenge existing regional and global integration projects. To date, regional discussion on migration issues have been framed in terms of controlling criminal activity or liberal human rights (access to social service, freedom from detention) (Pellerin 1999). However, the persuasive abuse of migrants can raise issues about the economic contradictions which force and sustain such flows and treatment. They also raise issues about the relationship between citizens within regions and the distribution of citizenship rights. Large-scale migrations such as Hispanics into the US may also change the nature of politics and allow for a redefinition of national interest in the integration process. The mobilisation of undocumented workers and Latinos in the US against changes to immigration and employment laws in the Spring of 2006 may be evidence of such a trend (Flaccus 2006).

The creation of regional economic agreements and the movement of business activity across state borders have also generated transnational labour political organisation. Some analysis of the role of trade unions in regional integration derives the possibility of labour agency directly from the structure of regional integration itself. For example, Abbott's comparative study of regional trade unions in Europe and the Asia-Pacific regions argues that European trade unions moved from ideological to political imperatives as the European Union developed out of the European Economic Community (Abbott 2000). In contrast, he argues that the lack of political institutions dooms Asian regional trade unions to focus upon ideological, rather than political or industrial concerns. In this context ideological concerns are used to refer to strategies which rely upon advocating particular norms of behaviour in order to rally support.

While there is no doubt that some trade union activity is heavily conditioned by what social movement theorists (Tarrow 1998) would call the political opportunity structures of regional integration, an overly deterministic view is unwarranted. Of course, trade unions do respond to the structures of regional political institutions. In Europe, the European Trade Union Confederation has a symbiotic relationship with the institutions of the European Union. In the Asia-Pacific region, the International Confederation of Free Trade Unions (ICFTU) had to create a new organisation (the Asia-Pacific Labour Network) to mirror APEC because its existing regional organisations covered only one side of the Pacific or the other. The NAALC has fostered increasing interchange between unions in North America as they seek to use its meagre provisions to cope with transnational business activities.

However, responding predictably to the structure and content of formal integration arrangements is only one element of the story. Labour groups continue to exercise choice about their responses. Thus, while it is true that unions in sectors exposed to intra-European competition are more likely to opt for European solutions, it is also true that there are a wide variety of trade union positions within trade sensitive and non-sensitive sectors (Bieler 2005). Some labour groups in similar situations choose to transnationalise and others do not. The increased competitive pressure brought on by regional and global competition has prompted some unions and labour groups to seek out alternative models and responses. Returning to the example of Asia, Abbott's analysis of the ICFTU's Asian and Pacific Regional Organisation (APRO) is correct in highlighting its limitations. However, APRO's limitations might also be explained with reference to its Cold War legacy and relatively conservative approach to labour issues. Indeed, frustration with existing union structures and strategies has led to the creation of more action-oriented networks. These networks may be more capable of launching action targeted at particular multinationals or state policies.

An example of one such organisation is the Southern Initiative on Globalization and Trade Union Rights (SIGTUR). Originally called the Indian Ocean Initiative, SIGTUR has pulled together a number of leftist southern trade union and NGO activists from around Australia, South Africa, South Asia and Southeast Asia (Lambert and Webster 2001). It is regional in a sense, but does not correspond to any of the traditional macro regions. It aspires to be more campaign- and action-oriented than existing trade union structures.

In the Americas, trade unions have joined a broad coalition of civil society groups opposing the creation of a neoliberal Free Trade Area of the Americas. Their response to the inter-state initiative has been to propose an alternative vision for the Americas where trade and investment liberalisation is subordinated to human rights, and environmental, labour and social concerns (HSA 2002). This take on integration has increasingly received state backing as several Latin American states have elected leaders from the left of the political spectrum. In April 2006, the government of Bolivia released a document entitled 'A People's Trade Agreement' (Morales 2006) which stressed themes raised by many civil society groups. While such an approach to regional integration would not be acceptable to the dominant states of the hemisphere, it is noteworthy that an alternative vision springing from labour, peasant and social groups is now finding some resonance in the inter-state arena.

This section has argued that the activities of labourers, whether they be migrants or trade unions, contribute to regional integration. Crucially, however, the regions they experience and the regions they would like to build diverge substantially from the regions brought into being through the formal regional integration projects.

Conclusion

This chapter has argued that from a labour perspective, formal regional integration agreements tend not to be positive developments. Although there are particular variants in different regions, the one thing they share is the drive to create larger and deeper markets. In most cases the form of regulation governing this market expansion either ignores labour rights, puts in place systems that do not improve upon state regulation, or undermines labour rights. The drive for market expansion and the marginalisation of worker protections are similar to globalisation trends. Moving away from formal integration, the migration of workers within regions has proved to be an increasingly significant economic and social development. Yet, the conditions that the majority of these workers operate under are hardly more favourable than economic migrants from other parts of the world. There are few privileges given to people from the region.

So, what does this brief overview of labour's interaction with formal and informal macro regions tell us about the subject matter? With regards to the relationship between regionalisation and globalisation, one should conclude that these are similar, rather than contradictory processes. Both generate similar unequal institutional arrangements governing the rights of capital and labour. Indeed, if one were to shift the scales again and look at the national level, a similar erosion of labour rights can be found (in terms of decreasing secure employment, falling rates of unionisation in developed states). Regional integration and economic globalisation are the extension of national struggles over wealth creation and production. Moreover, the global level is often used as the justification for putting in place regional arrangements that undermine labour rights. It is alleged that global pressures are so intense that labour markets must be made more flexible (EU), transnational regulation would be counter-productive (NAFTA) and labour should be pushed into following state prescriptions for productivity or adopt a passive role (Asia).

Thus, it is helpful to see regional projects in their various forms as the next step in a very long historical process of the enlargement of capitalist markets from local to national to regional and global realms (Cocks 1980). Although there is a greater social element to the European project than in the Americas or Asia, each regional development is primarily about expanding markets for investors. In this, they are very similar to the push to globalise economic activity across regions.

For labour, the region is a necessary arena of political conflict, but it holds no particular virtue. Regions are not the answer to labour's struggles. Regional arrangements, similar to national and global restructuring, are designed to undermine labour rights in the name of competitiveness and flexibility. There is very little evidence of regional arrangements improving labour's position and overwhelming evidence of these arrangements entrenching corporate rights. This applies to the legal frameworks created by inter-state negotiations and the conditions under which labour is attracted into regions and employed in them.

A third point is that the activity of labour groups themselves is contributing to increasing regionalisation. Migrants moving across state borders are tying families and communities together across regions. Labour activists – from grassroots organisations to traditional trade union structures – are struggling to respond to corporate activity and state initiatives. Both migrants seeking expanded rights and transnational labour groups are pressing for a form of regional integration that supports social development. This opens up the possibility of developing a different type of regional project that is not as informed by neoclassical economic principles. However, that project should be seen as intimately linked to national and global struggles rather than an alternative to globalisation.

References

Abbott, K. (2000) 'Why Ideology Dominates Regional Trade Unionism in the Asia Pacific', *Asia Pacific Business Review*, 6: 15–33.

ASEAN (2000) *ASEAN Labour Minister's Vision Statement*, Association of Southeast Asian Nations. Available at: http://www.almm.sg/index.php (accessed 6 May 2006).

Ayers, J. (2004) 'Power Relations under NAFTA', *Studies in Political Economy*, 74: 101–23.

Bieler, A. (2005) 'European Integration and the Transnational Restructuring of Social Relations: The Emergence of Labour as a Regional Actor?', *Journal of Common Market Studies*, 43(3): 461–84.

—— (2006) *The Struggle for a Social Europe*, Manchester: Manchester University Press.

Canales, A. (2000) 'International Migration and Labour Flexibility in the Context of NAFTA', *International Social Science Journal*, 52: 409–19.

Cocks, P. (1980) 'Towards a Marxist Theory of European Integration', *International Organization*, 34(1): 1–40.

Compa, L. (2001) 'NAFTA's Labor Side Agreement and International Labor Solidarity', in P. Waterman and J. Wills (eds) *Place, Space and the New Labour Internationalisms*, Oxford: Blackwell, pp. 147–63.

da Motta Veiga, P. and Lengyel, M. (2003) *International Trends on Labor Standards: Where Does Mercosur Fit In?* Buenos Aires: Latin American Trade Network.

Ellerman, D. (2005) 'Labour Migration: A Developmental Path or a Low-Level Trap?' *Development in Practice*, 15: 617–30.

Flaccus, G. (2006) '1M Immigrants Skip Work for Demonstration', *The Washington Post* 2 May, Online edn. Available at: http://www.washingtonpost.com/wp-dyn/content/article/2006/05/01/AR2006050100151.html

Gamble, A. and Payne, A. (eds) (1996) *Regionalism and World Order*, London: Macmillan.

Greenwood, J. (2003) 'Trade Associations, Change and the New Activism', in S. John and S. Thomson (eds) *New Activism and the Corporate Response*, New York: Palgrave, pp. 49–66.

Harrod, J. (1987) *Power, Production and the Unprotected Worker*, New York: Columbia University Press.

Haworth, N. and Hughes, S. (2002) 'International Labour and Regional Integration in the Asia-Pacific', in J. Harrod and R. O'Brien (eds) *Global Unions? Theory and Strategies of Organized Labour in the Global Political Economy*, London: Routledge, pp. 151–64.

Herod, A. (1997) 'Labor as an Agent of Globalization and as a Global Agent', in

K.R. Cox (ed.) *Spaces of Globalization: Reasserting the Power of the Local*, New York: Guilford Press, pp. 167–200.

Hobson, J.M. and Seabrooke, L. (n.d.) 'Introducing Everyday IPE: Decentring the Discipline – Revitalising the Margins', in J.M. Hobson and L. Seabrooke (eds) 'Everyday International Political Economy: Non-Elite Agency in the Transformations of the World Economy', unpublished manuscript.

HSA (2002) *Alternatives for the Americas*, Hemispheric Social Alliance. Available at: http://www.commonfrontiers.ca (accessed 5 May 2006).

IDB (2004) *Sending Money Home: Remittances to Latin America and the Caribbean*, Washington, DC: Inter-American Development Bank.

Lambert, R. and Webster, E. (2001) 'Southern Unionism and the New Labour Internationalism', in P. Waterman and J. Wills (eds) *Place, Space and the New Labour Internationalisms*, Oxford: Blackwell pp. 33–58.

Morales, E. (2006) 'A People's Trade Agreement', Available at: http://www.commonfrontiers.ca/Single_Page_Docs/Current_Activity_Updates/Apr26_06_Peoples Trade.html (accessed 5 May 2006).

O'Brien, R. (1998) 'Shallow Foundations: Labour and the Selective Regulation of Free Trade', in G. Cook (ed.) *The Economics and Politics of Interntational Trade*, London: Routledge, pp. 105–24.

—— (2000) 'Labour and IPE: Rediscovering Human Agency', in R. Palan (ed.) *Contemporary Theories of Global Political Economy*, London: Routledge, pp. 88–99.

—— (2005) 'The Agency of Labour in a Changing Global Order', in R. Stubbs and G. Underhill (eds) *Political Economy and the Changing Global Order*, Toronto: Oxford University Press.

Pellerin, H. (1999) 'The Cart Before the Horse? The Coordination of Migration Policies in the Americas and the Neoliberal Economic Project of Integration', *Review of International Political Economy*, 6: 468–93.

Piper, N. (2004) 'Rights of Foreign Workers and the Politics of Migration in Southeast and East Asia', *International Migration*, 42: 71–97.

Price, J. (2000) 'Challenging APEC: The Asia Pacific Labour Network and APEC's Human Resource Development Working Group', *Asia Pacific Business Review*, 6: 34–53.

Scharpf, F.W. (2002) 'The European Social Model: Coping with the Challenges of Diversity', *Journal of Common Market Studies*, 40(4): 647–70.

Schmitt-Egner P. (2002) 'The Concept of Regions: Theoretical and Methodological Notes on its Reconstruction', *European Integration*, 24: 179–200.

Scholte, J.A. (2005) *Globalization: A Critical Introduction*, New York: Palgrave.

Sell, S. (2003) *Private Power, Public Law: The Globalization of Intellectual Property Rights*, Cambridge: Cambridge University Press.

Söderbaum, F. (2005) 'The International Political Economy of Regionalism', in N. Phillips (ed.) *Globalizing International Political Economy*, London: Palgrave, pp. 221–45.

Stevis, D. (2002) 'Unions, Capitals and States: Competing Internationalisms in North American and European Integration', in J. Harrod and R. O'Brien (eds) *Global Unions? Theory and Strategies of Organized Labour in the Global Political Economy*, London: Routledge, pp. 130–50.

Tarrow, S. (1998) *Power in Movement: Social Movements and Contentious Politics*, Cambridge: Cambridge University Press.

Teague, P. (2003) 'Labour-standard Setting and Regional Trading Blocs: Lesson Drawing from the NAFTA Experience', *Employee Relations*, 25(5): 428–52.

Weeks, J. (2000) 'Have Workers in Latin America Gained from Liberalization and Regional Integration?' *Journal of Development Studies*, 16: 87–114.

Wills, J. (2004) 'Re-Scaling Trade Union Organisation: Lessons from the European Front Line', in R. Munck (ed.) *Labour and Globalisation: Results and Prospects*, Liverpool: Liverpool University Press, pp. 85–104.

Part III
Security considerations
The changing nature of
strategic regionalism

8 Regionalisation and responses to armed conflict, with special focus on conflict prevention and peacekeeping

Kennedy Graham

Introduction

The world of the early twenty-first century CE[1] would be scarcely recognisable to the framers of the United Nations (UN) Charter. Emerging from the ashes of a devastating global conflict that trumped even the concentrated carnage of its predecessor only a quarter of a century before, the world leaders of the day redrew a universal institutional framework designed to avert any third recrudescence. The concept of collective security to guard against inter-state aggression remains the underpinning of the international community to this day, based on the cardinal principles of sovereign equality, territorial integrity and the non-use of force save in the common interest.

In stark contrast with the 1940s, today's reality reflects 60 years of economic, political and social evolution – whose pace of change has intensified in the past two decades in an ineluctable and dynamic process widely known as 'globalisation'. But in response to the economic and technological dimensions of that change, the process of 'political globalisation' – in terms of an adaptive security framework and legal precepts that might respond to the 'new threats and challenges' of today – remains mired in controversy and some obfuscation.

An integral part of the process of globalisation is the phenomenon of regionalisation. The security dimension of regionalisation – the role of regional organisations in maintaining international peace and security in their own regions – is under intensive discussion and review at present, both within the United Nations and within the regional organisations themselves. Recent developments have generated hard discussion on how best to tackle the 'regional crises' in Kosovo, in Somalia and Darfur, in Afghanistan and Haiti; and how to integrate the new threats (weapons of mass destruction [WMD] proliferation, terrorism, transnational crime, and socio-economic-environmental stress). Strengthening the operational collaboration between the United Nations and regional organisations in conflict prevention, peace-making, peacekeeping, peace enforcement and peace-building is one of the most urgent tasks at hand.

This chapter seeks to assess the phenomenon of regionalisation as it pertains to the response of regional organisations to the threat of armed conflict in its 'post-modern' form. The first requirement is to clarify some conceptual and definitional issues. With this clarification, it is then proposed to review the theoretical basis of the response mechanism to armed conflict, at both the global and the regional levels, identifying any significant differences in this respect. The chapter then reviews the regional experience – both the constitutional basis for collaboration, the operational experience and the efforts at building a partnership with the United Nations. Finally, some prescriptive comments are advanced for the future UN-regional partnership – how to clarify the relationship and make it more efficient and effective.

The principal contention advanced is two-fold:

1 That once the true regional (and sub-regional) organisations are distinguished from other intergovernmental organisations, and their respective roles are clarified under the separate provisions of the UN Charter, the partnership will be freer to attain maximum comparative advantage for the vision of a 'regional-global security mechanism' as articulated by the UN Secretary-General in July 2003.
2 That a coordinated effort is necessary to ensure that the organisational, operational and resource capacities of the regional and sub-regional organisations are developed in a rational and planned manner so that a uniformly distributed capacity for peace and security exists across all regions alongside the United Nations.

Definitions: a conceptual clarification

An analysis of regionalisation and its response to armed conflict requires, in the first instance, some definitional attention. The three principal concepts of this chapter – regionalisation, conflict prevention and peacekeeping – are therefore explored below.

Regionalisation: Regional organisations in context

Regionalisation is the process through which governmental polities, civil society and the corporate sector share interests and combine resources to agreed common ends at the regional, as distinct from the national or global, level. The distinction is important, but largely overlooked, between processes of this kind that are truly regional and those that are cross-regional or transnational. As will be shown, this has implications, especially for the maintenance of peace and security, and not least conflict prevention and peacekeeping.

Regionalism can be analysed by two principal dimensions: objective and method.[2] The objective comprises the consciously articulated end-state which the regional constituency aspires to attain. In the broadest sense, the objective of regionalism may be of two kinds – total or partial. Total regionalism envisions political union in which formerly separate and discrete (sovereign) entities unite into one. Partial regionalism is confined within more delineated and focused parameters – in the security or socio-economic areas.

The method takes two procedural forms through which the objective is to be attained: cooperation or integration. Depending on the scale involved, security regionalism is usually confined to cooperation among sovereign states, although it can envisage integration. Socio-economic regionalism may commence with cooperation (free trade agreements) but usually proceeds beyond this to integration (common industrial base; customs union; labour mobility; fiscal and monetary union). Socio-economic integration may serve as a prelude to an intended political union (defence and foreign policy; ultimately a confederated state), or it may be an end in itself.

It is within this broad context that regional organisations have developed. There is, as yet, no formal definition of a 'regional organisation'. The UN Charter does not define 'region', its framers having decided, after much effort, against any self-restricting ordinance of that kind. A definition advanced during the San Francisco Conference in 1945 and voted down, however, gives as good a conceptual notion as is perhaps necessary:

> There shall be considered, as regional arrangements, organizations of a permanent nature grouping in a given geographical area several countries which, by reason of their proximity, community of interests or cultural, linguistic, historical or spiritual affinities make themselves jointly responsible for the peaceful settlement of any disputes which may arise . . . as well as for the safeguarding of their interests and the development of their economic and cultural relations.
>
> (cited in Russett 1967: 4)

It is generally accepted that the practical distinction between 'agency' and 'arrangement' concerns whether an inter-governmental organisation exists as a legal entity with a functioning secretariat and address (an 'agency') or whether it is simply an arrangement by sovereign states through treaty-making (an 'arrangement') (Simma *et al.* 1995: 694). It has been suggested that little distinction exists between the two (ibid.).

Peace and security: conflict prevention and peacekeeping in context

Over the past century, and especially in the latter half that comprises the UN era, the international community has laboured to construct an architecture of peace and security. Part of that architecture – the blueprint rather than the building material – is comprised of conceptual and doctrinal precepts, intended as normative, and occasionally binding, guidance for the behaviour of states.

All concepts pertaining to international peace and security in the current era must be derived from, and be compatible with, the Charter of the United

Nations. Some concepts in modern usage are to be found in the Charter itself, while some have entered into modern parlance in recent years. What are these?

In pursuit of its purposes, the United Nations and its members identify in the Charter seven principles that have defined, in theory, international order in the contemporary age. The two that govern the maintenance of international peace and security are pacific settlement and the non-use of force (Article 2).

The three principal methods for implementing these principles involve collective measures for:

1   prevention and removal of threats to the peace;
2   suppression of breaches of the peace (including acts of aggression);
3   the peaceful adjustment or settlement of international disputes (Article 1.1).

Each of these 'methods' warrants a separate chapter in the Charter for a global response to the problem of armed conflict: pacific settlement in Chapter VI, collective measures for enforcement action against threats or breaches to the peace and aggression in Chapter VII, and procedures for judicial settlement in Chapter XIV (see Articles 2.5 and 5).

Pacific settlement is comprised of six functions: negotiation, enquiry, mediation, conciliation, arbitration and judicial settlement (Article 3.1). Enforcement action is comprised of three broad functions:

1   provisional measures (which are left unspecified, and may involve peaceful or military means) (Article 40);[3]
2   peaceful measures (economic, transport, telecommunications and diplomatic sanctions) (Article 41);
3   military measures (demonstrations, blockade, or use of armed force) (Article 42).

Thus, a fairly elaborate fabric of peace exists to handle the ever-changing nature of global security. It cannot be said that the mechanism for ensuring peace at the global level does not exist. Yet to a significant extent the actions of the international community in peace and security are tethered only loosely to this framework. The global and regional responses to armed conflict are required to adapt to the continuous change in threats and instabilities in practical political and military terms while keeping the faith with the legal framework that is more immutable. This is accomplished by means of a 'dynamic' interpretation of the Charter and flexibility of institutions, both global and regional.

It may be queried whether such theoretical subtleties of legal and normative dimension have any meaning in today's hegemonic world of overwhelming military preponderance where unilateralism and exceptionalism prevail. The answer is that respect for and adherence to the law are of critical importance for precisely that reason.

Reflecting that dynamism, new concepts and terms pertaining to peace and security have come into use since 1945. The most notable, *peacekeeping*, was introduced in the 1950s, but the 1990s saw a number of inter-related concepts that are aimed at responding to the new realities which, if employed through institutional preference by different organisations, can risk some uncertainty and confusion.

In the past decade, the UN has developed a 'framework for peace' that reflects a more sophisticated approach to the complex security challenges of the modern world than the collective security response to inter-state aggression formalised in the Charter. Since the end of the Cold War, with the spread of intra-state conflict and the experience the UN has gained, a lexicon for the increasingly diverse peace operations has been developed. The concepts employed are not rigorously distinguished for academic purposes but they broadly suffice for operational clarity.[4] From its principal reports (United Nations 1992b, 1995, 2001; Brahimi 2000) and also from its website, the UN has developed a natural meaning for five principal operational concepts that comprise an inter-woven 'fabric of peace'.[5] They are: conflict prevention,[6] peacemaking,[7] peacekeeping,[8] peace enforcement[9] and peace-building.[10]

A natural, albeit rough, chronology accompanies these five operational concepts. Conflict prevention is designed to ensure that imminent conflict does not erupt into violence. If this fails, peacemaking efforts are undertaken to cease hostilities through peaceful means. If peacemaking fails, peace enforcement may be used to force a party to negotiate or withdraw from a conflict area. Once hostilities end, even through a temporary cease-fire, peacekeeping is undertaken.[11] Once a peace settlement is concluded, peace-building commences to ensure non-recidivism.

While these concepts are operationally adequate, their precise relationship to the UN Charter is less clear and there remains some overlapping in their meaning. The degree of imprecision commensurately retards the natural strengthening of a 'regional-global security mechanism' for responding to armed conflict.

Since the UN Charter was framed, however, the nature of the threats to international peace and security has metamorphosed in fundamental ways. Table 8.1 gives an impressionistic portrayal of the extent to which this has occurred in terms of the principal threat perception at the global level, in the form of the UN Security Council's judgements, as gleaned from an analysis of its myriad resolutions.[12]

Table 8.1 depicts the global perception of the threat to peace in terms of risk of armed conflict and the stakes involved. The regional perceptions do not necessarily mirror this. Each regional perception, moreover, is different. A table can be constructed for each region (begging the question of what is a 'region' and stressing the inherently subjective, or even existential, nature of

Table 8.1 Metamorphosis in global threat perception (1945–2006)

	Inter-state aggression	Intra-state instability	Inter-region instability	Terrorism	WMD proliferation	Organised crime	Socio-economic instability
	Nature of threat to international peace and security (perception of UN Security Council)						
1945	A	C	C	D	C	D	D
1955	A	C	C	D	C	D	D
1965	A	C	C	D	B	D	D
1975	A	B	B	B	B	B	D
1985	B	B	B	B	B	B	C
1995	C	A	A	A	A	A	C
2005	C	A	A	A	A	A	B

Key: A = primary threat; B = significant threat; C = modest threat; D = minor threat

that regional perception). Table 8.2 shows the threat perception that might be recognised as prevailing for different regions of the world in 2006.

These differences in threat perception generate different regional responses to armed conflict in terms of the type of threat for which a regional organisation judges it necessary to develop a conflict prevention mechanism, and appropriate (or not) to develop a peacekeeping or enforcement mechanism. A conflict prevention mechanism to avert conflict deriving from poverty, environmental degradation, a skewed trading system and post-colonial ethnic confusion, for example, is likely to differ from one focusing on terrorism, weapons of mass destruction and inter-state power struggles. Sub-regional conflict prevention mechanisms may develop along quite different lines, as can be seen in comparisons between, for example, Southeast Europe, West Africa, South America and Southeast Asia.

Institutional arrangements

Associated with the conceptualisation of the 'fabric of peace' is the institutional (and political) question of who does what. The Charter is quite clear on this. The principal actors in this respect are: the governments of member states, the UN Security Council (and in some circumstances the General Assembly), and the 'regional arrangements or agencies'. Each has a different role, and the role of regional organisations in response to armed conflict or threat thereof is more finely tuned than is generally appreciated.

Pacific settlement reflects a loose hierarchy of roles undertaken by these various parties. The Charter calls upon member states to engage by themselves in pacific settlement in the first instance (Article 33). In the event the member states fail to settle a dispute by themselves, the Security Council may become involved through investigation (Article 34), referral (Articles 35 and 37),[13] and recommendations (Article 38).

Table 8.2 Incidence of regional threat perceptions (2006)

	Nature of threat to regional peace and security (perception of region)						
	Inter-state aggression	Intra-state instability	Inter-region instability	Terrorism	WMD proliferation	Organised crime	Socio-economic instability
North							
North Americ	D	D	A	A	A	B	D
Europe	B	C	A	A	A	B	C
South							
Sub-Saharan Africa	B	A	C	C	D	D	A
Arab World	C	A	A	B	C	D	B
Asia	A	C	C	B	C	C	C
Pacific	D	B	D	C	D	C	A
Carib/Lat. Amer.	C	C	C	C	C	B	B

Key: A = primary threat; B = significant threat; C = modest threat; D = minor threat

Regional organisations, for their part, are encouraged under Chapter VIII to be proactive and undertake pacific settlement before referring disputes to the Security Council. Article 52 implies that a mechanism for pacific settlement is a necessary feature of a regional agency. By implication, this applies also to sub-regional agencies.

Other inter-governmental organisations (transnational or cross-regional)[14] may undertake pacific settlement efforts on their own initiative as well. This would be seen as measures undertaken on behalf of the United Nations under Chapter VI.

Enforcement action is treated quite differently. The use of armed force is confined to two circumstances only: the first is action by member states in self-defence (only *ex post* notification to the Security Council is required) (Article 51). The second is by organisations or member states acting under the authorisation of the Security Council, under two situations determined by the Council (a threat to, or breach of, the peace including any act of aggression). Strictly, self-defence is not enforcement but rather a legitimate preliminary use of force until UN-authorised enforcement takes over. Regional agencies undertaking enforcement must gain Security Council authorisation (Article 53). An enforcement capacity is an optional feature of a regional agency – not all have this or aspire to it.

Theoretical responses to armed conflict: global and regional differences

In the event that pacific settlement fails and armed conflict occurs, what is the response in terms of legitimate enforcement action?

An important if rather arcane distinction needs to be drawn between collective security and collective defence, because this carries implications for security at the regional and global levels. Collective security is conceptually designed to prevent or control state aggression among member states of a closed system, whether regional or global. Collective defence is designed to do the same in an open system, against a non-member state from outside the membership.

The distinction has implications for both organisational and doctrinal aspects of regionalism. Thus:

- Regional collective security pertains to controlling aggression from one's own membership of a regional organisation; and global collective security pertains to controlling aggression from any nation-state of the international community, institutionalised through the United Nations.
- Regional collective defence pertains to deterring or controlling aggression from a non-regional state beyond one's own regional organisational membership. There is, however, no such thing as 'global collective defence' since the world is a closed security system.

Collective security

Change and innovation in the methodology of peace in the UN era have come from *ad hoc* and pragmatic developments. The original response mechanism against inter-state aggression was planned as a collective security armed force operating on the basis of national contingents under UN command and flag. The United States, largely responsible for the concept, was ready in the mid-1940s with a major military contribution.[15] Agreements were to be reached between the UN and member states over the provision of national contingents.

The Korean crisis of the early 1950s represented the first, flawed, expression of collective security against inter-state aggression. But the global response to conflict there was due to the tactical absence of a major power from the Security Council, and subsequent Cold War vetoes undermined the efficacy of collective security as the central doctrinal strut of world order for four decades. The world retreated into regional collective defence structures for order and stability. During this period, inter-state aggression was prevented, not by collective security with conventional force, but by nuclear deterrence at both global and regional levels. The UN, with its Security Council relegated to the sidelines of strategic planning for global stability, acted as a forum and a venue for ratification rather than legislator and executor of global policy.

Peacekeeping

In such a situational context, the UN metamorphosed into a global agent of peace rather than of order as originally intended – nurse and social worker rather than policeman and judge. No further thought was given to concluding 'Article 43 agreements' for military contributions. In its stead the UN developed in the 1950s, through middle-power innovation and personal vision, an entirely new conceptual role for itself that reflected its 'softer' and marginalised function – peacekeeping.

As a pragmatic innovation unforeseen by the planners of post-war order, peacekeeping has never fitted easily into the UN Charter. It was famously characterised early on by Hammarskjöld as 'Chapter six-and-a-half' – that is to say, beyond pacific settlement but short of enforcement. Traditional peacekeeping responded to the prevailing threat perception and security situation of the time, namely inter-state aggression. Once hostilities ceased through negotiation and a ceasefire was declared, the separation of belligerent forces was governed by the UN peacekeepers comprising the 'thin blue line'. The peacekeepers were lightly armed and mandated to use force only in self-defence – observers and monitors of policy rather than its makers and executors.[16]

This is not to say, however, that the UN had been rendered redundant in the maintenance of peace and security. While the UN had been rendered ineffectual in enforcement, it had from the outset been active in conflict prevention. The use of the Secretary-General's good offices in mediation, under

Article 95, was well received from the late 1940s (Greece/Turkey) through the 1950s (American airmen hostages in China), the 1960s (Cuban missile crisis), 1970s (Vietnam), and 1980s (Lebanon; Iran-Iraq war).

Conflict prevention was given renewed attention and higher profile in the post-Cold War environment of the early 1990s. As the global enforcement mechanism transmogrified from bipolar deterrence to unipolar hegemony, hope was renewed that the UN would be freed from Cold War paralysis to become more active in both conflict prevention and enforcement.

The unacknowledged revolutions: Security Council summit (1992) and the Agenda for Peace

The first and seminal Security Council summit of January 1992 laid down, without fanfare or due attention, much of the basis of the post-Cold-War order (United Nations 1992a). The ending of apartheid and the expulsion of Iraq from Kuwait had reinvigorated the United Nations. The Council welcomed the role the UN had been able to play, under the Charter, in progress towards settling long-standing regional disputes, and would work for further progress towards their resolution.

To further strengthen the collective security system at such a time of opportunity, the Council invited the Secretary-General to submit recommendations on ways to strengthen and make more efficient the capacity of the United Nations for preventive diplomacy, peacemaking and peacekeeping. These were to cover the role of the UN in identifying potential crises and areas of instability, as well as the contribution to be made by regional organisations in accordance with Chapter VIII of the UN Charter in helping the work of the Council (ibid.).

The Council also addressed the other two issues of principal concern to regional and global stability: terrorism and WMD proliferation. In a move with far-reaching implications, the Council determined that the proliferation of weapons of mass destruction 'constituted a threat to international peace and security'.

This last determination was unprecedented, being the first time the Council had identified a hypothetical generic event as a threat to the peace, rather than an actual and specific event such as territorially-confined conflict, as originally envisaged by the framers of the Charter. In taking this action, the Council thereby empowered itself to engage in enforcement action on its judgement in the event that a non-permanent member moved to acquire nuclear, chemical or biological weapons. Empowering itself for the first time proactively rather than reactively, and generically rather than specifically, the Council signalled its intent to evolve into a prototype body of global governance rather than remain a narrowly focused instrument simply to combat inter-state aggression.[17]

In this remarkable assertion of policy, the international community commenced the journey from regarding the UN Security Council as a traditional instrument of twentieth-century statecraft for war-avoidance to a prototype mechanism of global governance. Since that date (January 1992) the Council, emboldened by the acquiescence of the global community to its growing assertiveness of policy, has taken it upon itself to declare as a 'threat to the peace' a variety of global and regional problems that were beyond the natural political imagination of the framers of the UN Charter.[18]

Such a novel construct of global governance was accorded a theoretical dimension in the form of the Secretary-General's *Agenda for Peace*, although his innovative proposals were designed more to revive some of the Charter's original intentions for collective security rather than buttress the Council's newly-acquired powers. The *Agenda*, produced in 1992 in response to the Council's request, proposed some far-reaching innovations in conflict prevention, peacekeeping and enforcement. Specifically it developed some conceptual distinctions that had hitherto been lacking, between 'classical' peacekeeping and two kinds of enforcement – peace enforcement and collective security enforcement against aggression.

Peacekeeping is now seen as of two kinds: 'traditional' and 'modern'. They are distinguished by two characteristics pertaining to a mission's mandate: breadth and strength. That is to say: whether its mandate is narrowly focused on ceasefire verification alone or encompasses a broad range of post-conflict activities; and whether it constrains the use of force to self-defence only or allows force to be used, on the mission's initiative, to 'enforce an end to hostilities'.[19]

'Traditional' peacekeeping pertains to the verification of mutually agreed ceasefires following a truce and with the consent of the belligerent parties. Force is to be used only in self-defence. It is intended essentially as a tool for conflict containment – creating space for further negotiations even at the cost occasionally of freezing the conflict for a considerable period.

'Modern peacekeeping' – involving missions that have been deployed in the post-Cold War era – differs from its traditional counterpart in two ways. First, such missions are 'multidimensional' in that their mandates extend beyond ceasefire verification to encompass a broad range of post-conflict activities, viz. disarmament; demobilisation; repatriation and rehabilitation; police and armed forces training; humanitarian delivery assistance; civilian protection; human rights promotion; electoral assistance; and judicial reform (United Nations 2003: 1). Second, some of these missions are 'robust' in that they are given an enforcement mandate to use force beyond strict self-defence (the 'all necessary means' formula used in the Security Council resolutions). These mandates characterise missions that are implementing final, comprehensive peace agreements. Such missions are deployed into unstable and insecure environments, which can occur even in post-agreement situations. The 'robust' enforcement mandates are required to enforce the agreement against 'minor order challenges' such as those mounted by spoilers, bandits, loosely commanded forces or splinter movements.

The distinction is important for constitutional reasons in distinguishing between global and regional responses to armed conflict. If 'traditional peace-keeping' is seen as part of Chapter VI of the Charter ('Chapter six-and-a-half'), then it is part of pacific settlement, and regional agencies are free to undertake such missions on their own initiative under Article 52 without Security Council authorisation. A 'peace enforcement' mission, however, using 'all necessary means', is authorised under Chapter VII. A regional agency undertaking such enforcement action, therefore, requires advance authorisation of the Council under Article 53.

Reflecting the optimism and the sense of urgency of the early 1990s, the proposal advanced by the Secretary-General was that 'peace enforcement' would fill the void that existed between pacific settlement activities (under Chapter VI) and inter-state collective security measures (under Chapter VII). Collective security was envisaged, in 1945, as a heavy military response by national armies against inter-state aggression – the full and final application of force. Peace enforcement was envisaged, in 1992, as the more controlled response to national (intra-state) or regional (cross-border) emergencies – the judicious application of lighter military force against 'threats of a lesser order'. Collective security was envisaged under Article 42 (military action); 'peace enforcement' under Article 40 (provisional measures). The latter, however, would still come under Chapter VII, involving the use of force and requiring a determination by the Security Council of a threat to peace, triggering its binding powers.

The concept is, however, fraught with difficulties. The present operational concept of 'peace enforcement' should be distinguished from the 1992 vision of UN 'peace enforcement units'. The idea in *Agenda for Peace* was that 'peace enforcement units' would be under UN command, made available from member states on a volunteer basis, highly trained and more heavily armed than peacekeeping forces. As such they would fulfil a function that had hitherto been lacking. The idea gained immediate positive attention when first advanced.[20]

Retreat from revolution: The Supplement to the Agenda, 1995

No such units materialised, however, and as noted, the negative experiences with 'peace enforcement' using traditional national military contingents in Bosnia-Herzegovina and Somalia soured the concept. These setbacks prompted a policy reversal by the United States from support for, to antipathy towards, UN peace enforcement.[21] By January 1995, the *Supplement to Agenda for Peace* had signalled a clear retreat from the ambitious concept of 'peace enforcement units'. Since then, UN operations have continued to receive peace enforcement mandates from the Security Council under Chapter VII but they have been implemented by means of the same operational arrangements as before – national contingents made available on a voluntary basis by troop-contributing countries.

Effort has been invested, however, to streamline this practice. In 1994, a UN

Stand-By Arrangement System (UNSAS) was established in which member states would make conditional pledges to contribute specific resources for UN peacekeeping within agreed response times. Some 83 States are participating, of which 43 have signed memoranda of understanding (MOUs) pledging contributions involving light infantry, helicopter and personnel carriers. UNSAS has been useful in planning for over 14 peace operations (United Nations 2000: para. 14). Within UNSAS, 15 countries belong to the Standby High Readiness Brigade for United Nations Operations (SHIRBRIG), a co-ordinated arrangement for the rapid deployment of an integrated multi-national high-readiness brigade. SHIRBRIG was deployed as a precursor for the United Nations Mission in Ethiopia and Eritrea (UNMEE) in the conflict of 2000. Both UNSAS and SHIRBRIG, however, are restricted to 'classical peacekeeping' operations, not as yet deployable for 'peace enforcement' operations.

All of the above operations – UN and multinational – are focused on what are now termed 'complex emergencies', national and regional. These are distinct from the traditional inter-state conflicts of the kind that preceded the UN and for which the UN was fundamentally designed to handle. The question of the international community's capability to respond to inter-state aggression through collective security arrangements has always been uncertain. The Charter envisaged 'Article 43 agreements' in which member states would enter a binding commitment to make available their designated armed forces which the Security Council could rely upon. Because such agreements were never concluded, the Council can only rely upon voluntary commitments.

In the early 1990s when hopes were high for a reinvigoration of the UN's collective security system, an attempt was made to rectify this. Under the *Agenda for Peace*, the Secretary-General called for agreements to be concluded by member states with the UN, as originally envisaged in Article 43, to make available 'on call' national armed forces for immediate response to 'outright aggression, actual or imminent' authorised by the Security Council under Article 42. This call also went unheeded. Once the ambitious proposals of *Agenda for Peace* were nullified by the US policy change of 1994, no serious thought was thereafter given to national contingents of armed forces for collective security as originally envisaged by the framers of the Charter.

Developments of the past decade (1996–2005)

Since the 1995 *Supplement*, the UN has pursued a less ambitious, more practical course in strengthening its response capacity to armed conflict. Two reports in particular advanced this goal – the Brahimi Report of 2000 and the Secretary-General's Report on the Prevention of Armed Conflict of 2001. The Brahimi Report called for stronger and clearer mandates for 'robust peacekeeping', better training and equipment and financing of missions, and above all a renewal of political will to stay the course on the part of member states. The Secretary-General's Report built on this and took it a step further.

One of its 29 recommendations concerned the role of regional organisations in conflict prevention. The Secretary-General recalled the series of high-level meetings he had convened with regional organisations since 1994 and urged member states to implement the conclusions reached on conflict prevention and peace-building (United Nations 2001).

During the same decade, however, the global threat perception itself became an issue of contention. The hitherto dominant Western influence over what threatened the international order and what was required to respond became subject to increasing challenge. First, notions of 'soft security' ranged along-side those of traditional 'hard security'. The more uniform input of all con-stituent parts of the international community into global policy-making ensured greater concern than hitherto for poverty alleviation, sustainable development and related socio-economic advancement as component parts of 'human security', captured in the Commission on Human Security Report of 2003. This increasingly sophisticated approach to conflict prevention needed to factor such broader notions of security into the doctrinal and institutional changes at the UN and in regional organisations.

Second, the dominant threat perception of 'hard security' mutated a sec-ond time, from intra-state instability to terrorism. Although the terrorist phenomenon has been felt by many societies, it was the United States that suffered perhaps the most dramatic terrorist action in September 2001, which responded the most forcefully with military force (in Afghanistan) and which continues to feel the most vulnerable in ways wholly novel to its citizenry. The US-proclaimed 'war on terror', however, draws varying coali-tions of the willing and the reluctant into a military operation against not a cause but a tactic. Operating in part *ultra vires* the Charter, such operations lack political authenticity and multilateral legitimacy; some are patently illegal. The notion of conflict prevention against private groups determined to wreak havoc on establishment thinking and hardware through terrorist actions against civilians raises entirely new issues – in particular, whether the root causes of terrorism should attract equal attention to the issue of response measures, and whether such response measures should be prosecuted as a global police action or an international military operation. When it was first made aware of the terrorist issue in the early 1970s, the UN General Assembly had emphasised the need to investigate the causes of terrorism.

The constitutional basis for regional response to armed conflict

Historically, the prototype security architecture of the Westphalian era of sovereign nation-states took the form of regional security arrangements through the Concert of Europe and the Monroe Doctrine in the Americas.

Differences were, however, discernible between the two. The Concert sought an internal regional security arrangement though a dynamic balance of power based on shifting alliances. The Monroe Doctrine was an external regional defence arrangement designed principally to deter one region (Europe) from any continuing predation on another (America) – regional collective defence rather than regional collective security.

Each arrangement proved to be a precursor to twentieth-century global collective security – a somewhat ironic development since President Wilson had consciously sought to translate the American experience (collective defence) onto the world stage.

In the UN era of the past 60 years, the nature of the security challenge has changed and with it the design of the security architecture to deal with it. That metamorphosis is apparent in the different structures and roles of regional organisations whose ages delineate the trend in security perceptions and thinking. Thus:

- The older organisations of the 1940s (League of Arab States [LAS], 1945; Organization of American States [OAS], 1948) combined both collective security and collective defence in an age when inter-state aggression was the principal threat perception immediately after the two world wars.
- The 'cross-regional' organisations of the 1950s (North Atlantic Treaty Organization [NATO], 1949; Australia-New Zealand United States Defence Arrangement [ANZUS], 1951; Southeast Asian Treaty Organization [SEATO], 1954; Warsaw Pact 1955; Central Treaty Organization [CENTO], 1959) were created solely for the purposes of regional collective defence against inter-state aggression during the Cold War.
- The younger regional organisations (Organization of African Unity/ African Union [OAU/AU], 1964/2002; Association of Southeast Asian Nations [ASEAN], 1967; Pacific Islands Forum [PIF], 1971) and cross-regional organisations (Commission on Security and Cooperation in Europe/Organization for Security and Cooperation in Europe [CSCE/ OSCE], 1975/1992) of the 1960s and 1970s focused on inter-sectoral regional cooperation to promote stability in an age when security problems derived from complex national and regional emergencies rather than simple inter-state aggression.
- The latest generation of regional (Commonwealth of Independent States [CIS], 1991) and cross-regional organisations (Shanghai Cooperation Council [SCO], 2001; Collective Security Organization [CSTO], 2003) reflect contemporary security perceptions by focusing principally on terrorism and transnational crime.

Standing separately from this complex mosaic are the two European organisations, the Council of Europe [COE] (1948) and the European Economic Community/European Union [EEC/EU] (1957/1992). The former is a regional organisation of 46 European countries that focuses on the promotion of societal stability through the rule of law and human rights. The latter is a sub-regional organisation which, alone around the world, originally sought integration of its member states' economies and now contemplates political union of some indeterminate kind.

One of the main challenges in analysing the regional response to armed conflict is to determine the extent to which a regional organisation has acquired a constitutional authority, and developed an operational mechanism, for conflict prevention and peacekeeping. The executive functions of UN Chapter VIII are identified in the Table 8.3.

The historical experience of regional response to armed conflict

The historical experience of regional response to armed conflict can be analysed in two contexts: the operational experience of regional organisations in the field and the efforts at forging an operational partnership with the United Nations.

Operational experience

The record to date of regional and sub-regional agencies in peacekeeping and peace enforcement is shown in Table 8.4. The record of regional, sub-regional and other agencies in peacekeeping and peace enforcement reflects the rather haphazard and *ad hoc* manner of the 'partnership' between the United Nations and its partners in the maintenance of peace and security. In terms of the most recent missions, the issue has arisen of the competence of the regional

Table 8.3 Chapter VIII executive functions

Executive function	Yes		No
	Agency	*Statutory reference*	*Agency*
Internal dispute settlement §52	AU	AU-PSP,[a] Art. 7.1 (a and b)	COE
	OAS	OAS Charter, Arts 24–7	EU
	CIS	CIS Charter, Art. 17	SAARC
	ASEAN	ASEAN-TAC,[b] Arts 13–17	
	LAS	LAS Charter, Art. V	
	PIF	Rarotonga Decl. paras 7–14	
Internal enforcement §53	AU	AU-PSP, Art. 7.1 (e)	ASEAN
	OAS	OAS Charter, Arts 28–9	COE
	CIS	CIS Charter, Art. 18	EU
	LAS	LAS Charter, Art. VI	SAARC
	PIF	Biketawa Decl. paras 1–2	
External self-defence §51	AU	AU-Const. Act, para. 4 (d)	COE
	OAS	OAS Charter, Arts 28–9	EU
	CIS/CST[c]	CIS Charter, Art. 12	SAARC
	LAS	LAS Charter, Art. VI	ASEAN
			PIF

Notes: (a) Protocol Relating to the Establishment of the Peace and Security Protocol of the African Union (AU-PSP).
(b) Treaty on Amity and Cooperation in Southeast Asia (ASEAN-TAC).
(c) Commonwealth of Independent States Collective Security Treaty (CIS/CST).

Table 8.4 Executive roles of regional, sub-regional and other agencies to date[a]

Organisation	Peacekeeping	Peace enforcement[b]	Collective security
OAU/AU	Chad 1981 Burundi 2003	Sudan 2004	
Economic Community of West African States (ECOWAS)		Liberia 1990 Sierra Leone 1997	
Southern African Development Community (SADC)	Lesotho 1998		
International Governmental Development Authority (IGAD)[c]			
LAS	Lebanon 1983		
COE			
EU	Macedonia 2003	DR Congo 2003	
CIS	Georgia 1994 Tajikistan 1994		
South Asian Association for Regional Cooperation (SAARC)	n.a.	n.a.	n.a.
ASEAN	n.a.	n.a.	n.a.
PIF		Solomon Is. 2004	
OAS		Dominican Rep. 1965	Cuba[d] 1962
Organization of East Caribbean States (OECS)		Grenada 1983	

Notes: (a) The roles identified above include peacekeeping (under Chapter VI) and peace enforcement and collective security (under Chapter VII); but exclude the peacemaking role (under Chapter VI).

    (b) Peace enforcement requires permission to use 'all necessary means' to achieve mission objectives granted by the Security Council acting under Chapter VII.

    (c) COE, SAARC, IGAD and ASEAN have to date undertaken no executive actions of any kind. In the first two cases, this is statutorily excluded.

    (d) During the Cuban crisis, the OAS resolved to take measures, individually and collectively, 'including the use of armed force', to ensure that the Cuban Government would not continue to receive military material from the Sino-Soviet powers.

or sub-regional organisation to resort to force. The UN Charter (Article 53) requires the approval of the Security Council before armed force can be used. In the case of ECOWAS, however, (notably Liberia 1990) the agency resorted to force in advance of a Council resolution. In fact, the first ECOWAS Monitoring Group (ECOMOG) was originally conceived as a peacekeeping force in the classic sense of governing a ceasefire, but was instantly transformed into a 'robust' enforcement version upon being met on arrival by armed resistance;

Not only the UN but ECOWAS itself was obliged to 'upgrade' the force's mandate retroactively. This and related experiences have prompted debate over the merits of advance Security Council authorisation, with some recommending a certain flexibility for regional organisations.[22] The UN's High-Level Panel on Threats, Challenges and Change, however, was quite clear on the matter: 'In relation to regional organizations: Authorization from the Security Council should in all cases be sought for regional peace operations' (United Nations 2004b).[23]

A similar issue arises when a regional organisation undertakes armed force on the basis of 'individual or collective self-defence' (such as the US-OAS action over Cuba in October 1962 and the Russian-led CIS intervention in Tajikistan in April 1993), with claimed justification of Article 51 of the Charter. The intervening states are required only to notify the Council of the action taken without further obligation to explain. Such experiences raise uncertainties over the relationship of regional organisations to the Security Council.

A further recent issue concerns the 'responsibility to protect' and the right of the international community – the Security Council or the regional organisation – to intervene if a government has failed in its primary responsibility to protect its citizens. In this respect the World Summit Outcome Document resolved:

> The international community, through the United Nations, also has the responsibility to use appropriate diplomatic, humanitarian and other peaceful means, in accordance with Chapters VI and VIII of the Charter of the United Nations, to help protect populations from genocide, war crimes, ethnic cleansing and crimes against humanity. In this context, we are prepared to take collective action, in a timely and decisive manner, through the Security Council, in accordance with the Charter, including Chapter VII, on a case-by-case basis and in cooperation with relevant regional organizations as appropriate, should peaceful means be inadequate and national authorities are manifestly failing to protect their populations from genocide, war crimes, ethnic cleansing and crimes against humanity.
>
> (United Nations 2005b: para. 139)

Thus the effectiveness of regional organisations becoming involved in peace operations, either in collaboration with the United Nations, or acting under its authority, or on occasion taking the initiative to engage militarily without authorisation, has become both complex and problematic.

Construction of UN-RO partnership

Since the mid-1990s the United Nations has taken the initiative in developing a partnership with regional organisations in the maintenance of international peace and security. The Secretary-General has convened six high-level meetings (HLM) with regional, sub-regional and other intergovernmental organisations with a view to building what might be called a 'regional-global security mechanism'.[24]

These meetings have resulted in a series of broad guidelines for operational measures in conflict prevention and peace-building. In recent years, the work surrounding the fifth HLM (July 2003) and sixth HLM (July 2005) has intensified. Meetings are henceforth to be regional, supported by an inter-sessional Standing Committee and served by a number of working groups.

Also in the past few years the Security Council has undertaken initiatives in strengthening the partnership. It has now held three meetings with regional and other organisations (April 2003; July 2004; October 2005), the most recent of which adopted a Council resolution on the UN relationship with regional organisations for the first time. The Council expressed its determination to take appropriate steps to further the development of cooperation with regional and sub-regional organisations in maintaining international peace and security consistent with Chapter VIII of the Charter. It stressed the importance for the UN of developing the ability of regional and sub-regional organisations in pacific settlement and also their ability to deploy peacekeeping forces in support of UN operations or other Security Council-mandated operations. And the Council invited the Secretary-General to submit a report on the opportunities and challenges facing the cooperation between the UN and regional and sub-regional organisations in maintaining international peace and security (United Nations 2005c). Thus the stage is now set for the operational partnership between the UN and RO/SROs to be realised.

This new focus on a UN-regional partnership has been given some prominence by the high-level process leading up to the World Summit of September 2005. The 2004 UN High-Level Panel noted the important role the regional organisations had to play in international peace and security and called for more formalised agreements between them and the UN. In his report *In Larger Freedom*, the Secretary-General declared his intention to conclude a series of memoranda of understanding with partner organisations (United Nations 2005a). This was noted and endorsed by the World Summit.

The latent potential of regionalism for responding to armed conflict

Despite these significant developments, the partnership between regional organisations and the UN in building a response to armed conflict remains stronger in the potentiality than actuality. The relationship remains in the declaratory rather than the substantive operational stage, although there are signs that it is on the cusp of transforming from one to the other. What is required to realise this?

First, it should be possible to identify those organisations that are 'regional' in nature in the sense of their membership covering a clearly defined jurisdictional area – a 'security region' – and sub-regions within it. These organisations could be accepted as regional and sub-regional agencies 'within the meaning of Chapter VIII' to cite the terminology employed by the UN's High-Level Panel of 2004.

Beyond this group, all other 'partner organisations' could be seen as cooperating with the UN under other provisions of the Charter – Chapter VI in pacific settlement, Chapter VII in enforcement, and Chapter IX in peace-building. In contrast to 'Chapter VIII regional organisations', these other bodies (cross-regional, transnational organisations) would be free to act, on behalf of the UN, 'out-of-area', as indeed two organisations (NATO, EU) currently do. This could include, in the future, the CSTO and the SCO.

Who gets to decide which organisations might be 'regional' under Chapter VIII? This in itself is not clear and the Charter is silent on the matter. The potential indicators for such decision-making are also ambivalent. Some regional organisations are official observers at the UN General Assembly but not all; not all observers are regional organisations. The Security Council has on occasion referred to 'regional organisations' in calling for assistance in the maintenance of peace and security, but not often and not consistently. The Secretary-General has extended invitations to the high-level meetings to organisations that have developed a partnership relationship with the UN in peace and security. But the range of bodies invited is all-encompassing; some of the twenty or so organisations that turn up are palpably not 'regional' and a few freely declare themselves not to be part of Chapter VIII.

A fourth way of identifying 'regional organisations' involves self-proclamation. The OAS states in its statute that it is an agency under Chapter VIII. The OSCE declared in 1992 (then as the CSCE) its understanding that it was a 'regional arrangement in the sense of Chapter VIII'. The General Assembly welcomed this understanding without according it any official imprimatur. Others have signalled a similar self-perception. In 2002, for example, the LAS adopted a resolution on the Iraq crisis, 'acting in accord-ance with Article 54 of the [UN] Charter', and conveyed it to the Security Council. The danger of self-proclamation is its scope for abuse – without some objective criteria and judgement, any entity could, as it were, 'gain entry'.

Relating global and regional responses to armed conflict: a UN-regional partnership

The 'Chapter VIII regional organisations', once identified, could develop an operational partnership with the Security Council. They could perform both institutional and executive functions within that context. Institutional functions could include both representational and reporting action. A repre-sentational action would mean that each organisation would represent its region on the Council (through the member states elected onto the Council at any one time). It would also be responsible for reporting to the Council on the security situation within its region – both through its 'representative member states' (by right) or by the organisation's head (by invitation).

The executive function would include a mechanism for regional pacific settlement in each case under Article 52 of the Charter. Under this provision, regional organisations (and their member states) are empowered to take initiatives in this respect, and the Security Council is authorised to encourage such initiatives. In contrast, an enforcement function is optional under Article 53 – as noted earlier, no regional organisation is obliged to develop such a capacity.

Implications for UN reform

The recent failure of the international community to agree on an expansion of the Security Council has been taken, not for the first time, as a serious setback to progress in UN reform. The need for greater legitimacy of the Council through more representative membership, as well as more transparency and accountability and improved decision-making procedures, is widely recognised. National rivalries assigned the aspirations of permanent membership by the Group of Four (G4) to failure.[25] Political tensions ran high during the diplomatic swordplay over Security Council composition in 2005.

This problem will recur every time the issue of Council expansion is re-opened on the basis of national membership. The self-evident political insight regarding the Security Council is that the future legitimacy of the body, which rests on a broader and more equitable representation, can by achieved only through some form of regional institutional representation of an inclusive nature rather than national rivalry that ensures the exclusion of many. It would be misguided to undertake any further attempt at Council enlargement on the basis of permanent national membership.

Once the political dust settles from the failed 2005 attempt, consideration should be given to a different approach to the goal of an enlarged Security Council – through regionalism. An expanded Council of 24 or 25 States could be elected entirely through a regional electoral framework that would replace the current obsolete electoral groupings that are a relic of the Cold War. Such a framework could include the five existing permanent Council member states.

The framework could be based on the regional organisations that currently cooperate with the UN: Sub-Saharan Africa could be represented through the AU; the Arab world, geographically comprising North Africa-West Asia, could be represented through LAS; Europe could be represented through the COE; Caucasia-Central Asia (including Russia) could be represented through CIS; South Asia could be represented by SAARC;[26] Southeast Asia could be represented by ASEAN; the Pacific could be represented by PIF; and the Americas (including the United States) could be represented by the OAS.

One region, East Asia, would remain unrepresented at present, since no regional organisation exists for this. If the above regional mosaic were to be fully developed, an organisation would need to be created by East Asian States – China, the Koreas, Japan and Mongolia. Given the tensions in the area this would not prove easy, yet other regions (Africa, Europe, South Asia) have successfully created and developed regional organisations despite, indeed because of, regional tensions and the need for regional crisis management. Recently China has floated the idea of an East Asian Community.[27]

The number of seats on a Council of 25 could be allocated in a way that ensures more democratic legitimacy to the Council. Africa could be allocated 4 seats, the Arab world 2 seats, Europe 3, Caucasia-Central Asia 2, South Asia 4, East Asia 3, Southeast Asia 2, the Pacific 1, and the Americas 4 seats. The 'regional spread' of such an arrangement would be considerably more equitable in terms of both population per Council seat and number of regional states per Council seat.[28]

The five permanent Council members could continuously retain one seat in their relevant groups – Europe (France, UK), Caucasia-Central Asia (Russia), East Asia (China) and the Americas (US). The other 20 seats would be allocated across the groups as identified above. Scope would exist for the G4 permanent aspirants to be re-elected in their relevant group as often as the group judged appropriate.

This would fall short of the current aspirations of the G4, and some time would need to pass before wounded national pride subsides in a few cases. But there is no way out of the stalemate if an expanded Council continues to mix new permanent membership with perennial national competitiveness.

The above regional approach contains certain shortcomings, but this or some variant on the theme is likely ultimately to prove to be the only viable and universally acceptable way of reforming the representational shortcomings of the Security Council in the twenty-first century.

As the United Nations emerges from its current woes and proceeds with administrative and structural reform, new and vigorous leadership over the next decade should give impetus to some qualitatively new approach to the question of Council expansion.

An invitation by the UN Secretary-General?

The need now exists to clarify the basis of the developing partnership between regional organisations and the United Nations in peace and security. This includes the need to identify which organisations operate 'for the purposes of Chapter VIII of the UN Charter', to quote the UN High-Level Panel. It will be incumbent on the United Nations, through the Secretary-General, to take the initiative.

Criteria may need to be developed for determining which organisations are 'Chapter VIII regional organisations' and which organisations operate under other chapters and provisions of the Charter. Such criteria could include the following:

1   A clearly-defined territorial area that responds to the normal meaning of a 'region'.
2   A basic document of a legal nature on which the regional organisation was founded or re-established.
3   An organisational structure – including a permanent secretariat.
4   A formal pacific settlement mechanism, comprised of both a legally-binding instrument and an executive decision-making capacity.
5   A territorial focus for all its executive functions for peace and security within the jurisdictional zone delimited by its own membership.
6   A declaration of intent to cooperate, with the United Nations in conflict prevention (and, optionally, peacekeeping).

On the basis of these criteria, the UN Secretary-General could take the initiative to identify regional and sub-regional organisations suitable to such a partnership, inviting them to declare themselves to be organisations for the purposes of Chapter VIII of the Charter. The formal recognition of such a status would be accorded by the Secretary-General. A group of eminent persons could act as an advisory panel to the Secretary-General for determining which would be so formally designated. Such a process could avoid any embarrassment by preliminary negotiation in advance of self-declarations by the serious organisations. At a subsequent stage, the Security Council could, for its own part, consider developing a similar relationship with such Chapter VIII organisations.

What is the point of developing the distinction between Chapter VIII and other chapters of the Charter? There is a need to respond to the original vision of the framers that envisaged a separate and close partnership between true regional organisations and the United Nations. And in a related way, because of the need to proceed beyond the continual rhetoric of 'comparative advantage' and 'complementarity' and to translate that into operational 'default mode' for reporting to the Security Council on conflict prevention. Enforcement would remain with the Security Council which retains sole authority to authorise such action by any organisation – whether regional, cross-regional or transnational.

Such a framework would refine the operational mechanism most appropriate for each specific UN-regional relationship that accurately reflects the different threat perceptions held be each regional organisation.

Conclusion

The relationship between the global and the regional responses to armed conflict remains somewhat invertebrate yet full of potential. The present confusion over which organisations are regional and which are other intergovernmental organisations needs to be clarified. The regions themselves remain at different stages of institutional development and of different political perceptions and persuasions, and this must be respected. But it is nonetheless possible for a broad framework to be developed that could lend structure to the development of an operational partnership for conflict prevention, peacekeeping, and indeed enforcement and peace-building over the next decade.

Notes

1 In this chapter, the Christian calendar is employed for ease of reference, but in deference to inter-cultural sensibilities the term Common Era (CE) is used.

2 The relationship between regionalisation and regionalism itself warrants consideration. Regionalisation is the process – the array and sequence of events – by which regionalism (the state of, and attitudes towards, regional identity) is advanced. That process may be politically purposeful, or not. Regional organisations act on behalf of their constituents, the nation-state, as facilitators of regionalism.

3 In the *Agenda for Peace* of June 1992, the Secretary-General called for the establishment of 'peace enforcement units', which would be established under Article 40.

4 The United Nations goes to great lengths to disown responsibility for the precision or significance of its terminology. Its website disclaimer describes the material therein as the 'findings, interpretations and conclusions' of the UN staff, consultants or advisers who prepared the work which does not necessarily represent the views of the UN. It makes no representations as to the accuracy of the material and carries no liability for any damage resulting from use of the site.

5 Beyond the five concepts, however, the UN also refers to 'conflict management' and 'conflict resolution' without defining these two concepts (see http/// www.un.org/Depts/dpa/prev_dip/fr_prev_dip_introduction.htm, accessed August 2004). It is concluded here that 'conflict management' is synonymous with 'peace enforcement' and 'conflict resolution' is synonymous with 'peacemaking'.

6 Conflict prevention comprises:

- preventive diplomacy: mediation, conciliation, negotiation;
- preventive deployment: the fielding of peacekeepers to forestall probable conflict;
- preventive disarmament: destroying old weapons and reducing small arms in conflict areas;
- structural prevention: political, institutional and developmental efforts at root causes.

7 Peacemaking refers to the use of diplomatic means to persuade parties in conflict to cease hostilities and negotiate a pacific settlement of their dispute. It includes:

- Security Council recommendations of ways to resolve a dispute.
- Secretary-General's envoys or missions for fact-finding or negotiation.
- Secretary-General's mediation between disputant parties.

8 Peacekeeping can cover any of the following four purposes:

- conflict prevention: deploy to prevent the outbreak of conflict or spillover of conflict across borders;
- ceasefire verification: stabilise conflict situations after a ceasefire, to create an environment for the parties to reach a lasting peace agreement;
- peace implementation: assist in implementing comprehensive peace agreements;

- governmental transition: lead states or territories through a transition to stable government, based on democratic principles, good governance and economic development.

9　Peace enforcement refers to the use of force against one of the parties to enforce an end to hostilities. The Security Council may authorise member states to use 'all necessary means', including force, to achieve a stated objective in situations where consent of the parties is not required. This has occurred on seven occasions, viz., Korea in 1950; Iraq in 1990, Somalia in 1993, Rwanda in 1994, Bosnia-Herzegovina in 1995, Albania in 1997, and East Timor in 1999.

10　Peace-building refers to assistance to countries and regions in the transition from war to peace. It includes:

- demilitarisation;
- institution-building, including police and judicial systems;
- human rights promotion;
- election-monitoring;
- political participation;
- rehabilitation;
- economic and social development.

11　Operationally, some complexity arises with regard to the concept of 'peace-keeping' since it can be undertaken in conflict prevention and peacebuilding phases of UN operations as well as being undertaken in its own right. Its principal functions, however, are to verify temporary cease-fires or assist in implementation of permanent peace agreements.

12　The threat clusters identified reflect the judgement of the 2004 UN High-Level Panel on Threats, Challenges and Change (United Nations 2004b). The intensity of threat perception identified in Table 8.1 reflects the author's own judgement.

13　The General Assembly may also become involved.

14　The typology of inter-governmental organisations used here is as follows. *Regional*: those that have an operational focus on a region and whose membership equates totally or near-totally with the region, with no external membership. *Sub-regional*: those that have operational focus on a sub-region within a 'parent region', and whose membership equates totally or near-totally with the sub-region, with no external membership. *Transnational*: those with membership from all or many regions of the world but whose membership is confined to a selective criterion that precludes universality (political, religious, cultural). *Cross-regional*: those that have operational focus on one region but whose membership extends beyond the region.

15　The US spoke of contributing, under Article 43, 20 divisions (300,000 troops), 1,250 bombers, 2,250 fighters and a large naval force (see Urquhart 1994).

16　An exception to this was the UN's force in the Congo in the mid-1960s, a controversial adventure by Hammarskjöld into 'robust peacekeeping' that was to prove premature as a generic security concept, but a harbinger of operational policy three decades later.

17　The policy statement of 31 January 1992 had the status of a presidential statement only and is thus not binding in international law. But such statements carry considerable weight, being the product of consensus of all 15 member states. And in this particular case, it has provided the foundation for the seminal resolution S/RES/1540 (United Nations 2004a) in which the Council, acting under Chapter VII, refers to the 1992 Statement, and then decides that all states shall refrain from providing any form of support to non-state actors that attempt to develop, acquire, manufacture, possess, transport, transfer, or use nuclear, chemical or biological weapons and their means of delivery.

18 The Council has proceeded since then to frame other generic threats (terrorism, 2001; implications of global health pandemics, 2001). It has also begun to focus on individuals, hitherto not subjects of international law (arrest warrants for Somalia warlords, 1994; Al Qaida operatives, 1999) and to direct state behaviour on domestic issues (threats of sanctions against Syria for non-cooperation over assassination investigations, 2005).

19 For a definition of 'peace enforcement', see http://www.un.org/Depts/dpa/prev_dip/fr_peacemaking.htm.

20 According to Urquhart (1994):

> It is essential to give the necessary authority and strength to the Security Council to deal with [crisis] situations more effectively in the future. The capacity to deploy credible and effective peace enforcement units, at short notice and at an early stage in a crisis, and with the strength and moral support of the world community behind them, would be a major step in this direction. Clearly, a timely intervention by a relatively small but highly trained force, willing and able to take combat risks and representing the will of the international community, could make a decisive difference in the early stages of a crisis.

21 US Presidential Decision Directive PDD-13 would have committed large numbers of US combat forces to UN command as part of the early Clintonian policy of 'assertive multilateralism'. Following Somalia, and just as Rwanda was breaking, PDD-25 reversed that approach, requiring instead stringent criteria for any US involvement in UN operations and a clear exit strategy. Since then the US has effectively eschewed UN peace operations as the best means of maintaining international security, preferring coalitions or unilateral action.

22 See, for example:

> In strict terms . . . the letter of the Charter requires action by regional organisations always to be subject to prior authorisation. But . . . there are certain cases when approval has been sought *ex post facto* . . . and there may be certain leeway for future action in this regard.
>
> ('The Responsibility to Protect', Report of the International Commission on Intervention and State Sovereignty, p. 54)

23 Recommendation 86 (a).

24 According to Annan (2003):

> I believe we can develop a new vision of global security. A vision that respects human rights while confronting the threats of our age, including the threat of terrorism. A vision that draws upon the resources and legitimacy of a network of effective and mutually reinforcing multilateral mechanisms – regional and global – that are flexible and responsive to our rapidly changing and integrating world.

25 The Group of Four (Germany, Japan, India and Brazil), seeking permanent membership of the Security Council, circulated a draft UN General Assembly resolution in July 2005. This was quickly followed by a 'United for Consensus' draft by the so-called Coffee Club composed of the 'second-tier rivals' – notably Italy, Pakistan and Argentina – with China also opposing Japan. A third proposal was put forward by the African Union. None proved successful.

26 If SAARC were to act as an executive agent for the Security Council, it would need to create a pacific settlement mechanism which is currently excluded under its

Statute. But there is nothing to prevent SAARC from operating as an electoral grouping at the UN.
27 At the tenth ASEAN Summit, in Vientiane, Laos, November 2004. The First East Asian Summit was held at the time of the tenth ASEAN Summit in Kuala Lumpur, December 2005. This meeting, however, included States from South Asia, Southeast Asia and Australasia as well as East Asia itself.
28 For a detailed exploration of such a regional electoral framework, see Graham and Felício (2006).

References

Annan, Kofi (2003) Opening Address to the fifth UN-RO High-Level Meeting, July.

Brahimi, Lakdhar (2000) *Report of the Panel on United Nations Peace Operations*, A/55/305, S/2000/809, 21 August.

Graham, Kennedy and Felício, T. (2006) *Regional Governance and Global Security: A Study of Interaction between Regional Organizations and the UN Security Council with a Proposal for a Regional-Global Security Mechanism*, Brussels: VUB Press.

Russett, Bruce (1967) *International Regions and International System: Study in Political Ecology*, Chicago: Rand McNally & Co.

Simma, Bruno, *et al.* (eds) (1995) *The Charter of the United Nations: A Commentary*, Oxford: Oxford University Press.

United Nations (1992a) 'Note by the President of the Security Council', Statement of the President of the Security Council adopted at the Council's Meeting of Heads of State and Government, S/23500, 31 January.

—— (1992b) *An Agenda for Peace: Preventative Diplomacy, Peacemaking and Peace-keeping*, A/47/277 – S/24111, 17 June, Available at: http://www.un.org/docs/SG/agpeace.html.

—— (1995) *Supplement to the Agenda for Peace: Position Paper of the Secretary-General on the Occasion of the Fiftieth Anniversary of the United Nations*, A/50/60 – S/1995/1, 3 January, Available at: http://www.un.org/Docs/SG/agsupp.html.

—— (2000) *Progress Report of the Secretary-General on Standby Arrangements for Peacekeeping*, S/2000/194, 8 March, Available at: http://daccessdds.un.org/doc/UNDOC/GEN/N00/333/10/IMG/N0033310.pdf?OpenElement.

—— (2001) *Prevention of Armed Conflict: Report of the Secretary-General*, A/55/985, S/2001/574, 7 June, Available at: http://domino.un.org/unispal.nsf/85255a0a0010ae82852555340060479d/b5bffcd5b649239585256caa006efab6!OpenDocument.

—— (2003) *Handbook on United Nations Multidimensional Peacekeeping Operations*, Peacekeeping Best Practices Unit, Department of Peacekeeping Operations, New York: United Nations. Available at: http://www.peacekeepingbestpractices.unlb.org/pbpu/handbook/Handbook%20on%20UN%20PKOs.pdf.

—— (2004a) *Security Council Resolution 1540*, S/RES/1540, 28 April, Available at: http://domino.un.org/UNISPAL.NSF/d744b47860e5c97e85256c40005d01d6/bc94a057247ad11085256e8500541fe5!OpenDocument.

—— (2004b) *A More Secure World: Our Shared Responsibility*, Report of the Secretary-General's High-Level Panel on Threats, Challenges and Change, A/59/565, 29 November, New York: United Nations.

—— (2005a) *In Larger Freedom: Towards Security, Development and Human Rights for All*, Report of the Secretary-General of the United Nations for decision by

Heads of State and Government, September. Available at: http://www.un.org/largerfreedom/.

—— (2005b) *2005 World Summit Outcome: Resolution Adopted by the General Assembly*, A/RES/60/1, 16 September, Available at: http://domino.un.org/UNISPAL.NSF/a06f2943c226015c85256c40005d359c/af5561450437805485257098 0054e21a!OpenDocument.

Urquhart, Sir Brian (1994) 'The United Nations' Capacity for Peace Enforcement', address, International Institute for Sustainable Development, Winnipeg, May. Available at: http://www.iisd.org/security/unac/urqudoc.htm.

9 Non-traditional security in Asia

The many faces of securitisation

Mely Caballero-Anthony

Introduction

Since the 1990s, there has been a growing interest in the study of non-traditional security (NTS) in Asia, especially in the light of the emerging challenges brought on by a host of factors, including the effects of globalisation. In East Asia[1] more generally, concerns about environmental degradation, outbreaks of infectious diseases, illegal migration, various types of transnational crimes and others have now been regarded as threats that endanger the security of states and society, and the regional and international community at large. Many of these non-military concerns are now categorised in the security studies literature as non-traditional security (NTS) threats/issues. The appropriation of the security label attached to these threats has been a significant development. It is significant in that there is increasingly a tendency by a number of actors – regional organisations, national governments, policy communities and civil society organisations – to designate and treat a growing list of national and transnational issues as security concerns. 'Security-framing' appears to be an effective way to bring attention to these threats, convey urgency and command resources at various levels – from the local to the regional and international – to address the complex challenges that arise as one responds to these security challenges.

The trend to frame these non-traditional issues as security threats or 'securitise' raises a number of salient issues. Let me cite two. The first one is the conceptual issue and its implication on the field of security studies and international relations. To be sure, securitisation has led to the mushrooming of various studies on the extension and re-conceptualisation of security. No longer is the meaning of security confined to the conventional military dimension of state and inter-state relations nor confined to strategic balance of power issues. With issues, for instance, like transnational crime and infectious diseases being framed as threats to the well-being and security of states and societies, the area of security studies is now also being re-defined as scholars are compelled to address the trend of broadening the concept of security. This led 'traditional' specialists of the field to lament the effects of including a long laundry list of issues to security which to them rendered the word (security) meaningless (see Del Rosso 1995: 190).

Nevertheless, while security specialists from the realist/neo-realist school stay true to their discipline of covering only issues that pertain to the state and its defence from external military attacks, several 'schools of thoughts' have emerged with their own approaches and frameworks in the study of security (see Smith 2002). Among these is the Copenhagen School of Security and Desecuritisation that attempts not only to examine the broadening conception of security, but also to provide a systematic framework in determining how and when a specific matter becomes securitised or desecuritised (see Buzan *et al.* 1995; Waever 1995). In understanding and coping with emerging non-traditional security issues, the Copenhagen framework (which will be discussed in more detail below) provides a useful analytical tool in examining how certain issues get onto the security agenda – i.e. 'securitised' – while others do not.

The second impact of securitising NTS is its implications on governance and policy responses of states, as well as non-state actors. An important question that needs to be asked is whether securitisation should be the way to go to respond to non-traditional security concerns, and at what level – national or regional? And if so, the related questions are: which NTS issues should be securitised, why, how and by whom? How should state and other non-state actors respond to these issues once they are 'securitised' and what are the indicators of successful securitisation? How can we balance the competing interests between state and non-state interests in responding to NTS challenges? Are regional responses more effective than domestic ones?

These questions indeed bring to the fore the inherent tensions between states and societies as attempts to securitise NTS issues differ and the processes involved in securitising them become more complex. Given the important place of NTS in the security agenda of many states in the region, it is therefore essential to focus more attention on understanding how these issues have become NTS issues besides mapping them out and examining the policies that have emerged and the mechanisms that have been crafted to deal with them. The aim of probing deeper in order to understand the securitisation process is also driven by the exigency of revisiting the question of whether framing these issues in security terms brings more negative than positive results. If it were more of the former, we would then need to examine the unintended consequences of securitisation.

Against these questions, the objectives of this chapter are two-fold. First, it examines how certain NTS issues have featured in the security agenda in Southeast Asia and how various actors have responded to the types of complex challenges (political, security, and economic) that have emerged. This section pays close attention to how state and non-state actors have framed these issues in security terms by applying the Copenhagen framework of securitisation. Second, in discussing these selected cases in which securitisation had either been successful or had failed, the chapter identifies key issues that arise in the process of securitisation. Some of the issues identified here are drawn from findings of the recently concluded research project on the 'Non-Traditional Security in Asia: Dynamics of Securitisation', undertaken by the Institute of Defence and Strategic Studies (IDSS), Singapore.[2]

There are two arguments that are being presented in this chapter. The first is that while 'securitisation' may make for a compelling approach to respond to urgent NTS security challenges, it also poses unintended consequences. These 'unintended consequences' present a number of policy dilemmas among different actors as they grapple with questions of how best to respond to NTS threats, especially when viewed against the competing practices of both state and civil society actors in the securitisation of these issues. The dilemma becomes starker when notions of security differ between states and society, especially when one confronts the questions: 'whose security?' and 'security for whom?' While one would submit that securitisation may be necessary in some cases for reasons of efficacy, this could in fact undermine gains made by the state towards democratisation, impede popular participation in addressing transnational issues and marginalise alternative voices and approaches to complex problems. Given these concerns, the second argument is, that in responding to certain NTS threats, different levels of 'securitisation' may need to take place in order to strike a balance between concerns for state and human security, while attending to the serious risks and vulnerabilities brought on by these security challenges.

Thus, understanding the dynamics of securitising NTS issues is pertinent to Southeast Asia[3] (and even beyond the region), particularly in the light of the series of crises that have hit the region. These include the debilitating impact of 1997–98 financial crisis on the members of the Association of Southeast Asian Nations (ASEAN), their experience with the health crises brought on by SARS and the looming threat of an influenza pandemic, and last but not least, the consequences of the 9/11 terrorist attacks in the United States followed by the rising incidents of terrorist bombings in the region. This spate of crises had created additional pressures and demands on governments and other non-state actors to protect the security of states and societies. And, while the trends in securitising NTS in the region may have largely been state-led, it is becoming increasingly clear that the processes of securitisation can no longer be the monopoly of the state.

The chapter proceeds as follows. Following the introduction, the second section presents a brief summary of the securitisation framework informed by the Copenhagen School. This section discusses the usefulness of applying the Copenhagen framework in identifying what and how certain issues have been identified as security concerns. This is followed by a third section which discusses how selected NTS issues – i.e. poverty and infectious diseases – have been securitised or partially securitised by different actors in the region, both state and non-state. The fourth section then proceeds to identify some of the problems that arise in the process of securitising these issues at the regional and the domestic levels. To explore whether domestic factors impact on the way NTS issues are securitised and addressed at the regional (ASEAN) level, this section examines key factors that explain points of tensions, namely: (1) the role of the state; (2) competing notions of security, particularly human security; (3) the lack of capacity/resources; and (4) the lacunae in institutions that are critical to promoting better governance in addressing emerging security challenges. With these key issues that define the dilemmas of securitisation in ASEAN, the chapter concludes with some thoughts on how a more participatory and multi-level governance is the way to better address the NTS challenges confronting us today.

Securitisation and non-traditional security issues

Before we proceed to discuss some examples of NTS issues and examine how state and non-state actors in ASEAN have responded to them, either by securitisation or other means, we need first to explain what securitisation is and what this process involves. The Copenhagen School, through the works of Barry Buzan, Ole Waever and Jaap de Wilde, defined securitisation as a process in which 'an issue is framed as a security problem' (Buzan *et al.* 1995: 75). In operational terms, a political concern can be securitised through an 'act of securitisation' – i.e. a 'speech act' (Waever 1995: 55). The speech act refers to the representation of a certain issue as an existential threat to security. According to this framework, an important criterion to linking the understanding of security to the question of survival is whether an issue is considered to be an existential threat.

Securitising actors use speech acts to articulate a problem in security terms and to persuade a relevant audience of its immediate danger. The articulation in security terms conditions public opinion and provides securitising actors with the right to mobilise state power and to move beyond traditional rules of politics. The latter may require emergency measures and may justify actions outside the normal political procedures.

The securitisation process as defined by the Copenhagen School essentially involves two stages that explain how and when an issue is to be perceived and acted upon as an existential threat to security. First, it is not enough for a securitising actor to use the speech act. Beyond the speech act, he/she must be able to successfully convince a specific audience (public opinion, politicians, military officers or other elites) that a *referent object* – things/people that are seen to be existentially threatened and have a legitimate claim to survival – is existentially threatened. What constitutes an existential threat is viewed by the Copenhagen School to be a subjective question that depends on a shared understanding of what is meant by such a danger to security. The securitising actor may not necessarily be the referent object. It could be an actor that speaks on behalf of and acts to defend the security of the state, or a larger community or certain groups of people. Second, once the audience is convinced, securitisation proceeds when the presence of an existential threat allows and legitimises the breaking of conventional rules and the adoption of emergency measures.

In sum, securitisation refers to the classification of and consensus about certain phenomena, persons or entities as existential threats requiring emergency measures. In these circumstances, standard political procedures are no longer viewed as adequate and extraordinary measures may be imposed to counter the threat. Due to the urgency of the issue, constituencies tolerate the use of counteractions outside of the normal bounds of political procedure.[4]

The securitisation framework offered by the Copenhagen School becomes a useful tool in investigating how some issues of non-military concerns have now been classified as NTS issues. It is useful in that it allows us to ask the following relevant questions:

- Who and what are the referent objects? These can be individuals and groups (refugees, victims of human rights abuses, etc.) as well as issue areas (national sovereignty, environment, economy, etc.) that possess a claim to survival and whose existence is ostensibly threatened.
- Who are the securitising actors/or desecuritising actors?[5] These can be governments – political elites, military, and civil society – those actors who securitise an issue by articulating the existence of threat(s) to the survival of specific referent objects.
- How is a process of securitisation completed? This focuses on how securitising actors use the language of security (speech act) to convince a specific audience of the existential nature of the threat.

Moreover, as a conceptual tool, the securitisation framework eliminates the rigid distinction between what are 'traditional' and 'non-traditional' security issues since these issues would presumably be high on the security agenda of states.

The framework, however, has some limitations. While the framework tells us who securitises and how the process takes place, it does not address the question of why securitisation occurs. Aside from its tendency to be Eurocentric in its approach, it also does not pay attention to empirical application. For example, besides stressing the need to convince an audience about the existential threat, it failed to identify indicators of successful securitisation. In fact, its explanation of how an issue is securitised is focused entirely on a single mechanism – the speech act (see Caballero-Anthony *et al.* 2006). Nevertheless, in a recently concluded research study of securitisation of NTS in Asia, which employs a modified version of the Copenhagen model and examines and applies it to empirical cases of securitisation and desecuritisation, it is interesting to note that policy-makers, non-governmental organisations (NGOs) and other actors in the region do in fact engage in acts of securitisation but may not necessarily be aware of the processes involved, as well as its unintended consequences (ibid).

Thus, despite the limitations of this framework, it is still a relevant approach, given the growing trend in the region of 'securitising' non-traditional concerns as security threats. By adopting such a framework, we are prodded to probe further into how NTS challenges, once securitised, are dealt with domestically and regionally. More importantly, aside from asking the usual questions of what is being securitised, by whom and for whom – we are able to raise other related but equally salient questions that speak to the conditions of securitisation, i.e. nature of the threats, distribution of power, the nature of domestic political systems and the impact of local and international norms, and, not least, the effects and consequences of securitisation.

NTS issues and the dynamics of securitisation in Southeast Asia [6]

Why securitise?

Before we investigate how some issues have been securitised, we first address why NTS concerns are gaining more prominence in Asia – particularly Southeast Asia – given that the region's notions of security already reflect a broader, more comprehensive view of security. One could even argue that the idea of NTS is not really new, and had been already inherent in the security thinking in ASEAN and the broader East Asian region (see Alagappa 1998; Akaha 2004; Caballero-Anthony 2005). Moreover, the current attention given to issues such as economic security and energy security had already been part of the 'traditional' security concerns in the region.

However, one would also note that it was not until the early 1990s and particularly after the advent of the 1997 Asian financial crisis that the notion of NTS gained more urgency in the region (see Kim and Lee 2000; Tan and Boutin 2001). In fact, with the onset of infectious diseases such as Severe Acute Respiratory Syndrome (SARS) and the avian influenza, increasing incidents of terrorist attacks and transnational criminal activities, not to mention the impact of natural disasters like the Indian Ocean tsunami in December 2004, there is now a clear tendency by multiple actors to designate and treat these issues as security matters – or 'securitise' them. Thus, not only is the security language increasingly being employed more frequently in framing these issues as security threats, but the nature of the existential threats has also taken on different interpretations to include threats to national sovereignty and territorial integrity (as in the case of piracy, drug trafficking and other transnational crimes), and threats to human security (as in the case of poverty and infectious diseases).

These developments therefore raise two major issues that need to be addressed. These are: (1) the rationale for deploying the language of security on issues that are outside the traditional domain of security; and (2) the extent to which one can clearly show the security implications of these challenges. The next section will turn to a discussion of selected NTS issues that are gaining more attention in the regional security agenda. The issues chosen – poverty and infectious diseases – are two of the most frequently highlighted NTS issues in ASEAN. In what follows, we examine the 'securitisation' process by identifying who the securitising actors are; their motivations for 'securitising' an issue; and analysing the issues/problems that have emerged as a result of the securitisation process.

Re-securitising poverty (and economic development) in ASEAN

Poverty has often been portrayed as a case for economic security, a concern that is not new to the region. This issue, however, has again become a pressing concern and has been featured in the list of emerging NTS challenges in Asia, particularly within Southeast Asia. The pertinent questions to ask here are: 'How is poverty a security issue?' and 'How has this been securitised, and by whom?'

In the experience of ASEAN, the framing of poverty as a security issue is a common trend among its member states. However, ASEAN members have their own approach in securitising the issue, and often these are informed by the way their respective political elites have linked poverty to the different concepts of security found in the region, i.e. state security, comprehensive security or human security. Closely related to the process of securitising poverty in ASEAN are the dominant notions of security found in the region. And, it fact, it is through these varying 'paradigms' where we would also be able to discern the palpable tensions between states and societies in the many ways poverty has been securitised.

Comprehensive security

In ASEAN, security had always been regarded as multi-dimensional and comprehensive in nature. It is comprehensive in that aside from the military aspects of security, the political, economic and socio-cultural aspects are regarded as equally important by member states in ASEAN. This security thinking is well reflected in numerous ASEAN documents such as the ASEAN Concord, ASEAN Treaty of Amity and Cooperation, ASEAN 2020 and more recently, the ASEAN Community. Comprehensive security, however, is more often understood as the mutually constituted relationship between (regime) stability and economic development. In ASEAN, this is best illustrated in the notion of regional resilience which is an extension of its member states, e.g. Malaysia and Indonesia's doctrine of *Ketahanan Nasional* (national resilience).[7] National resilience can briefly be described as attaining political (regime) stability by putting a premium on achieving economic development. National resilience in turn underpins regional resilience, and can only be secured if member states in ASEAN are able to fit it in their own domestic domains.

At least prior to the 1997 financial crisis, the political elites in ASEAN had been conscious about the destabilising effects of poverty on regime stability. These had made state officials wary of domestic factors that could jeopardise their political survival. Hence, a critical agenda that had to be addressed in order to build political legitimacy and ensure regime stability was precisely to fight poverty and achieve rapid economic growth. Particularly for multi-ethnic societies in ASEAN like Malaysia and Indonesia, there was a shared understanding among political elites that poverty and inequality could threaten political stability, and exacerbate ethnic and religious differences. These issues were regarded as more threatening than any form of external military threats. National resilience therefore advanced the idea that eco-nomic development and security were two sides of the same coin and in turn, provides the foundation for regional resilience and stability (Alagappa 1989).

Regional trends in the securitisation of poverty: tensions between state and human security

Against this background, a pertinent question to ask is, how successful was ASEAN's securisation of poverty/economic development? One could suggest that until the 1997 crisis, ASEAN's doctrine of 'national resilience' was a successful means to securitise economic development. But, as noted earlier, the process of securitisation was mostly done at the national level, despite regional declarations that indicate the importance of economic development to the security of Southeast Asia. Moreover, as an intergovernmental organ-isation with no supra-national jurisdiction, ASEAN's efforts in this regard have largely been defined by the sum of its parts. It is important to note therefore that the securitising actors of poverty and economic development had mostly been the states represented by their ruling political elites.

Since the dominant security thinking was underpinned by the idea that national security depended on robust economic development, it was not dif-ficult therefore for many of the political leaders in ASEAN to 'securitise' their economies without the necessary acceptance by the audience (i.e. their own citizens) – even to the point where opposition to the idea of a develop-mental state was not tolerated in many states in the region. Such modalities, however, have led to unintended consequences. For instance, 'securitising' economic development meant that aside from developing the five-year devel-opment plans, state authorities (like in Malaysia and Indonesia) undertook strict policies with regard to labour rights, employment, media operations and others to protect the values associated with economic security. As a consequence, the states took on greater capacity to impose controls in the allocation of economic resources. Since economic development was also equated with regime stability, this gave the states wider latitude to alienate citizens who held contrarian views on the nature of their developmental pol-icies, while government critics were often branded as 'subversive elements'. 'Securitisation' of economic development also allowed for the enactment of 'emergency measures' to protect the interests of the state against possible threats. However, when non-state actors also attempted to securitise poverty, new tensions emerged at different levels, given the conflicting interests and divergence in security thinking. These so-called unintended consequences of securitising poverty are best illustrated in the respective experiences of Malaysia and Indonesia in their securitisation of poverty, before and after the 1997 financial crisis. This is discussed next.

The Malaysian experience

In Malaysia, one could cite the adoption of the National Economic Policy (NEP) as a visible 'securitisation' move to guarantee regime stability and economic development, while at the same time 'securitise' the conditions of the Malay ethnic group who at that time largely comprised the poorer segments of the society.[8] Against the country's experience of racial riots in 1969, the government introduced the NEP in 1970 which introduced a series of government regulations to help advance the plight of the majority Malay ethnic group, including an 'affirmative action' programme for them based on quotas in education, employment and the awarding of government contracts (see Milne and Mauzy 1999; Sundaram 1988; and Herderson *et al.* 2002). The securitising actors were the dominant Malay elites who have continued to dominate the Malaysian government.

Policies associated with the securitisation of the economy had significant repercussions on the minority groups. The problem became more acute when seen from the context of the security referent, for clearly in the multi-ethnic society, the question that emerged is 'Whose (economic) security?' In securitising the economic development of the state and the dominant ethnic group, the government had created security dilemmas for the minority ethnic groups (Malaysian Chinese, Indians and others). The NEP policy has resulted in unintended consequences, such as the resultant 'emergency' measures meted out to those who questioned racial policies since this subject had been considered taboo for public discussions. Hence, any citizen assemblies that discussed and/or questioned the policies of affirmative action for the ethnic Malays (Bumiputra) faced the risk of being perceived as inciting racial riots. Individuals involved also risked the possibility of being detained under the Internal Security Act, which justified detention without trial in the name of national security. Interestingly, many of these types of measures still remain in place, in a state that can arguably be considered as being no less democratic than its other neighbours, such as Thailand and the Philippines. And, while the above measures are unpopular, there are no overt moves by the Malaysian authorities to repeal these policies. This is despite the fact that other sectors of the society – NGOs and civil society groups – have been putting pressure on the government. In this regard, the successful securitisation of the economic rights of the ethnic Malays reflected the power differentials between the racial groups in the country.

The Malaysian story of a state-led securitisation of poverty and economic development, although problematic, nevertheless points to a number of considerations that justified an uneven securitisation for the sake of racial harmony. In so far as poverty is concerned, Malaysia has been one of the developing countries in Asia that had recorded an impressive and successful poverty reduction programme. The country's incidence of poverty has drastically declined over the past three decades. In 1970, while 49.3 per cent of the population were officially poor, this figure was brought down steadily to 20.7 per cent in 1985 and 8.7 per cent in 1995 and 5.1 per cent in 2002. Incidence of hardcore poverty was also reduced to 0.4 per cent in 2002. In spite of the Asian economic crisis in 1997, the poverty rate in 2003 stood at 4.5 per cent (see Economic Planning Unit 2005). At least from this angle, it could be argued that the state-led securitisation of poverty in Malaysia has been successful.

During the 1997–98 financial crisis, Malaysia once again securitised its economy by introducing capital controls. One analysis of the Malaysian government's decision to adopt the policy of capital controls defined it as an emergency move to 'securitise' the Malaysian economy from global financial pressures. Although perceived as an 'illiberal' move, the decision was justified as a necessary response to domestic political pressures to protect its currency from volatility. Thus, despite international concerns about the repercussions of such a policy on the prospects of its economy, one could suggest that there was societal support for such measures. In fact, the argument was that taking the decision to impose capital controls outside the realm of normal politics – e.g. doing away with public debate – was part of the 'emergency' measures that had to be taken to mitigate the impact of the spiralling economic crisis on the country's economy and welfare of its people.

The Indonesian experience

The Indonesian case brings another dimension to regional attempts at securitising poverty. Prior to the 1997 financial crisis, Indonesia did not have Malaysia's equivalent of the NEP. Nevertheless, Indonesia was one of the cases cited by the World Bank and the United Nations Development Program (UNDP) as having successfully improved its economic conditions through its focused national development programmes. In fact, the country's remarkable stride was reflected in the kind of positive ranking it received from the UNDP's human development index, categorising Indonesia as part of the medium-developed economies. Its average annual growth rate of gross domestic product (GDP) in the last decade before the 1997 crisis was more than 7 per cent with a relatively low inflation rate of below 10 per cent. The former Indonesian President Suharto was commonly referred to as *Bapak Pembangunan* (Father of Development) and his long stay in power was legitimised by the country's long decade of economic development – also known as the 'performance legitimacy'.

But the crisis proved to unravel the legitimation that economic development had for the regime's security/stability (Japan Centre for International

Exchange 1999: 56–7; Thiparat 2001). This was clearly illustrated in the way the economic crisis had unfolded in Indonesia. Briefly, the financial crisis put the Indonesian economy into a tailspin. There was hyper-inflation, with unemployment levels reaching as high as 24 per cent. This resulted in about 15 million people in the country being rendered unemployed. At the height of the crisis in mid-1998, poverty rates consequently shot up. It was estimated that about 37 per cent of the country's population, or 75 million people, were reduced to living below the poverty line (defined as US$1 per person per day). This dire economic condition was in stark contrast to pre-1997 period when Indonesia was cited by the World Bank as the only country in the world that had remarkably improved its Human Development Index (HDI), after having started from a very low base in 1975. In effect, the crisis reduced the country's economy to shambles and led to untold human misery.

The crisis also triggered political unrest. The government's economic restructuring policies led by the International Monetary Fund (IMF), which included the foreclosure of 16 banks and the steep price hike of basic commodities such as the 71 per cent increase in petrol prices, led to a number of student protests and public demonstrations staged in the several cities. The 10-day student demonstration at Trisakti University in Indonesia that saw four students killed sparked a wave of violent riots that raged through the country's capital, leading angry mobs to loot and burn buildings indiscriminately. Hundreds of deaths were reported and those who could fled the country as the capital came to a standstill (Indahnesiah, 1998). Outside Jakarta, there were reports of ethnic and religious conflicts, which came as a great shock to a country that was known for its religious tolerance. The violence that shook the country eventually led to the fall of President Suharto after 33 years in power.

The economic crisis was indeed a wake-up call to Indonesia and to other states in the region. Indonesia's neighbouring states, for instance, were not immune to the political turmoil that happened in Indonesia, particularly those that were badly hit by the crisis. In Malaysia, palpable cleavages emerged among its political elites, especially after the ousting of the former Deputy Prime Minister Anwar Ibrahim who was perceived, among others, as having endangered the state's economic security with his pro-IMF policies, which he introduced during the early stage of the crisis.[9] In Thailand, the government of Chaovalit Choonhavan was forced to resign when political confrontation deepened as the country's currency collapsed and as the devastation brought on by the crisis continued to wreak havoc to its economy. The impact of the economic and political events in badly hit economies reverberated across the region and dashed hopes for early economic recovery for the rest of ASEAN. It also exacerbated the loss of confidence in the region that was once the darling of foreign investors and other financial institutions. Moreover, the events brought a number of uncertainties to regional security, including bilateral frictions among ASEAN members resulting from the effects of economic recession.[10]

More importantly, the crisis in Indonesia also re-affirmed the close nexus between economics and security. It reinforced the idea that the economy had to be (re-)'securitised' if regime security was to be ensured. Yet, ironically, one of the lessons learned at the height of the crisis was that no matter how convincing the arguments were for regime and economic security through rapid economic development, these approaches had become dismally inadequate against the new types of security threats that transcended borders.

Against these stories of human tragedies, what was more interesting in the Indonesian story of securitisation was what happened during the periods of crisis (1997–98). As we note, the 'securitisation' of poverty/economy in the past was largely state-led; during the crises period the discernible process was led by non-state actors. This was in contrast to the Malaysian state-led securitisation of its security during the 1997–98 crisis period.

In a recent study on the securitisation of poverty in Indonesia, Bob Hadiwinata (2006) has argued that while the Indonesian government should have moved to securitise poverty, it failed miserably to protect the welfare of its people. As a result, some NGOs decided to intervene to provide succour to the plight of the poor especially against the severe impact of the IMF's structural adjustment policies (SAPs) that were adopted by the Indonesian government. These included the government's decision to substantially cut the state subsidies on food, health care, education, petrol, etc.

Hadiwinata's study showed that the impact of the SAPs on the poorer sectors of the populations, e.g. urban settlers – factory workers, shop assistants, street side traders, coolies who had lost their jobs – reduced them to living in squalid conditions. The government's failure to securitise their condition had, however, resulted in NGOs moving in to securitise the plight of the poor by 'claiming to be the legitimate security agencies in providing human security to the underprivileged and neglected' (ibid.). Thus, NGOs such as Suara Ibu Peduli, Kalyaamitra and the Urban Poor Consortium (UPC) initiated what Hadiwinata described as emergency measures, to provide the basic necessities to poor families. There were instances, however, when the NGOs' securitisation approach led to speech acts which could be regarded as inflammatory and subversive. Hadiwinata cited cases, for instance, when NGOs such as the UPC responded to the government's move to expel poor settlers from the *kampungs* (village) by mobilising the poor to demonstrate against the local government office with placards carrying slogans like: '*Pemerintah adalah musuh rakyat kecil!*' (The government is the enemy of the poor!). But there were other NGOs that preferred a more constructive approach. In contrast to the UPC, Hadiwinata cited the experiences of the Bina Swadaya Yogyakarta (BSY) and CD-Bethesda NGOs that advocated a more self-help approach by focusing on providing primary health care treatments to those families who had lost or had no access at all to medical care through the formation and training of village health cadres. The BSY, for example, organised and set up micro-enterprises to facilitate access and distribution of basic goods (food, petrol, water, etc.) to poorer communities through their PRA (participatory rural appraisal) programme.

In both these cases, Hadiwinata argued that as a result of absent state policies and intervention to alleviate the suffering of the poor, especially as a result of crises, spaces were opened for NGOs to offer alternative approaches to address the human insecurities of these marginalised groups. Yet, as Hadiwinata observed, the securitisation move by the NGOs was met with reservations not only by state actors but even some members of the public who questioned the legitimacy of their actions. In this case, a major challenge that non-state actors faced as 'securitising actors' was to convince the Indonesian public of their competence and sincerity. Thus, Hadiwinata's assessment of the NGOs' securitisation of poverty during the crises period was one that was only partially successful. It was partially successful because of the perceived lack of legitimacy of NGOs as an 'agency with the authority to declare an emergency situation and convince the government that poverty was an existential threat to the security of the poor'.

The above discussion of two different cases of securitisation reveals that there can be different levels of securitising poverty (or any NTS) in the region. The different dynamics, however, can best be seen not at the regional level but rather at the national/domestic level. This is largely because beyond the regional (i.e. ASEAN) pronouncements of the vital importance of poverty threats to national and regional security, most of the acts of securitisation were clearly done at the national level. One could surmise therefore that in keeping with the regional thinking on national resilience, the process of securitising poverty was regarded primarily as a national responsibility. This is not to claim, however, that there were no attempts at the ASEAN level to rally support, especially at the height of the financial crisis to stricken countries. But most of the types of assistance were done through bilateral arrangements, due the lack of regional capacity and mechanisms to provide emergency assistance in times of crisis.

At the national level, the differing levels of securitisation are also predicated on the role that different actors take in the processes of 'securitisation' and who/what they want to secure. For instance, in the case of state-led securitisation undertaken by Malaysia before and after the crisis, one could surmise that it was the state's security that was being 'securitised' while in the Indonesian NGO-led securitisation during the crises, it was the human security of the poor and vulnerable that was being protected. Nonetheless, one could see that in both cases, several problems emerged which are reflective of the competing interests and practices of securitising actors in the complex processes of securitisation.

Securitising infectious diseases in ASEAN

In the securitisation of infectious diseases in the region, we again see interesting dynamics in the different levels of securitisation, as illustrated in the following two cases of 'successful' securitisation and 'partial' securitisation. These dynamics are played out more clearly when we look at the nature of the process involved in the securitisation of SARS and AIDS.

The outbreak of SARS in 2003 turned out to be one of the most devastating and feared diseases in modern history. It was instructive in that it demonstrated how the pandemic was more than a health crisis. The news and narratives about SARS revealed the extent of the health crisis which was not limited to loss of life alone but extended to other areas – socio-economic, political, and security. The virus infected about 8,000 people worldwide and killed nearly 800.

The panic was, however, compounded by the fact that there was no known cure for SARS, and while the death toll of SARS was much lower than the quarter of a million casualties of the Boxing Day tsunami, many of the victims were health-care workers. The psychological impact was significant. In the words of Dr. Cecilia Chan, Director of the Centre for Behavioural Health at HKU), 'when doctors and nurses cannot take care of themselves – [become victims], the whole community panics' (*Asian Wall Street Journal* 2005: 3). To be sure, the SARS crisis put the region's medical capability to test.

The impact of SARS was not only psychological. It also hit where it often matters most – the economy. The extent of the economic impact of SARS was reflected in the sudden disruption of economic activity in several Asian economies. Although the crisis lasted for about five months, the economic loss was estimated to be US$50 billion for the region and about US$150 billion worldwide (see *Far Eastern Economic Review* 2003; Asian Development Bank 2003). These losses were largely due to losses in the tourism and travel sectors that were badly hit when people began to shy away from travelling to SARS-affected countries such as China, Hong Kong, Singapore, and Vietnam. Topping all these was also the huge slump in the retail industry, which had seen a 20–50 per cent decrease in business for many countries (ibid.).

Moreover, SARS caused political ripples that had the potential to impact negatively on the government's legitimacy and perceived ineffectiveness. A case in point was China, which was initially blamed for mismanaging the outbreak. Beijing's poor handling of SARS in the early stages undermined its credibility, and led to international calls for more transparency and accountability. For instance, the former Director General of the World Health Organization (WHO) Gro Harlem Brundtland remarked in a press statement that had Chinese authorities acted earlier and with more openness, the outbreak of the disease would have taken a different course (*Straits Times* 2003). In order to win back confidence from the international community, Chinese health officials consequently held press conferences on a daily basis to assuage concerns about SARS transmission in the country and assure the international community that the situation was under control.

The case of SARS

The SARS episode presents some interesting indicators of how the infectious disease was securitised. First was the clear speech act. In the statements and press briefings coming from officials of Singapore, Vietnam, Malaysia, and the Philippines, SARS became 'a national security concern'. The national security adviser of the Philippines for instance even went to the extent of saying that '[the] SARS threat . . . was greater than any threat of terrorism in the country' (*The Inquirer* 2003; *The Star* 2005).

Second were the crisis management measures that were adopted, particularly the mandatory quarantine that was imposed in some states. For example, the Singapore Health Ministry invoked the Infectious Diseases Act to isolate people who were known to have been in contact with those who had fallen sick with SARS. Similar measures were adopted in SARS-stricken countries in the region, including closure of schools and entertainment centres and other areas known to spread infection. Although China was severely criticised for initially playing down the seriousness of the problem and its belated response in containing the spread of infection, the Chinese government eventually took action including the drastic step of controlling the movement of people in and out of the capital, Beijing, which had been a site for local transmission of the disease.

There were also strict immigration and border controls. Several countries adopted stringent measures to screen and control visitors from SARS-affected countries into their own countries. Thermal imagers were installed in airports to scan and bar passengers with fevers from entering and leaving airports and other points of entry-exit. There were also other more stringent measures introduced that later were on reconsidered. Within ASEAN, for example, Thailand and Malaysia had at one point banned entry of tourists coming in from China but withdrew it after quiet protests from China which in turn 'retaliated' by preventing its citizens from travelling to Malaysia, Singapore and Thailand. But the policy to require their own citizens arriving from China and other SARS-affected areas to go on voluntary quarantine for about a week to 10 days stayed in place until the WHO gradually removed the countries from its list of SARS-affected areas where the travel advisory applied (see Caballero-Anthony 2005).

The response to the SARS crisis was a good illustration of successful securitisation of infectious diseases at the regional level. For badly hit countries in Southeast Asia such as Singapore, Vietnam and even the Philippines, the speed and efficiency with which governments responded to SARS were commendable.

Securitisation at the wider regional level

As far as regional responses to contain SARS were concerned, the crisis generated unprecedented coordination among countries in ASEAN, together with China, Japan and Korea (ASEAN + 3), as seen by the hastily convened meetings among heads of governments and officials. Singapore Prime Minister Goh Chok Tong and Thai Prime Minister Thaksin Shinawatra led the initiatives to gather their regional counterparts to address the crisis. Following the ASEAN + 3 health ministers meeting held in Kuala Lumpur on 26 April 2003, the Special ASEAN Summit on SARS as well as the Special ASEAN-China Leaders Meeting were held back to back in Bangkok on 29 April 2003. During these meetings several measures were outlined to put in place regional mechanisms to address the multiplicity of issues brought on by the SARS crisis.

The immediate measures agreed upon involved the exchange of information and best practices in containing infectious diseases; strengthening of cooperation among front-line enforcement agencies such as health, immigration, customs, transport and law enforcement; and harmonisation of travel procedures to ensure proper health screening at the points of origin. Another significant measure was the protection of foreign nationals who may be suspected or probable SARS cases (see ASEAN 2003a, 2003b, 2003c).

The short-to-mid-term measures involved deepening cooperation between ASEAN and the WHO, as well as exploring the possibility of developing a regional framework of rapid response to outbreaks of infectious diseases. Malaysia, for example, proposed setting up a regional centre of disease control, while efforts are underway to further develop the ASEAN-Disease Surveillance Net, which coincidentally was set up in April 2003 at the height of the SARS crisis.

Securitising HIV/AIDS

While the response to SARS (or its securitisation) was effective in containing the spread of the disease, hence the argument for successful securitisation of infectious diseases, the responses to HIV/AIDS both at the national and regional level provide some interesting contrasts. Attempts at securitisation have brought mixed results. In a study by Ilavenil Ramiah (2006) on the securitisation of AIDS in Asia, she argues that despite the grave situation in the region, addressing the spread of HIV/AIDS is not getting the kind of urgency that it should be receiving. And, this is despite the fact that a number of actors, including state actors, have campaigned to securitise AIDS.

Ramiah's point is that while there are already several actors that have attempted to securitise AIDS, the results have not been effective. This, she argues, is a case of 'partial securitisation'. The author's views on partial securitisation are underlined by the argument that if AIDS were 'adequately securitised', there would have been more mechanisms to manage the disease both domestically and regionally and there would also be a declining trend in the rate of infections. The picture in Asia, however, paints a grim picture. It is estimated, for example, that there are about 8.2 million people living with HIV at the end of 2004 (see UNAIDS 2004: 38). In China, the Head of the

Department of Disease Control of the Ministry of Health had warned that if the AIDS epidemic were not dealt with efficiently by the year 2010, there could be more than 10 million HIV/AIDS patients in the country (see *Straits Times Interactive* 2002a).

Meanwhile, the figures are equally alarming in India. WHO's estimates placed the HIV infections in India at 5.1 million, while current reports from New Delhi's AIDS charity group, Naz Foundation, placed the figure closer to 15 million (*Time Magazine* 2005). In Cambodia, HIV/AIDS is now reported to be the country's 'killing field'. A senior Cambodian health official has said that by 2010, more than half a million of the country's 11.5 million population will suffer or die from AIDS (see *Straits Times Interactive* 2002b). Similarly, the WHO cites Myanmar as another country which has one of the most serious HIV epidemics in Asia, adding that HIV has already become 'entrenched in lower-risk populations in several parts of Myanmar' (UNAIDS 2004: 43).

To Ramiah, successful securitisation of AIDS goes beyond the 'speech act' of declaring AIDS as a national crisis. More importantly, these speeches should result in the creation of a national authority for HIV/AIDS that is responsible for policy formulation and coordination in the monitoring of the disease. This would also require the formulation of a framework for action that 'drives the alignment of all partners' – state officials, NGOs, and other civil society organisations – which would then lead, among others, to: (1) the establishment of standardised monitoring and evaluation for the prevention, care and treatment of AIDS; and (2) the mainstreaming of fighting HIV/AIDS into a major national development agenda (Ramiah 2006).

Reflections on securitisation in Southeast Asia

From the preceding discussion on the two cases of securitisation, we now examine some of the key issues that have emerged in the complex process of securitisation in the region. These issues, in turn, reflect the dilemmas that securitisation presents as a means to addressing a number of other non-traditional security issues as well.

A key issue in any securitisation process is the identity and role of the securitising actor. The two cases have reinforced the idea that the state is a critical actor in most of the securitisation process that is taking place in Southeast Asia. With resources at its disposal, the state plays the dominant role in deciding which issues are to be securitised – poverty, economic development, infectious disease, illegal migration, etc. Beyond the state's speech act, the state can also ensure the successful process of securitisation by carrying out concrete policies and undertaking the necessary institutional and structural adjustments to see the process through. In the Malaysian example on securitising poverty, we saw how the state had acted to securitise the plight of the ethnic Malays in Malaysia (post 1970s), and in the process securitise its economic and political stability, as well as the decision of the Malaysian leaders to impose capital controls in 1997 to insulate its economy from currency volatility caused by the financial crisis. Similarly, in case of securitising infectious diseases, we saw the critical role that different governments played in stemming the transmission of SARS by introducing emergency measures such as quarantines, and immigration and border controls.

On the other hand, while states are powerful actors in the securitisation of NTS issues, they could also be obstacles in attempts to securitise other NTS issues. As mentioned in this chapter, when the SARS crisis began to spiral, China was accused of trying to conceal the extent to which the transmission of infection was taking place in some of its provinces until the situation got out of hand. Similarly, in the current fight against the possible outbreak of the avian influenza, the poor health infrastructure of some states in ASEAN seriously affects both local capacity and regional capacity to institute reliable regional surveillance measures to stop the spread and transmission of the disease. For example, it was reported that Indonesia hid the information about infection for about two years until the number of infected avian influenza cases shot up (*Straits Times* 2005b).

The above cases highlight the problem of securitising certain issues that bring attention to the domestic conditions of state capacity and governance. In this regard, the interventions of regional organisations are critical in responding more effectively to the different kinds of challenges that could arise when NTS issues are not addressed adequately at the national/domestic level. The case of SARS and the continuing threat of avian flu are good examples of why regional responses are critical in supporting efforts at the national level for health and human security. Looking at the regional efforts in this regard, we note for instance that in December 2004, ASEAN established a task force to respond to the spread of avian flu in the region. In the spirit of this task-sharing arrangement, responsibility was divided among the five original members of the group with each country taking on a specific role. Indonesia was to harmonise vaccination and culling procedures; Malaysia was to draft action plans to contain the disease, boost emergency preparedness and establish disease-free zones within the region; the Philippines was to increase public awareness about the problem; Singapore was to establish an information-sharing system; and Thailand was to create surveillance systems to detect the disease and ensure rapid exchange and analysis of virus samples. This plan was reinforced in October 2005 with the establishment of a regional fund for avian flu and a three-year action plan (*Straits Times* 2005a). Funds are also being established beyond ASEAN to ASEAN + 3 as Southeast members look to their partners Japan, South Korea and China to assist in supplementing the amount (ibid).

Aside from regional organisations, a critical role is also played by NGOs and international organisations as securitising actors. But in certain NTS cases, however, some problems do arise given that states will prefer to seek alternative strategies to address a threat so as not to weaken their legitimacy. NGOs or international organisations may then find it difficult to proceed in securitising an issue if there is resistance from the state. What this means is that securitisation can run directly counter to the strong norm against internal interference that extends across the region.

Nevertheless, based on the experience of the region, there are exceptions to the centrality of the state in the securitisation process, especially in times of unexpected crises. As shown in the case of securitising poverty in Indonesia during the 1997 crisis, NGOs and civil society groups 'entered the arena' and became the main securitising actors, providing the necessary intervention (food and health care) at a time when the state failed to attend to the emergency needs of the poor. To be sure, this securisation had heightened the growing tensions between state and NGOs, especially at a time when the state was already weakened as a result of the crises. However, it is significant to note that in a democratising state such as Indonesia, despite competing interests, NGOs were allowed the space to intervene and draw on their own resources to respond to security concerns of certain sectors in the society without having to clash directly with the interest of the state. What is therefore equally significant is the fact that different actors with different resource constraints also account for differing levels of securitisation.

Another key issue, and closely related to the above role of securitising actors, are the normative tensions that emerge from the securitisation process. While it can be argued that securitisation may be good for reasons for efficacy – meaning that by securitising an area like poverty, actors may be able to draw attention to the issue and mobilise more resources – it could have unintended consequences. These can also come in various forms, especially when there are differing levels of securitisation as in the case of Malaysia which securitised economic development but, in the process, also gave preference to a particular referent object by securitising the plight of the dominant ethnic group. As a result, this led to the marginalisation of other members of the society. In the Indonesian case during the crisis period, one could see how the state, in the process of 'securitising' the economy by adopting SAPs, caused the dislocation of millions of workers and added more problems to the already suffering poor in the country.

The same concerns also apply to other NTS issues, such as illegal migration. Regardless of who is being protected, state or individual, securitising illegal migration could lead to greater abuse of state authority and repression of the rights of individuals. One could also argue that securitising the issue is not only bad on normative grounds but could also be counter-productive since this does not necessarily lead to more efficient solutions to the problem of illegal migration.

A third issue that is related to uneven securitisation is the nature of the NTS threat and the urgency that it commands. This can be seen in the different ways SARS (and now, avian influenza) have been 'securitised', as compared with how HIV/AIDS had been managed. While one could argue that the two types of infectious diseases are equally fatal, the impact that SARS had on the economy in so short a time and the virulence of the disease led many states, including international organisations like the WHO, to give utmost priority to addressing the problem. But given the fact that compared to SARS and AIDS, deaths from malaria are estimated to reach 3,000 daily (James 2003), and that about 1,000 people die of tuberculosis every day (*Philippine Star* 2005), one need not go any further to appreciate the need to securitise all types of infectious diseases. Yet, unlike SARS, these diseases are still essentially treated like medical problems rather than one of security. In this instance, we see two different levels/degrees of securitisation: one is the 'securitisation' of SARS and avian influenza and the other is still the 'medicalisation' of HIV/AIDS and other infectious diseases.

A related issue to the differences in threat perception is the varying impact on concerns for governance and human rights. What was interesting in the 'securitisation' of SARS was that while the emergency measures taken respectively by each states were draconian to some extent, there was less furore about the violation of human rights when quarantine orders were issued. Although the securitising actors were largely the states, there was also societal support to securitise SARS in order to respond urgently to the health threats to people and states. One could therefore suggest that the 'successful' securitisation of SARS may have more to do with the urgency posed by the security threat rather than about good governance, transparency and accountability. As the SARS experience revealed, it did not take much to convince anyone that SARS presented a clear and present danger to human lives, an unseen 'enemy' that had to be securitised.

Finally, a salient factor that needs to be highlighted in the securitisation of NTS in the region is the different conceptualisation of security that has had an important bearing on deciding what issues should be securitised, how this was going to be done and by whom. More often than not, the choice of which NTS to securitise, be it economic security, infectious diseases, or others, is predicated on the dominant conception of security, i.e. comprehensive security and state-centric security rather than human security. And since the dominant actor in the region remains the state, and thus becomes the main 'securitising' actor, it follows that securitisation of any NTS issue is still largely defined by the kinds of issues which are considered vital to the political survival of the regime or state (Alagappa 1998: 680). This was illustrated in the way economic development rather than poverty became the main focus of securitisation in most countries in the region. It also explains why on a salient issue like illegal migration, this continues to be regarded as a major NTS threat to the state. Clearly, against this trend, the idea of human security – drawing attention to the insecurities of individuals and societies – cannot advance further.

In conclusion, if the aim of securitisation was to better address emerging NTS concerns, against the dilemmas that arise from the uneven processes of securitisation, a better alternative might be to give more attention to building the capacity of institutions at all levels of governance that could best address and cope with the huge list of NTS concerns that confront the region.

Notes

1 East Asia in this chapter covers the ten states of Southeast Asia/ASEAN, and three Northeast Asian states: China, Japan and Korea.
2 For more information on the IDSS NTS project, see http://www.idss-nts.org.
3 The regional domain examined in this chapter is limited to Southeast Asia or ASEAN.
4 The Copenhagen School indicates, however, that the success of the act of securitisation does not depend solely on the adoption and implementation of such extraordinary actions.
5 Desecuritisation is the reverse process of securitisation. It involves the 'shifting of issues out of emergency mode and into the normal bargaining processes of the political sphere' (Buzan *et al.* 1995: 4).
6 In this chapter, I shall use Southeast Asia and ASEAN interchangeably.
7 Similar security doctrines can also be found in other ASEAN countries like Singapore and Thailand.
8 Until the 1970s, studies had shown that the poor in the country has been concentrated largely in the Bumiputra population and found living in the poorer regions of Kelantan, Terenggany, Kedah and Perlis and also in Sabah and Sarawak. The Malays also held about 1.5 per cent of the country's equity, while the Chinese held around 23 per cent and the rest was owned by foreign investors.
9 Before his unceremonious dismissal, former Deputy Prime Minister Anwar Ibrahim was also Malaysia's Finance Minister. He played an active role in stemming the economic crisis in the initial stages before he was fired from his official position. For more on the Malaysian crisis, see, for example, Jomo (2003) and Hilley (2001).
10 As recession began to bite in Thailand and Malaysia, both countries began deporting hundreds of foreign workers, most of them illegal, back to Myanmar and Indonesia. Some quarters in Indonesia had expressed disquiet over the timing of the repatriation of these workers given the volatile labour situation in the country. See Caballero-Anthony (1999).

References

Akaha, Tsuneo (1998) *Asian Security Practices: Material and Ideational Influences*, Stanford, CA: Stanford University Press.
—— (2004) 'Non-Traditional Security Cooperation for Regionalism in Northeast Asia', paper based on talk delivered at Waseda University, Tokyo, on 27 November 2003. Available at: http://www.waseda-coe-cas.jp/paper/20040116_akaha_eng.pdf.
Alagappa, Muthiah (1998) 'Comprehensive Security: Interpretation in ASEAN Countries', in Robert Scalapino *et al.* (eds) *Asian Security Issues: Regional and Global*, Berkeley, CA: Institute of East Asian Studies, University of California, pp. 50–78.
ASEAN (2003a) *Joint Statement on the Special ASEAN-China Leaders Meeting on SARS* Bangkok, 26 April.
—— (2003b) *Joint Statement of the Special ASEAN Leaders Meeting on SARS*, Bangkok, 29 April.
—— (2003c) *Joint Statements of ASEAN + 3 Ministers of Health Special Meeting on SARS*, Kuala Lumpur, Malaysia, 26 April.
Asian Development Bank Regional Economic Monitor (2003) 'Economic Impacts of the SARS Outbreak on East Asia: An Initial Assessment', 5 May.

Asian Wall Street Journal (2005) 'What Ails Asia', *The Asian Wall Street Journal*, 22 April.

Buzan, Barry, Waever, Ole and de Wilde, Jaap (1995) *Security: A New Framework for Analysis*, Boulder, CO: Lynne Rienner.

Caballero-Anthony, Mely (1999) 'Challenges to Southeast Asian Security Cooperation', in Guy Wilson-Roberts (ed.) *An Asia-Pacific Security Crisis? New Challenges to Regional Stability*, Wellington: Centre for Strategic Studies.

—— (2004) 'Revisioning Human Security in Southeast Asia', *Asian Perspectives*, 28 (3):155–89.

—— (2005) 'SARS in Asia: Crisis, Vulnerabilities and Regional Responses', *Asian Survey* 45(3) May/June, pp. 475–95.

——, Emmers, Ralf and Acharya, Amitav (eds) (2006) *Non-Traditional Security in Asia: The Dilemmas of Security*, Oxford: Ashgate.

Del Rosso, Stephen J. (1995) 'The Insecure State: Reflections on the "State" and "Security" in a Changing World', *DAEDALUS*, 124, cited in Paul B. Stares (ed.) (1998) *New Security Agenda: A Global Survey*, Tokyo: Japan Centre for International Exchange.

Economic Planning Unit (2005) *Mid-Term Review of the Eighth Malaysia Plan 2001–2005*, Putrajaya: Economic Planning Unit, Prime Minister's Department, Government of Malaysia. Available at: http://www.epu.jpm.my/New%20Folder/development%20plan/midterm-RM8.htm.

Far Eastern Economic Review (2003) 'The Cost of SARS: US$11 Billion and Rising', *Far Eastern Economic Review*, 24 April.

Hadiwinata, Bob (2006) 'Poverty and the Role of the NGOs in Protecting Human Security in Indonesia', in M. Caballero-Anthony *et al.* (eds) *Non-Traditional Security in Asia: The Dilemmas of Security*, Oxford: Ashgate.

Herderson, Jeffrey, Hulme, David, Philips, Richard and Ainur M. Nur, Noorul (2002) 'Economic Governance and Poverty Reduction in Malaysia', Working Paper, Available at: http://www.gapresearch.org/governance/MalaysiaReportMay2002.pdf.

Hilley, John (2001) *Malaysia: Mahathirism, Hegemony and the New Opposition*, London and New York: Zed Books.

Indahnesiah.com (1998) 'Ten Days that Shook Indonesia', Available at: *Indahnesiah.com:* http://www.indahnesia.com/DB/Story/Item.php (accessed 10 February 2004).

Inquirer (Philippines) (2003) 'Macapagal Bares Tough Measures to fight SARS', 25 April.

James, Barry (2003) 'Besides Malaria, SARS Pales as a Killer', *International Herald Tribune*, 26 April.

Japan Centre for International Exchange (1999) *The Asian Crisis and Human Security*, Tokyo: Japan Centre for International Exchange.

Jomo, K.S. (2003) *My Way: Mahathir's Economic Legacy*, Kuala Lumpur: Forum.

Kim, Dalchoon and Lee, Jung-Hoon (eds) (2000) *Comprehensive Security: Conceptions and Realities in Asia*, Seoul: Yonsei University Press.

Milne, R.S. and Mauzy, Diane (1999) *Malaysian Politics under Mahathir*, London: Routledge.

Philippine Star (2005) 'Healthcare Reforms, Growth-Stifling Diseases in Asia', *The Phillippine Star Online edn*, Available at: http://www.philstar.com/philstar/NEWS_FLASH090520021_1.htm.

Ramiah, Ilavenil (2006) 'Securitising the AIDS Issue in Asia', in Mely Caballero-

Anthony *et al.* (eds), *Non-Traditional Security in Asia: The Dilemmas of Securitisation*, Oxford: Ashgate.

Smith, Steve (2002) 'The Contested Concept of Security', Institute of Defence and Strategic Studies Working Paper No. 23, Singapore: Institute of Defence and Strategic Studies.

Star (Malaysia) (2005) 'SARS: A National Security Matter', 5 April.

Straits Times (2003) 'China: It's Cooperating Now: by WHO', 8 April.

—— (2005a) 'Fund Set Up to Fight Flu in S-E Asia', 1 October.

—— (2005b), 'Jakarta "Covered up" Bird Flu for 2 Years', 22 October.

Straits Times Interactive (2002a) 'China on the Verge of AIDS Epidemic', 6 September. Available at: http://straitstimes.asia1.com.sg.

—— (2002b) 'More than 500,000 Aids Victims in Cambodia by 2010', 30 September. Available at: http://straitstimes.asial.com.sg.

Sukma, Rizal (1999) 'Security Implications of the Economic Crisis in Southeast Asia', in Guy Wilson-Roberts (ed.) *An Asia-Pacific Security Crisis? New Challenges to Regional Stability*, Wellington: Centre for Strategic Studies.

Sundaram, Jomo Kwame (1988) *A Question of Class: Capital, the State, and Uneven Development in Malaya*, New York: Monthly Review Press.

Tan, Andrew and Boutin, J.D. Kenneth (2001) *Non-Traditional Security Issues in Southeast Asia*, Singapore: Institute of Defence and Strategic Studies.

Thiparat, Pranee (ed.) (2001) *The Quest for Human Security*, Bangkok: Institute of Strategic and International Studies.

Time Magazine (2005) 'When Silence Kills', *Time* Magazine, 165(22), 6 June.

UNAIDS (2004) 'Global Summary of the HIV and AIDS Epidemic', *Joint United Nations Programme on HIV/AIDS (UNAIDS) 2004 Report on the Global AIDS Epidemic*, Available at: http://www.unaids.org/bangkok20004/GAR2004_html/GAL2004_03_en.htm.

Waever, Ole (1995) 'Securitization and Desecuritization', in Ronnie D. Lipschutz (ed.) *On Security*, New York: Columbia University Press.

Part IV

Governing structures

Managing contemporary
multilevel architecture

10 Making cultural policy in a globalising world

Patricia M. Goff

Introduction

Assessing globalisation's effects on culture has been a central component of the globalisation debate from the outset. The processes of globalisation have accelerated the reach, quantity, and intensity of the movement of people, ideas, and images, all key contributors to culture. For many, this is a positive development, bringing with it opportunities for exchange and learning across cultures. For example, Tyler Cowen argues that individual societies are much more diverse as a result of a larger menu of choice.

> What do we have to choose from? What options do we have? What kinds of opportunities do we have with our lives? When we ask ourselves, 'does globalisation bring more of this kind of diversity?', we find that the answer is usually yes.
>
> (Cowen 2000: 15)

On the other hand, others suggest that the consequences of globalisation for culture are negative. Rather than enhancing diversity, globalisation diminishes it as standardised products diffuse across national borders. As Redner puts it:

> with the onset of globalization in general, culture has assumed an unprecedented form, identical in all parts of the world – global culture . . . As a result, the still extant local cultures, some of them going back thousands of years, are being rapidly subverted and overwhelmed by the constant flood of such imports. This invasion seems impossible to stem in an era of globalization, with its open markets and porous borders and satellite communications. If this trend is allowed to continue for much longer there will soon be nothing left but the one pervasive global culture, the ultimate homogenization.
>
> (Redner 2004: 2)

These two examples are representative of the poles of the academic debate over globalisation and culture. Attenuated versions of these views are also reflected in cultural policy. Some policies look to harness the potential of globalisation; others aim to erect a bulwark against it and these are not mutually exclusive. While one might be able to discern an emphasis on one or the other approach in the cultural policies of a given national, regional, or municipal actor, in reality, strands of both are often present.

Our assessments of globalisation's effects on culture are at least partly contingent on how we define culture and how we define globalisation. For many, trade liberalisation generally and the World Trade Organization (WTO) specifically are symbols of globalisation. The WTO is perhaps even an agent of globalisation. It is one of the sites from which the negative cultural consequences of globalisation are said to emanate and it provides a pivot for my inquiry. Regardless of our definitions, it seems clear that local and national cultures will not be left unchanged by globalisation. But are regional responses likely to capture the benefits or provide shelter from the costs?

Regionalisation scholars have suggested that regional arrangements can be either a step along the way toward greater globalisation or a defence against it (Breslin and Higgott 2000). My analysis suggests that this dynamic may be more complex where culture is concerned. Government officials are simultaneously trying to reap globalisation's rewards and protect against its threats and their approach is multi-level. They take action on the global level to preserve national cultural prerogatives. They implement cultural policy at the local level to compete globally. Therefore, the local, national, regional, and global levels are all implicated and not always in straightforward ways. Regional-level activity is relevant, but it is not the most significant. In fact, the most significant responses to cultural globalisation appear to be at the global and local levels, in part because efforts at the regional level have proven unsatisfactory.

Think nationally, act regionally – Canada in North America

In the mid-1980s, the American and Canadian governments began talks that would lead to a comprehensive free trade agreement. The two countries were already each other's largest trading partners and barriers were quite low between them. Nonetheless, the 1980s recession prompted the Canadian government to seek *assured* access to the American market in the face of mounting US protectionism. While the Canadian government sought a comprehensive trade pact, Canadian negotiators indicated from the outset that 'culture was not on the table'. This would mean negotiating an exemption for culture industries from the provisions of the agreement, which Canadian negotiators successfully accomplished. This policy stance was motivated by a fear that Canadian culture industries would be unable to compete against American ones, threatening their existence and the country's identity and 'cultural sovereignty' along with it.

Then-Minister of Trade Patricia Carney, whom one might expect to emphasise economic concerns, acknowledged the cultural contribution of culture industries thus:

> Culture is an elusive and visceral concept because it is the way we know ourselves and each other. Cultural expression aims for excellence and self-knowledge, it is also the way we communicate among ourselves; Canada's cultural sovereignty is maintained and strengthened by the ability of Canadian cultural industries to produce, market, and distribute the products of our artists, our creative people; the dominance of U.S. firms on our sound recording, film, television and publishing sectors impinges upon our cultural sovereignty. This massive penetration of the Canadian market threatens the growth of Canada's cultural products which are the major demonstration of our identity as a separate nation.
>
> (Carney 1987)

The Office of the Trade Negotiator, acutely aware that this perspective would be unacceptable to the United States and would stall negotiations, defended the 'cultural exception' strategy for similar reasons:

> Canada's cultural policy objectives are not to keep U.S. culture out of Canada. Their objective is to ensure Canadians an opportunity to maintain their own unique identity, through film, records, broadcasting and publishing ... The future of Canadian culture, the future of Canada, is secure as long as Canadian artists, performers and writers, Canadian broadcasters and publishers, have the opportunity to reach their fellow Canadians.
>
> (Canada 1987: 1–2)

The Canadian government pursued the so-called 'cultural exception' strategy in the Canada-United States Free Trade Agreement (CUSFTA) and the North American Free Trade Agreement (NAFTA) negotiations by designating a list of culture industries that would be exempt from the national treatment obligations applied to other sectors. The assumption was that the 'cultural exception' strategy would allow the Canadian government to continue the range of domestic support measures – tax incentives, content quotas, etc. – it has implemented for decades to promote local cultural producers. These measures seek to compensate for the economic challenges facing Canadian cultural industries, including a small domestic market and the attendant difficulty of recovering production costs, smaller production budgets in broadcasting and filmmaking, and high unit cost for book publication.

Though the Canadian government succeeded in obtaining a cultural exception provision in CUSFTA and later in NAFTA, many analysts expressed scepticism about its ability to preserve some autonomy in Canadian cultural policy. For example, cultural industries are evolving in ways that put the internet and new media at the fore. These, however, are not mentioned on the list of exempted industries, suggesting that protection exists only for a limited list of cultural industries. In addition, the cultural exception was paired with a provision that permits limited retaliation, which was invoked in 1994 when the US contested a Canadian Radio-television and Telecommunications Commission (CRTC) decision to revoke the license of an American country music cable station and re-issue that license to Canadians.[1] The license had been issued to the American company ten years earlier, when no Canadians had sought to provide a country music programming service. However, the CRTC had anticipated entry of Canadian firms, mandating termination of non-Canadian competitors' licenses in that event. The threat of US retaliation was enough to produce a compromise. Nonetheless, the experience with the country music channel demonstrates from another angle the limited protections contained in NAFTA.

Many of these concerns about the content of the exclusion clauses became, to some extent, irrelevant in the 1990s when the United States sidestepped NAFTA dispute settlement arrangements completely, choosing to avail itself instead of the remedies afforded by the World Trade Organization. The American government took the Canadian government before the WTO to contest several measures supporting the domestic magazine industry, including postal subsidies; tax incentives for placing advertising in Canadian publications; and limits on split-run magazines like *Time* and *Sports Illustrated*. Split-runs recycle the majority of the content found in the American edition. Some Canadian content is added for the Canadian edition, but the cost of production is relatively low since most costs have already been recovered in the American market. From the standpoint of the Canadian periodicals industry, split-runs are at a significant cost advantage and support measures are necessary for domestic producers to offset this.

The 'periodicals case' convinced many in Canada that the cultural exception carved out in NAFTA was unreliable because it could do very little to prevent countries from opting to pursue their disputes in an alternative forum where similar protections are non-existent. Indeed, in response to the WTO periodicals case decision, the Canadian government changed its strategy and, to all intents and purposes, abandoned the cultural exception, recognising that, at best, it can be a limited, short-term solution. At worst, it may provide no protection at all.

This experience is instructive in considering the present inquiry into the relationship between globalisation and regionalisation. At the regional level in North America, culture is a key component of the debate on regionalisation. Most government officials and business leaders in North America support continental free trade. Yet in Canada few are willing to sacrifice national cultural policy autonomy. Therefore, while the production chains of a variety of commercial activities become continentalised or regionalised, actors of various stripes endeavour to keep culture as a national preserve by exempting it from the regional free trade agreement. The broader regional effort to harness the benefits of globalising markets is tempered in the cultural realm by efforts to guard national cultural sovereignty.

That this 'nationalist' current has predominated in Canadian cultural policy does not deny the fact that the federal government simultaneously seeks to reap benefits from developments associated with globalisation in the cultural sector. For example, one key feature of globalisation is the ease with which private actors can cross borders for commercial purposes. The Canadian government has encouraged this where culture is concerned in limited ways. The Production Services Tax Credit is the best example of this. It encourages the employment of Canadians in the film and video industry by allowing Canadian *or* foreign-owned entities to deduct a percentage of wages and salaries paid to Canadians. This program has fueled so-called 'runaway production' from California to Canada as American filmmakers come north to take advantage of cost savings, creating employment opportunities and community revenue for Canadians in the process.

The Canadian case suggests at least two things. First, cultural policy at the national level is complex. In Canada, a 'cultural track' that seeks to defend national identity is poised alongside an 'economic track' that seeks to reap the economic benefits of globalisation, though the former has historically been more prominent. This is an imperfect characterisation since there is no reason why policies with a cultural purpose cannot also stimulate economic return, and vice versa. Nonetheless, the various policies in place at the federal level in Canada, not surprisingly, suggest a selective embrace of globalisation in the cultural realm. Second, it may be difficult to make a general statement about the relationship between regionalisation and globalisation writ large. Instead, we may need to qualify our claims as we move from sector to sector. What might be true for the automobile manufacturing sector, for example, is certainly not true for the cultural sector. This is, in large part, due to the fact that the value of cultural products is measured in a range of ways beyond the commercial, suggesting a range of consequences from globalisation that do not touch other sectors. As a result, whether regionalisation can be a stepping stone to globalisation or a defence against it for producers and consumers of culture depends on a unique set of concerns.

Think nationally, act globally – the Convention on Cultural Diversity

The cultural exception strategies that Canada tried at the regional level were also tried by the Europeans at the global level in the Uruguay Round of the General Agreement on Tariffs and Trade (GATT) negotiations with different results. In the end, 'the European Union and the United States did not reach any substantive agreement concerning the audiovisual sector. The European Union and the United States merely agreed to disagree' (Cahn and Schimmel 1997: 8). This agreement to disagree meant that the EU could continue measures like the 'Television without Frontiers' directive, as well as other existing subsidies and quotas, with no requirements to change current policies and no restrictions on the nature of future policies. 'In other words, the European Union obtained an exemption from the application of the principle of non-discrimination' (ibid.):

While much of this was encouraging to the European cultural community, it would resemble the outcome in NAFTA in that the victory is partial and potentially short-lived. There is no explicit recognition that audiovisual products merit special consideration. Furthermore, within the context of the WTO system, the debate over audiovisual industries did not end with the Uruguay Round GATT agreement. Instead, audiovisual issues are still being debated in the context of services liberalisation as part of the General Agreement on Trade in Services (GATS). As Grant and Wood (2004: 358) explain:

> Broadcasting is a perfect example of a service. And although video tapes of television programs are, like release prints of films, 'goods' in a physical sense, the intellectual property of television programs was increasingly being transmitted by satellite, which involved no goods being imported at all.

To date, very few countries have made offers to liberalise their audiovisual services within the context of the GATS. GATS signatories that do not commit to opening their audiovisual services sector preserve the right to continue support measures to domestic actors, measures that, under other circumstances, might look like discriminatory practices. While this provides some measure of protection, GATS negotiations are ongoing. As Ivan Bernier explains with regard to audiovisual subsidies:

> [I]f the right of WTO members to freely subsidize their audiovisual services does not appear to be seriously challenged at the moment, this is largely due to the fact that the negotiations underway are not progressing as planned. However, there is no guarantee that at the end of the current negotiations, or at the end of other negotiations, a legal regime creating the multilateral disciplines necessary to avoid trade-distortive effects from the use of subsidies will not be established.
>
> (2003a: 10)

While there may be room for flexibility in requesting and offering market opening, there seems to be less flexibility once commitments to liberalise have been made, as New Zealand discovered 'to its later regret' (Grant and Wood 2004: 359). In the late 1980s and early 1990s, the National (conservative) Government in power undertook to commercialise and privatise New Zealand's state-owned broadcasting industry. As part of its overhaul, the government also made partial commitments at the GATS to open their audiovisual sector. Several years later, when the Labour Party was re-elected, it inherited this arrangement, finding their capacity to pursue an alternative broadcasting policy, including local content quotas, greatly circumscribed. Prime Minister and Minister for Culture Helen Clark explained her predicament:

> We have unilaterally disarmed ourselves on trade but very few others have been so foolish. We're now left with perfectly legitimate calls for local content and people saying 'You can't do that because of GATS'. This seems a bit ridiculous so we're just working out the best way to handle it.
> (quoted in Kelsey 2003)

The New Zealand government is not without options, though many of those options do involve risking a WTO dispute. Nonetheless, the broader lesson of New Zealand's experience is that commitments to liberalise are not easily reversible.

Those who concede that the capacity for choice with regard to audiovisual liberalisation in GATS offers greater range of motion than GATT where domestic cultural policy-making is concerned remain unconvinced that their interests can be adequately addressed inside the services trade regime. This skepticism lingers because cultural products defy straightforward definition as either goods or services. Is a television program, for example, a tangible good in the form of a videotape 'that can be dropped on your foot'? Or is the service of transmitting the program over the airwaves its defining feature? Nevertheless, reaching some consensus on this categorisation is decisive in determining whether the cultural sector will be regulated by the more permissive GATS agreement or the more restrictive GATT, with important consequences for cultural producers and consumers, as well as cultural policy-makers. Not surprisingly, the Americans have favoured an interpretation of most cultural products as goods, while the Europeans and Canadians have made a case for defining them as services. More recently, the United States has introduced the term 'virtual good' to capture audiovisual products, as well as software and e-commerce in the hopes that re-categorisation in this direction might bring these sectors under the auspices of the GATT. These various developments, in addition to the WTO dispute panel decision on Canadian periodicals policy, make many uneasy about the degree to which we should rely on the trading regime to protect national governments' domestic policy-making capacity to promote cultural diversity. Indeed, these realities prompted the Canadian government to rally like-minded governments at the global level.

The Canadian government initiated an effort to create an international convention that would have the effect of mitigating just the sorts of influences that the periodicals case suggested international institutions could have on national policy-making. In so doing, the Canadian government signalled that it found the protections that had been built into prevailing trade agreements to be insufficient. It could not rely on trade agreements or trade dispute panels to protect its interests when it comes to cultural policy-making. This realisation generated a demand for an international institution that would enshrine with binding legal force a government's right to use domestic policy to promote cultural diversity.

In 1998, one year after the WTO decision in the periodicals case, then-Minister of Canadian Heritage, Sheila Copps, launched the International Network on Cultural Policy (INCP), hosting culture ministers from around the world in Ottawa to grapple with the challenge posed to domestic cultural policy-making by trade commitments. Copps introduced to her counterparts an idea that had been presented to her by a panel of Canadian industry experts, assembled by the Department of Foreign Affairs and International Trade, called the Culture Industries Sectoral Advisory Group on International Trade (SAGIT). Among the recommendations articulated in the SAGIT report is the belief that the Canadian government should move away from the cultural exception strategy toward promotion of a 'new international instrument' – a convention, a treaty, perhaps even a brick-and-mortar institution – whose mandate is the promotion of cultural diversity. Such an instrument would put cultural diversity squarely onto the international agenda, alongside economic liberalisation, the environment, sustainable development, human rights and other key goals. It would require governments to recognise cultural diversity as an integral value to be taken into account in global-level policy-making activities and also to confirm the legitimate right of national governments to implement domestic cultural policy in the public interest. Canada's trade minister at the time, Pierre Pettigrew, captured the fine line that an INCP convention would hope to walk:

> the objectives for the Instrument were to respect trade obligations, keep markets open for cultural exports, recognize that cultural products have a greater role in society than other products, and enshrine with legal certainty the ability of government to pursue a domestic cultural policy.
>
> (in Bristow 2003: 25)

In 2003, the United Nations Educational, Scientific and Cultural Organisation (UNESCO) agreed to house the instrument and a draft convention was adopted by its membership in October 2005. Though it continues to be known by many as the Convention on Cultural Diversity, its official name is the Convention on the Protection and Promotion of the Diversity of Cultural Expressions. As negotiations on the nature of the instrument evolved, many hoped for a binding instrument. However, the version adopted in 2005 is of a declaratory nature.

Observers and participants in the process have offered a range of responses to the Convention. Some hail the very appearance of such a treaty as a great accomplishment. The International Network of Cultural Diversity, the civil society group that has been leading the charge, called the convention a 'rather weak shield against continuing pressure in the multilateral and bilateral trade negotiations to eliminate or amend policies and measures which promote a diversity of cultural choices' (Neil 2005). At the same time, they note that the Convention could have value as a 'political tool' that could 'become a rallying point for civil society groups and governments that remain concerned about how the trade and investment agreements are being used to stifle cultural policies' (ibid.). For its part, the United States offered a scathing attack of the draft Convention, calling it 'deeply flawed and fundamentally incompatible with UNESCO's Constitutional obligation to promote the free flow of ideas by word and image'. The American statement goes on to say that

> it could impair rights and obligations under other international agreements and adversely impact prospects for successful completion of the Doha Development Round negotiations. In so doing, it will set back progress toward the economic liberalization that has done so much to increase prosperity throughout the world.
>
> (Martin 2005)

Whether the strategy embodied in the Convention to protect cultural diversity will be successful remains to be seen. Many issues are yet to be resolved, in part because the United States did not ratify the agreement. This is significant in that US policy is, in many respects, the target of the agreement, but it will not be bound by it. The treaty is a relatively new entrant to the field of international law, so its relationship with existing laws and institutions – especially the World Trade Organization – is also yet to be determined.

The Convention does contain a non-derogation clause that reads: 'Nothing in this Convention shall be interpreted as modifying rights and obligations of the Parties under any other Treaties to which they are parties.' However, it also contains language saying that signatories are not subordinating this Convention to any other treaty, as well as a clause that states: 'when interpreting and applying other treaties to which they are parties or when entering into other international obligations, Parties shall take into account the relevant provisions of this Convention' (cited in INCD 2005). This combination of provisions makes predictions about how the Convention might be applied in conjunction with the GATT very difficult indeed.

The existence of the Convention on Cultural Diversity reflects an important strategy on the part of national governments to maintain some domestic regulatory independence. Governments are indeed finding that their ability to continue traditional domestic regulatory programs is limited by their membership in international institutions. As such, forces associated with globalisation appear to be affecting state authority and autonomy where state-led cultural policy is concerned. These same national governments are returning to the level from which these new constraints emerge to make offsetting global commitments that can create a space for favoured domestic regulations. In effect, they are working to circumscribe the consequences of globalisation generally, and trade liberalisation specifically, by establishing that there are products and practices that should fall outside of the multilateral trading regime. These products and practices require ongoing policy-making by national governments to ensure that domestic socio-cultural interests are not impinged upon by international agreements. This national policy-making seems to require an international justificatory framework that the Convention seeks to provide and that regional-level arrangements failed to guarantee.

Think regionally, act regionally – culture in the European Union

The integration of Europe began in the economic sphere with the lowering of national barriers to the movement of goods and services. The founders assumed that political integration would naturally follow, but this has proven to be elusive, in part because of the variety of languages spoken across member states and because of the range of interests pursued by their governments.

As early as 1973, at the Copenhagen Summit, this issue was broached in terms of identity, with the Declaration on European Identity. Uniting Europe at the level of identity could potentially serve many purposes, including legitimating the institutions of the Community as its jurisdiction expands, strengthening Europe as an international actor, and justifying economic transfers from richer to poorer member states (Garcia 1993). Originally based on the assumption that there is an (already existing) European identity to evoke, this strategy later evolved toward the notion that there is an identity to cultivate. Later, the Treaty on European Union, signed in Maastricht in 1992, promised to 'mark a new stage in the process of European integration ... creating an ever closer union among the peoples of Europe'. This implied evoking among citizens of member states a collective consciousness of their status as Europeans without trampling meaningful national and sub-national attachments. The Maastricht Treaty also included a provision that expanded the jurisdiction of the institutions of the European Union to the cultural sphere. Section 128 'is an expression of the Community's obligation to consider cultural objectives in all its activity' (ibid.). It officially recognises that it is not possible to develop a cultural policy within institutions designed to create economic union. It provides 'a legal basis specific to culture [that] signifies that Community action with regard to culture will henceforth be of a permanent nature and become an acknowledged branch of Community activity' (ibid.).

In order to promote European identity, the European Union has taken a number of cultural initiatives in recent decades. It has subsidised translations of major works of European literature and financed the preservation of architectural treasures. It has supported the ERASMUS program – the European Community Action Plan for the Mobility of University Students – which gives college level students the opportunity to study in another member state. Since 1985, it has named one city annually as the European City of Culture. 'But it is in the audio-visual sphere that the Community has made the most effort and had the most impact' (Hutchison 1993: 439).

The audiovisual policy of the European Union has been driven by two major objectives: the establishment of a 'European area' for audiovisual services so that 'most of the work disseminated by European broadcasters is European'; and the reinforcement of the European program production industry (Commission 1996). The publication of the Hahn Report[2] in 1983 was an early sign that audiovisual policy would play a central role in European unification strategy, pointing to transnational communication and audiovisual industries as the cornerstone of the cultural initiative toward political union. 'The Hahn Report argued that "information is a decisive, perhaps the most decisive factor in European integration" and judged that integration was unlikely to be achieved whilst "the mass media is controlled at national level" ' (Collins 1994: 94). The report advocates a Community broadcasting policy and supports satellite technology to facilitate the establishment of European television.

If the Hahn Report is the first move toward European audiovisual policy, the 1984 Green Paper, which led to the 1989 Commission Directive 'Television without Frontiers', remains the most important. Indeed, Theiler notes that many on either side of the audiovisual debate in Europe attributed to television 'an almost magical ability to mould popular attitudes' (2006: 87). Many in the Commission and the Parliament, in particular, had perhaps 'too uncritical a faith in the ability of technology to act as a European identity forger' (ibid.: 111). The directive creates a single broadcasting market across European member states, in addition to establishing quota requirements for European content. As a 'directive', it is enforceable by European Union law. However, implementation is at the discretion of each member state 'where practicable'. European officials explicitly acknowledge its potential contribution to European integration.

> European unification will only be achieved if Europeans want it. Europeans will only want it if there is such a thing as a European identity. A European identity will only develop if Europeans are adequately informed. At present, information via the mass media is controlled at the national level.
>
> (European Parliament 1982)

EU level action can be significant by contributing to 'the bottom-up development of a dynamic European identity' (Commission 2004: 10), assuming it has adequate *means* to make such a contribution. The audiovisual industry is among the favoured means:

> The social and cultural impact of the audiovisual sector exceeds that of any other medium. This impact is its defining feature and is evident from the role of television alone. Household penetration of television sets in Europe is of the order of 98% and the average European watches more than three hours of television a day. For children the figure is even higher.

> The audiovisual media play a fundamental role in the development and transmission of social values. The audiovisual sector has a major influence on what citizens know, believe and feel and plays a crucial role in the transmission, development and even construction of cultural identities.
>
> (Commission 2004: 13)

If broadcasting is one key component in the EU strategy, program production is the other. In 1986, the European Commission proposed the MEDIA program (Measures to Encourage the Development of the Audiovisual Industry) and launched it five years later as a complement to 'Television without Frontiers'. It has been renewed twice. MEDIA is designed to ensure that there is enough programming content to fill the quotas set by the 'Television without Frontiers' directive. MEDIA responds to structural weaknesses in European audiovisual industries by promoting cooperation among Europeans in programming, financing and distribution. It supports training initiatives, production assistance, promotion, and multilingualism of programming. It emphasises the pre- and post-production phases of creation and encourages production companies to improve their organisational structure and to seek European partners. 'Priority is given to small- and medium-sized undertakings and to those countries whose languages and cultures are less widespread than others within the Community' (Hutchison 1993: 446). In the area of project development, MEDIA supports film and television drama, documentaries and animation. In addition, it provides assistance for script-writing, obtaining financing, and training (Commission 2003: 2). Among other measures, MEDIA supports pilot projects by providing up to 50 per cent of the cost of the undertaking as seed money that must then be matched by professional institutions or private sponsors.

MEDIA promotes distribution of films within the European Union by offering incentives for several distributors to come together to promote a single film throughout Europe. In 1996, 50 films were distributed widely throughout the member states under this program (Commission 1997: sec. 3.4). The European Union further supports distribution by supporting film festivals. 'The festivals play a prime cultural role as an alternative method of film distribution to the commercial cinema circuit, and enable the public to see films which would otherwise not have been distributed widely, if at all' (ibid.: sec. 3.6). Festivals subsidised by the European Union generally show upwards of 80 per cent European content.

Theiler (2006) argues that the original hope among EU officials was to promote genuinely European, 'denationalised' products. This did not materialise in part due to national resistance to EU activity in the cultural sphere. Instead, EU measures promoted greater national cultural production, as well as greater circulation of national cultural products within the EU. That this is true reminds us that European cultural policy is, of course, not strictly about building a European identity. Each member state guards its prerogatives where national cultural policy is concerned. In addition, in a moment when many European countries are running high unemployment rates, the cultural sector can also be an important source of jobs and, of course, there is an important public service component, both of which the EU acknowledges. Therefore, as is true for other levels of government in Europe and elsewhere, EU cultural policy seeks simultaneously to harness the forces of globalisation and to protect against them. Regional efforts provide a vehicle to do both of these, though I might stop short of saying that regionalisation is a stepping stone to greater globalisation where the European cultural sector is concerned. While national and regional policies do seek to promote European cultural industries that can compete globally, they also aim to produce a regional cultural community that corresponds to the regional single market. Once again, we are faced with the complexity of the cultural sector when it comes to making a statement about the relationship between regionalisation and globalisation. Policies suggest that governments at the national and regional level see limited benefits to be derived in the cultural realm from globalisation. As a result, they pursue policies at the national, regional and global levels designed to reap those limited benefits while minimising the costs.

Think globally, act locally – the global city

The national, regional, and global levels are not the only levels where activity is taking place with regard to culture. The local level is increasingly important. Local activity represents an effort to embrace the new globalizing environment, often with the support of sub-national, national, and regional governments; however, this embrace sidesteps the regional level and functions most actively at the level of the city.

The debate about globalisation has had as one of its major foci the question of whether national sovereignty and national borders are being made obsolete by globalisation. According to some, national governments are increasingly unable to exert control over the flows of goods, services, and money that are transcending national borders. If national governments are unable to exert control, then government more broadly must be playing a diminished role in the governance of the globalised economy.[3] Many have taken issue with this argument by showing that the national government is still relevant and powerful and that it is not weakening. For our purposes, though, it is Saskia Sassen's response that is most informative.

Sassen argues that transnational flows do not render governments or place obsolete. She shows that these flows do indeed have to 'touch down' somewhere at some point because 'the capabilities for global operation, coordination and control contained in the new information technologies and in the power of transnational corporations need to be produced' (Sassen 2001: xxii). The difference is that the relevant unit for this production is the city. While some have assumed that the weakening of the national state, the most significant contributor to governance in recent memory, implies the weakening of governance more broadly, Sassen, on the other hand, suggests that the weakening of the state as a result of globalisation has created the conditions for other spatial units to rise in importance.

> The territorial dispersal of current economic activity creates a need for expanded central control and management ... The fundamental dynamic posited here is that the more globalized the economy becomes, the higher the agglomeration of central functions in a relatively few sites, that is, the global cities.
>
> (Sassen 2001: 4)

Indeed, she goes so far as to suggest that 'key structures of the world economy are *necessarily* situated in cities' (ibid.) because the types of transactions and services that power the global economy rely on the close proximity and simultaneous participation of key specialists (lawyers, accountants, computer programmers, etc.). This practical need is compounded by the fact that such workers are apparently more attracted to the amenities of urban centres.

This last point anticipates Richard Florida's work (2002, 2005) on the creative city. Florida argues that three things promote economic growth in the current moment: technology, talent, and tolerance. He argues that attracting the first two components requires the presence of the third.

> What accounts for the ability of some places to secure a greater quantity or quality of these flows? The answer, according to the creativity theory, lies in openness, diversity, and tolerance. Our work finds a strong connection between successful technology- and talent-harnessing places and places that are open to immigrants, artists, gays, and racial integration.
>
> (Florida 2005: 7)

Florida devised a series of indices measuring the presence of artists, gays, and others that he claims are strong predictors of such things as presence of high-tech industry, highly sought-after knowledge workers, and employment growth.

Important for Florida is why people concentrate in certain centres. 'Why do creative people cluster in certain places? In a world where people are highly mobile, why do they choose some cities over others and for what reasons?' (ibid.: 33). He finds that firms cluster in areas where there are rich talent pools and talent clusters in areas where there is tolerance. Though Florida is not without his detractors, city planners across the world have taken his work very seriously and devised strategies that reflect this thinking. From Bilbao to London to Los Angeles, cities that either seek to revitalise regions caught in the decline of manufacturing or that hope to attract knowledge workers or tourists have embraced the notion that the culture of a city may be the key to its economic growth. Toronto is one of those cities and I use it as an example here.

In 2003, the City of Toronto ratified the Culture Plan. 'The Culture Plan demonstrates that Toronto's arts, culture and heritage assets are essential to Toronto's economic future as well as its quality of life, and that our competitors are already moving on these fronts' (City of Toronto 2003: 4). Competitors in this new formulation are cities like Chicago, Milan, Barcelona, Montreal and San Francisco. Echoing Sassen, the Plan notes that the current context is not characterised by cities in the same region battling for industry. Rather, cities across the globe compete with each other for people (ibid.: 8). The Plan goes on to note that 'in a globalized world, great metropolises are the major engines of economic growth . . . Toronto's culture is the dynamo that turns the biggest economic motor in the country' (ibid.: 7).

According to the Plan, 'Toronto's arts, culture and heritage will help to attract the educated, mobile newcomers we want, keep our best and brightest at home and make our economy among the strongest anywhere. Arts, culture and heritage will be the future Toronto's heart and soul' (ibid.: 7). The City Council defined two goals for the Culture Plan: 'to position Toronto as an international cultural capital, and to define culture's role at the centre of the economic and social development of the city' (ibid.: 8).

> In a globalized world, only cities with a strong and particular sense of place will stand out and succeed. Our cultural heritage and our physical heritage create our sense of place . . . In other words, in order to keep our best at home and entice their counterparts from around the world to visit or move right in, we must become more intensely Toronto and less like everywhere else.
>
> (ibid.: 10)

The City of Toronto's effort to mobilise culture for the sake of economic growth is a commendable and unsurprising policy. Given that it seeks quite explicitly to harness the energy of globalisation, it is an interesting complement to national, regional, and global-level efforts that emphasise the protection of national identities and practices from the homogenising forces of globalisation. Of course, Toronto's Culture Plan can also contribute to the ongoing redefinition and strengthening of Canadian identity, simultaneously serving as a means to defend against the cultural ravages of globalisation as it delivers cultural and commercial returns.

What do we make of this? At least two observations are in order. First, consideration of culture prompts a complex answer to the question about the relationship between regionalisation and globalisation. Does regionalisation provide a bulwark against globalisation or does it offer a stepping stone? Where culture is concerned, the short answer is 'both'. Governments everywhere seem to be working to protect themselves from the negative effects of globalisation at the same time they seek to exploit its potential. Culture may occupy a unique position in these debates, suggesting that our understanding of these new dynamics requires a sectoral, or at least an issue-specific, approach. In other words, what may be true about the relationship between regionalisation and globalisation when observed primarily through the lens of commercial activity may not be true when socio-cultural considerations come into play. Second, national governments are still central to debates about culture in the context of both regionalisation and globalisation. Local governments are increasingly prominent and global initiatives cannot be ignored. A clearer understanding of culture's place in the globalisation debate requires a multilevel lens. Making cultural policy in a globalising world requires a complex set of initiatives at all levels of government. Relying on the dynamic between globalisation and regionalisation as our theoretical framework provides only a partial picture.

Notes

1 Note that, while the US invoked the right to retaliate in NAFTA, it did not use official NAFTA dispute settlement mechanisms to pursue its grievance.
2 Officially known as the *Interim Report on Realities and Tendencies in European Television: Perspectives and Options*, COM(83) 229 final, Brussels, 25 May 1983.
3 For a detailed examination of these trends in GATT and NAFTA, see Goff (2000).

References

Bernier, Ivan (2003a) 'Audiovisual Services Subsidies within the Framework of the GATS', paper prepared for the Ministry of Culture and Communications, the Government of Québec. Available at: http://www.mcc.gouv.qc.ca/international/diversite-culturelle/eng/update.html.
—— (2003b) 'A UNESCO International Convention on Cultural Diversity', paper prepared for the Ministry of Culture and Communications, the Government of Québec. Available at: http://www.mcc.gouv.qc.ca/diversite-culturelle/eng/pdf/update0303.pdf (accessed 10 July 2006).
Breslin, Shaun and Higgott, Richard (2000) 'Studying Regions: Learning from the Old, Constructing the New', *New Political Economy*, 5(3): 333–52.
Bristow, Jason (2003) *Symbolic Tokenism in Canada-U.S. Cultural Sector Trade Relations*, Orono, ME: Canadian-American Center on Public Policy, University of Maine.
Cahn, S. and Schimmel, D. (1997) 'The Cultural Exception: Does it Exist in GATT and GATS Frameworks? How Does it Affect or Is It Affected by the Agreement on TRIPs?', *Cardozo Arts & Entertainment Law Journal*, 15(2).
Canada (1987) 'Overview of the Agreement', *Canada-US Free Trade Agreement*, Ottawa: Canadian Trade Negotiations Office, Archival Records, 5420–1.
Carney, Patricia (1987) 'Arts and Cultural Industries', Notes for Minister of Trade Carney's Briefing Book – Meeting with SAGIT's chairpersons, Ottawa: Canadian Trade Negotiations Office, Archival Records, 5420–1, 23 June.
City of Toronto (2003) *Culture Plan for the Creative City*, Toronto: Department of Economic Development, Culture and Tourism, Culture Division.
Collins, Richard (1994) 'Unity in Diversity? The European Single Market in Broadcasting and the Audiovisual, 1982–92', *Journal of Common Market Studies*, 32: 89–102.

Commission of the European Communities (1996) 'Audiovisual Policy,' in *First Report on the Consideration of Cultural Aspects in European Community Action*, COM(96) 160 final, Brussels, 17 April.

—— (1997) *The European Film Industry under Analysis*, Second Information Report, Brussels: Directorate of Culture and Audiovisual Policy.

—— (2003) *Report from the Commission on the Implementation and the Results of the MEDIA II Programme (1996–2000)*, COM(2003) 802 final, Brussels, 18 December

—— (2004) *Making Citizenship Work: Fostering European Culture and Diversity through Programmes for Youth, Culture, Audiovisual and Civic Participation*, COM-(2004) 154 final, Brussels.

Cowen, Tyler (2000) *Culture in the Global Economy*, Hans L. Zetterberg Lecture. Stockholm: City University of Stockholm.

—— (2002) *Creative Destruction*, Princeton, NJ: Princeton University Press.

European Parliament (1982) *Report on Radio and Television Broadcasting in the European Community on Behalf of the Committee on Youth, Culture, Education, Information and Sport*, Document 1–1013/81, Brussels, 23 February. Available at: http://aei.pitt.edu/3120/01/000057.pdf (accessed 10 July 2006).

Florida, Richard (2002) *The Rise of the Creative Class*, New York: Basic Books.

—— (2005) *Cities and the Creative Class*, New York: Routledge.

Garcia, Soledad (1993) 'Europe's Fragmented Identities and the Frontiers of Citizenship', in Soledad Garcia (ed.) *European Identity and the Search for Legitimacy*, New York: Pinter.

Goff, Patricia M. (2000) 'Invisible Borders: Economic Liberalization and National Identity', *International Studies Quarterly*, 44(4): 533–62.

Grant, Peter S. and Wood, Chris (2004) *Blockbusters and Trade Wars*, Toronto: Douglas and McIntyre.

Hutchison, David (1993) 'The European Community and Audio-visual Culture', *Canadian Journal of Communication*, 18(4). Available at: http://www.cjc-online.ca/viewarticle.php?id=197&layout=html (accessed 10 July 2006).

INCD (2005) 'UNESCO Convention Process', International Network for Cultural Diversity (INCD), *Newsletter*, 6(6).

Jenkins, Barbara (2005) 'Toronto's Cultural Renaissance', *Canadian Journal of Communication*, 30(4): 169–86.

Kelsey, Jane (2003) 'Lessons from New Zealand: The Saga of the GATS and Local Content Quotas', paper for the Conference on Cultural Diversity, Paris, 2–4 February. Available at: http://www.arena.org.nz/gatspari.htm (accessed 10 July 2006).

Martin, Robert S. (2005) 'Final Statement of the United States Delegation on the Draft Cultural Diversity Convention', Paris: The Permanent Mission of the United States of America to UNESCO, 3 June. Available at: http://www.usunesco.org/texts/Cultural_Diversity_Final.pdf (accessed 10 July 2006).

Neil, Garry (2005) 'Updates on UNESCO Convention Process; Report from Garry Neil', International Network for Cultural Diversity (INCD), *Newsletter*, 6(5).

Redner, Harry (2004) *Conserving Cultures*, Lanham, MD: Rowman and Littlefield.

Sassen, Saskia (2001) *The Global City*, 2nd edn, Princeton, NJ: Princeton University Press.

Theiler, Tobias (2006) *Political Symbolism and European Integration*, Manchester: Manchester University Press.

11 Regionalism in global governance

Realigning goals and leadership with cultures

Martin Albrow and Colin I. Bradford

Introduction

The development of regional agreements that assert common values and also adopt the Millennium Development Goals (MDGs) appear to jeopardise the achievement of the goals if regions are aligned along civilisational divides. We find, however, there are several principles, including congruence with values, complementarity, comparative advantage and added value, that are already evident in practice that can allow for enhanced and effective co-operation on goals even where values differ. National acknowledgement, in all sectors, of the MDGs, and that includes the United States (US), expresses an active global society and this is consistent, rather than in conflict with growing regional participation as a key feature in global governance. In that framework, national leaders giving effective voice to popular concern in their regions on global issues will enhance regional purpose and profile.

Governance and global issues

The governance concept has helped to lever open many of the boxes into which an earlier generation sought to force a new world order. It has lifted the lid on corporations to let in democracy, exposed governments to transparency requirements and promoted civil society within the United Nations (UN). But governance is just one among many disturbances to old ideas of corporate personality, sovereignty or world government.

Ultimately it is the globality of the current challenges to humankind that drives the overhaul of twentieth-century social scientific concepts (Albrow 2004). Even if the imagery of variable geometry may be too technocratic for some, it reflects the agitation of a world where the human species can envisage its own extinction. No theories or institutional structures are exempt from critical review and renewal.

Globalisation as a concept could itself be regarded as part of that renewal, if it were not so frequently assimilated to, and treated as, an extension of modernisation. Regionalisation, serving as both counterpart and contradiction to globalisation, substantially mitigates the danger of that kind of regress to earlier modes of thinking. It helps to defeat the notion of globalisation as a one-way street. Anything can be globalised: trade, but also regulation; American culture, but also anti-Americanism. Globalisation in itself has no direction. The paradox is crystallised in the globalisation of the anti-globalisation movement.

Processes, even those like globalisation, then, do not necessarily produce new structures. They may equally well replicate old ones, but in any case it is transformation the world requires for an adequate response to global challenges. Transformation goes beyond process. It is prompted by events and crises, but may also result from policies. New forms of global governance need to emerge, not just a reflex of globalisation processes, but as calculated products of collaboration between countries and agencies developing credible policy responses to the challenges of climate change, environmental degradation, nuclear proliferation, terrorism, AIDS and hunger.

Among the multifarious agencies (corporate, civil society, national, international and transnational) that share global concerns, the region is gathering recognition as a possible locus for global governance. The Economic and Social Council of the United Nations (ECOSOC 2005), for instance, recently suggested to the UN summit that the region should assume a place within UN voting structures. But its potential to play a significant role in global governance is both underestimated, in so far as it is seen as purely reactive and defensive in the face of globalisation, and contested when seen as a power base to rival the United States, or indeed the national interests of any country. We only have to think of the precarious balance of the most developed regional organisation, the European Union (EU), in relation to its own members and to the US, to realise why global governance might be the least of its concerns. David Held has drawn attention to the risk that regional governance structures will not foster the open regionalism within which global social democracy could flourish (Held 2004: 166–8).

Beyond the concerns about security and global markets that regionalism raises, there is a deeper worry about its consequences for global governance as such if it serves to focus rival world views and values. A world of regions might be less able to agree on, let alone meet, global challenges than one of multilateral institutions, a worry that receives the maximum theoretical underpinning when the region becomes a proxy for the civilisation. Europe as a trading area sits more easily in a global market frame than Europe as Christian civilisation in a set of shared global values.

A world view in which abiding common values are the wellspring of collective identity regards regionalism with apprehension. Samuel P. Huntington has long been the most provocative exponent of the centrality of values for creating both solidarity within and conflict between the main global actors. His *Clash of Civilizations* (1996) with its multipolar world organised around deeply divergent value systems has as its counterpart his *Who Are We? America's Great Debate* (2004) that envisages a weakened United States should it separate from its own roots in settler Christian values.

Civilisations are the problem for global governance in Huntington's account. Our purpose here is to examine the extent to which their value diversity is less a problem and more a positive contribution to finding solutions to global challenges. His treatment of regions (Huntington 1996: 130–5) sees them formed of relatively loose bonds between contiguous trading partners and unthreatening up to the point where they develop patterns of co-operation based on the deep trust that springs from common culture. Then, however, they begin to equate with civilisations, with rather little room for supervening common interests and allowing only a thin multipolar commonality on which he precariously bases the international order.

A recent ambitious attempt to take issue with Huntington's thin commonality and replace it with an elaborated architecture of global governance is Amitai Etzioni's *From Empire to Community* (2004). He introduces a significant place for regions in global governance, with a dozen or so regional communities occupying a greatly enhanced role in the United Nations (ibid: 204). He suggests a triple test for the use of American power: convergence of interests with other powers, legitimacy, and input into constituting global regimes (ibid: 116), a test that can equally apply to other powers.

Etzioni also envisages 'global authorities' including an upgraded International Criminal Court and World Trade Organization, and new bodies for Health, Welfare and Environmental Protection. Again, he sees 'no principled reason why such authorities cannot be promoted by powers other than the United States' (ibid: 172) provided they supply the resources to run them and do not challenge big power interests. Presumably regional communities could take on the task with that proviso.

The somewhat incidental nature of Etzioni's sole proviso on resources is, however, something that should give pause for thought. A list of further provisos might include at least recognition by other agencies, enforcement capacity, mission credibility and popular legitimacy. Governance is after all only one of many means to an end, and structures that are inadequate for their tasks, or for tasks for which there is little support, may survive, but do little more. It is telling that for Etzioni the prototype success story for a global authority is the Global Antiterrorism Authority for which the US is the 'key and controlling member' (ibid: 123). What other authorities will command the same punch? Where is the authority of the authority?

We are not saying that this is a straight conflict between realism and idealism. Certainly Huntington plays more on fear and Etzioni on hope, but the latter also reflects the reality of a vast complex of inter-governmental and transnational agencies and networks that the former either ignores or regards as ineffective. He is also more expansive on the conditions for achieving regional communities that are more than the sum of their members. In his terms they need legitimate control of the means of violence, ability to distribute resources among members, and to command loyalty to the community.

Even with those conditions, however, we can still ask how the regional community can rise to global challenges. What will it deliver for the globe, humankind as a whole, that is not provided by its members? Is it appropriate at all as an agency for those tasks? After all, the European Union's project has been to provide peace and prosperity for its members, objectives on which it can claim considerable success. It is still only slowly adjusting to the idea that globalisation is not just a threat but may also provide opportunities. Is it not a stretch to imagine it taking on a global mission too?

The potential global role of regions

If the region is to become an accepted component of global governance, we need to establish just what kind of entity it is. For Huntington, it reaches full international status as a civilisation, with a set of self-contained values that are binding and exclusionary, with goals that are ideally defensive and non-imperial. For Etzioni, the region as a community is a platform for global governance but its relation to global goals is unspecified. They both then leave open the issue of how regions might commit to global goals and contribute to their attainment and it is this we begin to address in this chapter.

As entities, regions appear very differently for specialists coming from different disciplines. Huntington and Etzioni are in some ways typical, though outstanding, representatives of international relations and sociology. Neither of them consider the land area particularly interesting, but in the first instance that is what regions are for geographers. Their mapping of the earth's surface into regions appears to work on the basis of three criteria: (1) no area of territory should be excluded; (2) regions cannot share space; and (3) boundaries are chosen by judging on a balance of qualities; topographical, cultural, and political. On that basis, one current textbook (Marston *et al.* 2005) identifies ten world regions: the US and Canada; Latin America; Europe; the Middle East and North Africa; Sub-Saharan Africa; the Russian Federation, Central Asia and Transcaucasus; East Asia; South Asia; Southeast Asia; and Australasia and the South Pacific. They define world regions as 'large-scale geographic divisions based on continental and physiographic settings that contain major clusters of humankind with broadly similar cultural attributes' (ibid: 5). However, further analysis beyond simple mapping provides that the distinctive attributes of a region are clear at the core, dominant in a broader domain, but in a wider sphere are merely present, creating the possibility of overlap.

The possibility of overlap is inherent in Huntington's (1996: 42–5) insistence that there are no clear boundaries to civilisations. In fact, his prioritisation of language, history, religion, customs and institutions omits reference to territory, somewhat odd in view of the importance of landscape and environment for understanding the American experience of the frontier or the Monroe Doctrine, the Chinese homeland notion of the Middle Kingdom, and indeed current defence and strategic issues like Taiwan. And it is instructive to compare his list of contemporary civilisations with the geographers' world regions. He splits East Asia into Sinic and Japanese, but links

Southeast Asia exclusively to the Sinic; his Hindu categorisation belongs to South Asia; his Islamic covers Middle East and North Africa, as well as Central Asia and parts of South and Southeast Asia; Latin America and Africa (possibly) coincide with geographic regions; and, finally, he has the West covering North America, Europe and Australasia. Orthodox Russian culture may just make the civilisation grade, which would make up eight major contemporary civilisations. Geography has surely played an unacknowledged part in drawing these boundaries.

Economists have a quite different fix on regions. The primacy of exchange and rationality as core concepts means markets are bounded only by information and transaction. In the history of capitalism, territorial integrity and the self-sufficiency of local units were the earliest casualties. However, the early political economists were emphatic that certain straightforward environmental conditions favoured the development of trade. For Adam Smith (1776 [1868] Bk 1, Ch. 3: 9) the Mediterranean was the cradle of civilisation because of the ease of navigation between nations. Inland navigation as in China, India or Ancient Egypt did not favour international trade. Note, however, that the nation is his unit of analysis, and defence, justice, the facilitation of commerce and education were for Smith main and proper reasons for sovereign expenditure and the raising of taxes. Political economy has always accepted that trade follows the flag, and the intimate relation between state and capital has been the priority theme for political economists through Marx to current theories of the international division of labour and the world system.

Regions result from configurations of labour and productive capital within that system. In a global market all regions then are, in terms of their ultimate interdependency, global, and that applies to hot spots like Silicon Valley as much as to declining rust belt areas. In that context the nation-state's domestic role in guaranteeing a degree of social security and social order remains as important in the global age as it was at the high point of the modern welfare state. But the factors behind the rise of big trading agreements that we also call regional, like the EU, Mercosur or the Association of Southeast Asian Nations (ASEAN) are different from those that create the economic identities of North-East England (viewed as a global region in Sadler 1992) or the Mezzogiorno.

The question of the future of the nation-state under globalised conditions is no longer a live issue: diminished sovereignty with extended strategic responsibilities might be a broadly acceptable answer (see Paquet 2001). The same cannot be said about regional trade pacts. Some argue that these are alternatives to, others that they are consistent with globalisation. They are prominent issues within vigorous globalisation debates in the EU countries, replicated in the developing regional arrangements like ASEAN, Mercosur, and the North American Free Trade Agreement (NAFTA).

The further possibility in economic terms is that regionalisation and globalisation reinforce each other. Anne Krueger (1998: 273), summing up an edited volume (Frankel 1998) on the regionalisation of the world economy, observed that most preferential trade agreements arose with a concurrent increased openness in most economies, and while regional integration was proceeding at a faster rate than global integration, it was not stopping the growth of the latter. The WTO Annual Report of 2002 noted that more than half of world trade was within regional integration agreements and since 1995 there had been an average of 15 such agreements registered with it each year (see Das 2004: 88).

Economics allows for reciprocal advantages to arise over any distance and Saavedra-Rivano (2001) argues that it has to be developmental affinities of culture, religion and ethnic alliances that consolidate regions. Without them the economic advantages of integration, even for close neighbours, are ignored. If, as Bhagwati (2002) asserts, there are no good economic arguments for anything less than global multilateral arrangements, the regional arrangements between neighbours and their boundaries must arise from other reasons. The origins of the European Union are in the aspiration of securing lasting peace between nations. The value of Mercosur for its members goes far beyond economic considerations (Saveedra-Rivano 2001).

Taking these disciplinary contributions to understanding regions together we see how they can be as small as the Scottish Highlands or as large as NAFTA and have equally diverse cultural, economic and political underpinnings. In fact, what none of these accounts provides for adequately is the sheer importance of policy, not driven or determined by factors beyond control, but as a creative and innovative response to challenges. If we regard the European Union as the most developed example of the region, then it represents the mobilisation of people to ends that go beyond the merely reactive. There is a vision, even if support for it is uncertain.

Huntington's requirements for a region to qualify as a civilisation resonate in the current debates in Europe, but it is only in the context of the potential entry of Turkey that common Christian roots have been headlined as the primordial bonding of Europe. Up to now it has been a vision of the future that has inspired, perhaps too predominantly, a European technocratic elite. In the formalisation of the big regional agreements (Coleman and Underhill 1998), we see how important policy decisions are for taking a degree of control over both economic and non-economic drivers. It is then crucial for social scientists to recognise that the future belongs not to academic disciplines but to collective aspirations to make the world fit for human beings. Björn Hettne postulates a set of stages through which regions may pass until they achieve the level of 'acting subject with a distinct identity, actor capability, legitimacy and structure of decision making' (Hettne 2000: 158).

In this sense, the emergence of the region as a potential global actor is only assured when it has a place in the grand narrative that has hitherto belonged to nation-states, but they are unlikely to relinquish their pride of place so easily. The status of the nation-state within the regional agreement is the most hotly debated domestic issue in Europe. We can see this vividly in the relation between the United Kingdom and the EU and in the European Constitution impasse. In these debates 'What is the EU for?' is a repeated question. Is it just for economic benefit or does it have a wider vision? Is it for the benefit of the members only, or can it raise its eyes to global issues? In arguing for a global Europe the British assert the importance of open frontiers but of broader global responsibilities for health, poverty reduction and attending to the consequences of global climate change. They do not go on to generalise this by advocating a generalised regional role in global public policy. That could of course imperil their membership of the United Nations Security Council.

But, in the end, which agencies can adopt which goals is a matter of legitimacy, of their command of public support, and trust and confidence in their capacity to deliver what they promise. There are now global goals at large in the public domain and no agency, not even the United Nations, can claim exclusive rights to them. We need to ask how and under whose auspices those goals have emerged before we can consider a claim from regions to pursue them.

The emergence of global goals

Even in the absence of a coherent global governance process, global goals nevertheless emerged over a series of summits in the 1990s (Jomtien, Rio, Cairo, Vienna, Copenhagen, and Beijing) to generate a set of goals which were ratified by 189 heads of state and head of government at the Millennium General Assembly in New York in September 2000. The main challenges articulated in the Millennium Agenda were framed into five baskets: security; human rights; democracy and governance; poverty and development; and environmental sustainability. In the UN Financing for Development Summit in Monterrey, Mexico, in March of 2002, a set of Millennium Development Goals (MDGs) were affirmed that set specific targets for the realisation of global goals in poverty, gender equality, education, health and environment. The overarching goal is reducing the proportion of people living in poverty by half its 1990 level by the year 2015.

The UN Millennium Summit Plus Five has just taken place in New York to assess global progress toward the five Millennium Agenda baskets and the seven multisectoral MDGs. The problems of implementation, execution and achievement across these functions constitute the priority fields of action over the next decade. But behind these still is the problem of legitimacy and popular support, and hence of global governance.

The frame within which global goals have emerged, the international development goals and the MDGs, is richly instructive about the weakness of the present system. Goals arising from the Group of Eight (G8) meetings – not part of the UN process – that are subsequently adopted by the UN, is the reverse order that one would expect in a democratic decision-making process. It is the G8 that should be implementing the will of the UN; the UN can implement nothing, except through its members. It provides legitimacy that is only undermined when it undertakes tasks it cannot execute. The G8 has no legitimacy to represent the globe as a whole, only the powerful member governments who could choose to exercise their influence, but refrain from doing so. Arising out of the needs of the economically dominant, the G8 has staked a broader role in policy sectors beyond the economic. However, its legitimacy is derived from no more than its member electorates – a small proportion of the world's population, and even at that they contain considerable internal dissent. In these circumstances it will be remarkable if global goals are achieved.

Representativeness is a key factor in securing legitimacy and there are proposals to expand the number of countries that are permanent members of the G8. One proposal for summit reform envisions incorporating the major emerging market economies (EMEs) into permanent membership of the summit grouping as a means of enhancing representativeness. This proposal rests on the notion of a multipolar world comprised of large dynamic economies such as those already involved in the G20 finance ministers grouping. The G20 is composed of the G8 plus Australia and the EU president as well as ten EMEs – China, India, Indonesia and Korea in Asia, Argentina, Brazil and Mexico in Latin America, and Turkey, Saudi Arabia, and South Africa.

Whereas elevating the G20 finance ministers to a Leaders Twenty (L20) summit is a vast improvement over the G8 in terms of the scope of representational legitimacy, it has its own drawbacks (see Cooper, Chapter 12 in this volume). The larger countries in this proposal purport to speak for regions but their claim to do so rests on size rather than on cultural identity or a representational process such as election or rotation or regional leadership. A note of caution is in order here. Governance may be defective and the goals may have arisen by a dubious process. That does not in itself invalidate them, and support for the goals may be much more widespread than respect for their main sponsors and agents.

If, as was the case in the Millennium Summit of 2000, 189 national leaders declare their support for the MDGs, the fact of goal-setting at this level and the nature of the goals involve the lodging of global goals in both public policy discourse and in public opinion in an unprecedented manner. The UN Millennium Campaign seeks to enlist the support of civil society organisations worldwide for the same goals. The language of timetables and targets, hitherto the preserve of national governments and corporations, extends into individual awareness worldwide as well as the G8. In 2005, the Make Poverty History campaign sought to make a media event of popular pressure on the G8 discussions in Gleneagles, with the connivance of leaders themselves.

These high profile news management exercises certainly spread awareness of global goals, and do not invalidate them. For instance, the first MDG, the eradication of poverty and hunger, cannot be dismissed as a spin project. But the sheer prominence of the goals makes governance a more, not less, important issue, to guard against false claims, spurious accounting and their treatment as ephemeral news items. The Make Poverty History campaign reflects the weakness of global governance and in itself should not be necessary if world leaders were genuinely representing the will of their people and sincere in their determination to achieve the goals.

Yet in a multipolar world the civilisational divides may be more important than the stated commitments of national leaders. A view of development dominated by Western concepts of globalisation and free markets will necessarily arouse the suspicions of the rest of the world. Global goals provide for the first time the possibility of self-direction for global society, but global governance must address cultural divides if there is to be a chance of success. The incorporation of regions within global governance, as Etzioni proposes, has to take Huntington's analysis seriously, which means we need to review the relation between global goals and the cultural basis of regions.

Congruence and complementarity in relating goals and cultures

We owe it to Huntington for making so many of the premises of his argument transparent. His multipolar world depends on the integration of its several units around their respective common values and for their cultures correspondingly to determine their stance in the world. Commonalities across cultures, like moral concepts of truth and justice, are only 'thin' (1996: 318).

Yet, if we take a concrete case like the 1994 Cairo International Conference on Population and Development, as Andrew Cooper did, to test the applicability of the civilisational thesis, we find that the major clash was not across civilisations, but between secular individualists and traditionalist religious believers within the West (Cooper 2004: 182), while particularistic identities did not outweigh economic self-interest, issues of common concern or the 'opportunism of state officials' (ibid.: 154).

For opportunism, we can, more often than not, substitute professionalism. In a world of multilateral negotiations, public officials in one department in one country often find they have more in common with their counterparts abroad than with colleagues in other departments at home. They focus on issues of common concern and share professional outlooks acquired from similar education and training. The Washington Consensus owed as much to professional solidarity as it did to American or even Western interests. These transgovernmental networks (Slaughter 1997; Reinecke 1998) are a well-recognised element in developing global governance.

They also illustrate one of the key contrasts between modernity and globality, the functionally integrated nation-state of the former and the decentred, de-linked systems of the latter (Albrow 1996: 122). We no longer assume the concentricity and congruence of culture, economy, and society in the contemporary nation-state. Sovereignty and identity are ever more negotiable than they were and the relatively free floating nature of functional spheres of life: production, leisure, education, even law, allows public officials more greatly enhanced freedom of scope in shaping policy than they simply gain from professional independence.

We can find an alternative interpretation of contemporary trends in Alain Touraine's (2005) account of the globalisation of market capitalism, arguing it has undercut the role of the state and provided the individual with access to technologies which permit personal detachment from the social context. Culture, human rights, and individualism triumph over society, responsibilities and community. 'Nous ne sommes pas tous citoyens du même monde, car celui-ci n'est pas une unité institutionnelle et politique définissant les droits et les devoirs de chacun' (Touraine 2005: 295). The units of articulation and mediation are the self and global consumer culture, with intermediary agents having been peeled away by the globalisation of market capitalism, consumerism and communications. The privacy of the individual and the impersonal forces of global market capitalism dominate, weakening society and governance as balancers. This 'new paradigm' opens to analysis the linkages between cultural forces and forms of economic systems (Amable 2005).

Once such analysis (Lodge and Vogel 1987) arrayed rules, laws and values along a community/individual dominance dimension that allows for different kinds of tensions and trade-offs for different economic cultures. Another underlying cultural dimension is interiority/exteriority, the extent to which the inner, spiritual life is prioritised as against material success, similar to the 'this world/other world' distinction Max Weber used in his sociology of religion that allowed him to account for the paradox of the Puritans' pursuit of worldly wealth linked to the quest for personal salvation. This widely accepted account of the motivation behind Western capitalism itself has been challenged by the success of the Far East. But Japanese literature exhibits 'the sometimes restless interior feelings of central characters . . . [and] the strength of this inward thrust of narrative over the centuries remains one crucial constant in the Japanese tradition' (Rimer 1995: 6) and this suggests how the strong community values of the Asian miracle countries may be channelling personal energies quite as effectively as Western individualism.

The success of an economic system, capitalism, in crossing civilisational boundaries, on different cultural drivers and accommodating to different kinds of social organisation suggests that there are many possibilities for the MDGs to lodge in different cultures in a variety of ways. So far, their boundary crossing of countries has been mainly issue-led, responses to challenges, rather than value-led. They reflect career investments of people belonging to transnational professional communities. And they have the support of many thousands of transnational and national non-governmental organisations. The question we are asking here, however, is, are they equally strengthening the case for regionalism in global governance? For while the widespread acceptance of the MDGs may appear to contradict the cultural divides in forming global public policy, it does not follow that regional organisations have either adopted the goals or are appropriate agents for their delivery.

The evidence for their adoption is substantial. The EU Commission and its member states issued reports on their contribution to attaining the MDGs which were synthesised in the EU's contribution to the UN 2005 review (EU Commission 2005b). The Commission declared its commitment to strengthening its role in the eighth MDG (MDG8) – the Global Partnership for Development – and reported that it and virtually all member states have conducted a review of their development policies to bring them more into line with MDG8. The goal reported a strengthened resolve to fight global poverty, above all in Sub-Saharan Africa (ibid.: 81–2). Many reports also argue for an extension of the goals.

ASEAN met with the Secretary-General of the United Nations on 13 September 2005. In their joint communiqué, there is a general affirmation of the need to extend and intensify co-operation on the MDGs. Paragraph 13 is of particular interest as evidence of the penetration of the goals:

> We welcomed the initiatives and activities to enhance learning among key stakeholders from the government, civil society, and the business community to deal with poverty in a comprehensive and integrated manner, and to share and exchange views on how best to mainstream MDG processes into normal development functions of governments, and to establish linkages nationally and regionally for mutual support in achieving poverty reduction initiatives.
>
> (ASEAN 2005)

The EU identified ASEAN as a key economic and political partner in September 2001 and there have been regular meetings of the foreign ministers of their respective members every other year since 1978. In their fifteenth meeting in Jakarta in March 2005, the MDGs were discussed as well as the Kyoto Protocol and the WTO (EU Commission 2005b). These bilateral relations between regions could be illustrated further for instance by EU/ Mercosur, Mercosur/NAFTA, African Union/ASEAN and more. The global positioning of regional organisation is further established by UN High Level meetings with Regional and Inter-Governmental Bodies, the sixth of which was held on 25–26 July 2005, to which 23 such bodies were invited (UN Information Service 2005). (The fact that the EU alone was represented three times over by the Commission, the Presidency and the Council indicates the pride of place it enjoys among regional organisations.)

The EU is the test case for regional organisation in so many respects. For a start, its invitation to Turkey to join in entry talks flouts the civilisational divide. It also challenges old conceptions of national sovereignty. Stephen Krasner (2001), reviewing challenges to sovereignty, suggests that the rest of the world cannot imitate the EU, implying that it is largely the creature of American post-war policy towards the Soviet threat and that Mercosur and NAFTA are largely limited to trading agreements. That is overstated, but undeniably the relation with the US is vital to understanding the EU. In the words of Commission President Barroso: 'The relationship between the

United States and Europe constitutes the world's strongest, most comprehensive and strategically important partnership' (EU Delegation of the EU Commission to the USA 2005).

The EU delegation to the US declares the two to be 'the greatest powers on the world scene' (ibid.: 2005) disingenuously suggesting that there might be more than one superpower. But certainly it confirms that the EU is an interlocutor, if not a military partner with the US. This is not the place to review the deep ambivalence the US has towards Europe, oscillating as it does between wanting it to build its defence capacity and anxious that it might aspire to real strategic capability. At times, the Bush administration appeared to relish the split in Europe as much as it did the idea of intervening in Iraq. The roots of this ambivalence lie deep in four hundred years of history; indeed, they arguably represent a civilisational divide of the same order as that between Europe and Orthodox Russia.

The EU/US relation has special significance because the disparity of the partners in military power is matched by an implicit recognition of the counter-balancing soft power of the EU. The EU's influence on world public opinion, with its commitment to capitalism, but greater emphasis on social and development goals, coupled with critical support for the US, make it a valuable intermediary with the rest of the world. Within the global frame it suggests an incipient division of labour. This has become even more explicit in the increasing prominence the EU is giving to sustainable development and environmental sustainability in recent years. On the issue of climate change the EU and current US administration do not yet inhabit the same planet and at the current rate may not inhabit this one much longer.

The emergence of clear policy divides between the US and Europe on global issues, given Europe's market leader status in regionalisation, may suggest that interests divide even where values are shared. But it also indicates that there are advantages to be gained from parties to a relationship concentrating their efforts on their strengths. There certainly have been advantages to Europe in allowing the United States a near monopoly on military power, and the EU may yet persuade the US that health is too important to be left to market forces. It is a division of labour that suggests complementarity may be as important as harmonisation when it comes to co-operation on common goals.

The European report on the MDGs stresses that its member countries are concerned about strengthening the complementarity of their efforts. Most EU donors have focused on fewer priority partners and sectors; the report cites Finland's explicit consideration of the added value of its own development policy and the Greek national plan that identifies areas of comparative advantage (EU 2005b:11). If responses to global issues may be co-ordinated in this way within a region, we may ask if the same may not be possible across the regions. In other words, instead of regarding value difference as an impediment to goal achievement, may it not also represent a diversity asset?

In the divided civilisation model there is an assuption of congruence between values and goals, as in military values producing aggressive foreign policy. But in a decentred, de-linked world, policy goals may cross value divides. For instance, in an area as contested as population policies, the goal of zero population growth can be agreed upon, even where there is profound value conflict. Complementarity can be as important a principle as congruence if the MDGs are to be achieved. Even with goal/value congruency the parties may simply agree to go their separate ways where they differ on those values. These distinctions need to be borne in mind in considering the contributions regions or civilisations might make to achieving global goals.

Thus there is a clear case of congruence between goals and values in suggesting that the economic and technological dynamism resulting from the individualistic, competitive, and action-oriented culture in the US sustains the strongest set of military, organisational and logistical skills appropriate for leadership on military security issues. The more nuanced versions of capitalism in continental Europe have historically been more explicit about the non-economic dimensions of economic life, especially social and environmental issues, which makes the leadership of Europe on environmental sustainability seem appropriate. There is a clear case of congruence here too, and the bonus of complementarity with the US role. At the same time, military values have arguably played a considerable part in European identity formation too: it is comparative advantage that decides that there is a common interest between the US and Europe, the latter concentrating on sustainability.

The case of ASEAN is of particular interest given the emphatic insistence by Malaysia in recent years on a distinctive set of Asian values. The President of Indonesia, Dr. Yudhoyono, delivered a lecture on its thirty-eighth anniversary on 8 August 2005, where he cited his country's Vision 2020, prefiguring a 'community of caring societies', arguing that community took on a special meaning for ASEAN, with a we-feeling based on its values. (Certainly the European Community never achieved that). He moved directly from that to a discourse on economic integration (Yudhoyono 2005).

Certainly the extraordinary experience of Pacific Asia in demonstrating exceptional economic performance based on high degrees of coherence in the relationship of the public and the private sector, the State and the market, and the goals of growth and equity, make their experience something to emulate for those societies searching for ways to bring family and local community values into the social cohesion seemingly now so potent in driving economic growth. Pacific Asia is also a major force in world finance and an arbiter in global imbalances. For Yudhoyono, these are all issues of empowering the people, but equally for him they support the MDGs and explain why some ASEAN governments have already exceeded MDG targets on poverty. In this way he claims ASEAN provides 'added value' to global efforts (ibid.).

Distinctive Asian values gain recognition within UN circles too. The United Nations Environment Programme (UNEP) engaged in an Asian-Pacific Civil Society consultation on 12–13 November 2003, discussing water, sanitation and human settlements with representatives from 23 countries. They agreed to emphasise the spiritual dimension of sustainable development and to assert that one of the principles guiding policy formulations in the area should be that 'an insistence on the harmony between land, air and earth rights and economic, social and environmental justice could provide that distinct affirmation of traditional Asia values' (UNEP 2003). Whether Asian values best contribute to the MDGs in reducing poverty or enhancing sustainable development is determined then by the principle of comparative advantage with other regions. But on the surface the congruence of values and goals is clear-cut and not in conflict with other regions.

Latin America has a much more ambiguous position on the relation of values to economic life. For decades, Latin America has flirted with a wide variety of institutional forms, economic systems and political ideologies, only to be seemingly left now in a muddled position. Neither adherence to the individualism and economic liberalisation of the West nor significant efforts at reforming the role of the State, coordinating economic activity, forging coherent development strategies and advancing a social agenda have transformed the region's trajectory in a sustained way. In Bruno Amable's formulation of five capitalisms (Amable 2005) – Anglo-Saxon, social democratic, Asiatic, European continental and Mediterranean – no distinctive Latin American model of capitalism appears. Colonialism, Catholicism and indigenous cultural forces have not congealed generally into a distinctive development model, impulse or result, leaving Latin America without a well-defined profile in the international community.

Yet this very hybridity and irresolution of multiple tendencies (see the various works of Octavio Paz) have been represented in distinguished contributions to world literature and art and could mark the region as a logical locus for leadership in education and gender equality in global arenas. The social impact of high enrolment rates in primary and secondary school and greater gender equality than other regions position it well to provide insights and experience on these challenges for the global community. The nemesis of high inequality in Latin America makes education a major instrument not only for economic advancement but also, as human capital, for changing the distribution of assets. Innovations linking nutrition and income to school attendance have had dynamic effects on poverty reduction in Latin America. These kinds of advances can be a major source of transformational change to other countries and regions.

Islamic countries would seem to demonstrate the clearest case of close alignment of culture and regional identity. Some 56 states in the Organization of the Islamic Conference (OIC), established in 1969, combined to safeguard the interest and ensure the progress of Muslim people worldwide. In this case there is an overt political objective, to support the Palestinian people, and the founding principles are concerned primarily with regulating relations between members. This faith-based region appears to offer much grist to the mill of the civilisational divide. Yet recently its Secretary-General spoke to the Council of Europe on education and religion, emphasising inter-cultural dialogue and common international values of human rights, as well as a commonality of values between monotheistic religions (OIC 2005). OIC particularly values its relations with the United Nations Educational, Scientific and Cultural Organisation (UNESCO) and its contribution to global goals through education would appear one of the most promising routes towards complementarity on global issues.

These beginning remarks on the congruence and complementarity of global goals and cultures are indicative only, and certainly not comprehensive. India, China, Japan, Australasia, and Russia all require analysis, but we cannot conclude without mention of Africa, simply because it is regarded more as a target rather than a partner. The EU, for instance, has made a focus on Sub-Saharan Africa central to its contribution to the MDGs (EU 2005b). To receive and never to give is not good for self-esteem, and there can be a wider benefit if Africa can be shown to contribute to a new global regime. We need in this case to think beyond congruence and complementarity to co-optation, an invitation to assume a role where the region's development needs are also channelled into a positive contribution to global goals. The options here need careful review, but if this continent, plagued with internecine strife, were to develop effective models of society building on the basis of the governance of diversity (Albrow 2001), this would be a major contribution to human welfare, from which the rest of the world could draw lessons. Initiatives to this end are not primarily resource dependent, and could well take the issue of African values as a starting point.

The regions and the US

The argument we have advanced is that the cultural affinities that differentiate regions, far from hindering the achievement of global goals, may actually provide the basis for enhanced co-operation based on principles such as congruence, complementarity, added value, comparative advantage, and co-optation. We have found evidence for the application of these principles within regional groupings, and since they are based on the bridging of value divisions rather than value consensus, we see no reason why they cannot also be applied between regions.

There is already a widespread acceptance of the role of regional bodies in international settings. The EU has representation though no vote in the UN and often a voice at G8 meetings. The UN has high-level meetings with regional bodies. The Economic and Social Council (ECOSOC) meeting on 27 July 2005 sent a message to the World Summit of the need to implement the UN's development agenda including the MDGs. The fifth of seven elements of the message was: 'the session has stressed the importance of regional co-operation and the need to better integrate regional bodies in global processes' (ECOSOC 2005).

The advantages to the global community of regional organisation are many. Etzioni stressed one particularly, namely the reduction in the number of voices at meetings, ten representatives from regions averaging 20 countries would have a far easier job reaching agreement than 200 country representatives (Etzioni 2004: 192). At the moment the US and European countries find it much more effective to deal with trade issues through the European Commission.

This is not to deny that the Commission has immense difficulty in bridging the divergent interests of its members, not just between countries, but also between cross-EU interest groups, such as farmers and consumers. But the burden of our argument is that the unity of the region forged out of the pragmatic resolution of differences is a much better model of positive governance, and more suitable for emulation in global governance, than one that depends on finding some primordial unity of values.

In an earlier phase of his distinguished career Etzioni was an exponent of organisational theory, where span of control is a key element in theorising organisational effectiveness. That was the early 1960s. Later in the decade he moved on to advocating the active society (Etzioni 1968). The rise of global goals exactly fulfils a key requirement for such a society.

Where global issues transcend civilisational difference, regional bodies can give them effective voice. After 9/11, the OIC met in Qatar on 10 October 2001. It condemned the 'brutal terror attacks that befell the United States', stressed they were 'opposed to the tolerant divine message of Islam' and called for an international conference 'under the auspices of the United Nations'. At the same time it called on the United States to achieve 'security and justice for the Palestinian people' (Takeyh 2002: 70–1). It invokes a governance frame that has no place for the later invasion and occupation of Iraq.

We now have an active global society, namely a worldwide web of social relations in which people of all kinds from civil society, business and public bodies are committing themselves to finding solutions to global problems. The task is to find the forms of governance that will be most effective in translating aspirations into achievements. This chapter offers no ideal blueprint. We have drawn both on evidence of movement towards greater regionalism in global governance and on principles that can provide a rational basis for its further development. But we have to develop models that start from the present circumstances, and in the first instance that means being realistic about American power.

As we noted, the development of the EU as a regional actor has been bound up intimately with the United States. From the beginning of their relations America and Europe have viewed each other in New World/Old World terms. They are the interlocutors in the West's grand narrative, and while their relative power has changed over time, they are locked in a relationship and tell a story where influence flows two ways. The same logic with different histories applies for the rest of the world. Europe and Asia, for instance, go back to Herodotus. Etzioni says the way the United States treats regional bodies 'reflects which global architecture the United States is seeking to advance' (Etzioni 2004: 191). We would add, 'and how regional bodies respond'. As he says, to advance a global community the US 'cannot ride roughshod over 200 nations'. Regionalism does not stem just from the will of the US, it has roots in global consciousness-building and in globalisation that transcend American borders and control. In our view, the US and those nations are now party to a process of global society building that is bigger than any of them, and can be arrested only by a massive reversal of public opinion, dismantling of institutions, catastrophe or madness.

The nations are demonstrating how they can contribute to regionalising global governance and national leaders play a key role here. Their main current task is to rectify the democratic deficit in regional governance while articulating the region's contribution to global needs. That is the key issue for all regional bodies, not just Europe, well illustrated by Indonesian President Yudhoyono's (2005) speech to ASEAN. The debacle over the proposed European Constitution is directly related to this question – it failed to tap the well spring of popular feeling for big issues and left open the question of what Europe is for. Prime Minister Blair made an effective pitch for leadership in his speech to the European Parliament at the beginning of the British Presidency. We wait for the follow-through. National leaders can occupy the global stage with both dignity and effectiveness, and a world of regions requires only few Mandelas, Brundtlands, or Brandts, while American Presidents, current or past, only need to aspire to that role if they are comfortable with it. North America is bigger than the United States. Perhaps in the fullness of time we will hear a Canadian or Mexican speak for a newly formed North American region in a governing council of the United Nations.

References

Albrow, Martin (1996) *The Global Age: State and Society beyond Modernity*, Cambridge: Polity.
—— (2001) 'Society as Social Diversity: The Challenge for Governance in the Global Age', in OECD, *Governance in the 21st Century*. Paris: OECD, pp. 149–82.
—— (2004) 'The Global Shift and its Consequences for Sociology', in Nikolai Genov (ed.) *Advances in Sociological Knowledge over Half a Century*, Wiesbaden: VS Verlag für Sozialwissenschaften, pp. 33–50.
Amable, Bruno (2005) *Les cinq capitalismes: diversité des systèmes économiques et sociaux dans la mondialisation*, Paris: Seuil.
ASEAN (2005) *Joint Communiqué of the Second ASEAN-UN Summit*, New York, 13 September. Available at: http://www.aseansec.org/17711.htm.
Bhagwati, Jagdish (2002) *Free Trade Today*, Princeton, NJ: Princeton University Press.
Coleman, William D. and Underhill, Geoffrey R. D. (1998) 'Introduction: Domestic Politics, Regional Economic Co-operation and Global Economic Integration', in W.D. Coleman and G.R.D. Underhill (eds) *Regionalism and Global Economic Integration*, London and New York: Routledge, pp. 1–16.

Cooper, Andrew F. (2004) *Tests of Global Governance: Canadian Diplomacy and United Nations World Conferences*, Tokyo: United Nations University Press.

Das, Dilip K. (2004) *Regionalism in Global Trade*, Cheltenham: Edward Elgar.

ECOSOC (2005) 'Statement by Mr. José Anonio Ocampo, Under Secretary-General for Economic and Social Affairs at the Closing of the 2005 Substantive Session of ECOSOC', New York, 27 July. Available at: http://www.un.org/docs/ecosoc/meetings/2005/docs/Ocampo-Closing.pdf

Etzioni, Amitai (1968) *The Active Society*, New York: The Free Press.

—— (2004) *From Empire to Community*, New York: Palgrave Macmillan.

EU Commission (2005a) *The EU's Relations with ASEAN*, 5 October 2005, Available at: http://europa.eu.int/comm/external relations/asean/intro.

EU Commission (2005b) *Staff Working Document* SEC(2005) 456. Brussels.

EU Delegation of the EU Commission to the USA (2005) 'EU/US Relations', 5 October 2005, Available at: http://63.77.220.100/partner/euusrelations/transcorpdocs.htm.

Frankel, Jeffrey A. (ed.) (1998) *The Regionalization of the World Economy*, Chicago: Chicago University Press.

Held, David (2004) *Global Covenant: The Social Democratic Alternative to the Washington Consensus*, Cambridge: Polity.

Hettne, Björn (2000) 'Global Market versus Regionalism', in David Held and Anthony McGrew (eds) *The Global Transformations Reader*, Cambridge: Polity, pp. 156–66.

Huntington, Samuel P. (1996) *The Clash of Civilizations and the Remaking of World Order*, New York: Simon and Schuster.

—— (2004) *Who Are We? America's Great Debate*, New York: Simon and Schuster.

Krasner, Stephen D. (2001) 'Sovereignty', *Foreign Policy*, 122: 20–9.

Krueger, Anne O. (1998) 'Overview', in J.A. Frankel (ed.) *The Regionalization of the World Economy*, Chicago: University of Chicago Press, pp. 259–74.

Lodge, George C. and Ezra F. Vogel (eds) (1987) *Ideology and National Competitiveness: An Analysis of Nine Countries*, Cambridge, MA: Harvard Business School Press.

Marston, Sallie, Knox, Paul L. and Liverman, Diana M. (2005) *World Regions in Global Context*, Upper Saddle River, NJ: Prentice Hall.

OIC (2005) 'Education and Religion', speech to the Parliamentary Assembly of the Council of Europe' by H.E Professor Ekmeleddin Ihsanoglu. Available at: http://www.oic-oci.org/press/english/october2005/sg-cu-speech.htm.

Reinecke, Wolfgang (1998) *Global Public Policy: Governing without Government?* Washington DC: Brookings Institution.

Rimer, J. Thomas (1995) 'Japanese Literature: Four Polarities', in Nancy G. Hume (ed.) *Japanese Aesthetics and Culture: A Reader*, Albany, NY: State University of New York Press, pp. 1–25.

Saavedra-Rivano, Neantro (2001) 'Developmental Affinities in Regional Integration', in N. Saavedra-Rivano, A. Hosono and B. Stallings (eds) *Regional Integration and Economic Development*, Basingstoke and New York: Palgrave, pp. 91–101.

Sadler, David (1992) *The Global Region: Production, State Policies and Uneven Development*, Oxford: Pergamon.

Slaughter, Anne-Marie (1997) 'The Real New World Order', *Foreign Affairs*, 76(5): 183–97.

Smith, Adam (1776 [1868]) *The Wealth of Nations*, London: Nelson.

Takeyh, Ray (2002) 'Two Cheers from the Islamic World', *Foreign Policy*, 128: 71–2.

Touraine, Alain (2005) *Un nouveau paradigme: pour comprendre le monde d'aujourd-'hui*, Paris: Fayard.

UNEP (2003) 'UNEP Asia Pacific Civil Society Consultation', Chair's Summary of Session 6, Asian Institute of Technology, Phatum Thani, Thailand, 12–13 November.

UN Information Services (2005) 'United Nations, Regional Organization to Agree on Stronger Partnerships in Facing Peace, Security Challenges', *Press Release*, New York, 21 July. Available at: http://www.unis.unvienna.org/unispressrels/2005/pi1668.html.

Yudhoyono, Susilo B. (2005) 'On Building the ASEAN Community: The Democratic Aspect', lecture on the occasion of the 38th Anniversary of the Association of Southeast Asian Nations, Jakarta. Available at: http://www.aseansec.org/17656.htm.

12 Executive but expansive

The L20 as a project of 'new' multilateralism and 'new' regionalism

Andrew F. Cooper

Introduction

'The Taming of Globalisation' as a thematic construct cuts into a massive number of issues pertaining to the dynamics of global change (Held and Koenig-Archibugi 2003). What is to be tamed and by whom? Are we focusing on the well-recognised patterns of power in a more integrated world economy? Or do we give equal billing to the globalisation of other forms of public goods (and 'bads') along with the multiplication of actors, both state and non-state? How should the response to globalisation take place: as a form of retreat to slow down the pressures of 'turbo-capitalism' and insulate what are perceived to be the marginalised losers left behind by this process? Or should we place the emphasis on better efforts for collective forms of management – and heightened participation – on a global scale?

Equally salient is the question of where this response should take place. One site of value is as a form of 'new' multilateralism. Using the space available for agency this project highlights both a widening agenda and repertoire of activities for advancing a more regulatory approach to global affairs (O'Brien *et al.* 2000; Knight 2000; Cooper *et al.* 2002). Another site is as an expression of 'new' regionalism: political projects aimed at region-building in different parts of the world (Hettne *et al.* 1998; Breslin and Higgott 2000). Cast in a more discrete if not localistic mode, new regionalism can be utilised as both a means of resisting and adapting to the pressures of globalisation.

It is tempting to see these two projects as opposites in design and rivals for predominance. The regional project privileges to some extent physical space in that few projects of this type – with the European Union (EU) and the North American Free Trade Agreement (NAFTA) as the archetypes – have some element of territorial contiguity attached to them. New multilateralism by way of contrast privileges functionalism – bringing together coalition partners on an issue-specific basis through initiatives on landmines, the International Criminal Court (ICC), child soldiers, or the Kimberley process on blood or conflict diamonds. What Robert Cox terms their 'collective images' (1997) – never mind their institutional typologies – are bound therefore to be in many ways quite divergent.

Still, notwithstanding these essential differences, it is the parallels, not exclusively the juxtaposition between these projects that should merit attention. Playing up their dichotomous attributes and their competitive nature is problematic intellectually and practically unproductive. Digging deeper than an appreciation of their elements of distinctiveness allows the two projects to stand out as two sides or twins of the same phenomenon and as alternative mechanisms in terms of multi-level governance.

This sense of 'we-ness' as opposed to apartness emerges in a range of features that help define these projects in a comprehensive fashion. In terms of the scope of activity what distinguishes both projects is how far they extend beyond economics – into areas of security, the environment, and social policy. In terms of actors, if both still place states at the centre of the project, ample room has been made available for a wider range of actors. Both projects profile the manner by which a network approach – using technology and norm advocacy – has risen to the forefront with respect to their toolkits. In terms of operational style, both projects are highly flexible in outline, doing away with the element of rigidity associated with traditional forms of state-centric regionalism and diplomatic method. Moreover, both have some element of spontaneity built into them, putting some onus on sudden bursts of activity. Finally, in terms of delivery, as essentially political projects, opportunities are available not only for striking (and often unanticipated) successes, but for failure on both tracks. Few would have predicted the multiple advances over the past decades in new regionalism or in more recent times on new multilateralism. Yet, the obstacles to these projects have not gone away as viewed in recent events in the EU or in the failure to copycat on other initiatives the success achieved on the landmines and the ICC cases. Above all it is the non-compulsory and global contours that stand out – distancing these 'new' projects from their older counterparts.

This chapter examines the Leaders' Twenty (L20) initiative, intended to expand the Group of Eight (G8) into a larger forum, as a manifestation of some components of both new multilateralism and new regionalism. As will be laid out at the outset of this contribution, the L20 is in some ways an awkward and incomplete fit into both these types of design structures. Far from the classic bottom up form of multilateralism – with a mixed constituency of middle and small states together with NGOs – the L20 has some embedded characteristics of what Michael Zurn (2005: 37) terms 'executive' multilateralism.

In other ways, however, the L20 initiative has the possibility of going further than the accumulated roster of initiatives showcasing new multilateralism up to now. On almost every count, this potential of the L20 lends itself to an expansionary format and vision that calls for closer scrutiny. On agenda items the ambit of the L20 would be far more diverse than the issue-specific initiatives that have distinguished new multilateralism to this point of its advance. On actors, the L20 is explicitly a leaders' summit. Nonetheless, as we will explore, there is some room for the L20 to transform itself from this 'club' approach into a networked form of multilateralism. In operational style some hazards (such as self-selection and status seeking) may come into play. But these features are in character little different than those found in a wide range of other initiatives (including the successful initiatives such as landmines and the ICC). At its core the L20 remains a voluntary if still elite-oriented exercise (see English *et al.* 2005).

In tandem with its intersect with new multilateralism, the connect between the L20 and new regionalism poses perhaps a longer stretch. The essence of the L20 is that it is a cross-regional project. However, while a departure from the spatial component of classic regionalism – and these primary forms of 'we-ness' – in other ways it is precisely this component that provides the L20 with so much of its creative potential. At an instrumental level, the L20 strives according to its most common plan to bring together the leaders of key regional hubs on a global basis. This is true not only in terms of the EU (through the representation of the UK, France, Germany, and Italy), but the presence of all three NAFTA countries, the two major entities within Mercosur (Brazil and Argentina), China and India (regional as well as global powerhouses), and a variety of members from the Asia-Pacific Economic Cooperation (along with China, Japan, South Korea, Indonesia – also a key member of the Association of Southeast Asian Nations – and Australia), South Africa (the pivotal member of the Southern African Development Community), along with two key members from the Middle East (Turkey and Saudi Arabia).

In symbolic terms though, the potential of the L20 goes much further. If it is too bold to see this initiative as an enterprise that operates (and allows discussion) as a cosmopolitan channel across 'civilisational' divides prevalent in global politics (see Cox 2002: 139–56; Held 2003: 160–86), there is a strong bias in the project to use this mechanism as a bridge between North and South. What forum we now have at the apex of global politics – via the centrality of the G7/8 – is not only a very restrictive club structure but one that is highly North-centric. Notwithstanding its elite design, the L20 breaks out of this mid-1970s grip and pushes us towards a structure that mirrors the global and regional reality of the twenty-first century.

To signpost this logic is not to escape the bias in this architecture to an asymmetrical order (with the rising powerhouses being rewarded as opposed to giving the 'laggards' in the system an enhanced status). This is not to ignore some other measures that can be incorporated into the L20 project that can compensate for these defects, both in terms of a rotational and a representational component. But as on the multilateral side it must be acknowledged that for all of the cross-regional attractions grounded in an L20, a global governance gap would remain with its implementation.

Extending 'new' multilateralism

As suggested above, the L20 will remain a highly contested form of new multilateralism. From one angle it is an explicitly top-down, executive mode of institutional reform. Not only is the initiative state-centric in origin, it is leader-centric. The mantra of the most avid proponents of the L20 notion is that leaders – whether in the North or South – are different. Individual leaders – as evidenced indeed by Paul Martin, the former Prime Minister of Canada, who has assumed the position as the leading champion of the L20 – can act as entrepreneurs of ideas (Martin 2004). They can look at the big picture, unlike those with ministerial responsibility. They can break down administrative silos, and overcome bureaucratic infighting. They can take political risks, and engage in a new form of political engagement where it counts.

From another angle the L20 appears to constitute a classic form of plurilateralism (Cerny 1993; Väyrynen 2002: 110–11), not new multilateralism with a comprehensive membership via the United Nations (UN) system. Far from being universalistic in form, the L20 has a highly restricted composition picked on a hierarchical basis. Looked at historically, it has some commonalities with past attempts to develop concerts of dominant powers in eras of turbulence and transition.

The L20 initiative, however, has an innovative quality that allows it to transcend many if all not all of these deficiencies. In common with the other forms of new multilateralism via the cases of the landmines, the ICC, and child soldiers it is a departure from concert plurilateralism across the continuum of who belongs, how it would operate, and what it would do. Whatever its flaws, it is an initiative based not on the status quo but on a reformist model.

In terms of membership, the whole premise of the L20 is to go beyond the tightly defined limits of the G8. What is more, this extension is based on an extension of the equality of membership (although arguments flare up about the exact modalities of how this goal should be achieved). Operating on the basis of this principle is very different from the concept of 'outreach' as advocated by the defenders of the concert in place. Nicholas Bayne recommends, for example, that leaders should maintain the practice, begun at Okinawa in 2000, of inviting a group of leaders from developing countries to meet them before the summit proper. He argues that the admission of new members to the G8 itself, however, should be approached with caution. He characterises the G8's great merit as the fact that 'it is small and compact enough for the leaders to have a direct exchange around the table. This quality would be lost if extra members were added in the interest of making the G8 more widely representative' (2001).

The second feature that adds weight to the progressive credentials of the initiative is the global – and interregional – dimension of the L20. All of the other plurilateral initiatives have had an element of 'we-ness' about them.

In terms of concert plurilateralism, it is precisely the informality of the crucial top-down case – the G7/8 – that produces the club-like atmosphere of the summit. Although tested by disagreements on a wide number of issues (most recently, of course, on the Iraq War), the glue that has held this forum together has been a shared mindset concerning basic rules and processes.

With respect to bottom-up cases of new multilateralism, the bond between the actors has been a form of 'like-mindedness'. In addition to the amplified role of many established middle powers, including the Nordics, Canada, Australia, and New Zealand, an extended group of activist states became involved. Of these countries, the new diplomatically active model citizen South Africa stands out. Taking a cue from the classic middle power copybook, it played a huge role both on the landmines campaign and within the 'Lifeline Nations', a group of states advocating an independent court and independent prosecutor as opposed to an ICC under the control of the Security Council.

Extending the G7/8 to a group of highly 'unlike' states therefore is an idea that is both ambitious and risky. At an instrumental level, the logic is unassailable from a reformist (albeit not transformational) perspective: to absorb rising powers such as China, India, Brazil and others from the South into the longstanding club with all its informal rules, patterns of socialisation, and voice and participation opportunities. This integrative motivation is tied up in turn with the high level of anxiety about the future global order not only from the peripheral actors but also from the core of the global system. For from an institutional point of view it is clear that if these emerging/ emergent powers are not brought in and accommodated, they could concentrate their activities on other clubs (such as the WTO group of 20 developing countries and the India-Brazil-South Africa (IBSA) Forum) and competitive activity with respect to rule-making (Narlikar and Tussie 2004).

A third feature of the L20 that lends it some credibility as an agent of change is its concern with legitimacy as well as effectiveness (see Hurd 1999; Zurn 2000). The greatest source of weakness (as well paradoxically as its strength in terms of club cohesion) was its self-selected (and un-elected) status. To China and India as well as most other outsiders it was precisely this feature that demarked the G8 as an illegitimate body in contrast to the universal form of multilateralism via the UN system (with all its formalism).

The G7/8 was meant to function as a body coordinating the practices of its own membership. As Putnam and others described a long time ago, this role was performed in a dualistic fashion: with a keen eye on both the one big G7/8 table and on the individual domestic tables back at home (Putnam 1988). But it has been a role that all of the members have had a huge stake in performing. In terms of managing the affairs of the rising powers, however, the G7/8 has little credibility (as shown by the disconnect between the G7/8 and China on currency questions). The G7/8 could not simply dictate to affect change. It had to engage with the 'upstarts' in the system.

The way forward – both in terms of cause and effect – came with respect to the creation of the G20 Finance Ministers forum as a result of the 1997/8 Asian Financial crisis. This crisis revealed that universal multilateralism – or at least the 'solutions' crafted through the International Financial Institutions – did not have the answers at a time of turmoil (criticism which was repeated by the slowness of the International Monetary Fund (IMF) to react to the 2001 financial crisis in Argentina). But it also demonstrated that the G7/8 as a plurilateral club had neither the right membership nor the authority to manage the situation successfully. Triggered by the thinking and actions of key members of the Clinton administration – and Finance Ministers such as Paul Martin, German Finance Minister Hans Eichel, and Gordon Brown in the North and South Africa's Trevor Manuel from the South – the G20 was not only able to deliver some immediate tangible deliverables in terms of its core concerns (managing financial shocks and working towards crisis prevention). It was able to build momentum on a much wider agenda, most notably the action plan on terrorist financing with special attention to freezing terrorist assets and the implementation of an international strategy as a result of the September 11 tragedy in 2001.

Instead of being an impediment, the larger number of members proved (at least for the practitioners) to be the recipe for success. While major lender countries retained a seat at the table so did many of the most prominent creditor countries. This mix of actors was more appropriate for dealing with the issues of financial shocks and crisis prevention. Beyond this one triggering issue, from the standpoint of legitimacy – as well as effectiveness – the composition of this group was also appropriate for facilitating an action plan for combating terrorist financing, as it had representation from both core members of the G7/8 and from frontline countries such as India, Indonesia, and Saudi Arabia (see Kirton 2002).

Just as importantly, the G20 had to show that it could balance the efficiency agenda with some concern for equity. Again we should not exaggerate this tendency to seek a balance between the economic market and the social, but nor should we ignore the importance attached by the G20 – and even more so the putative agenda of the L20 – to focus on the need to try to 'shape' globalisation in the interests of society. Nor in its declaratory or operational agendas is there any triumphal sense contained within the G20 of market forces or even the other norms often associated with globalisation (human rights, above all). Rather there is very much a 'double movement' feel attached to the initiative – with the need for selective intervention and regulation at both the global and national levels.

On substance, the G20 has reinforced the impression that it takes the social side of the agenda – on a global foundation – seriously by extending its ambit beyond the restrictive limits of the Washington Consensus. Acting on the wider purview of the Montreal Consensus, the G20 expanded its range of interest to a broader mandate taking in poverty reduction, development assistance and the UN Millennium Development Goals (MDGs) (see Bradford and Linn 2004).

The L20 offers in principle the prospect of extending this range of policy interests. Paul Martin, even after his defeat in the Canadian election, has continued to argue for the L20, not on the exclusive basis of economic or strategic issues but on the need to deal collectively with social/health agenda items such as Avian flu (Martin 2006; Jaura 2006).

This shift allows the G20 – and an L20 – to have some considerable advantages over rival forms of plurilateralism. From a top-down perspective, the G7/8 appears beyond its sell-by date. Klaus Schwab, for instance, dismissed the G8 as the guardians of the status quo, reflecting an outdated vision of the industrialised past (2004). From a bottom-up perspective, the L20 represents a signal that the status quo is too exclusionary – and that it needs to change. If still exclusive, the forum is opened up considerably. It is one thing to criticise the G7/8 – and use it as a lightning rod for protests – as an executive committee at the core of the international system. It is harder to see an L20 – with representation from both North and South – in this same stark negative light. Paradoxically, the criticism would more likely come from conspiracy-oriented voices on the right.

Although still highly divergent in terms of goals of what can be considered authentic civil society, the L20 proposal demonstrates the fact that states are not willing to be passive actors. After all, the main target of the global dissent movement is not national states but the neo-liberal vision linked to corporate expansion over the realm of governance and the entrenchment of a homogenous 'one size fits all' agenda. As one contribution to this debate argues, while the proposal for the creation of an extended summit of leaders may be viewed as part of a process of political globalisation far removed from the ordinary concerns of individual citizens, 'nothing could be further from the truth . . . By delegating authority to increase sovereignty, political globalization will overcome the democratic deficit and give governments the power to implement the policies their citizens demand' (Harmes 2004).

To put a positive hue on the L20 is not to say that the official model cannot be refined substantially in a variety of ways. The G20 – like the G8 – operates fundamentally as a club of state representatives (albeit an enlarged one including members from the South and also representatives from the IFIs and the EU). Indeed, it is this club-like atmosphere that is the enticing feature for the champions of an extended G20 into a Leaders' Twenty Summit. As Paul Martin (2004) has concluded:

> [The G20 avoids] the 'us' versus 'them' mentality that bedevils so many international meetings, and it has worked remarkably well – because peer pressure is often a very effective way to force decisions. We believe a similar approach among leaders could help crack some of the toughest issues facing the world. We need to get the right mix of countries in the same room, talking without a set script.

It is this aspect of the framework that fundamentally differentiates the L20 initiative from the bottom-up projects of new multilateralism, such as the landmines and ICC. All of these initiatives operated as fluid networks, with only rudimentary formal institutionalism (as illustrated by the establishment in 1999 of the so-called Lysøen Group with respect to human security). Links between mixed state and non-state like-minded actors were honed and consolidated, whether through one central group (the International Campaign to Ban Landmines) or multiple partners (diverse groups such as Amnesty International, Human Rights Watch, to the Lawyers Committee for Human Rights on the ICC).

A key question before the L20 concerns this type of scenario. Anne-Marie Slaughter most notably expands the debate about a Leaders' Twenty Summit not just as a contrast with the prevailing status quo but as the centrepiece of and conduit to what she terms a 'network of networks' (Slaughter 1997, 2004, 2005). An L20 would thus act as an informal hub or steering committee, with ideas and practices flowing both out from and into the L20, to and from other networks. As she concludes: 'An L20 has the potential [to demonstrate] how a government network can in fact be more inclusive than existing international institutions . . . in terms of balance of power' (2005: 294).

Such an approach is rife with questions, not the least of which being the formidable bureaucratic obstacles standing in the way of opening up the process to non-state actors. But the model also contains a huge amount of opportunities to move out ahead of the curve in innovative thinking and design. As Ramesh Thakur (2004) has summarised, cast in networking or brains trust terms, the attractions of an L20 are increased still further as this type of expanded summit

> would be a better forum for framing the issues, outlining choices, making decisions for setting, even anticipating, the agenda; for framing, the rules, including for dispute settlement; for pledging and mobilizing resources; for implementing collective decisions; and for monitoring progress and [receiving] mid-term corrections and adjustments.

Adding a further incentive for this notion is the utility of networking for making the plurilateral L20 more compatible with specific elements of the universalistic UN system. It is here that a proposed caveat to the L20 initiative by Thomas Fues and myself comes to the fore. In order to formalise the link to the UN system, ensuring focused access to the L20 by the Secretary-General and the ECOSOC presidency becomes a priority. To increase the representative nature of the body, one or two poor countries of the LDC category might also be included. All in all, membership could go up as high as 24: the number considered in the ongoing reform of the Security Council, the issue to which we now turn (Cooper and Fues 2005).

Playing off 'new' regionalism

Any form of plurlilateral project – at least in declaratory terms – is a second best option to the universal model as symbolised by the UN system. Indeed, as galvanised by the report, *In Larger Freedom* from UN Secretary-General Kofi Annan, an ambitious set of proposals have moved in play for upgrading this core system (Annan 2005).

The paradox of this universalist project – at least with respect of reform of the Security Council (SC) – is that it is has floundered on the rocks of internal regional machinations. The push by Germany for membership in a revamped SC has run up against the opposition of Italy and Spain. Ditto for Brazil and Mexico and Argentina, Japan *vis-à-vis* China and South Korea, and India and Pakistan and Bangladesh.

Can the L20 play more attractively to regional dynamics? The regional hub notion – with the L20 as a meeting place on an interregional basis between the central members (or more precisely their leaders) of the 'core' regions and the up and coming regions (see Hettne 2004) – provides the L20 with a more stable platform. In part, this is a function of the level of sensitivity between reform of the UN and the G8. Few voices of dissent would be available for the choice of China, India, and Brazil as the core candidates for either an expanded G8 – or for that matter, a stand-alone forum of leaders drawn from the North and South. The stakes are simply not as high as the L20 would still lack the imprint that would go along with Security Council accession – with all its formalism. States and their leaders have some considerable range of choice to become members (or not) of most clubs. But for most countries the UN is exceptional – as a meeting place of supposedly sovereign equals.

Yet, there are some 'permissionary' elements as well in enhancing the L20's design if the criterion for inclusion is as regional hubs. All of the core members of an L20 fit the profile of classic big emerging markets and/or regional powerhouses, all of which are becoming increasingly integrated into the world economy (Goldman Sachs 2003). Indeed, by many criteria, the leading candidates for inclusion into the forum would provide better fits than Russia, the most recent state to have graduated into the G7/8.

This structural prowess goes hand-in-hand with diplomatic recognition. As suggested by John Humphrey and Dirk Messner in their innovative work on what they term 'anchor countries', the size of the economies of these hub countries must be blended with their capacity to 'actively participate in global dialogue' that is crucial for this analysis (2005).

As part of the outreach described above by Nicholas Bayne, these regional hubs have become hybrids in the working of the G7/8: still formally outside but with on-going access to the 'big' club operations. The French state chose to showcase these regional hubs – with the leaders from China, India and Brazil (along with those from other L20 potential members including Mexico and Saudi Arabia) at Evian in 2003. The UK, with a similar model in mind, invited the same core countries (albeit without Middle East representation) to discuss climate change at Gleneagles in 2005.

A similar framework was used in key ancillary bodies. Most noticeably, the G7/8 forum of finance ministers was opened up to the upper echelon of the core group. The finance ministers from China and India attended the two 2005 meetings in St. Petersburg and London.

So entrenched did this hub approach become that it operated with little critical comment. At the societal level, protestors targeted many aspects of the G7/8 for criticism but the outreach component slid under the radar. At the societal level, the main focus for reproach was not because of their inclusion but when this core group appeared to be excluded. French President Jacques Chirac publicly rebuked the United States, most obviously, for not being more inclusive to these regional hubs at the 2004 Sea Island summit: 'We cannot discuss major economic issues nowadays without discussing these issues with China, with India, Brazil, South Africa' (G8 Information Centre 2004).

Pressure to integrate more fully the so-called 'Big 5' (China, India, Brazil, South Africa and Mexico) into the G8 process intensified from the Gleneagles to the Heiligendamm summit. In part, this reflected the concerns of world leaders, most notably summit hosts UK Prime Minister Tony Blair and German Chancellor Angela Merkel, with specific functional issues, such as global poverty climate change. Underneath this dynamic, however, a legitimacy deficit provides the momentum. With the credentials of Russia as a G8 partner under increasingly critical scrutiny, the exclusion of selected hub countries from the South appears deeply flawed on a representative basis (Elliott and Wintour 2006).

If habit-forming, this regional hub or powerhouse approach raises as many questions as possible answers for the future of the global system. Is this the right model for representation? Even among the G7/8 members there appeared to be some disagreement about what the right model should be. As noted, France and the UK took the lead in adopting the hub approach. Other members, by way of contrast selected a more explicit but limited regional model with which to work. Italy and Canada – under former Prime Minister Jean Chrétien – took what might be termed an African-centric approach. The respective meetings they hosted – in Genoa and Kananaskis – picked a form of representation that put the primary emphasis on the attendance of leaders from the African continent and the implementation of the NEPAD agenda. Japan at the earlier 2000 Okinawa summit took a similar line, inviting Algeria, South Africa, and Nigeria into the mix (with Thailand added in as well). And Tony Blair played the African card as well at Gleneagles.

Other countries took a divergent track. As mentioned, the US did things its own way at Sea Island, moving from an approach that downplayed outreach altogether to one that placed the emphasis on the Middle East. The response rate, however, proved low for this invitation: Afghanistan, Bahrain, Iraq, Jordon, Tunisia, Turkey and Yemen said yes. But Saudi Arabia, Kuwait, Pakistan, Egypt and Morocco said no. Consequently, the Bush administration scrambled in the last six months to bring together a blend of African states to Sea Island (see Lyman 2004).

Notwithstanding all its limitations, the regional hub concept has a good number of advantages over the other models. For one thing, this model provides the most appropriate form of compensation for failure on the first best option: universalistic reform via the UN. Almost all the leading candidates for a permanent seat on the SC would be accommodated in this model (most notably, India and Brazil). Likewise there is room for a number of SC possibilities (Indonesia, for example) and for some strong blockers (Mexico, Argentina).

This is not to minimise the position of the losers. But in the case of the L20 this group would be concentrated among the states that already have a high element of status at the apex of power even without SC membership (Germany and Japan). As such, their deprivation would be a relative one in having to share an expanded club with a new set of members. If and when the push for SC reform is rekindled, these two states would once more – it must be added – be in the front of the line.

For another thing, the regional hub notion has the greatest possibility for providing continuity to the process. One problem with the African-centric approach is that it builds up momentum (and expectations) that can be dissipated quickly. After solid championship by Italy, Canada, and the UK (and to some extent by the US), what happens with a Russian host that has little or no interest in pursuing this agenda? Another problem is that this approach creates gaps. Even with the dual approach of the Blair government – with both 'core' and African representation – the UK found itself in a position where it had no Middle East representation at Gleneagles (a missing element that was made more glaring by the July 2005 London bombings).

The regional hub notion doesn't eradicate these gaps. As in the other models, the devil is in the details about any equitable composition of the L20. If South Africa is moved to the top of the slate (and, after all, President Thabo Mbeki has attended all of the G7/8 summits since 2000 – more than the majority of the G7/8 leaders themselves!), does this ranking leave Nigeria out (a very contentious issue among African states)? In a similar vein, does India's presence come at the expense of Pakistan? Is Indonesia kept on as it is with the G20 at the expense of Malaysia or even Thailand? And on what justification are these choices made? Saudi Arabia makes sense for the G20 but is a less credible selection for a Leaders' Twenty Summit. Should Turkey be chosen over Egypt or another state such as Algeria (which might be championed by France)? Is there an overrepresentation of Western European states because of the legacy of the G7/8 and the presence of the EU Commission? Or should a European state with a middle-power diplomatic tradition (the Netherlands or Sweden) be added to buttress the presence of good international citizens? Should Russia remain as the one and only Eastern European state in the composition? Or should another state such as Poland be added?

Still, it can be argued quite persuasively that this regional hub or power-house model lessens these deficiencies to a considerable extent. At a minimum, the model provides a structure that allows all regions to have some represen-tation. In a more ambitious mode, this model opens some considerable possibilities to mediating regional issues.

On this basis the other regional dimensions that could possibly be played out through the L20 would be a bonus. One dimension of this extended typology would be some provision for an asymmetric form of representation within the L20. As Colin Bradford denotes, this model would mean an enlargement of the G8 with the core members identified above (the regional hubs or powerhouses). Another group would be added on a supplementary basis 'depending on the issue being worked on . . . This is called variable geometry' (Bradford 2005).

Do the advantages of such a formula trump these pitfalls? Maybe. Amidst all the flaws of the UN system the constituency system has taken hold. More-over, some of the flaws in that system are avoided. Due to the absence not only of formal veto power but formal voting as well, the level of sensitivity pertaining to the inequality built into this system will perhaps be reduced. A number of regionally in-between countries could be accommodated. And the logic of the link between select states and issues might be so compelling as to reduce debate on composition. This might be true in the area of pan-demics (as the spotlight would be on certain states at the centre of the crisis such as Vietnam or Thailand in the case of Avian flu). It might also be true if the agenda was extended to other areas such as the prevention of natural disasters or fragile or failing states.

The obstacles go back to some of the regional flashpoints dominating the SC debate. After the French and Dutch 'no', it appears that any hope that the EU is ready to speak with one voice has been dashed. Instead of freeing up seats at the table for other regions in an L20, therefore, the battle might be to try to grab more (especially as an argument that a smaller 'good citizen' state such as the Netherlands or Sweden deserves a place in such a forum). NAFTA is not even open to this sort of debate, as the notion of any of these 'three amigos' representing each other on the global stage would be met by incredulity. Nigeria and South Africa can combine to take on Egypt and Algeria in the drive for SC reform, but they remain bitter rivals as to who speaks for Africa. Would a state such as Indonesia be the one permanent ASEAN country in the L20 with other members added on when needed? The list of delicate issues goes on and on.

Conclusion

The L20 remains very much a work in progress. Galvanising a process of reform in the global order is never easy. What is usually required is the advent of a new structural challenge and/or of a new settlement or order produced by a shape-shifting crisis. In the context of accelerated globalisation, faith in the pattern of global governance has clearly waned in terms of concerns both about who sets the rules of the game and why these rules are in place. Yet it is still unclear whether we are at the tipping point for morphing the core clubs of the twentieth century. There is an expanding consensus in both the North and South that we are facing a double deficit in terms of efficiency and legitimacy, yet the hold of the status quo is formidable.

With its parsimonious outline, the L20 does not offer a big bang solution with an agenda of sudden and comprehensive fashion. Instead of laying out an elaborate template in intricate detail, the construction of this design and its potential capability for addressing key world issues is laid out in sketch or draft format, to be debated and built on. Its top-down, executive-oriented contours, furthermore, depart from the tenets of those approaches that have become identified with the more common push for a new form of bottom-up, 'societal-led' multilateralism.

Still, if bounded by intent, the proposal is far from modest in either form or function. The proposal of a Leaders' Twenty Summit, in stylistic terms, is grounded on the need to overcome sluggishness in the global system. Not only are there important gaps to be filled, but impatience has also built up concerning the need to do things (and be seen to be doing them) quickly. Consistent with the 'just in time' quality found in new multilateralism, a quickened pace of delivery lies at the heart of the proposed framework for an L20. By focusing on broad niches (itself another feature of new multilateralism) the L20 would be able to prioritise those issues on which the forum should concentrate. By doing so, the L20 would act as a catalytic agent, a guide and a demonstration effect for other modes of reform.

In terms of its plurilateral orientation, the L20 blends some of the character of issue-specific new multilateralism with a keen appreciation of the new contours of regionalism. Retreating from the 'hyperglobalist' vision (Ohmae 1995), the L20 is firmly located in the architecture associated with the new regionalism no longer just situated in the EU and North America but concentrated on what have been fully accepted as regional hubs and power-houses and a narrow (but potentially valuable) form of inter-regionalism.

For some critics' tastes, of course, the model is still narrow in that it remains at odds with the universalist approach tied to the UN system (although the UN may be embedded in the 1945 model). For other critics, though, the model may still be too expansive, pushing the limits of a club structure with all the complexity of cultural, language, and political differences. Parsimony through this lens is crucial.

Whatever the 'right mix', if there is to be any claim that the forces of globalisation can be conditioned, the big rising/risen powers must be brought into the apex of power and responsibility. Executive multilateralism it may well be, but the L20 initiative rests on a expansive framework that is anything but a stylised and limited response to the challenges of legitimacy and delivery in the global system. Signalling a departure from the familiar script and mode of ownership, not only in terms of the actors involved but the potential agenda, this project has the potential to be utilised as a breakout in rethinking and reformulating the construct of global governance.

References

Annan, Kofi (2005) *In Larger Freedom: Towards Development, Security and Human Rights for All*. Response to the High-Level Panel Report. UN Doc. A/59/ 2005, 21 March. Available at: www.un.org/largerfreedom/contents.htm (accessed 12 July 2006).

Bayne, Sir Nicholas (2001) 'Concentrating the Mind: Decision-Making in the G7/G8 System', paper presented to the 2001 G8 Pre-Summit Public Policy Conference, 'Promoting Conflict Prevention and Human Security: What Can the G8 Do?', Rome, 16 July. Available at: www.g8.utoronto.ca/conferences/ 2001/rome/bayne-conflict.pdf (accessed 12 July 2006).

—— (2004) 'Prospects for the 2005 G8 Gleneagles Summit', presentation to the G8 Research Group, Trinity College, University of Toronto, 22 November.

Bradford, Colin I. (2005) 'Global Governance Reform for the 21st Century', unpublished paper. Available at: http://www.oecd.org/dataoecd/14/62/34983436.pdf

—— and Linn, Johannes F. (2004) 'Global Economic Governance: Governance at a Crossroads: Replacing the G-7 with the G-20', Washington, DC: The Brookings Institution, *Policy Brief*, no. 131, April.

Breslin, Shaun and Higgott, Richard (2000) 'Studying Regions: Learning from the Old, Constructing the New', *New Political Economy*, 5(3): 333–52.

Carin, Barry and Smith, Gordon (2005) 'Making Change Happen at the Global Level', in J. English *et al.*, *Reforming from the Top: A Leaders' 20 Summit*, Tokyo: United Nations University Press.

Cerny, Philip G. (1993) 'Plurilateralism, Structural Differentiation, and Functional Conflict in the Post-Cold War World Order', *Millennium*, 22(1): 27–51.

Cooper, Andrew F. *et al.* (eds) (2002) *Enhancing Global Governance: Towards a New Diplomacy?* Tokyo: United Nations University Press.

—— and Fues, Thomas (2005) 'L20 and ECOSOC Reform: Complementary Building Blocks for Inclusive Global Governance and a More Effective UN', *Briefing Paper*, Bonn: German Development Institute/DIE, 1–4 June.

Cox, Robert W. (ed.) (1997) *The New Realism; Perspectives on Multilateralism and World Order*, London/Tokyo: Macmillan/United Nations University Press.

—— (2002) 'Civilizations: Encounters and Transformations', in Robert W. Cox with Michael G. Schechter (eds) *The Political Economy of a Plural World: Critical Reflections on Power, Morals and Civilization*, London: Routledge, pp. 139–56.

Elliott, Larry and Wintour, Patrick (2006) 'Blair Wants Developing Nations in New G13 to Help Secure Key Deals', *The Guardian*, 13 July.

English, John, Thakur, Ramesh and Cooper, Andrew F. (eds) (2005) *Reforming from the Top: A Leaders' 20 Summit*, Tokyo: United Nations University Press.

G8 Information Centre (2004) 'Press Briefing by French President Jacques Chirac', Sea Island documents, 9 June.

Goldman Sachs (2003) 'Dreaming with BRICS; The Path to 2050', *Global Economics Paper*, no. 99, New York, October. Available at: www.gs.com/insight/research/reports/99.pdf (accessed 12 July 2006).

Harmes, Adam (2004) *The Return of the State: Protestors, Power-brokers and the New Global Compromise*, Vancouver: Douglas & McIntyre.

Held, David (2003) 'From Executive to Cosmopolitan Multilateralism', in David Held and Mathias Koenig-Archibugi (eds) *Taming Globalization: Frontiers of Governance*, Cambridge: Polity, pp. 160–86.

—— and Koenig-Archibugi, Mathias (eds) (2003) *Taming Globalization: Frontiers of Governance*, Cambridge: Polity.

Hettne, Björn *et al.* (eds) (1998) *Globalism and the New Regionalism*, New York: Palgrave Macmillan.

—— (2004) 'Interregionalism and World Order', paper presented to 'Section 33, States, regions and regional world orders', SGIR, Fifth Pan-European International Relations Conference, Netherlands Congress Centre, the Hague, 9–11 September.

Humphrey, John and Messner, Dirk (2005) 'The Impact of the Asian and other Drivers on Global Governance'. Available at: http://www.ids.ac.uk/ids/global/pdfs/AsianDriversGovernancepaper05.pdf (accessed 12 July 2006).

Hurd, Ian (1999) 'Legitimacy and Authority in International Politics', *International Organization*, 53(1): 379–408.

Jaura, Ramesh (2006) 'New Political Push Proposed', *Inter Press Service*, 10 June.

Kirton, John J. (2002) 'Guiding Global Economic Governance: The G20, G7 and IMF at Century's Dawn', in John J. Kirton and George Von Furstenberg (eds) *New Directions in Global Economic Governance*, Aldershot: Ashgate, pp. 143–67.

Knight, W.A. (2000) *A Changing United Nations: Multilateral Evolution and the Quest for Global Governance*, London: Macmillan.

Lyman, Princeton N. (2004) *Freedom, Prosperity, and Security: The G8 Partnership with Africa: Seal Island 2004 and Beyond*, New York: Council on Foreign Relations, Special Report, May.

Martin, Paul (2004) 'Speech by the Prime Minister', address on the occasion of his visit to Washington, DC, 29 April.

—— (2006) 'Forming Clubs in Order to Enhance Efficiency? G20 and L20 as "Main Committee" of World Politics', Presentation to the Development and Peace Foundation conference, 'Multilateralism in Transition: Fragmentation, Informalisation and Networking', Dresden, 8 June.

Narlikar, Amrita and Tussie, Diana (2004) 'The G20 at the Cancún Ministerial: Developing Countries and their Evolving Coalitions in the WTO', *The World Economy*, 27(7): 947–66.

O'Brien, R., Goetz, R.A.M., Scholte, J.A. and Williams, M. (2000) *Contesting Global Governance*, Cambridge: Cambridge University Press.

Ohmae, K. (1995) *The End of the Nation State: The Diffusion of Power in the World Economy*, London: HarperCollins.

Putnam, Robert D. (1988) 'Diplomacy and Domestic Politics: The Logic of Two-Level Games', *International Organization*, 48(3): 427–60.

Schwab, Klaus (2004) 'Disband G8 Order: WEF Chief', BS Corporate Bureau in New Delhi, 7 February.

Slaughter, Anne-Marie (1997) 'The Real New World Order', *Foreign Affairs*, 76(5): 183–97.

—— (2004) *The Real World Order*, Princeton, NJ: Princeton University Press.

—— (2005) 'Government Networks, World Order, and the L20', in J. English *et al.*, *Reforming from the Top: A Leaders' 20 Summit*, Tokyo: United Nations University Press, pp. 281–95.

Thakur, Ramesh (2004) 'How to Build a Better Brains Trust', *Globe and Mail*, 3 June.

Vyrynen, Raimo (2002) 'Reforming the World Order: Multi- and Plurilateral Approaches', in Björn Hettne and Bertil Oden (eds) *Global Governance in the 21st Century: Alternative Perspectives on World Order*, Gothenburg: Almqvist and Wiksell International, pp. 106–46.

Zurn, Michael (2000) 'Democratic Governance Beyond the Nation-State: The EU and other International Institutions', *European Journal of International Relations*, 6(2): 183–221.

—— (2005) 'Introduction: Law and Compliance at Different Levels', in Michael Zurn and Christian Joerges (eds) *Law and Governance in Postnational Europe: Compliance beyond the Nation-State*, Cambridge: Cambridge University Press.

Index

Abbott, Keith 151
Afghanistan 22, 159, 172, 258
Africa, Central and Western 5, 22, 31, 36, 66, 119, 164, 244; and regionalism 37, 68;
Africa, North 233, 234
Africa, Sub-Saharan 179, 233, 240, 244
Africa, West 164
African Union 27, 36, 37, 39, 184n, 240
Albrow, Martin 10
Algeria 258–260
Amable, Bruno 243
Andean Community 31, 32
Annan, Kofi 19, 24, 35, 40, 257
Argentina 147, 184n, 237, 251, 254, 257, 259
Asia 20, 28, 31, 115, 149, 150, 179, 180, 196, 233, 239, 246; Asian values 242, 243; and Europe 31, 32; financial crisis in 21, 192, 196, 254; and HIV/AIDS 202, 203; security in 9, 187, 189; Southeast 164, 188, 207n, 234
Asia-Pacific Economic Cooperation (APEC) 32, 46, 142, 145, 151; and new regionalism 44
Asia-Pacific region 143, 151, 152, 242; Asia-Pacific Basin 32;
Association of Southeast Asian Nations (ASEAN) 29, 31, 146, 179, 185n, 189, 193, 194, 201, 202, 207n, 234, 240, 243, 246; ASEAN + 3, 202, 204; and China 202; economic recovery in 197, 199; members of 189, 251, 201, 260; and SARS 202, 204; and securitisation 190, 192, 193, 199; as sub-regional organisation 27, 234
Australasia 185n, 233, 234, 244
Australia 152, 237, 251, 253

Bach, Daniel 68
Bangladesh 257
Bartlett, Christopher A. 107
Bayne, Nicholas 253, 257
Beamish, Paul W. 109
Bhagwati, Jagdish 120, 128, 235
Bina Swadaya Yogyakarta 198
Blair, Tony 246, 258, 259,
Bøås, Morten 72
Bradford, Colin 10, 260
Brazil 38, 147, 237; as regional hub 257; as rising power 253, 258; and the UN 184n, 257, 259
Breslin, Shaun 68
Bretton Woods 74
Brown, Gordon 254
Brundtland, Gro Harlem 200
Buckley, Peter J. 100
Bull, Hedley 17
Burma (Myanmar) 146, 203, 207n
Buzan, Barry 190

Caballero-Anthony, Mely 9
Cable, Vincent 71
Calleya, Stephen C. 50
Canada 130, 216, 217, 252, 258, 259; as middle power 253; CRTC 215; DFAIT 220; and the United States 4, 134, 147, 233
Caribbean, CARICOM 31; and Pacific Group of States 31
Carney, Patricia 215
CD-Bethesda 198
Chan, Cecilia 200
China 27, 29, 146, 168, 180, 200, 201, 203, 207n, 234, 236, 237, 258; and ASEAN + 3, 202, 204; and the G8 257; and L20 251; as rising power 253; and

SARS 200, 201, 204; and UN Security
Council 180, 184n
Choonhavan, Chaovalit 197
Chrétien, Jean 258
Christiansen, Thomas 67
civil society 1, 3, 6, 18, 19, 20, 32, 37, 152,
160, 187, 195, 231, 238; and
Convention on Cultural Diversity 220,
221; and global governance 24, 230,
246; as international actor 21, 58n, 66,
75, 205; and L20 255; and the UN 22
Clark, Helen 219
classical integration theory 7, 81–3, 84,
88, 92, 93, criticisms of 84, 86, 88, 91;
marginalised 7; and new regional
approach 55, 69, 84; purpose of 81, 90;
rehabilitation of 80, 87, 88, 92
Clinton, Bill 184n, 254
Cold War 83, 152; end of 26, 64, 163;
post-Cold War 82, 168, 169; and UN
167, 179
Collinson, Simon 108
Commission on Global Governance 1,
23
Common Market for Eastern and
Southern Africa 31
conflict diamonds 26, 249
Cooper, Andrew F. 11, 238
Copenhagen School of Security and
Desecuritisation 188, 189, 190, 191,
207
Copps, Sheila 220
country-specific advantages 100, 114
Cowen, Tyler 213
Cox, Robert W. 249

Delios, Andrew 109
Deutsch, Karl W. 82
Doha Development Agenda 119, 126,
132, 133, 137
Dow Jones 110, 111

Economic Community of West African
States (ECOWAS) 31, 33, 40, 175, 176
Egypt 234, 259, 260
Eichel, Hans 254
Etzioni, Amitai 232, 233, 238, 245
Europe 4, 10, 19, 46, 67, 76, 81, 90, 109,
119, 129, 148, 151, 164, 172, 173, 179,
225, 231, 235, 236, 241, 242; audiovisual policy of 223, 224; Council of
173, 244; and regional case studies 143,
233, 234, 246; regional integration in
46, 62, 65, 67, 69, 222; and regional

organisations 31, 179; and
regionalisation 7, 18, 241; and
regionalism 37, 44, 45, 64, 68, 119; and
the United States 19, 241, 245; and
Western European integration 25, 84
European Coal and Steel Community 25,
63, 81
European Commission 32, 46, 129, 244,
245
European Community 39, 63, 222, 242
European Court of Justice 22, 83, 148
European Union 5, 19, 31, 36, 37, 46, 47,
53, 67, 82, 85, 87, 129, 132, 134, 130,
135, 136, 137, 138, 147, 148, 222, 224,
225, 236, 237, 245; EU Commission to
the United States 237, 240, 241, 244,
245, 259; and Free Trade Agreements
126, 131; and integration
theory/studies 68, 69, 76; and L20 251,
261; and labour 142, 148; as regional
organisation 33, 37, 69, 80, 86, 178,
234, 241, 250; and Regional Trade
Agreements 122, 127, 130, 131; and
regionalism 4, 45, 46, 47; rules of 85,
129, 130; studies of 43, 44, 48, 49, 56,
57n, 67, 80–94

Felicio, Tânia 33, 185n
Florida, Richard 226
France 25, 180, 251, 258, 259
Free Trade Area of the Americas 152

Gamble, Andrew 65
de Gaulle, Charles 64
General Agreement on Tariffs and Trade
3, 71, 105, 119, 128, 129, 135, 217, 218,
221; and Regional Trade Agreements
120–2; and restriction to commerce
138, 219; rules of 119; Uruguay Round
129, 130, 132, 135, 136, 217, 218
General Agreement on Trade in Services
120, 131, 126, 218, 219; negotiations in
123, 131
Germany 25, 184n, 257, 259
Ghemawat, Pankaj 104
Ghoshal, Sumantra 107
Global Compact 148
global governance 1, 2, 6, 10, 11, 17, 22,
23–5, 32, 37, 168, 230, 232, 233, 238,
262; as coherent process 10, 236; form
of 11, 23, 231; framework of 20, 22, 37;
and L20 251; and regionalisation 1, 4,
5, 11, 29, 240, 245, 246; and the United
Nations 24, 231

Global Partnership for Development 240
Goff, Patricia 10
Government Procurement Agreement 131, 136
Graham, Kennedy 9, 33, 185n
Grant, Peter S. 118
Group of Eight (G8) 11, 236–7, 244, 250, 252, 253–4, 255, 257, 258, 260; Sea Island (2004) 258–9; Gleneagles (2005) 237, 258–9; St. Petersburg (2006) 258; Heiligendamm (2007) 258
Group of Four 38, 39, 179, 180

Haas, Ernst B. 53, 63, 64, 66, 81, 90
Hadiwinata, Bob 198, 199
Hahn Report 223
Hammarskjöld, Dag 167, 183n
Hayek, Friedrich A. von
Held, David 231
Henderson, David 71
Hettne, Björn 6, 7, 8, 43, 46, 48, 77n
Higgott, Richard 2
Hirst, Paul 100
HIV/AIDS 24, 39, 202, 203, 205, 206
Hobson, John M. 144
Hoffmann, Stanley 64, 78, 82, 83, 94
Humphrey, John 257
Huntington, Samuel P. 232, 233, 238
Hurrell, Andrew 1, 45
Hveem, Helge 53, 72,

Ibrahim, Anwar 197, 207n
India 109, 150, 195, 203, 234, 237, 244, 251, 258; and G7/8 254, 258; and G20 259; as regional powerhouse 251; as rising power 253; and the UN 257, 259
India-Brazil-South Africa Forum (IBSA) 253
Indonesia 150, 194, 195, 197, 204, 205, 207n, 237, 240, 242, 254, 259; financial crisis 196, 197, 198; and L/20 260
International Criminal Court 232, 250, 251–3, 256
International Labour Organization 147, 148, 149,
International Monetary Fund 21, 197, 254
Iraq 168, 178, 183n, 241, 245, 258; Iraq War (2003-) 253
Italy 184n, 227251, 257–9

Japan 115, 146, 180, 196, 239, 244, 251, 259; and ASEAN 202, 204; and China 184n, 234; Japanese MNEs 108, 109; and the UN 257, 258
Jessop, Bob 72

Kalyaamitra 198
Keohane, Robert 64
Krueger, Anne 234
Kuwait 17, 168, 258

Laursen, Finn 53
L20 (Leaders Twenty) 253, 254, 261; core of 251, 252; and G8 250; and G20 237, 255; members of 257, 259; and multilateralism 11, 252, 255; and Paul Martin 252, 255; and plurilateralism 255, 256; and regionalism 11, 251, 257, 260
League of Arab States 33, 173, 178, 179
Leonard, Mark 37
Lindberg, Leon N. 81

Maastricht Treaty 147, 222
Make Poverty History 237, 238
Malaysia 193–5, 201, 202, 203, 207n, 242; as developing country 196, 197; securitisation in 199, 206
Mansfield, Edward D. 68
Manuel, Trevor 254
Marchand, Marianne, H. 53, 72
Martin, Paul 252, 254, 255
Marx, Karl 235
Mattli, Walter 48, 53
Mbeki, Thabo 38, 259
Melo, Jaime de 71
Mercosur (Common Market of the South) 40, 147, 234, 235; and NAFTA 240, 251; as regional organisation 31, 32
Merkel, Angela 258
Messner, Dirk 257
Mexico 136, 146, 150, 236, 237, 257–9
Middle East 233, 234, 251, 258, 259
Millennium Development Goals 10, 230, 236, 237, 239, 241, 242, 243, 244; Millennium Development Summit 24, 236, 237; and the EU 240, 244
Milner, Helen V. 68
Milward, Alan 64
Mitrany, David 63, 82
Monnet., Jean 63
Monroe Doctrine 172, 233
Montreal Consensus 254
Multilateral Agreement on Investment 132

multinational enterprise 99, 100, 105–9, 115

new regionalism 43, 47, 48, 54; and EU studies 43, 44; and integration theory 49, 57n
New Zealand 218, 219
Nigeria 258–60
non-governmental organisations 17, 20, 21, 22, 191, 195, 198–9; as civil society 1, 203; as securitising actor 198, 204–5
North American Agreement on Labour Cooperation 146, 148, 151
North American Free Trade Agreement 4, 54, 104, 122, 126, 129, 131, 132, 136, 216, 235, 249, 251; and dispute settlement 137, 216, 228n; negotiation of 147, 150, 215; and regionalism 44, 147
Nye, Joseph 57, 64, 81

O'Brien, Robert 8, 9, 66
Odinkalu, Chidi 22
OSIRIS database 109, 110, 111
Organisation for Economic Co-operation and Development 121, 129, 148; plurilateral approach of 130, 132, 199
Organisation of the Islamic Conference 33, 243, 244, 245
Organisation for Security and Cooperation in Europe 33, 178

Pakistan 184n, 257, 259
Panagariya, Arvind 71
Payne, Anthony 65, 71
Paz, Octavio 243
Pettigrew, Pierre 220
Philippines 150, 195, 201, 204
Polanyi, Karl 73, 74, 75, 77
Pollack, Mark A. 89
Prebisch, Raúl 71
Putnam, Robert D. 253

Ramiah, Ilavenil 202, 203
Redner, Harry 213
Rosamond, Ben 7, 48, 67, 70, 77n, 89
Rugman, Alan 7, 8, 101, 104, 108, 115
Russia 21, 180, 241, 244, 257–9

San Francisco 161, 227
SARS (Severe Acute Respiratory Syndrome) 189, 200, 201, 202, 204, 206
Sassen, Saskia 226, 227

Saudi Arabia 237, 251, 254, 257–259
Schmitter, Phillipe 64, 81, 90,
Schuman, Robert 25
Schwab, Klaus 255
Seabrooke, Leonard 144
Shaw, Timothy, M. 44, 53, 72
Shinawatra, Thaksin 202
Singapore 136, 200, 201, 202, 204, 207n
Slaughter, Anne-Marie 22, 256
Slim, Hugo 21
Söderbaum, Fredrik 6, 7, 43, 46
Somalia 159, 170, 183n, 184n
South Africa 43, 237, 251, 253, 258–60
South Asian Association for Regional Cooperation 27, 29, 31, 179, 184n, 185n
South Korea 17, 146, 183n, 202, 204, 207n, 251, 257
Suara Ibu Peduli 198
Suharto, GCB 197

Taiwan 27, 233
Telò, Mario 48
Thakur, Ramesh 6, 8, 9
Thailand 195, 197, 201, 202, 204, 207n, 260
Theiler, Tobias 223, 224
Thompson, Graeme 100
Tong, Goh Chok 202
Turkey 168, 235, 237, 240, 258, 259
Tussie, Dianna 72

United Kingdom 110, 111, 180, 234, 251, 258; and L20 257, 259; UK MNEs 109, 110, 112, 113, 114
United Nations 3, 6, 9, 18, 23, 24, 32, 35, 38, 71, 168, 171, 180, 196, 230, 231, 232, 236, 242, 246, 252; membership of 28, 32; and regional organisations 34, 36, 159, 160, 174–81; responsibilities of 34, 182n; Secretary General of 37, 240
United Nations Charter 17, 34, 36, 160, 161, 162, 167, 168, 170, 171, 172, 175, 176, 177, 178, 179, 180, 181; framers of 159, 168, 169; and international peace and security 162–4
United Nations Educational, Scientific and Cultural Organization 220, 244; Convention on the Protection and Promotion of the Diversity of Cultural Expressions 221
United Nations Framework Convention on Climate Change 32–3

United Nations Security Council 23, 34, 168, 169, 177, 253; authority of 17, 166, 167; authorisation of 166, 170, 171, 175, 176, 179, 183n; composition of 32, 38, 39, 164, 179, 184n, 236; and dispute settlement 166, 182n; reform of 256, 257; and regional organisations 33–6, 176, 179, 181
United Nations University 19; Comparative Regional Integration Studies 77n, 121; World Institute for Development Economics Research 65
United Nations World Summit 40, 176, 177, 244
United States, and Canada 215; and CUSFTA 130, 215; and the EU 217; and Europe 19, 241; and GATT 219; Jacques Chirac 258; labour in 109; and MDGs 230; and NAFTA 46, 149, 216; in North America 246; policy of 170; and regionalism 30; terrorist attacks in 172, 189, 245; and the United Nations 231

Van Langenhove, Luk 6, 8, 9
Verbeke, Alain 104

Vietnam 150, 168, 200, 201, 260

Warleigh-Lack, Alex 6, 68, 69, 70, 77n, 80
Waever, Ole 190
Weber, Max 239
Westphalian System 28, 63, 64, 76, 171
de Wilde, Jaap 190
Wilson, Woodrow 173
Woods, Chris 118
Woolcock, Stephen 8, 139n
World Trade Organization (WTO) 3, 29, 32, 118, 121, 129, 132, 133, 138, 147, 149, 216, 218, 219, 220, 235; Codex Alimentarius 129, 130, 138; and globalisation 144, 214; and Kyoto Protocol 240, 258; members of 29, 105, 137; and Regional Trade Agreements 29, 120, 138, 139n; and regionalism 29, 105; rules of 118, 119, 129–35; SPS agreement 126, 129, 130
World War II 25, 26, 28, 67, 74

Yudhoyono, Susilo B. 242, 246

Zurn, Michael 250, 253